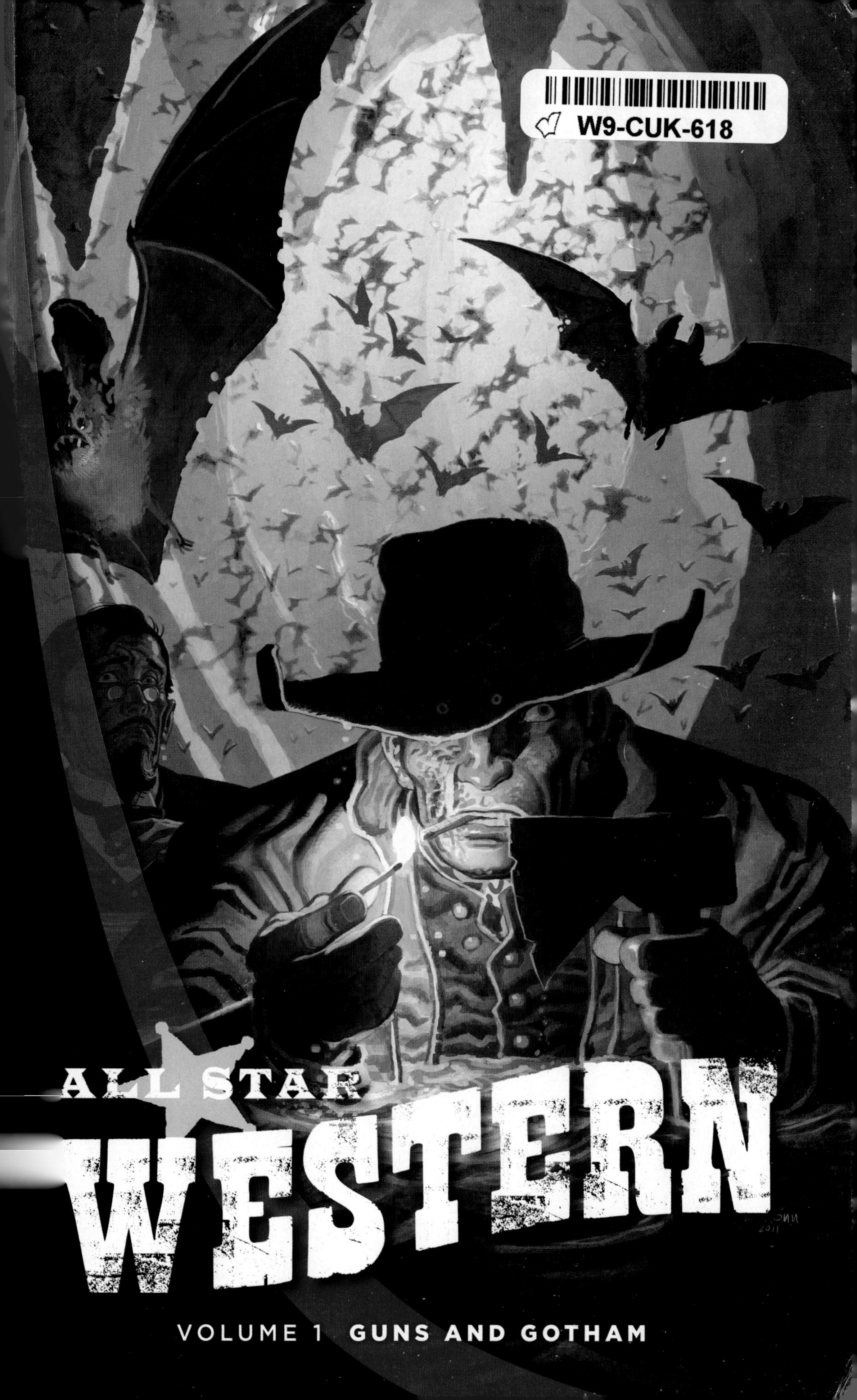
ALL STAR
WESTERN
VOLUME 1 GUNS AND GOTHAM

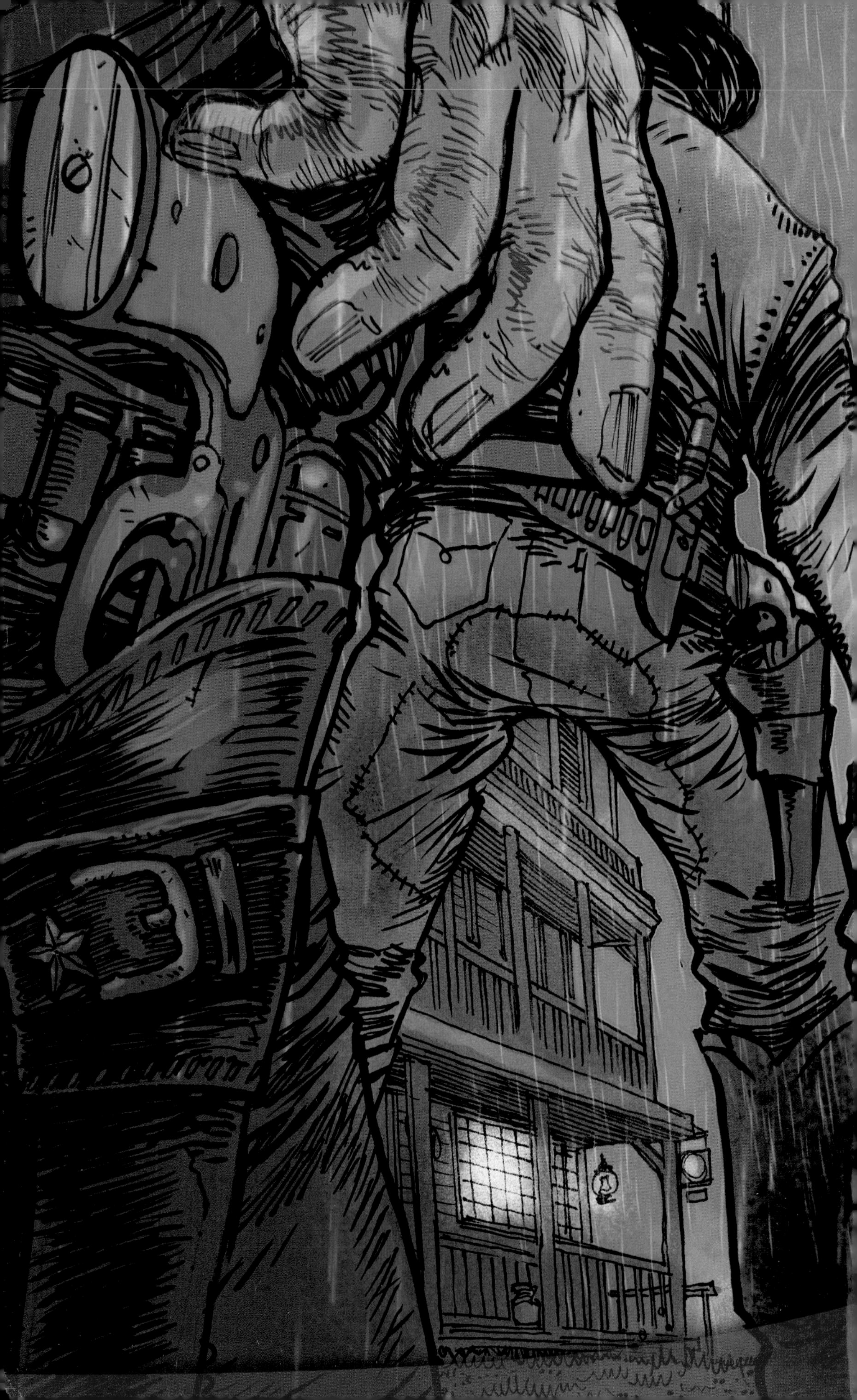

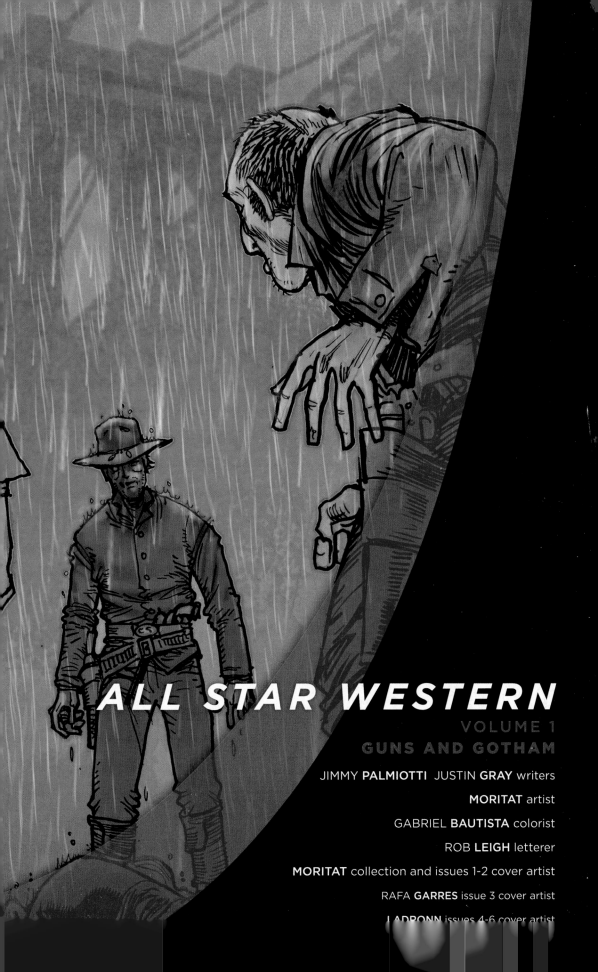

# ALL STAR WESTERN

## VOLUME 1
## GUNS AND GOTHAM

JIMMY **PALMIOTTI**  JUSTIN **GRAY** writers

**MORITAT** artist

GABRIEL **BAUTISTA** colorist

ROB **LEIGH** letterer

**MORITAT** collection and issues 1-2 cover artist

RAFA **GARRES** issue 3 cover artist

**LADRONN** issues 4-6 cover artist

JOEY CAVALIERI Editor – Original Series  KATE STEWART Assistant Editor – Original Series
ROWENA YOW Editor  ROBBIN BROSTERMAN Design Director – Books  ROBBIE BIEDERMAN Publication Design

BOB HARRAS VP – Editor-in-Chief

DIANE NELSON President  DAN DIDIO and JIM LEE Co-Publishers  GEOFF JOHNS Chief Creative Officer
JOHN ROOD Executive VP – Sales, Marketing and Business Development  AMY GENKINS Senior VP – Business and Legal Affairs
NAIRI GARDINER Senior VP – Finance  JEFF BOISON VP – Publishing Operations  MARK CHIARELLO VP – Art Direction and Design
JOHN CUNNINGHAM VP – Marketing  TERRI CUNNINGHAM VP – Talent Relations and Services
ALISON GILL Senior VP – Manufacturing and Operations  HANK KANALZ Senior VP – Digital
JAY KOGAN VP – Business and Legal Affairs, Publishing  JACK MAHAN VP – Business Affairs, Talent
NICK NAPOLITANO VP – Manufacturing Administration  SUE POHJA VP – Book Sales
COURTNEY SIMMONS Senior VP – Publicity  BOB WAYNE Senior VP – Sales

ALL STAR WESTERN VOLUME 1: GUNS AND GOTHAM

DC Comics, 1700 Broadway, New York, NY 10019
A Warner Bros. Entertainment Company.
Printed by RR Donnelley, Salem, VA, USA. 9/28/12. First Printing.

ISBN: 978-1-4012-3709-7

Library of Congress Cataloging-in-Publication Data

Palmiotti, Jimmy.
All star western volume 1 : guns and Gotham / Jimmy Palmiotti, Justin Gray, Moritat.
p. cm.
"Originally published in single magazine form in All Star Western 1-6."
ISBN 978-1-4012-3709-7
1. Graphic novels. I. Gray, Justin. II. Norman, Justin. III. Title. IV. Title: Guns and Gotham.
PN6728.A425P35 2012
741.5'973—dc23
2012023699

SUSTAINABLE
FORESTRY
INITIATIVE

Certified Chain of Custody
At Least 25% Certified Forest Content
www.sfiprogram.org
SFI-01042
APPLIES TO TEXT STOCK ONLY

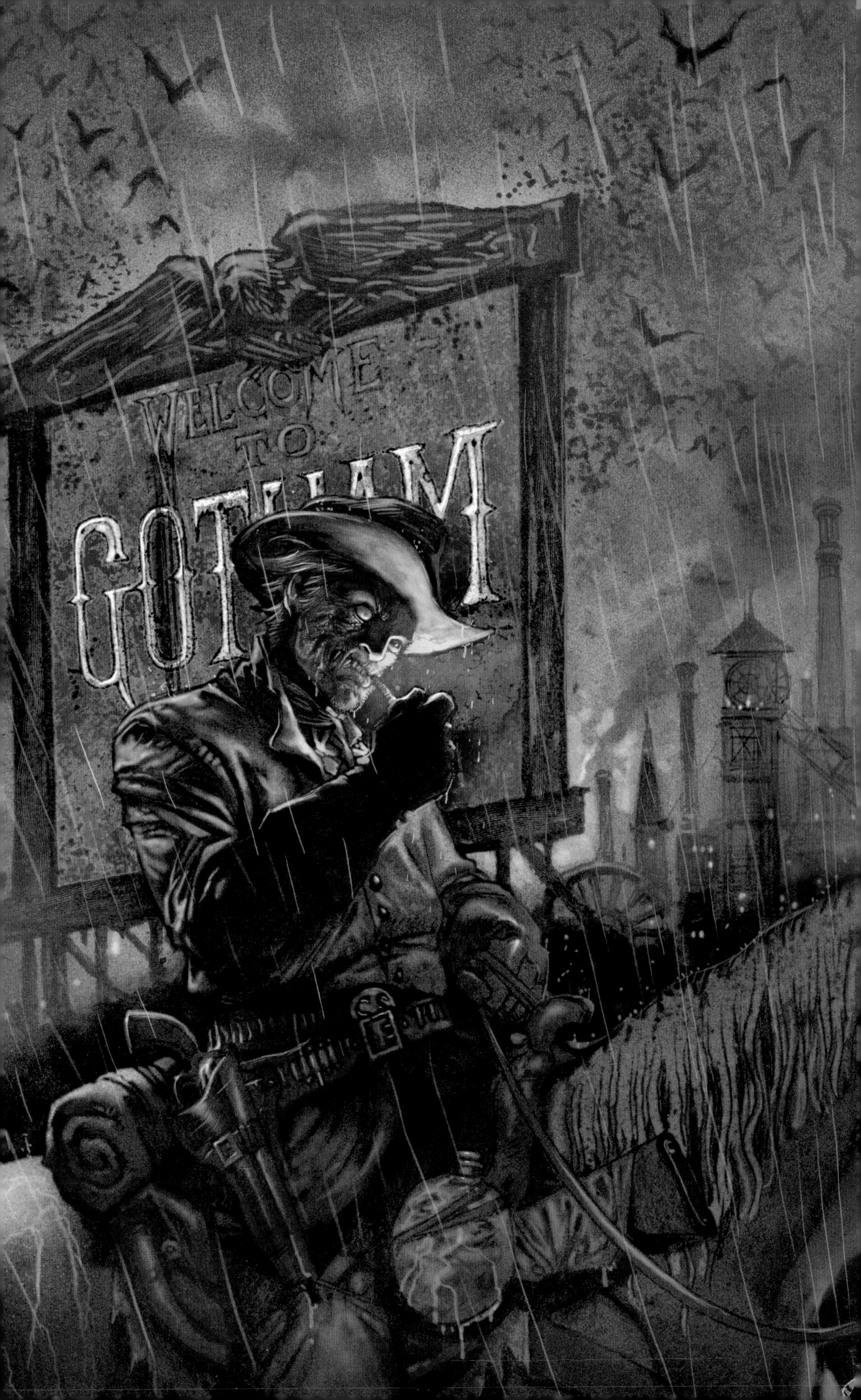
WELCOME
TO

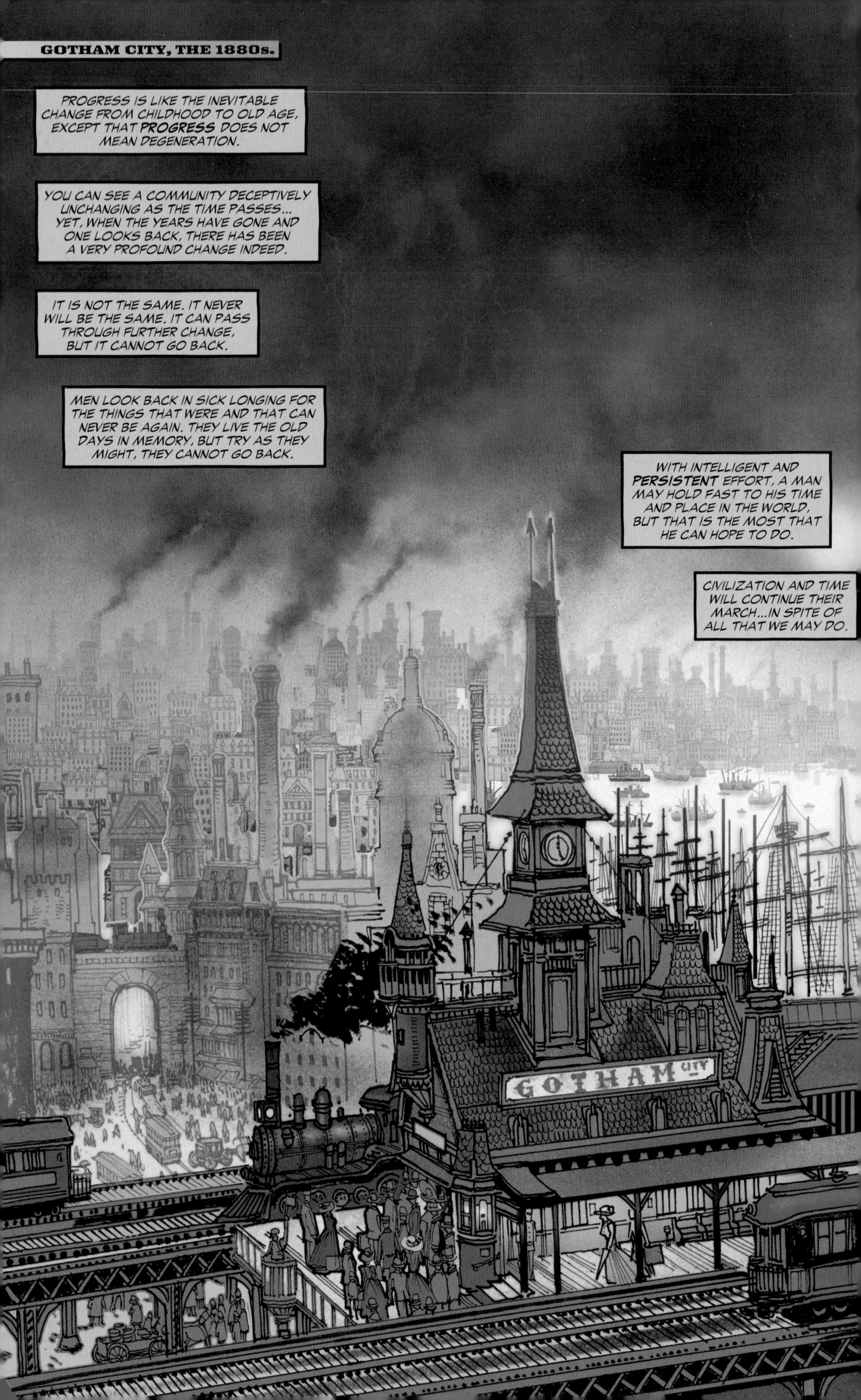
GOTHAM CITY, THE 1880s.
PROGRESS IS LIKE THE INEVITABLE CHANGE FROM CHILDHOOD TO OLD AGE, EXCEPT THAT PROGRESS DOES NOT MEAN DEGENERATION.
YOU CAN SEE A COMMUNITY DECEPTIVELY UNCHANGING AS THE TIME PASSES... YET, WHEN THE YEARS HAVE GONE AND ONE LOOKS BACK, THERE HAS BEEN A VERY PROFOUND CHANGE INDEED.
IT IS NOT THE SAME. IT NEVER WILL BE THE SAME. IT CAN PASS THROUGH FURTHER CHANGE, BUT IT CANNOT GO BACK.
MEN LOOK BACK IN SICK LONGING FOR THE THINGS THAT WERE AND THAT CAN NEVER BE AGAIN. THEY LIVE THE OLD DAYS IN MEMORY, BUT TRY AS THEY MIGHT, THEY CANNOT GO BACK.
WITH INTELLIGENT AND PERSISTENT EFFORT, A MAN MAY HOLD FAST TO HIS TIME AND PLACE IN THE WORLD, BUT THAT IS THE MOST THAT HE CAN HOPE TO DO.
CIVILIZATION AND TIME WILL CONTINUE THEIR MARCH...IN SPITE OF ALL THAT WE MAY DO.
GOTHAM CITY

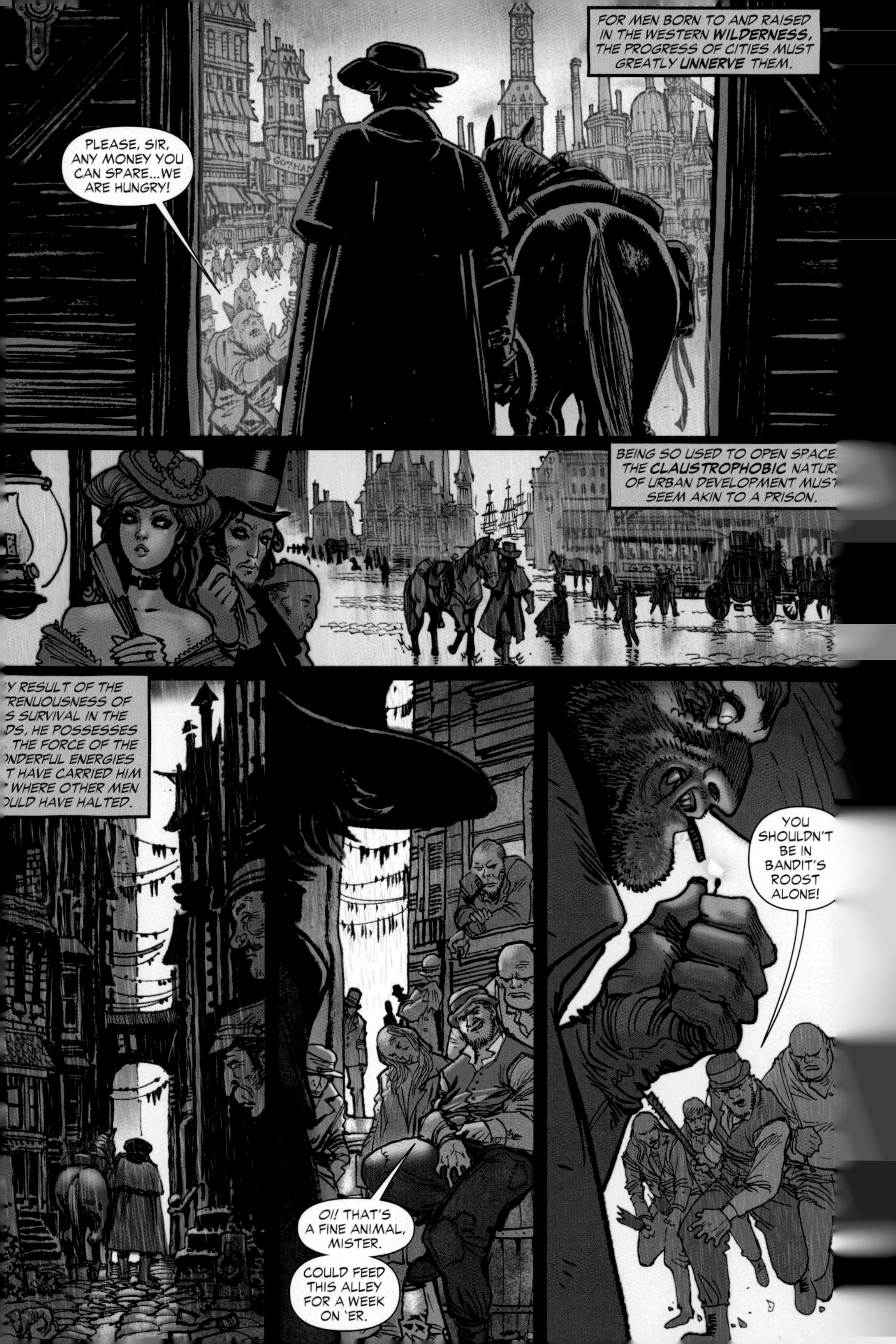
FOR MEN BORN TO AND RAISED IN THE WESTERN WILDERNESS, THE PROGRESS OF CITIES MUST GREATLY UNNERVE THEM.
PLEASE, SIR, ANY MONEY YOU CAN SPARE...WE ARE HUNGRY!
GOTHAM
BEING SO USED TO OPEN SPACE THE CLAUSTROPHOBIC NATUR OF URBAN DEVELOPMENT MUST SEEM AKIN TO A PRISON.
GOTHAM
Y RESULT OF THE TRENUOUSNESS OF S SURVIVAL IN THE DS, HE POSSESSES THE FORCE OF THE ONDERFUL ENERGIES T HAVE CARRIED HIM WHERE OTHER MEN OULD HAVE HALTED.
OI! THAT'S A FINE ANIMAL, MISTER.
COULD FEED THIS ALLEY FOR A WEEK ON 'ER.
YOU SHOULDN'T BE IN BANDIT'S ROOST ALONE!

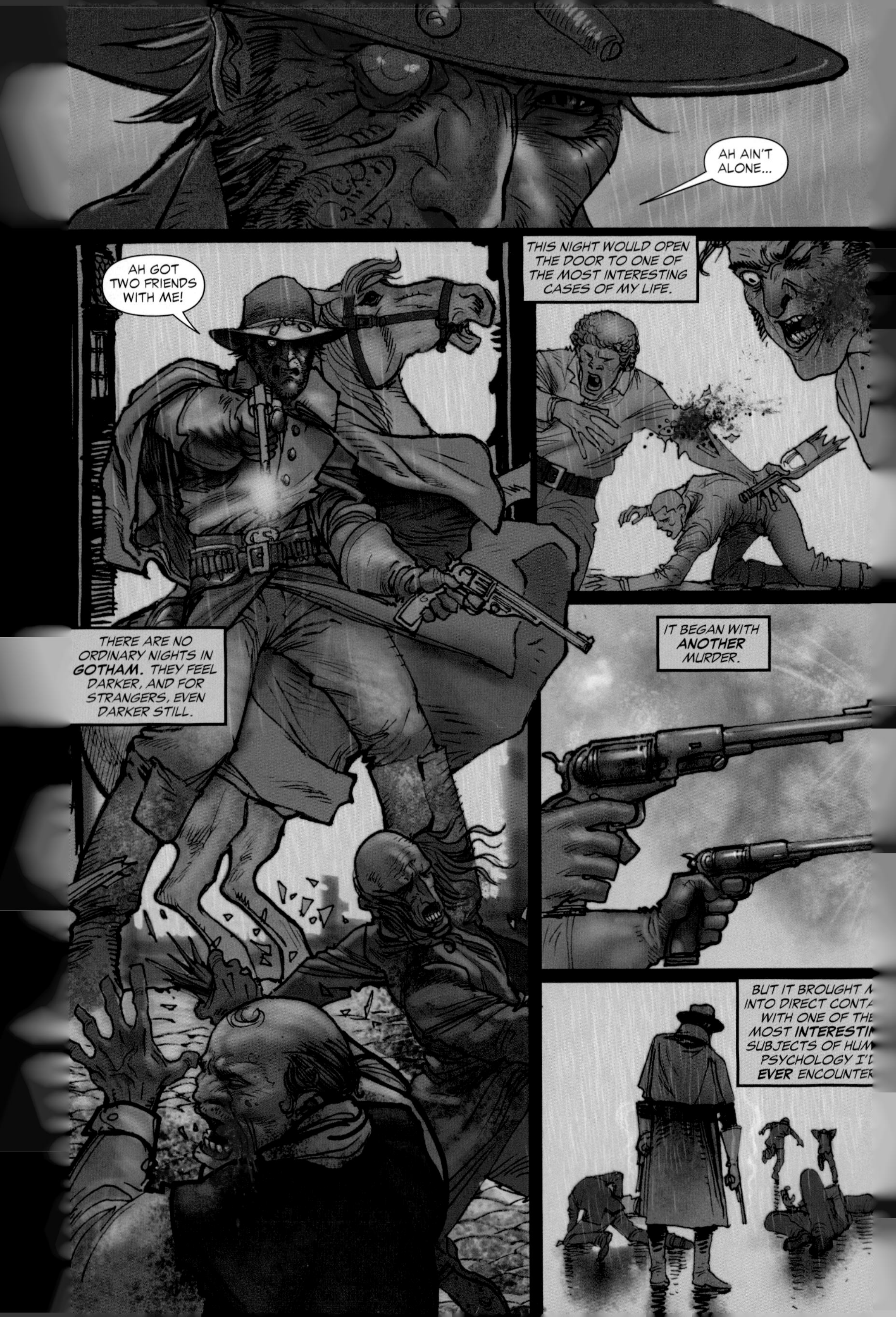
AH AIN'T ALONE...
AH GOT TWO FRIENDS WITH ME!
THIS NIGHT WOULD OPEN THE DOOR TO ONE OF THE MOST INTERESTING CASES OF MY LIFE.
THERE ARE NO ORDINARY NIGHTS IN GOTHAM. THEY FEEL DARKER, AND FOR STRANGERS, EVEN DARKER STILL.
IT BEGAN WITH ANOTHER MURDER.
BUT IT BROUGHT M
INTO DIRECT CONTA
WITH ONE OF THE
MOST INTERESTIN
SUBJECTS OF HUM
PSYCHOLOGY I'D
EVER ENCOUNTER

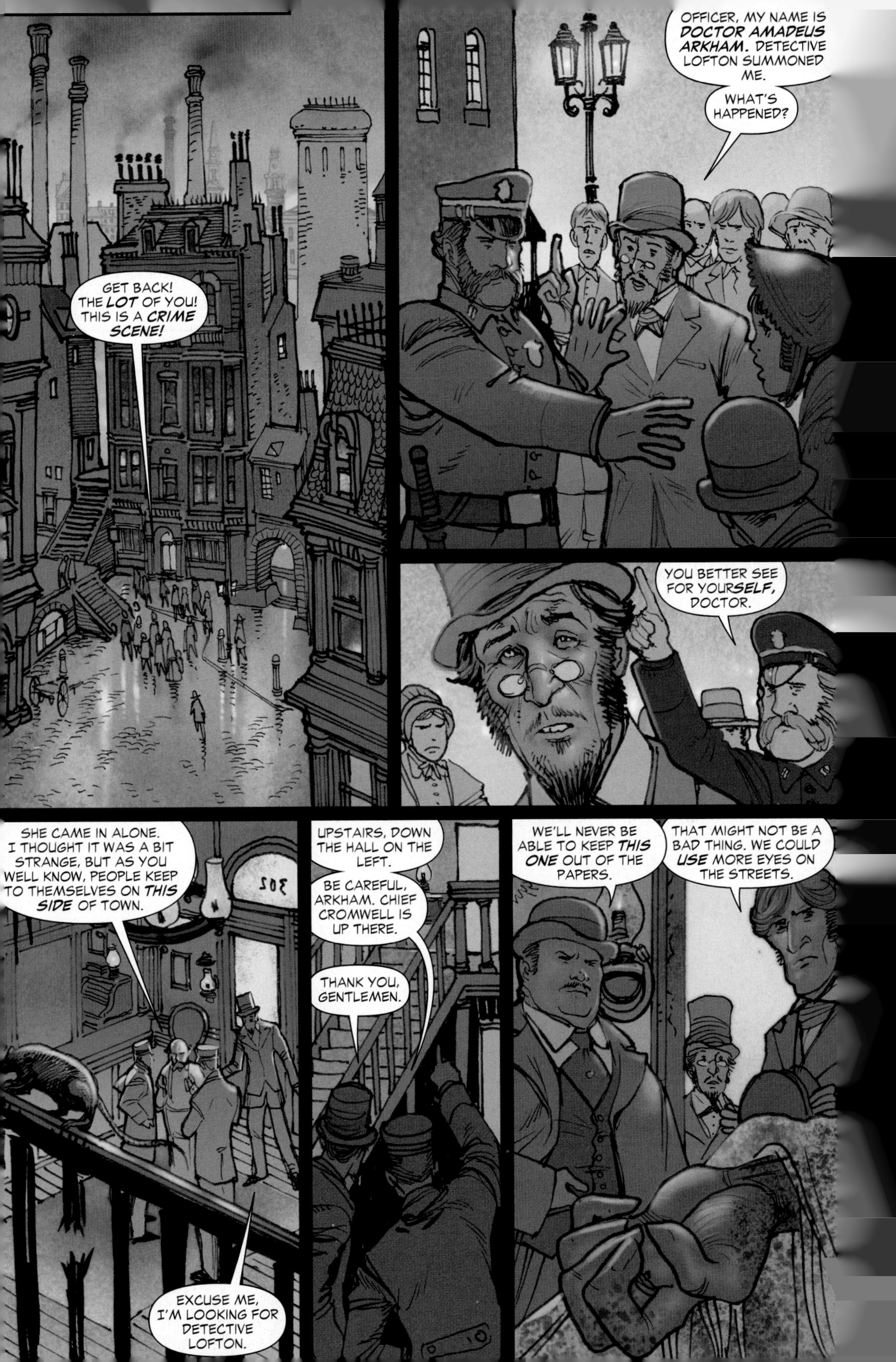
GET BACK! THE LOT OF YOU! THIS IS A CRIME SCENE!
OFFICER, MY NAME IS DOCTOR AMADEUS ARKHAM. DETECTIVE LOFTON SUMMONED ME.
WHAT'S HAPPENED?
YOU BETTER SEE FOR YOURSELF, DOCTOR.
SHE CAME IN ALONE. I THOUGHT IT WAS A BIT STRANGE, BUT AS YOU WELL KNOW, PEOPLE KEEP TO THEMSELVES ON THIS SIDE OF TOWN.
EXCUSE ME, I'M LOOKING FOR DETECTIVE LOFTON.
UPSTAIRS, DOWN THE HALL ON THE LEFT.
BE CAREFUL, ARKHAM. CHIEF CROMWELL IS UP THERE.
THANK YOU, GENTLEMEN.
WE'LL NEVER BE ABLE TO KEEP THIS ONE OUT OF THE PAPERS.
THAT MIGHT NOT BE A BAD THING. WE COULD USE MORE EYES ON THE STREETS.

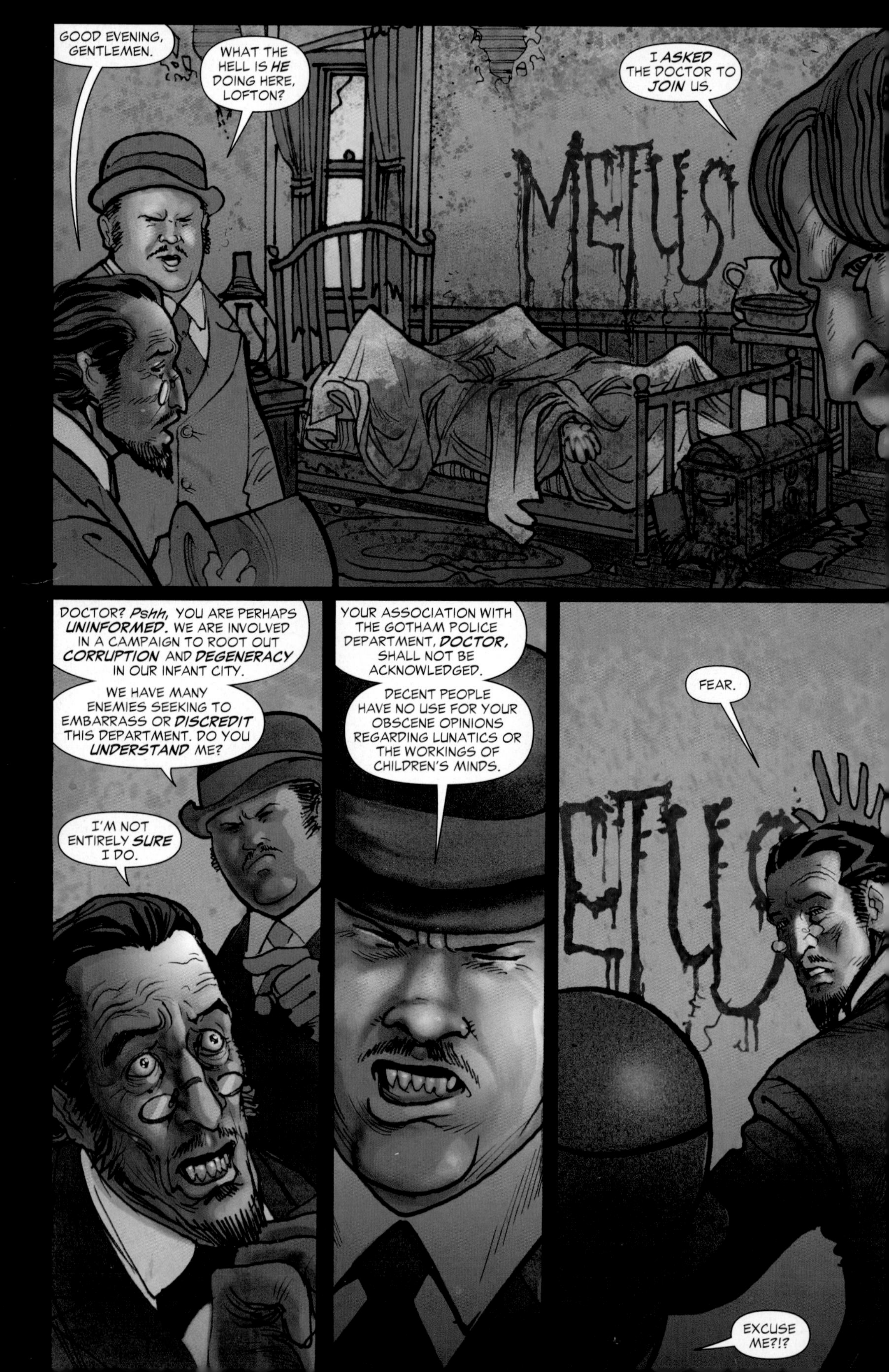
GOOD EVENING, GENTLEMEN.
WHAT THE HELL IS *HE* DOING HERE, LOFTON?
I *ASKED* THE DOCTOR TO *JOIN* US.
METUS
DOCTOR? *Pshh,* YOU ARE PERHAPS *UNINFORMED.* WE ARE INVOLVED IN A CAMPAIGN TO ROOT OUT *CORRUPTION* AND *DEGENERACY* IN OUR INFANT CITY.
WE HAVE MANY ENEMIES SEEKING TO EMBARRASS OR *DISCREDIT* THIS DEPARTMENT. DO YOU *UNDERSTAND* ME?
I'M NOT ENTIRELY *SURE* I DO.
YOUR ASSOCIATION WITH THE GOTHAM POLICE DEPARTMENT, *DOCTOR,* SHALL NOT BE ACKNOWLEDGED.
DECENT PEOPLE HAVE NO USE FOR YOUR OBSCENE OPINIONS REGARDING LUNATICS OR THE WORKINGS OF CHILDREN'S MINDS.
FEAR.
EXCUSE ME?!?

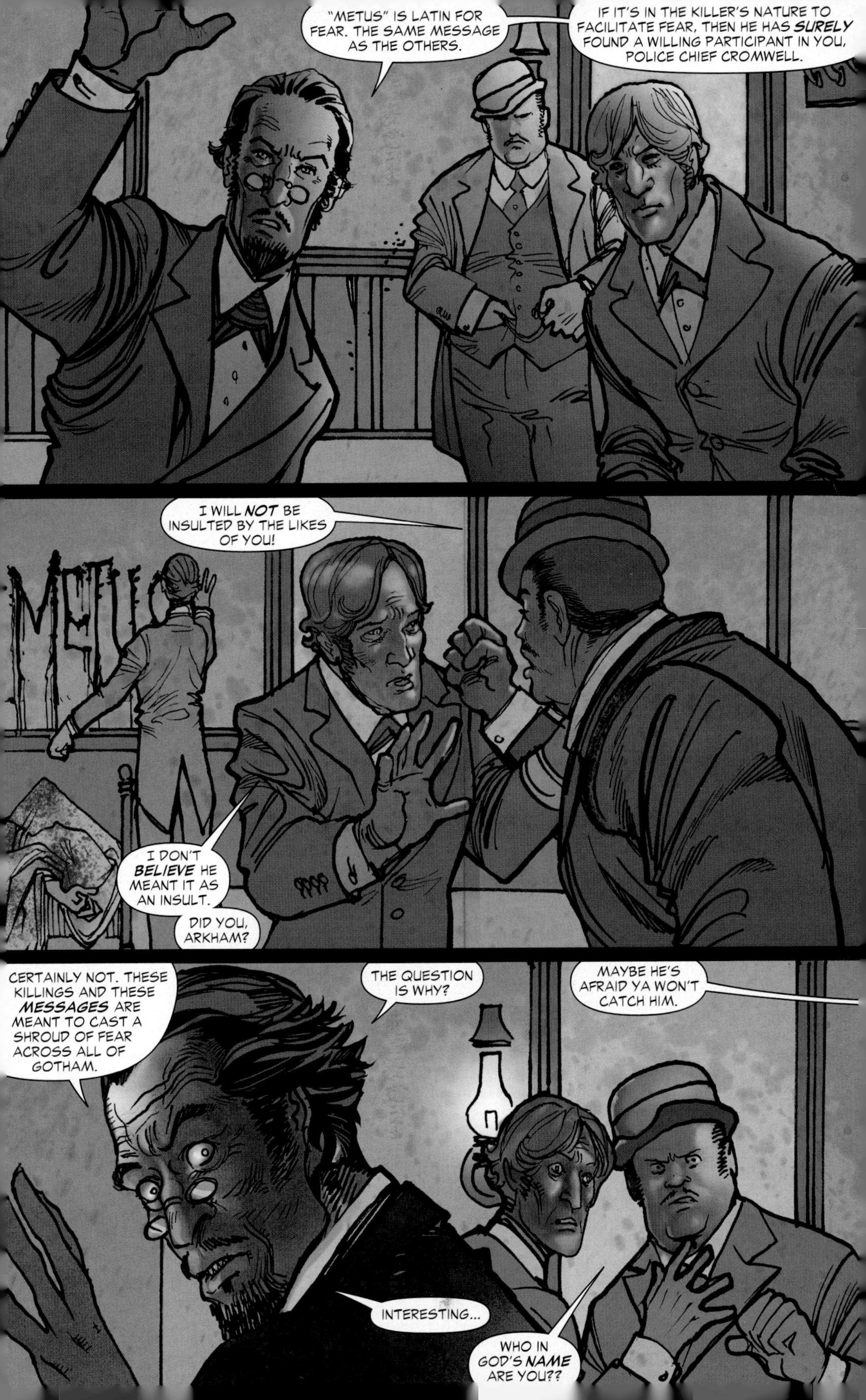
"METUS" IS LATIN FOR FEAR. THE SAME MESSAGE AS THE OTHERS.
IF IT'S IN THE KILLER'S NATURE TO FACILITATE FEAR, THEN HE HAS SURELY FOUND A WILLING PARTICIPANT IN YOU, POLICE CHIEF CROMWELL.
I WILL NOT BE INSULTED BY THE LIKES OF YOU!
METUS
I DON'T BELIEVE HE MEANT IT AS AN INSULT.
DID YOU, ARKHAM?
CERTAINLY NOT. THESE KILLINGS AND THESE MESSAGES ARE MEANT TO CAST A SHROUD OF FEAR ACROSS ALL OF GOTHAM.
THE QUESTION IS WHY?
MAYBE HE'S AFRAID YA WON'T CATCH HIM.
INTERESTING...
WHO IN GOD'S NAME ARE YOU??

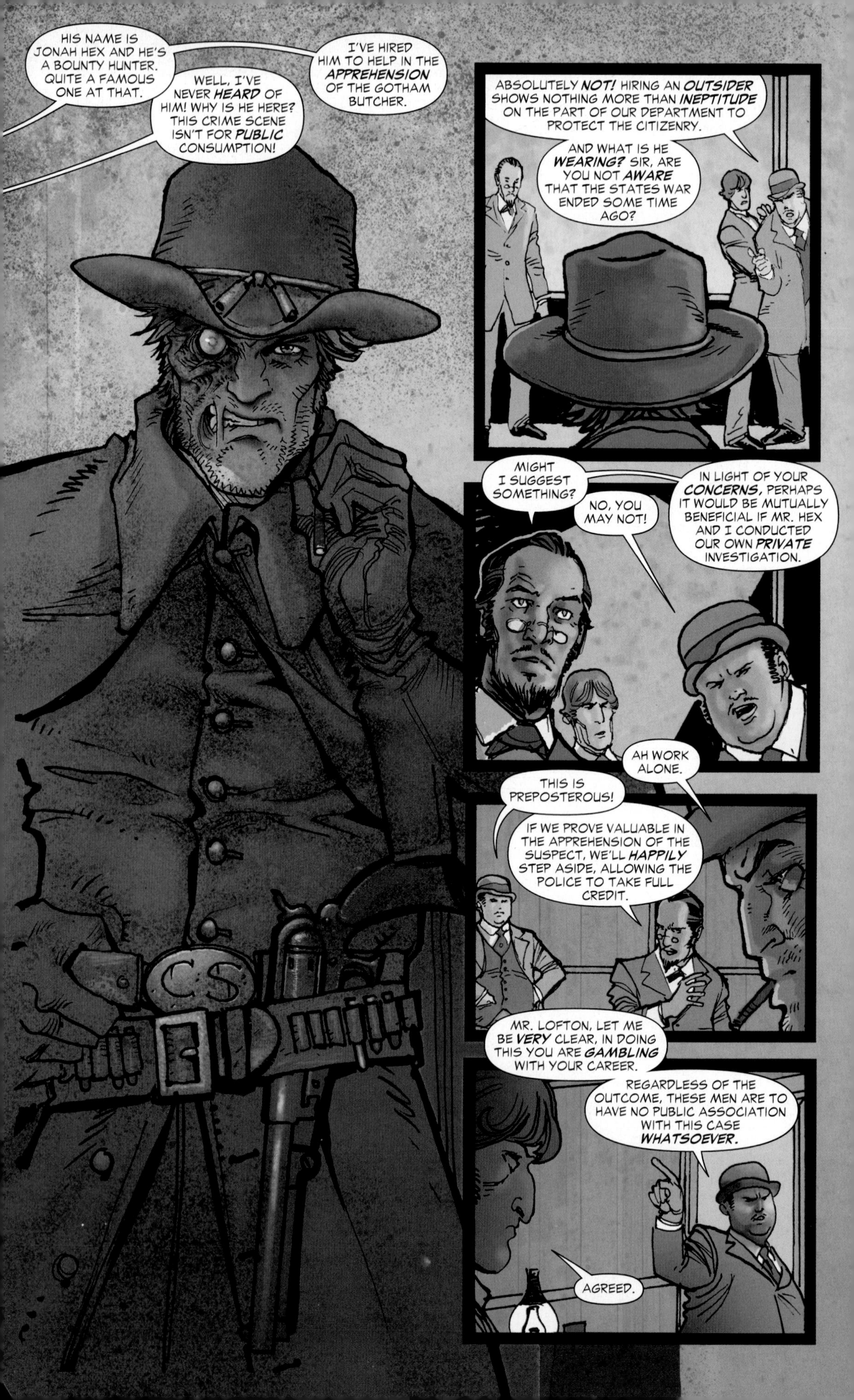
HIS NAME IS JONAH HEX AND HE'S A BOUNTY HUNTER. QUITE A FAMOUS ONE AT THAT.
I'VE HIRED HIM TO HELP IN THE APPREHENSION OF THE GOTHAM BUTCHER.
WELL, I'VE NEVER HEARD OF HIM! WHY IS HE HERE? THIS CRIME SCENE ISN'T FOR PUBLIC CONSUMPTION!
ABSOLUTELY NOT! HIRING AN OUTSIDER SHOWS NOTHING MORE THAN INEPTITUDE ON THE PART OF OUR DEPARTMENT TO PROTECT THE CITIZENRY.
AND WHAT IS HE WEARING? SIR, ARE YOU NOT AWARE THAT THE STATES WAR ENDED SOME TIME AGO?
MIGHT I SUGGEST SOMETHING?
NO, YOU MAY NOT!
IN LIGHT OF YOUR CONCERNS, PERHAPS IT WOULD BE MUTUALLY BENEFICIAL IF MR. HEX AND I CONDUCTED OUR OWN PRIVATE INVESTIGATION.
AH WORK ALONE.
THIS IS PREPOSTEROUS!
IF WE PROVE VALUABLE IN THE APPREHENSION OF THE SUSPECT, WE'LL HAPPILY STEP ASIDE, ALLOWING THE POLICE TO TAKE FULL CREDIT.
MR. LOFTON, LET ME BE VERY CLEAR, IN DOING THIS YOU ARE GAMBLING WITH YOUR CAREER.
REGARDLESS OF THE OUTCOME, THESE MEN ARE TO HAVE NO PUBLIC ASSOCIATION WITH THIS CASE WHATSOEVER.
AGREED.

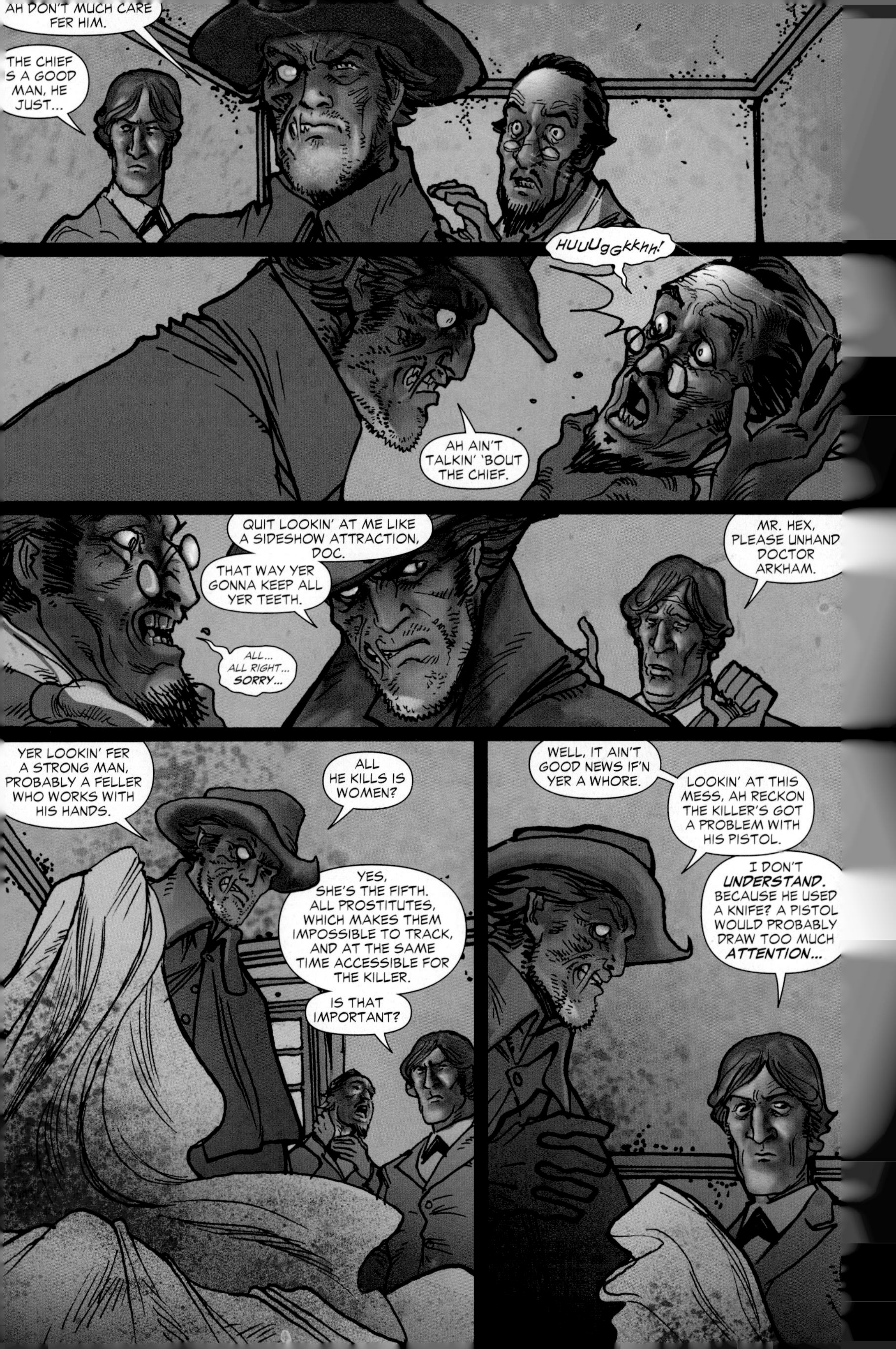
AH DON'T MUCH CARE FER HIM.
THE CHIEF S A GOOD MAN, HE JUST...
HUUUgGkkhh!
AH AIN'T TALKIN' 'BOUT THE CHIEF.
QUIT LOOKIN' AT ME LIKE A SIDESHOW ATTRACTION, DOC.
THAT WAY YER GONNA KEEP ALL YER TEETH.
ALL... ALL RIGHT... SORRY...
MR. HEX, PLEASE UNHAND DOCTOR ARKHAM.
YER LOOKIN' FER A STRONG MAN, PROBABLY A FELLER WHO WORKS WITH HIS HANDS.
ALL HE KILLS IS WOMEN?
YES, SHE'S THE FIFTH. ALL PROSTITUTES, WHICH MAKES THEM IMPOSSIBLE TO TRACK, AND AT THE SAME TIME ACCESSIBLE FOR THE KILLER.
IS THAT IMPORTANT?
WELL, IT AIN'T GOOD NEWS IF'N YER A WHORE.
LOOKIN' AT THIS MESS, AH RECKON THE KILLER'S GOT A PROBLEM WITH HIS PISTOL.
I DON'T UNDERSTAND. BECAUSE HE USED A KNIFE? A PISTOL WOULD PROBABLY DRAW TOO MUCH ATTENTION...

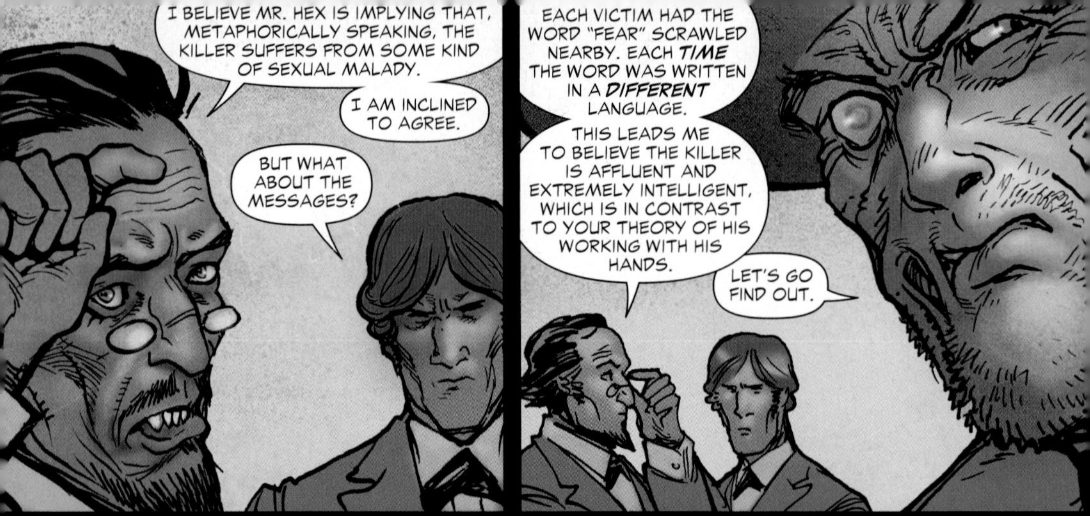
I BELIEVE MR. HEX IS IMPLYING THAT, METAPHORICALLY SPEAKING, THE KILLER SUFFERS FROM SOME KIND OF SEXUAL MALADY.
I AM INCLINED TO AGREE.
BUT WHAT ABOUT THE MESSAGES?
EACH VICTIM HAD THE WORD "FEAR" SCRAWLED NEARBY. EACH TIME THE WORD WAS WRITTEN IN A DIFFERENT LANGUAGE.
THIS LEADS ME TO BELIEVE THE KILLER IS AFFLUENT AND EXTREMELY INTELLIGENT, WHICH IS IN CONTRAST TO YOUR THEORY OF HIS WORKING WITH HIS HANDS.
LET'S GO FIND OUT.

# Things get bloody

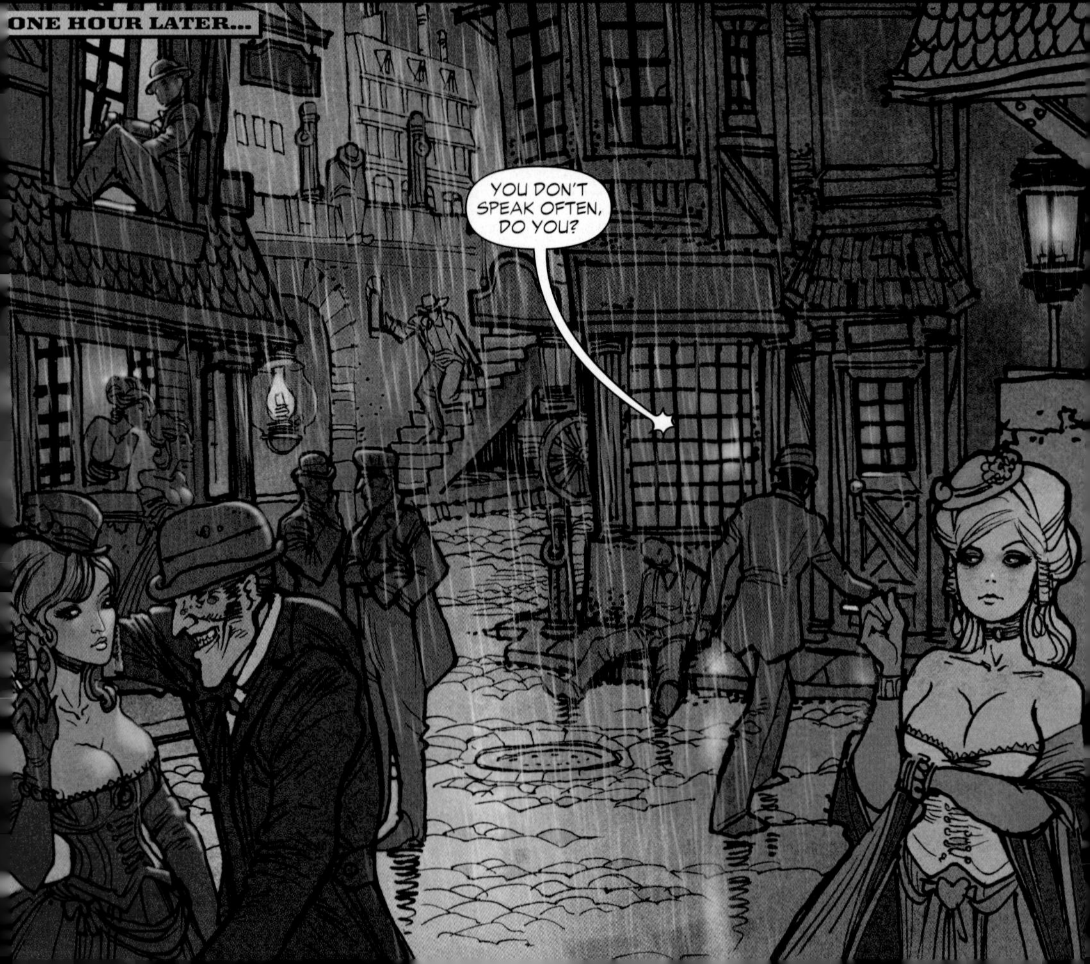
ONE HOUR LATER...
YOU DON'T SPEAK OFTEN, DO YOU?

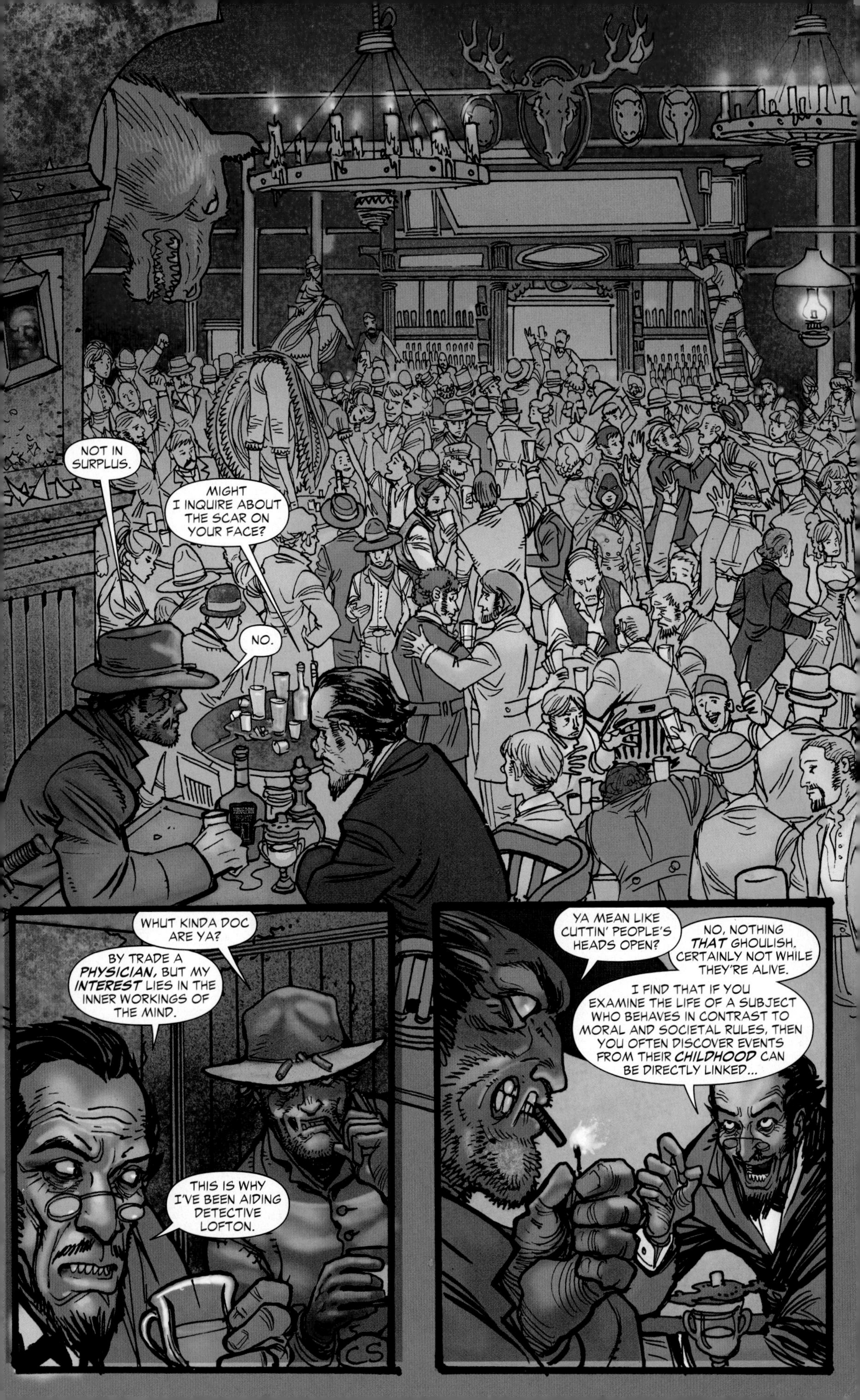
NOT IN SURPLUS.
MIGHT I INQUIRE ABOUT THE SCAR ON YOUR FACE?
NO.
WHUT KINDA DOC ARE YA?
BY TRADE A PHYSICIAN, BUT MY INTEREST LIES IN THE INNER WORKINGS OF THE MIND.
THIS IS WHY I'VE BEEN AIDING DETECTIVE LOFTON.
YA MEAN LIKE CUTTIN' PEOPLE'S HEADS OPEN?
NO, NOTHING THAT GHOULISH. CERTAINLY NOT WHILE THEY'RE ALIVE.
I FIND THAT IF YOU EXAMINE THE LIFE OF A SUBJECT WHO BEHAVES IN CONTRAST TO MORAL AND SOCIETAL RULES, THEN YOU OFTEN DISCOVER EVENTS FROM THEIR CHILDHOOD CAN BE DIRECTLY LINKED...

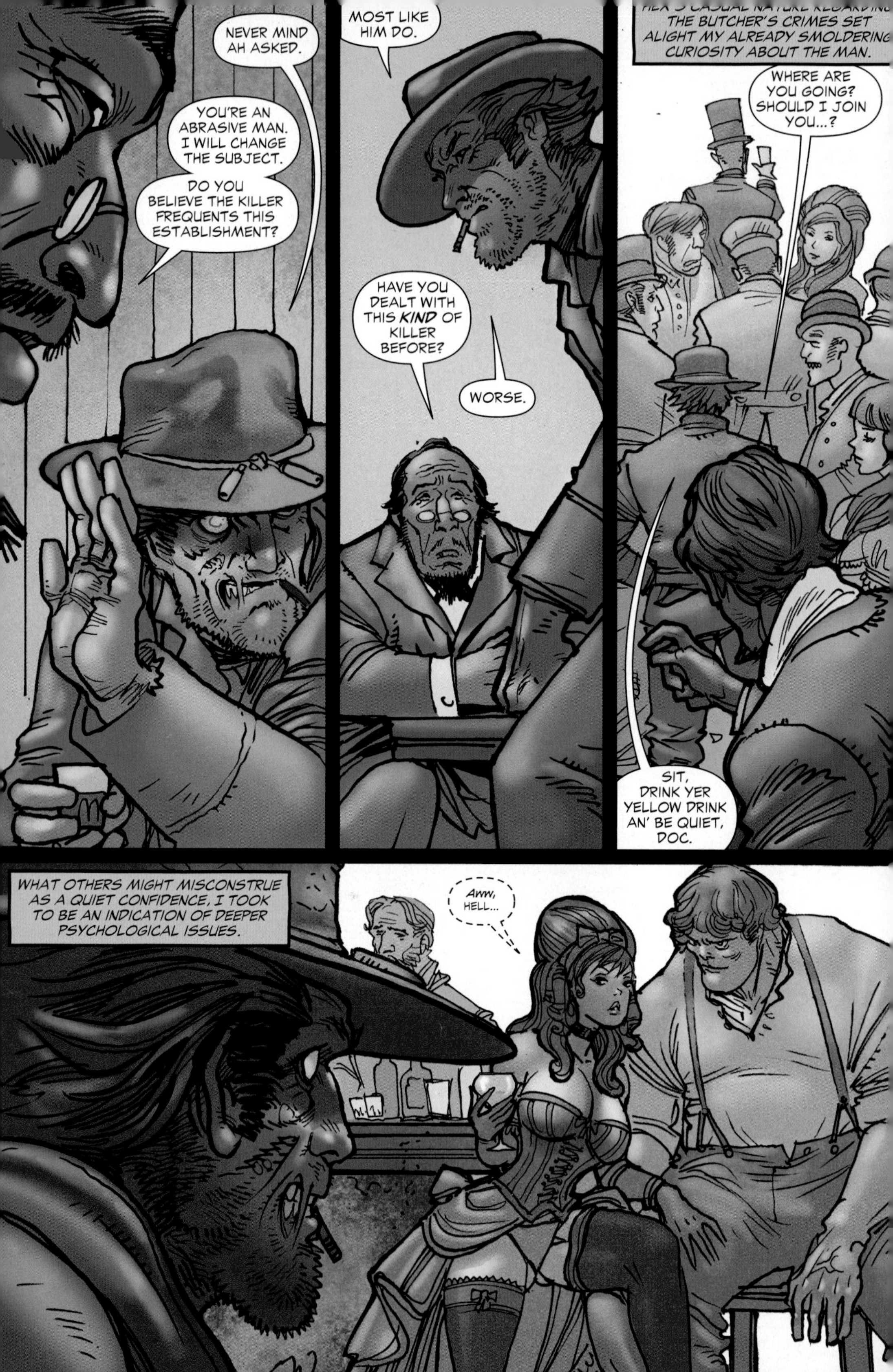
NEVER MIND AH ASKED.
YOU'RE AN ABRASIVE MAN. I WILL CHANGE THE SUBJECT.
DO YOU BELIEVE THE KILLER FREQUENTS THIS ESTABLISHMENT?
MOST LIKE HIM DO.
HAVE YOU DEALT WITH THIS KIND OF KILLER BEFORE?
WORSE.
THE BUTCHER'S CRIMES SET ALIGHT MY ALREADY SMOLDERING CURIOSITY ABOUT THE MAN.
WHERE ARE YOU GOING? SHOULD I JOIN YOU...?
SIT, DRINK YER YELLOW DRINK AN' BE QUIET, DOC.
WHAT OTHERS MIGHT MISCONSTRUE AS A QUIET CONFIDENCE, I TOOK TO BE AN INDICATION OF DEEPER PSYCHOLOGICAL ISSUES.
Aww, HELL...

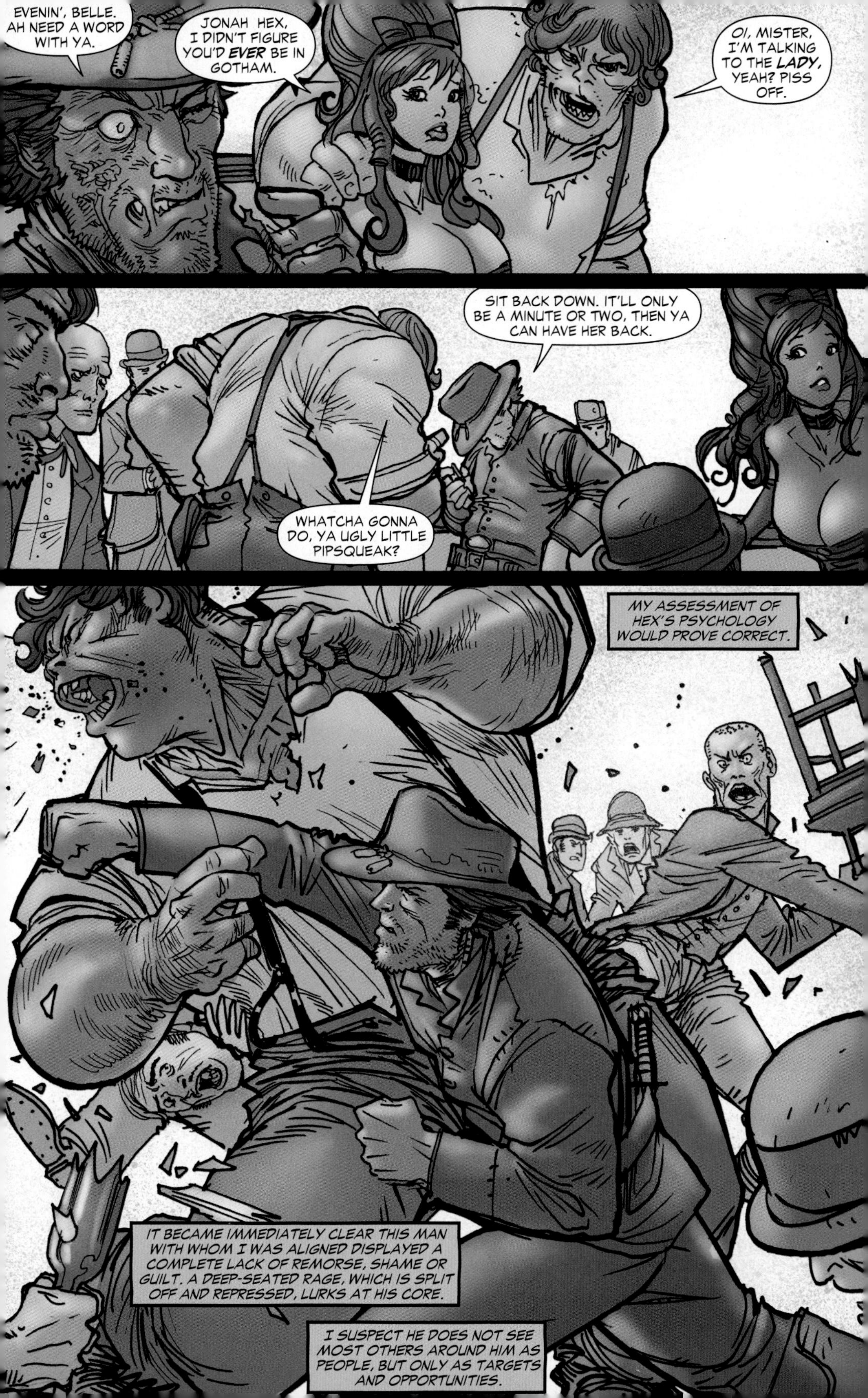

EVENIN', BELLE. AH NEED A WORD WITH YA.
JONAH HEX, I DIDN'T FIGURE YOU'D EVER BE IN GOTHAM.
OI, MISTER, I'M TALKING TO THE LADY, YEAH? PISS OFF.
SIT BACK DOWN. IT'LL ONLY BE A MINUTE OR TWO, THEN YA CAN HAVE HER BACK.
WHATCHA GONNA DO, YA UGLY LITTLE PIPSQUEAK?
MY ASSESSMENT OF HEX'S PSYCHOLOGY WOULD PROVE CORRECT.
IT BECAME IMMEDIATELY CLEAR THIS MAN WITH WHOM I WAS ALIGNED DISPLAYED A COMPLETE LACK OF REMORSE, SHAME OR GUILT. A DEEP-SEATED RAGE, WHICH IS SPLIT OFF AND REPRESSED, LURKS AT HIS CORE.
I SUSPECT HE DOES NOT SEE MOST OTHERS AROUND HIM AS PEOPLE, BUT ONLY AS TARGETS AND OPPORTUNITIES.

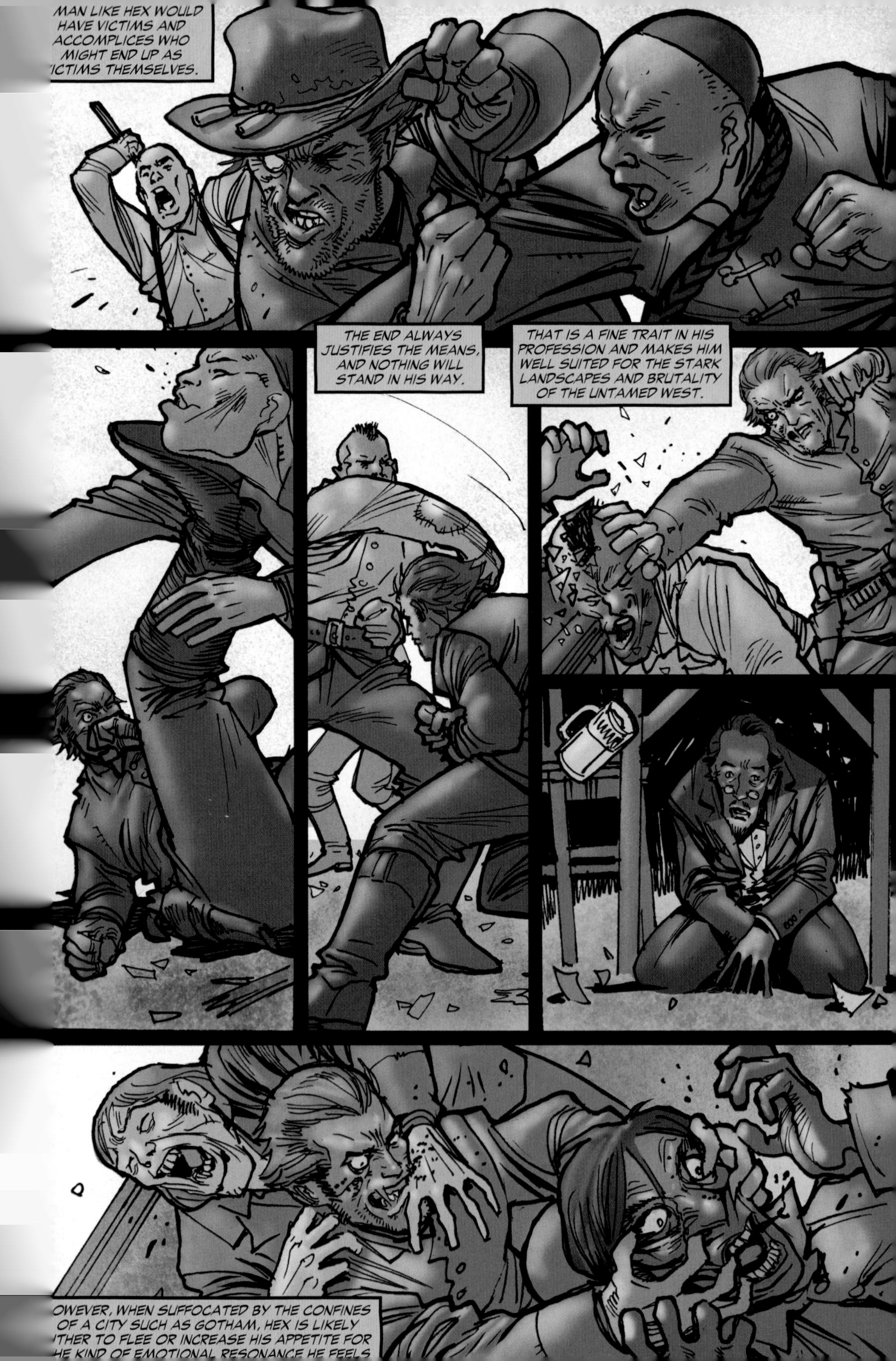
MAN LIKE HEX WOULD HAVE VICTIMS AND ACCOMPLICES WHO MIGHT END UP AS VICTIMS THEMSELVES.
THE END ALWAYS JUSTIFIES THE MEANS, AND NOTHING WILL STAND IN HIS WAY.
THAT IS A FINE TRAIT IN HIS PROFESSION AND MAKES HIM WELL SUITED FOR THE STARK LANDSCAPES AND BRUTALITY OF THE UNTAMED WEST.
OWEVER, WHEN SUFFOCATED BY THE CONFINES OF A CITY SUCH AS GOTHAM, HEX IS LIKELY ITHER TO FLEE OR INCREASE HIS APPETITE FOR HE KIND OF EMOTIONAL RESONANCE HE FEELS

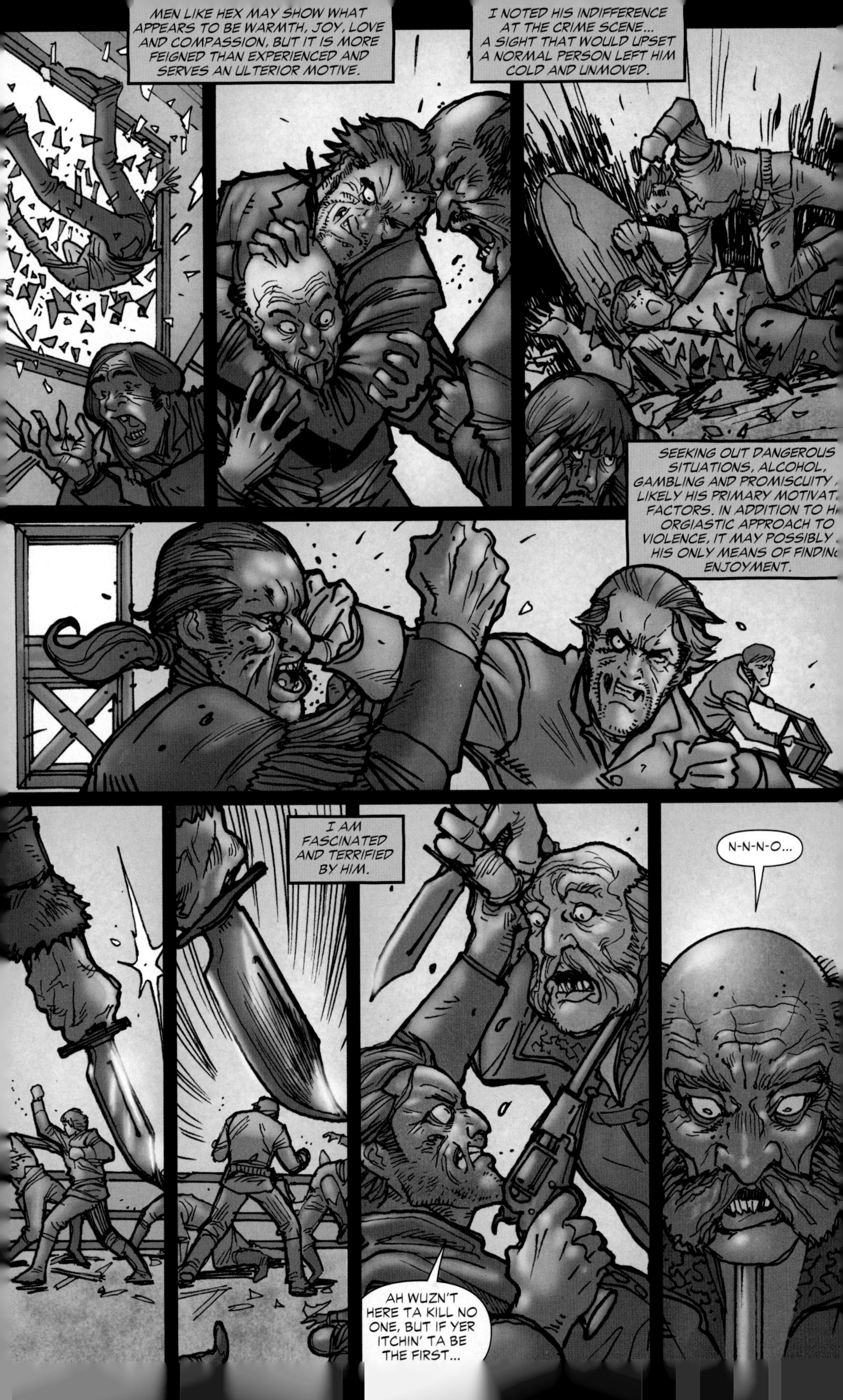
MEN LIKE HEX MAY SHOW WHAT APPEARS TO BE WARMTH, JOY, LOVE AND COMPASSION, BUT IT IS MORE FEIGNED THAN EXPERIENCED AND SERVES AN ULTERIOR MOTIVE.
I NOTED HIS INDIFFERENCE AT THE CRIME SCENE... A SIGHT THAT WOULD UPSET A NORMAL PERSON LEFT HIM COLD AND UNMOVED.
SEEKING OUT DANGEROUS SITUATIONS, ALCOHOL, GAMBLING AND PROMISCUITY LIKELY HIS PRIMARY MOTIVAT FACTORS. IN ADDITION TO H ORGIASTIC APPROACH TO VIOLENCE, IT MAY POSSIBLY HIS ONLY MEANS OF FINDING ENJOYMENT.
I AM FASCINATED AND TERRIFIED BY HIM.
AH WUZN'T HERE TA KILL NO ONE, BUT IF YER ITCHIN' TA BE THE FIRST...
N-N-N-O...

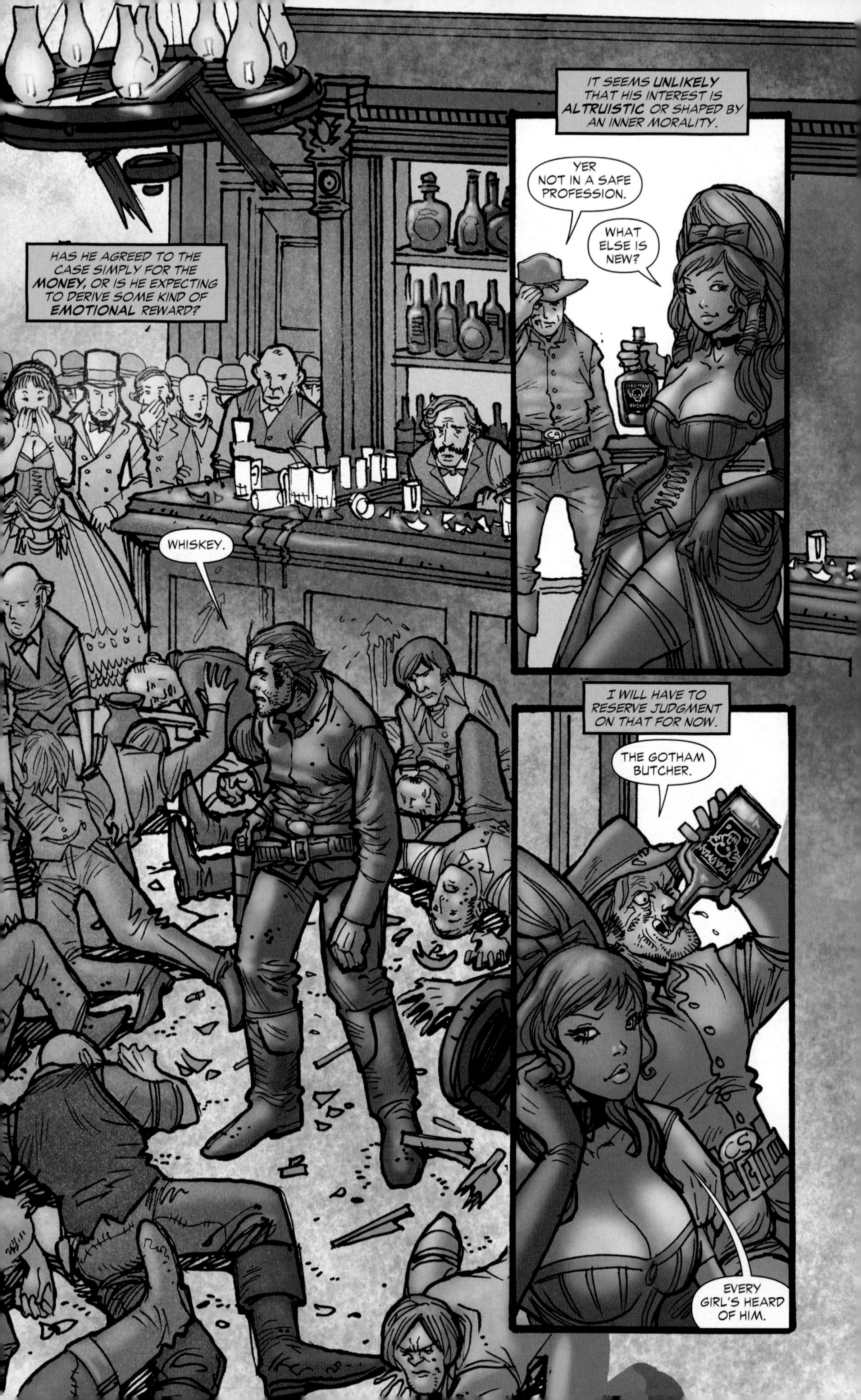
HAS HE AGREED TO THE CASE SIMPLY FOR THE MONEY, OR IS HE EXPECTING TO DERIVE SOME KIND OF EMOTIONAL REWARD?
WHISKEY.
IT SEEMS UNLIKELY THAT HIS INTEREST IS ALTRUISTIC OR SHAPED BY AN INNER MORALITY.
YER NOT IN A SAFE PROFESSION.
WHAT ELSE IS NEW?
I WILL HAVE TO RESERVE JUDGMENT ON THAT FOR NOW.
THE GOTHAM BUTCHER.
EVERY GIRL'S HEARD OF HIM.

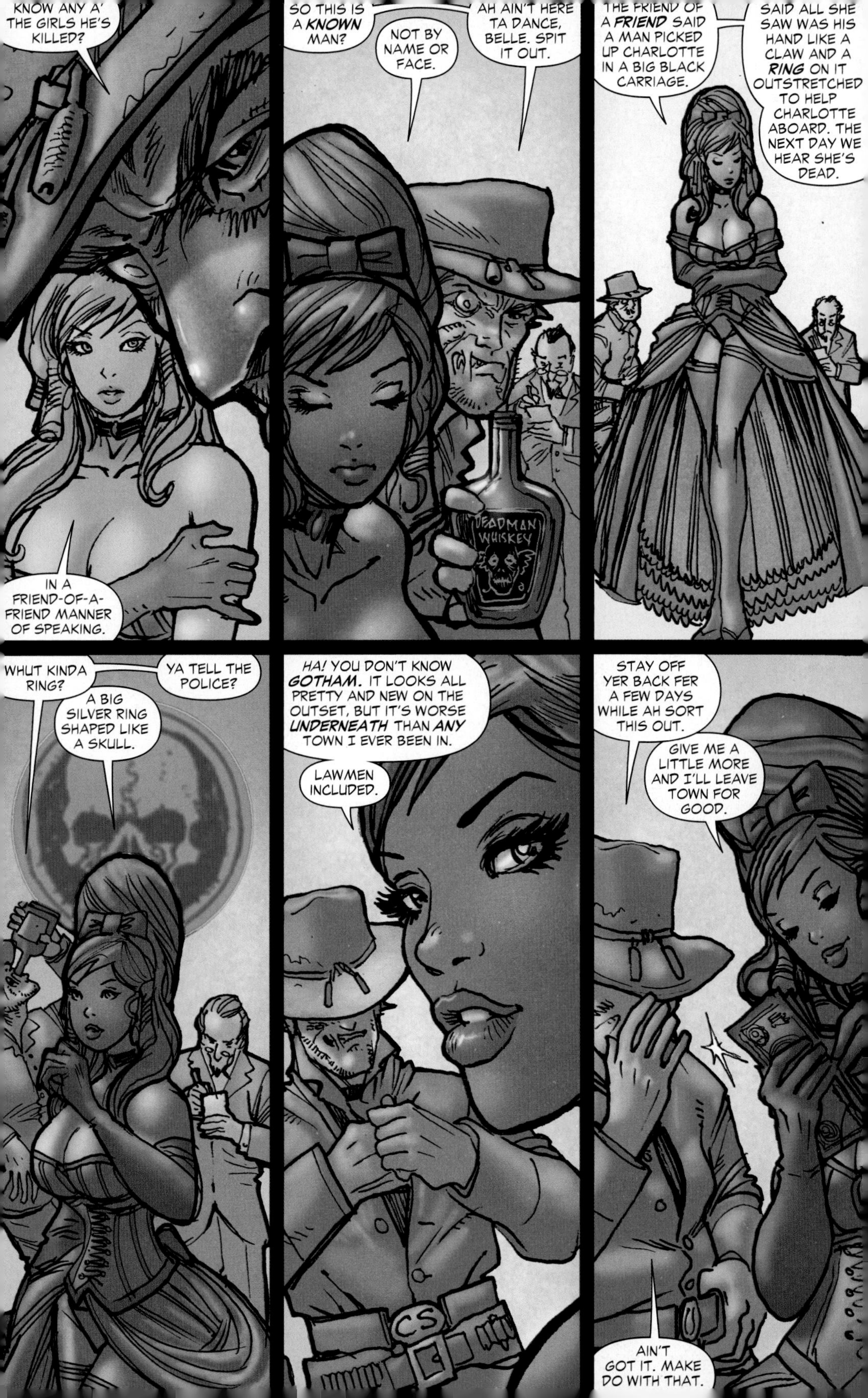

KNOW ANY A' THE GIRLS HE'S KILLED?
IN A FRIEND-OF-A-FRIEND MANNER OF SPEAKING.
SO THIS IS A **KNOWN** MAN?
NOT BY NAME OR FACE.
AH AIN'T HERE TA DANCE, BELLE. SPIT IT OUT.
DEADMAN WHISKEY
THE FRIEND OF A **FRIEND** SAID A MAN PICKED UP CHARLOTTE IN A BIG BLACK CARRIAGE.
SAID ALL SHE SAW WAS HIS HAND LIKE A CLAW AND A **RING** ON IT OUTSTRETCHED TO HELP CHARLOTTE ABOARD. THE NEXT DAY WE HEAR SHE'S DEAD.
WHUT KINDA RING?
YA TELL THE POLICE?
A BIG SILVER RING SHAPED LIKE A SKULL.
*HA!* YOU DON'T KNOW **GOTHAM.** IT LOOKS ALL PRETTY AND NEW ON THE OUTSET, BUT IT'S WORSE ***UNDERNEATH*** THAN ***ANY*** TOWN I EVER BEEN IN.
LAWMEN INCLUDED.
CS
STAY OFF YER BACK FER A FEW DAYS WHILE AH SORT THIS OUT.
GIVE ME A LITTLE MORE AND I'LL LEAVE TOWN FOR GOOD.
AIN'T GOT IT. MAKE DO WITH THAT.

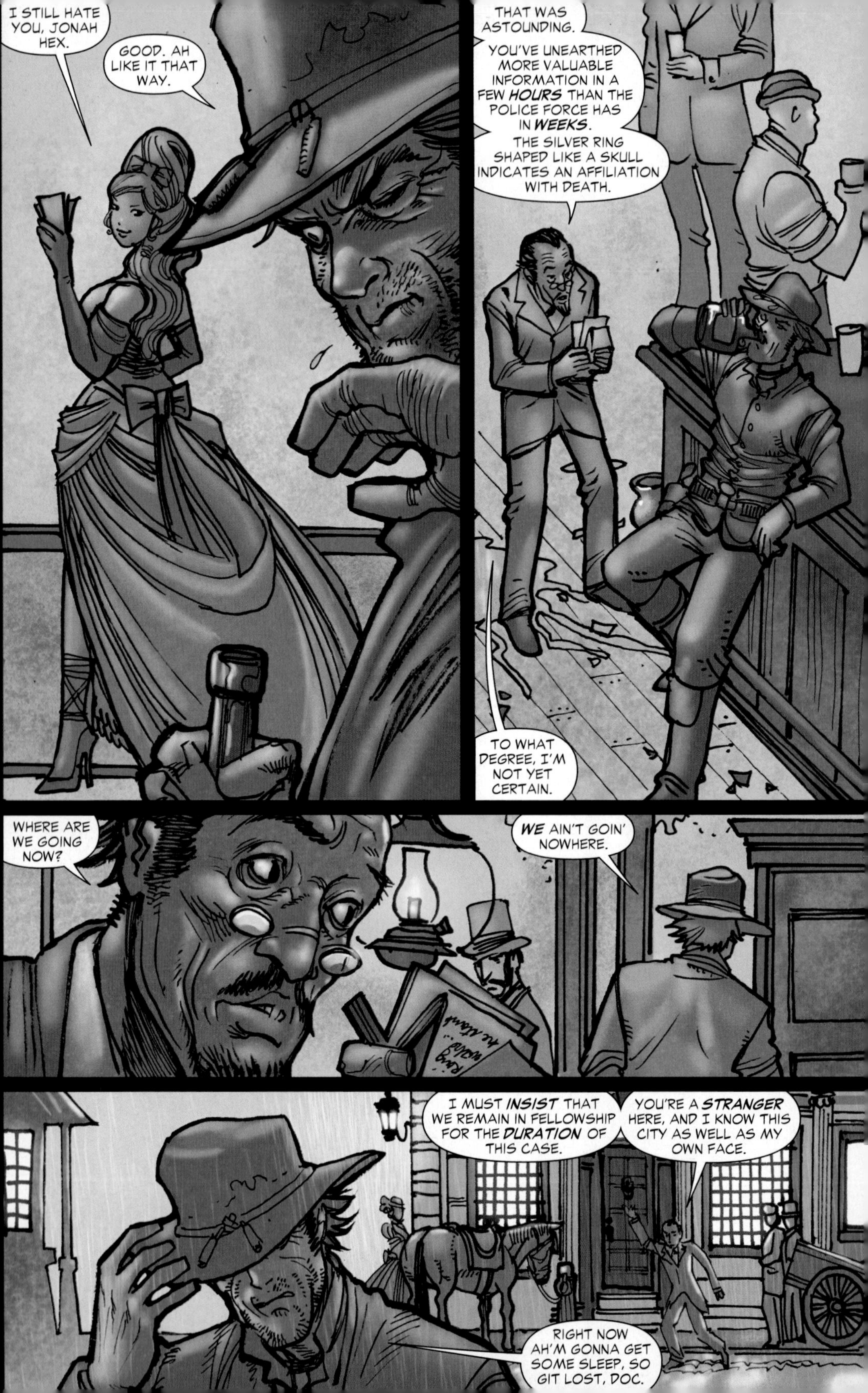
I STILL HATE YOU, JONAH HEX.
GOOD. AH LIKE IT THAT WAY.
THAT WAS ASTOUNDING.
YOU'VE UNEARTHED MORE VALUABLE INFORMATION IN A FEW HOURS THAN THE POLICE FORCE HAS IN WEEKS.
THE SILVER RING SHAPED LIKE A SKULL INDICATES AN AFFILIATION WITH DEATH.
TO WHAT DEGREE, I'M NOT YET CERTAIN.
WHERE ARE WE GOING NOW?
WE AIN'T GOIN' NOWHERE.
I MUST INSIST THAT WE REMAIN IN FELLOWSHIP FOR THE DURATION OF THIS CASE.
YOU'RE A STRANGER HERE, AND I KNOW THIS CITY AS WELL AS MY OWN FACE.
RIGHT NOW AH'M GONNA GET SOME SLEEP, SO GIT LOST, DOC.

# No rest for the wicked

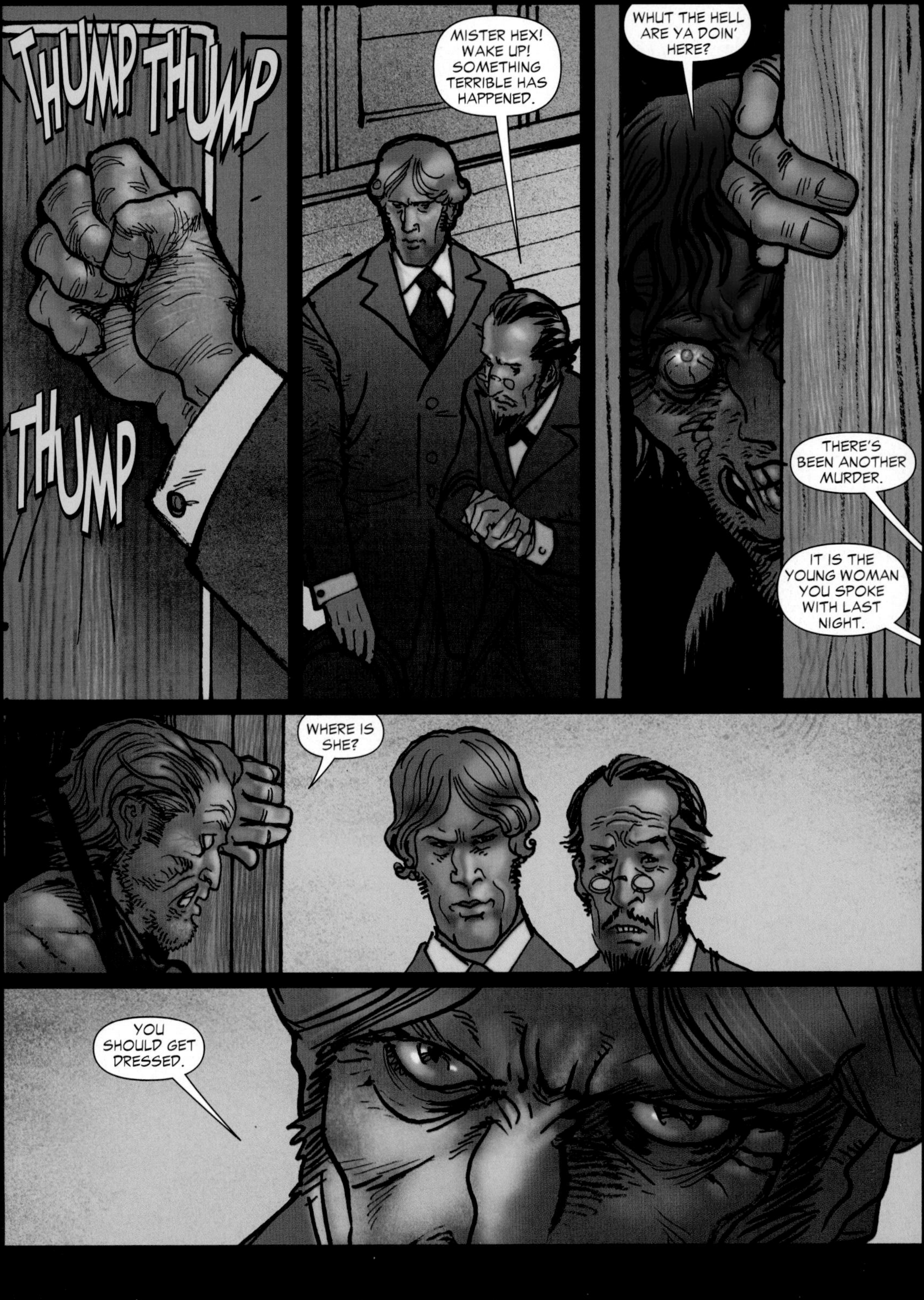
THUMP THUMP
THUMP
MISTER HEX! WAKE UP! SOMETHING TERRIBLE HAS HAPPENED.
WHUT THE HELL ARE YA DOIN' HERE?
THERE'S BEEN ANOTHER MURDER.
IT IS THE YOUNG WOMAN YOU SPOKE WITH LAST NIGHT.
WHERE IS SHE?
YOU SHOULD GET DRESSED.

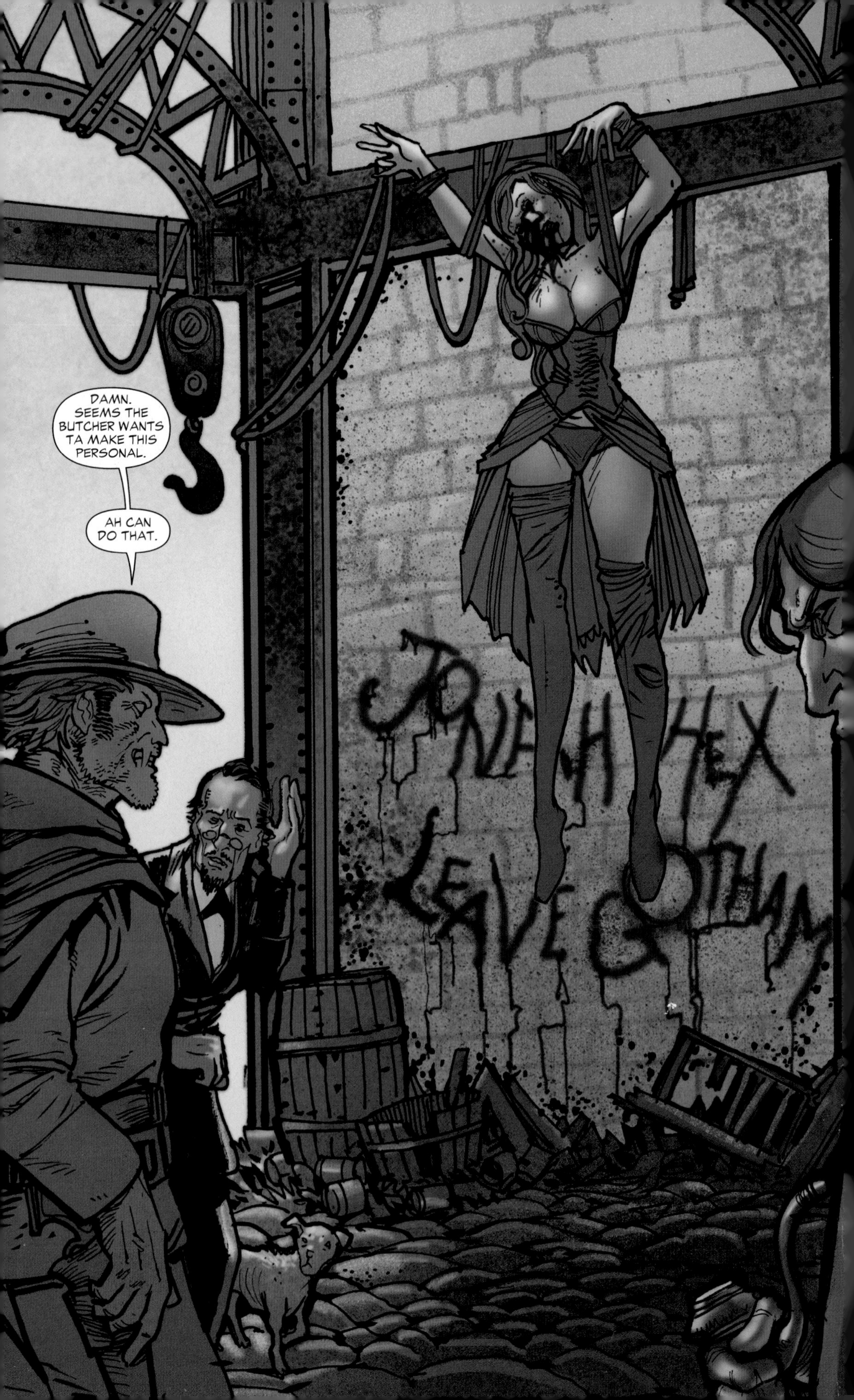
DAMN. SEEMS THE BUTCHER WANTS TA MAKE THIS PERSONAL.
AH CAN DO THAT.
JONAH HEX
LEAVE GOTHAM

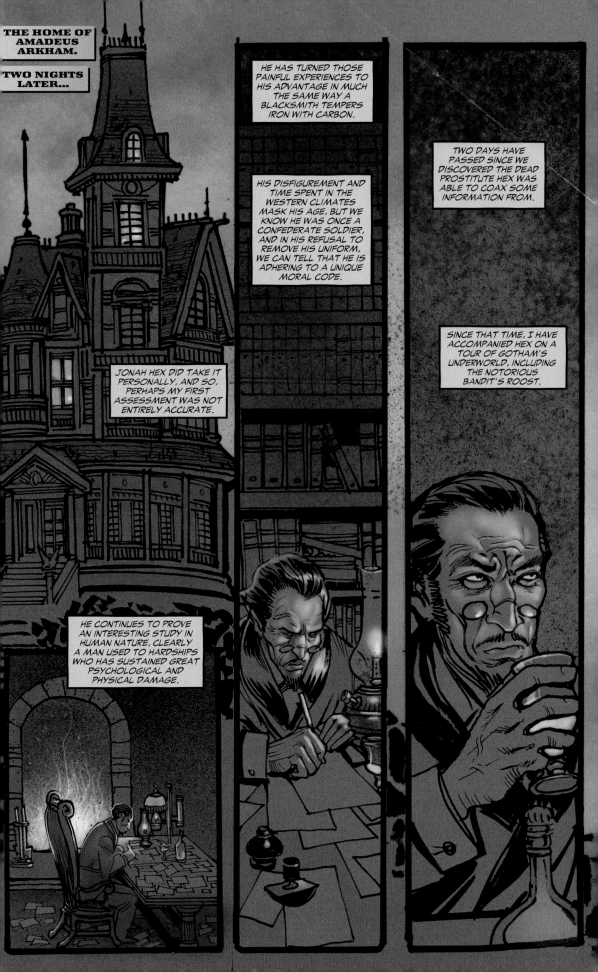

THE HOME OF AMADEUS ARKHAM.

TWO NIGHTS LATER...

HE HAS TURNED THOSE PAINFUL EXPERIENCES TO HIS ADVANTAGE IN MUCH THE SAME WAY A BLACKSMITH TEMPERS IRON WITH CARBON.

HIS DISFIGUREMENT AND TIME SPENT IN THE WESTERN CLIMATES MASK HIS AGE, BUT WE KNOW HE WAS ONCE A CONFEDERATE SOLDIER, AND IN HIS REFUSAL TO REMOVE HIS UNIFORM, WE CAN TELL THAT HE IS ADHERING TO A UNIQUE MORAL CODE.

JONAH HEX DID TAKE IT PERSONALLY, AND SO, PERHAPS MY FIRST ASSESSMENT WAS NOT ENTIRELY ACCURATE.

TWO DAYS HAVE PASSED SINCE WE DISCOVERED THE DEAD PROSTITUTE HEX WAS ABLE TO COAX SOME INFORMATION FROM.

SINCE THAT TIME, I HAVE ACCOMPANIED HEX ON A TOUR OF GOTHAM'S UNDERWORLD, INCLUDING THE NOTORIOUS BANDIT'S ROOST.

HE CONTINUES TO PROVE AN INTERESTING STUDY IN HUMAN NATURE, CLEARLY A MAN USED TO HARDSHIPS WHO HAS SUSTAINED GREAT PSYCHOLOGICAL AND PHYSICAL DAMAGE.

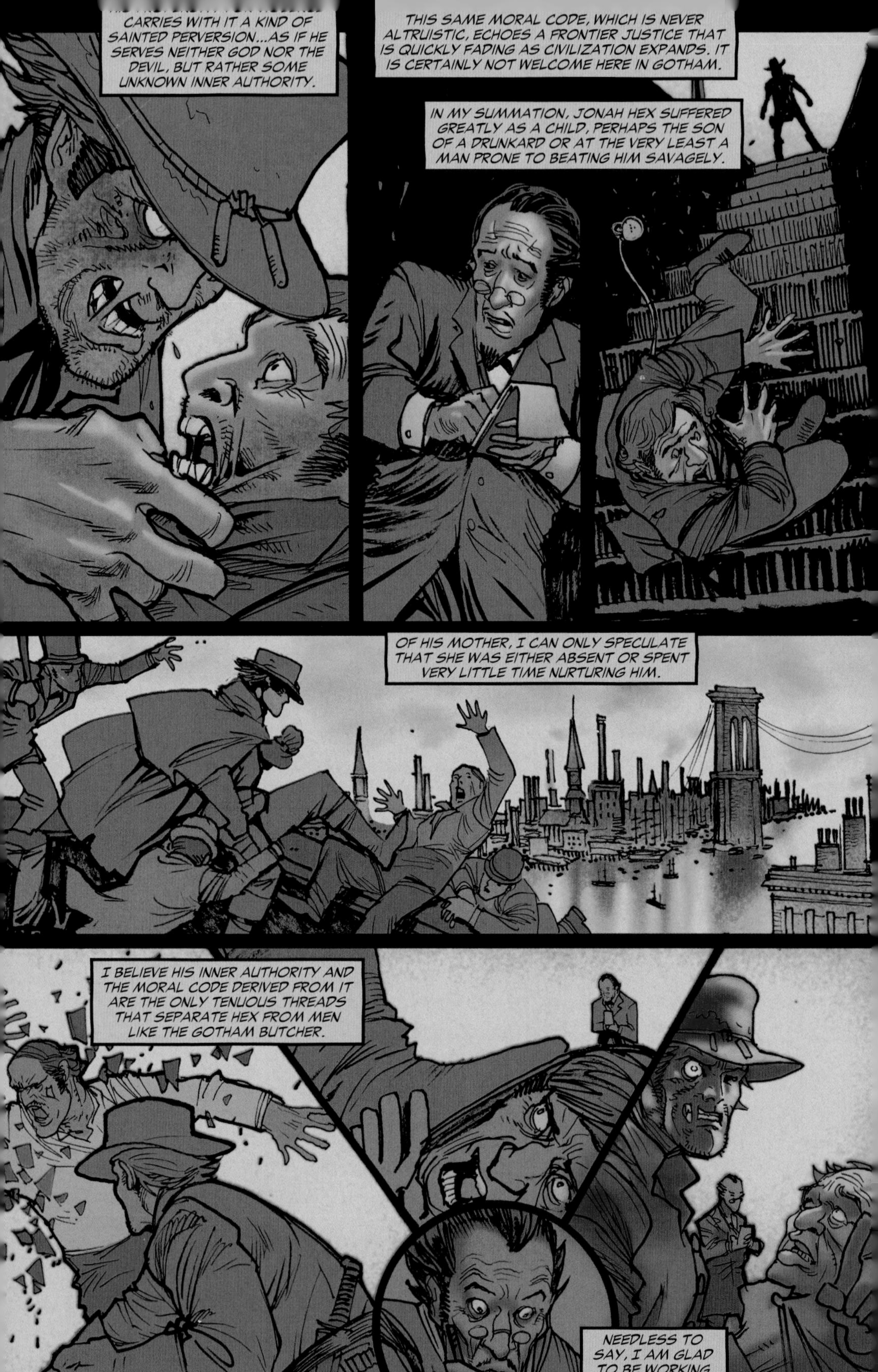
CARRIES WITH IT A KIND OF SAINTED PERVERSION...AS IF HE SERVES NEITHER GOD NOR THE DEVIL, BUT RATHER SOME UNKNOWN INNER AUTHORITY.
THIS SAME MORAL CODE, WHICH IS NEVER ALTRUISTIC, ECHOES A FRONTIER JUSTICE THAT IS QUICKLY FADING AS CIVILIZATION EXPANDS. IT IS CERTAINLY NOT WELCOME HERE IN GOTHAM.
IN MY SUMMATION, JONAH HEX SUFFERED GREATLY AS A CHILD, PERHAPS THE SON OF A DRUNKARD OR AT THE VERY LEAST A MAN PRONE TO BEATING HIM SAVAGELY.
OF HIS MOTHER, I CAN ONLY SPECULATE THAT SHE WAS EITHER ABSENT OR SPENT VERY LITTLE TIME NURTURING HIM.
I BELIEVE HIS INNER AUTHORITY AND THE MORAL CODE DERIVED FROM IT ARE THE ONLY TENUOUS THREADS THAT SEPARATE HEX FROM MEN LIKE THE GOTHAM BUTCHER.
NEEDLESS TO SAY, I AM GLAD TO BE WORKING WITH HIM, RATHER THAN AGAINST.

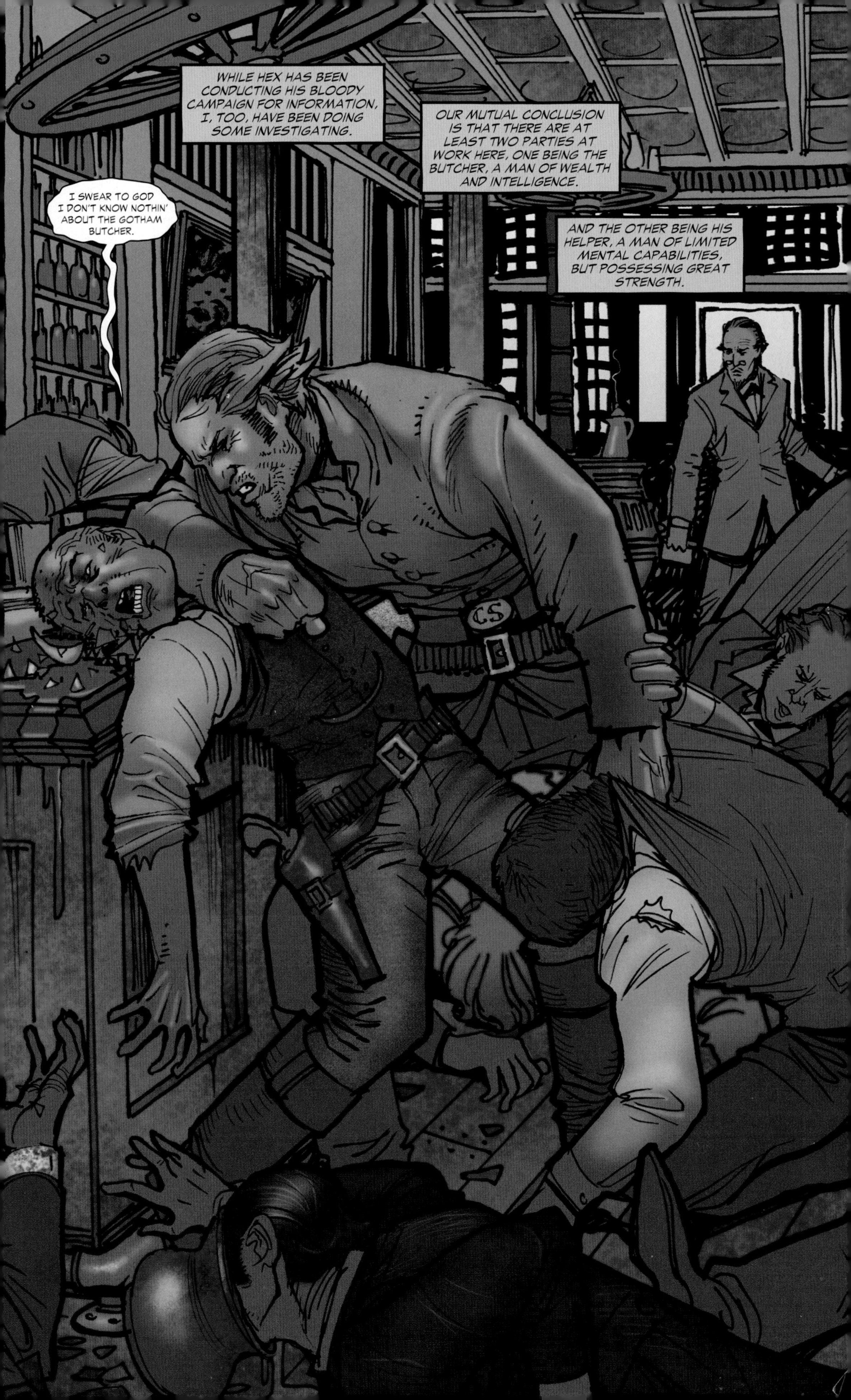
WHILE HEX HAS BEEN CONDUCTING HIS BLOODY CAMPAIGN FOR INFORMATION, I, TOO, HAVE BEEN DOING SOME INVESTIGATING.
I SWEAR TO GOD I DON'T KNOW NOTHIN' ABOUT THE GOTHAM BUTCHER.
OUR MUTUAL CONCLUSION IS THAT THERE ARE AT LEAST TWO PARTIES AT WORK HERE, ONE BEING THE BUTCHER, A MAN OF WEALTH AND INTELLIGENCE.
AND THE OTHER BEING HIS HELPER, A MAN OF LIMITED MENTAL CAPABILITIES, BUT POSSESSING GREAT STRENGTH.

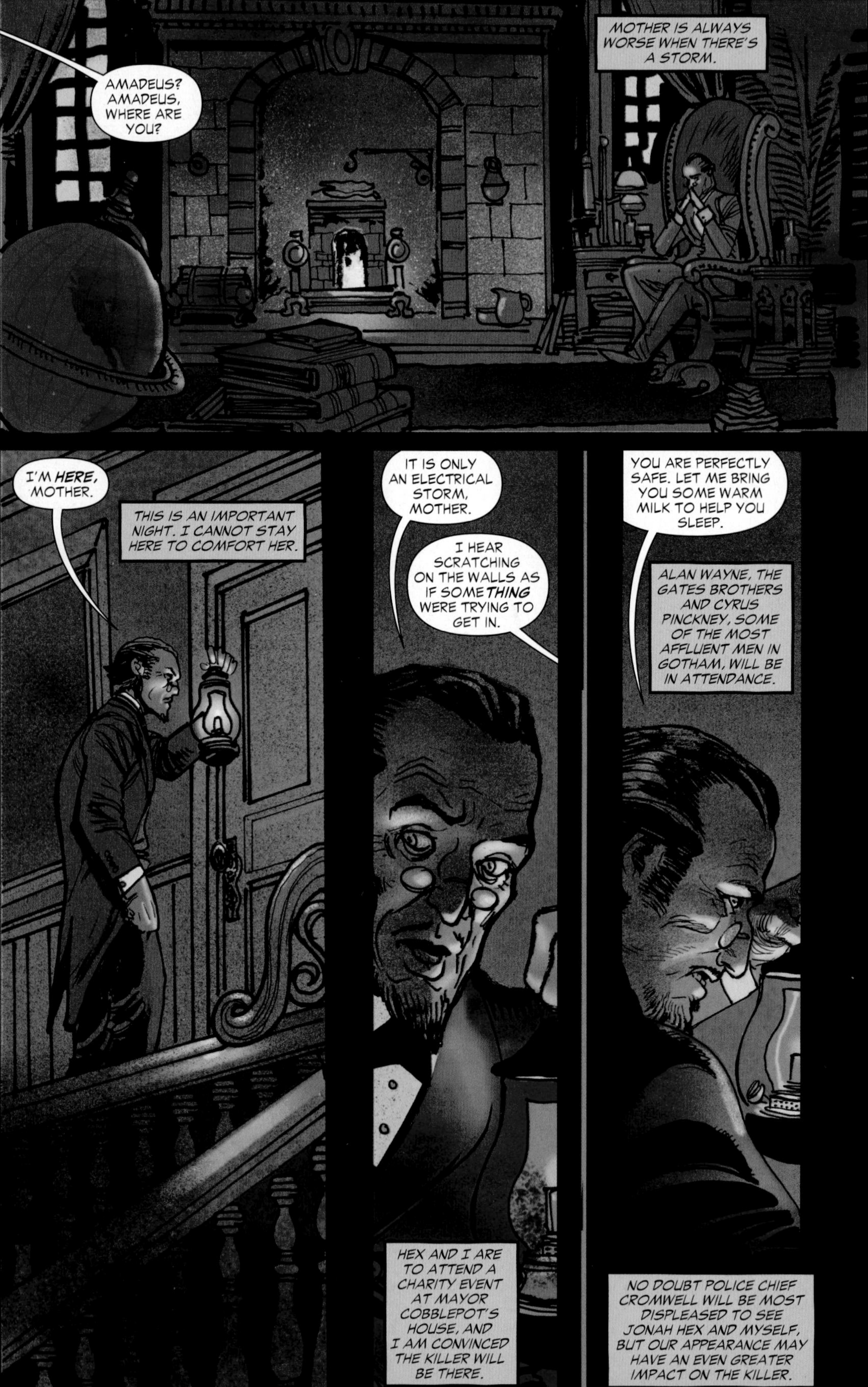
AMADEUS? AMADEUS, WHERE ARE YOU?
MOTHER IS ALWAYS WORSE WHEN THERE'S A STORM.
I'M HERE, MOTHER.
THIS IS AN IMPORTANT NIGHT. I CANNOT STAY HERE TO COMFORT HER.
IT IS ONLY AN ELECTRICAL STORM, MOTHER.
I HEAR SCRATCHING ON THE WALLS AS IF SOMETHING WERE TRYING TO GET IN.
HEX AND I ARE TO ATTEND A CHARITY EVENT AT MAYOR COBBLEPOT'S HOUSE, AND I AM CONVINCED THE KILLER WILL BE THERE.
YOU ARE PERFECTLY SAFE. LET ME BRING YOU SOME WARM MILK TO HELP YOU SLEEP.
ALAN WAYNE, THE GATES BROTHERS AND CYRUS PINCKNEY, SOME OF THE MOST AFFLUENT MEN IN GOTHAM, WILL BE IN ATTENDANCE.
NO DOUBT POLICE CHIEF CROMWELL WILL BE MOST DISPLEASED TO SEE JONAH HEX AND MYSELF, BUT OUR APPEARANCE MAY HAVE AN EVEN GREATER IMPACT ON THE KILLER.

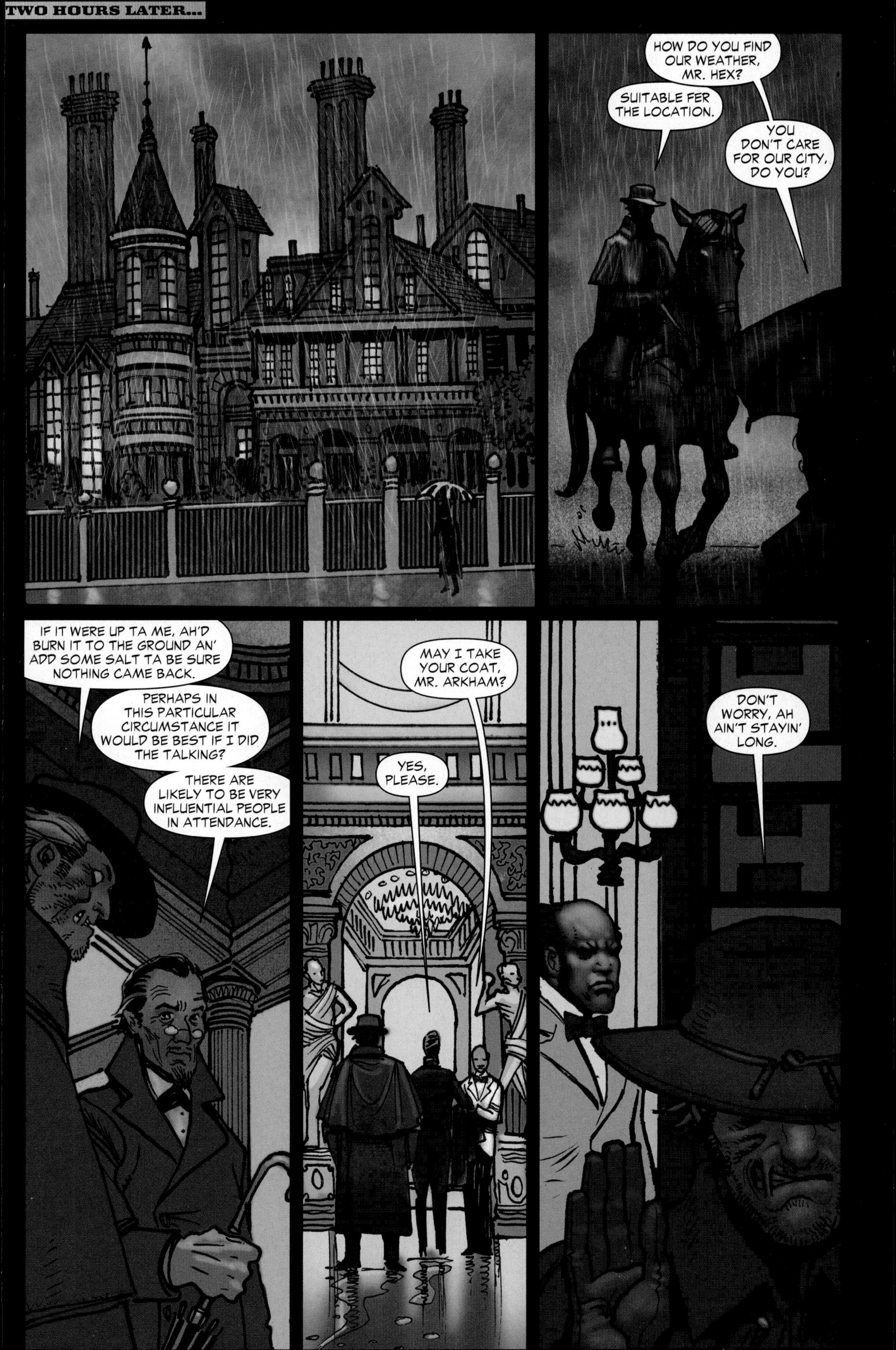
TWO HOURS LATER...
HOW DO YOU FIND OUR WEATHER, MR. HEX?
SUITABLE FER THE LOCATION.
YOU DON'T CARE FOR OUR CITY, DO YOU?
IF IT WERE UP TA ME, AH'D BURN IT TO THE GROUND AN' ADD SOME SALT TA BE SURE NOTHING CAME BACK.
PERHAPS IN THIS PARTICULAR CIRCUMSTANCE IT WOULD BE BEST IF I DID THE TALKING?
THERE ARE LIKELY TO BE VERY INFLUENTIAL PEOPLE IN ATTENDANCE.
MAY I TAKE YOUR COAT, MR. ARKHAM?
YES, PLEASE.
DON'T WORRY, AH AIN'T STAYIN' LONG.

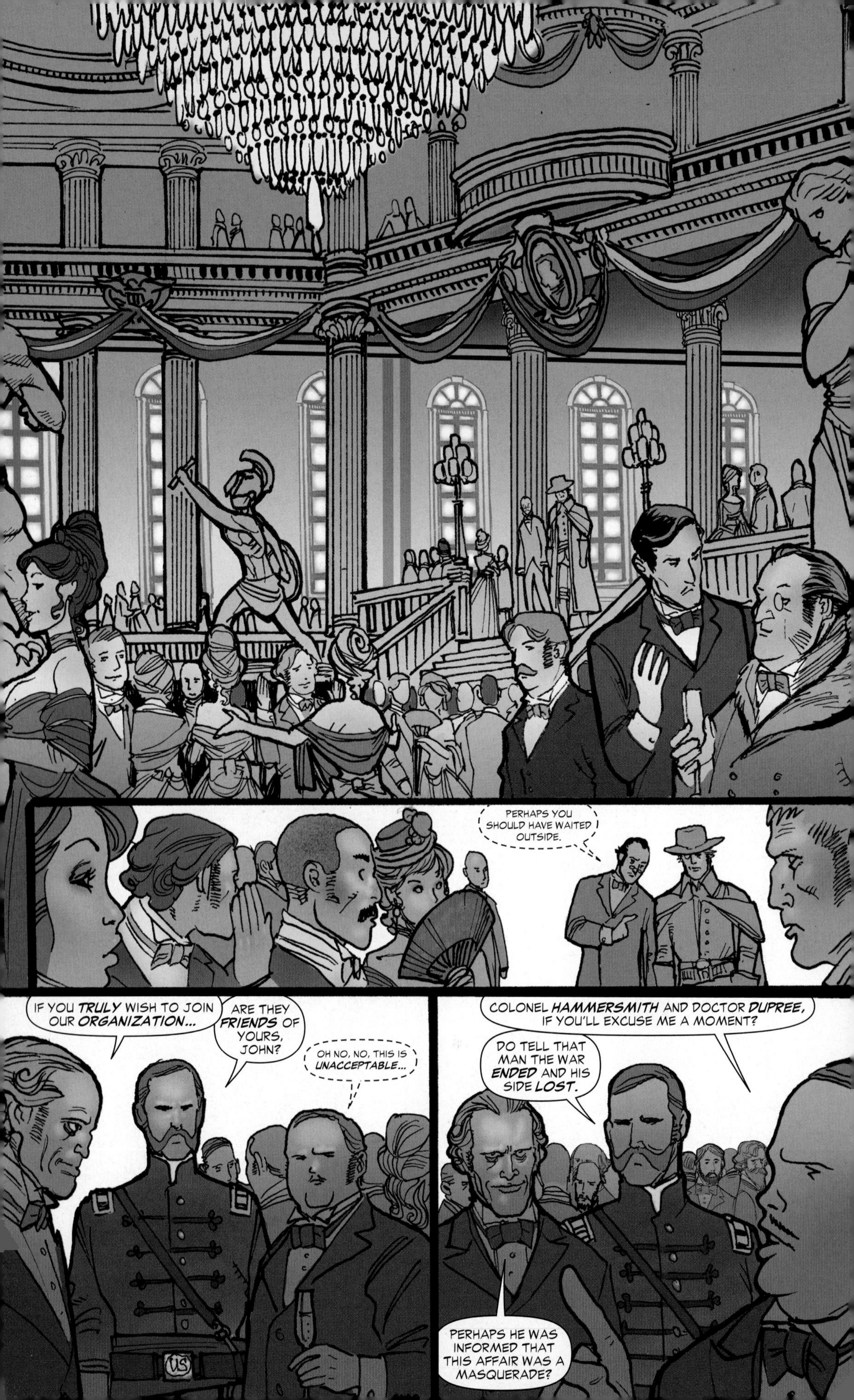
PERHAPS YOU SHOULD HAVE WAITED OUTSIDE.
IF YOU TRULY WISH TO JOIN OUR ORGANIZATION...
ARE THEY FRIENDS OF YOURS, JOHN?
OH NO, NO, THIS IS UNACCEPTABLE...
COLONEL HAMMERSMITH AND DOCTOR DUPREE, IF YOU'LL EXCUSE ME A MOMENT?
DO TELL THAT MAN THE WAR ENDED AND HIS SIDE LOST.
PERHAPS HE WAS INFORMED THAT THIS AFFAIR WAS A MASQUERADE?
US

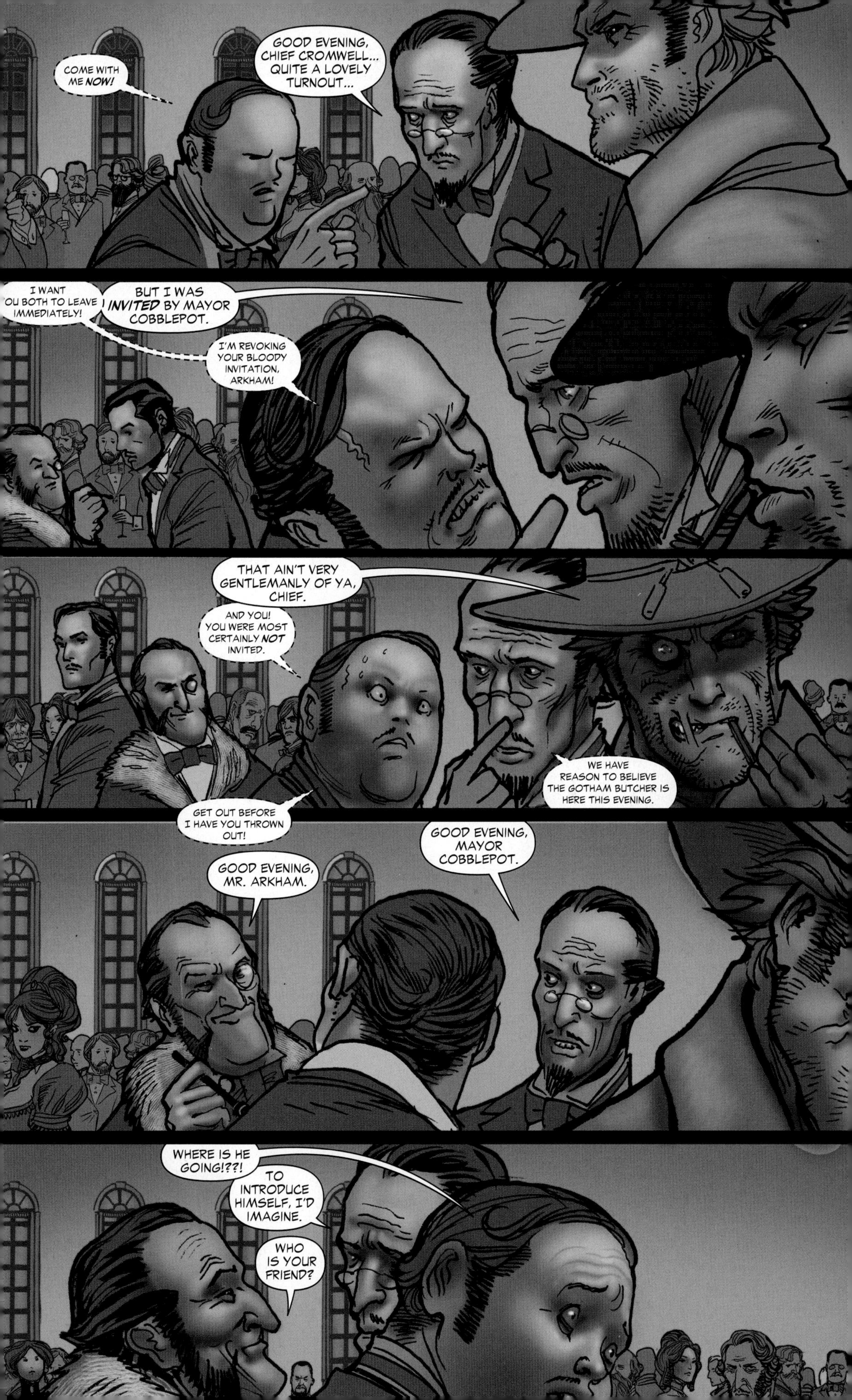
COME WITH ME NOW!
GOOD EVENING, CHIEF CROMWELL... QUITE A LOVELY TURNOUT...
I WANT OU BOTH TO LEAVE IMMEDIATELY!
BUT I WAS INVITED BY MAYOR COBBLEPOT.
I'M REVOKING YOUR BLOODY INVITATION, ARKHAM!
THAT AIN'T VERY GENTLEMANLY OF YA, CHIEF.
AND YOU! YOU WERE MOST CERTAINLY NOT INVITED.
WE HAVE REASON TO BELIEVE THE GOTHAM BUTCHER IS HERE THIS EVENING.
GET OUT BEFORE I HAVE YOU THROWN OUT!
GOOD EVENING, MAYOR COBBLEPOT.
GOOD EVENING, MR. ARKHAM.
WHERE IS HE GOING!??!
TO INTRODUCE HIMSELF, I'D IMAGINE.
WHO IS YOUR FRIEND?

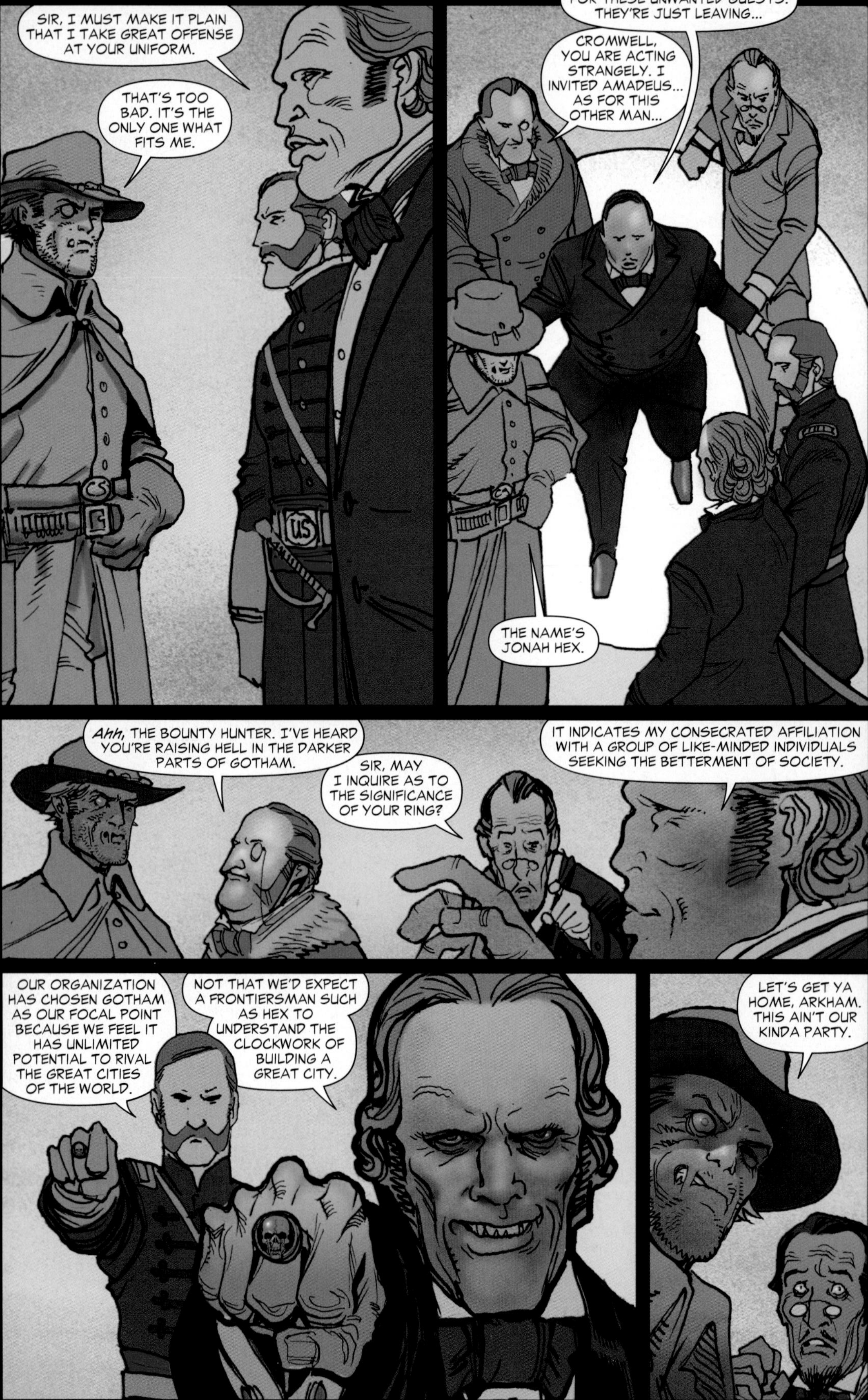
SIR, I MUST MAKE IT PLAIN THAT I TAKE GREAT OFFENSE AT YOUR UNIFORM.
THAT'S TOO BAD. IT'S THE ONLY ONE WHAT FITS ME.
GENTLEMEN, I APOLOGIZE FOR THESE UNWANTED GUESTS. THEY'RE JUST LEAVING...
CROMWELL, YOU ARE ACTING STRANGELY. I INVITED AMADEUS... AS FOR THIS OTHER MAN...
THE NAME'S JONAH HEX.
*Ahh,* THE BOUNTY HUNTER. I'VE HEARD YOU'RE RAISING HELL IN THE DARKER PARTS OF GOTHAM.
SIR, MAY I INQUIRE AS TO THE SIGNIFICANCE OF YOUR RING?
IT INDICATES MY CONSECRATED AFFILIATION WITH A GROUP OF LIKE-MINDED INDIVIDUALS SEEKING THE BETTERMENT OF SOCIETY.
OUR ORGANIZATION HAS CHOSEN GOTHAM AS OUR FOCAL POINT BECAUSE WE FEEL IT HAS UNLIMITED POTENTIAL TO RIVAL THE GREAT CITIES OF THE WORLD.
NOT THAT WE'D EXPECT A FRONTIERSMAN SUCH AS HEX TO UNDERSTAND THE CLOCKWORK OF BUILDING A GREAT CITY.
LET'S GET YA HOME, ARKHAM. THIS AIN'T OUR KINDA PARTY.

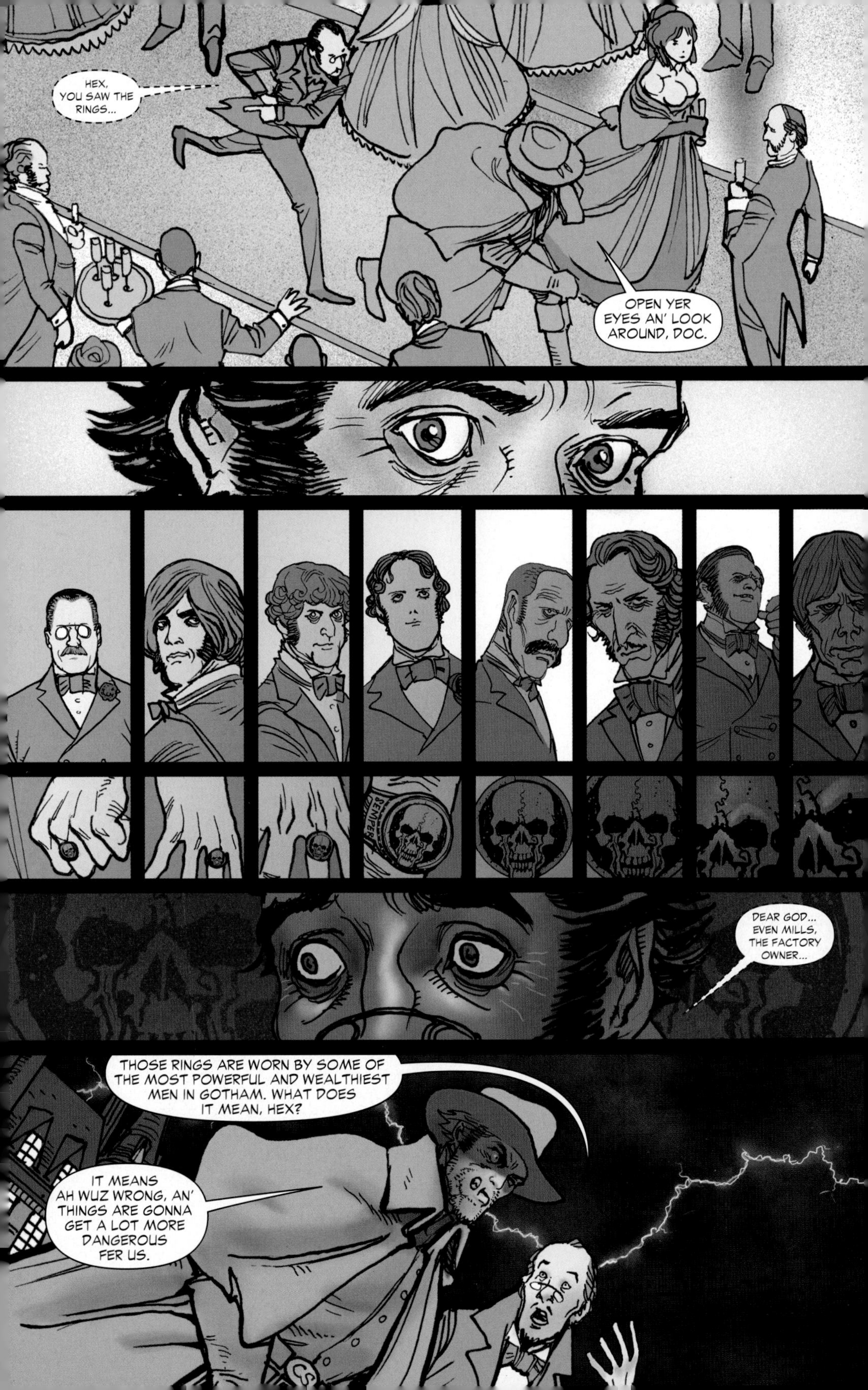
HEX, YOU SAW THE RINGS...
OPEN YER EYES AN' LOOK AROUND, DOC.
SEMPER
DEAR GOD... EVEN MILLS, THE FACTORY OWNER...
THOSE RINGS ARE WORN BY SOME OF THE MOST POWERFUL AND WEALTHIEST MEN IN GOTHAM. WHAT DOES IT MEAN, HEX?
IT MEANS AH WUZ WRONG, AN' THINGS ARE GONNA GET A LOT MORE DANGEROUS FER US.

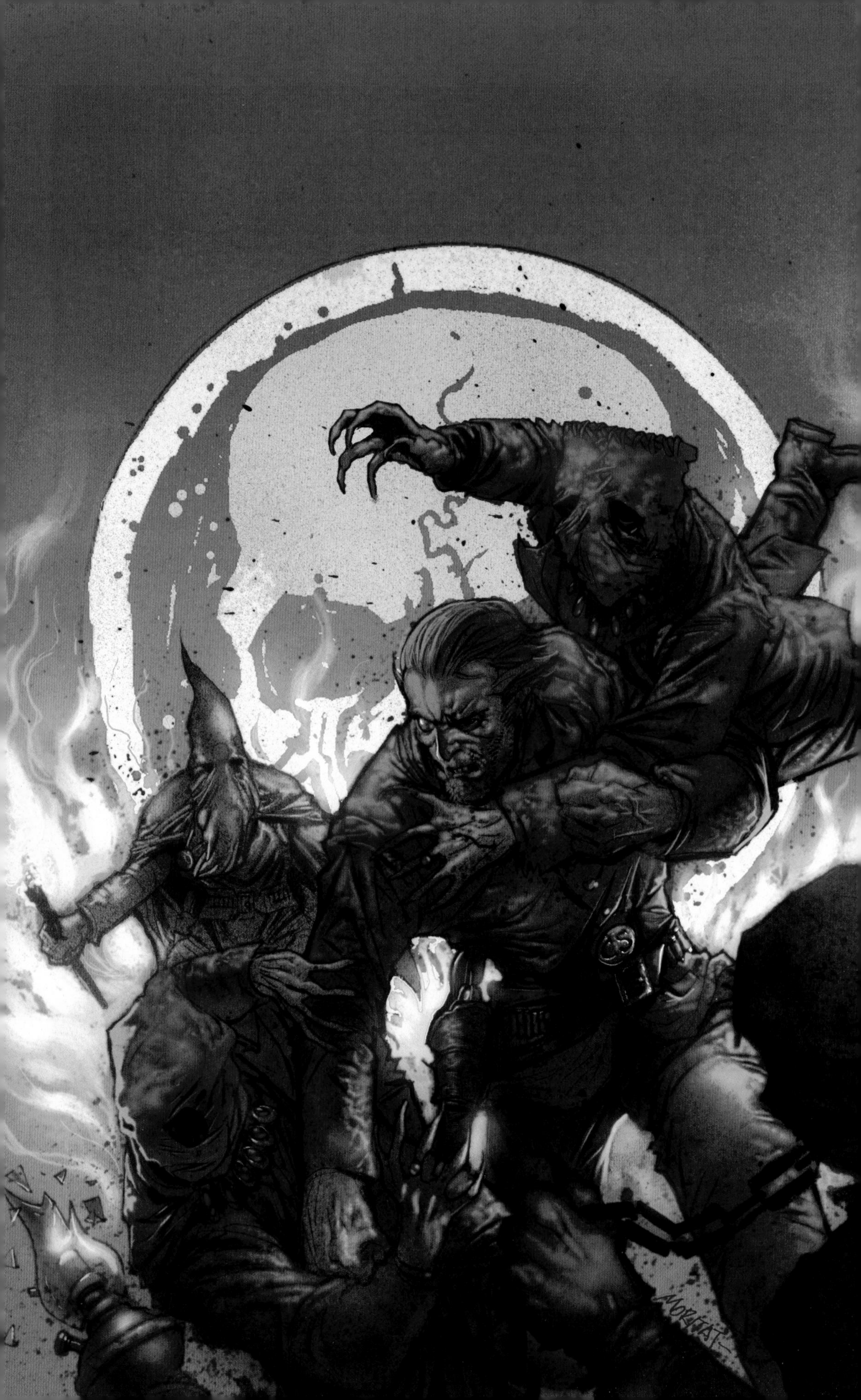

# Showdown at House Arkham

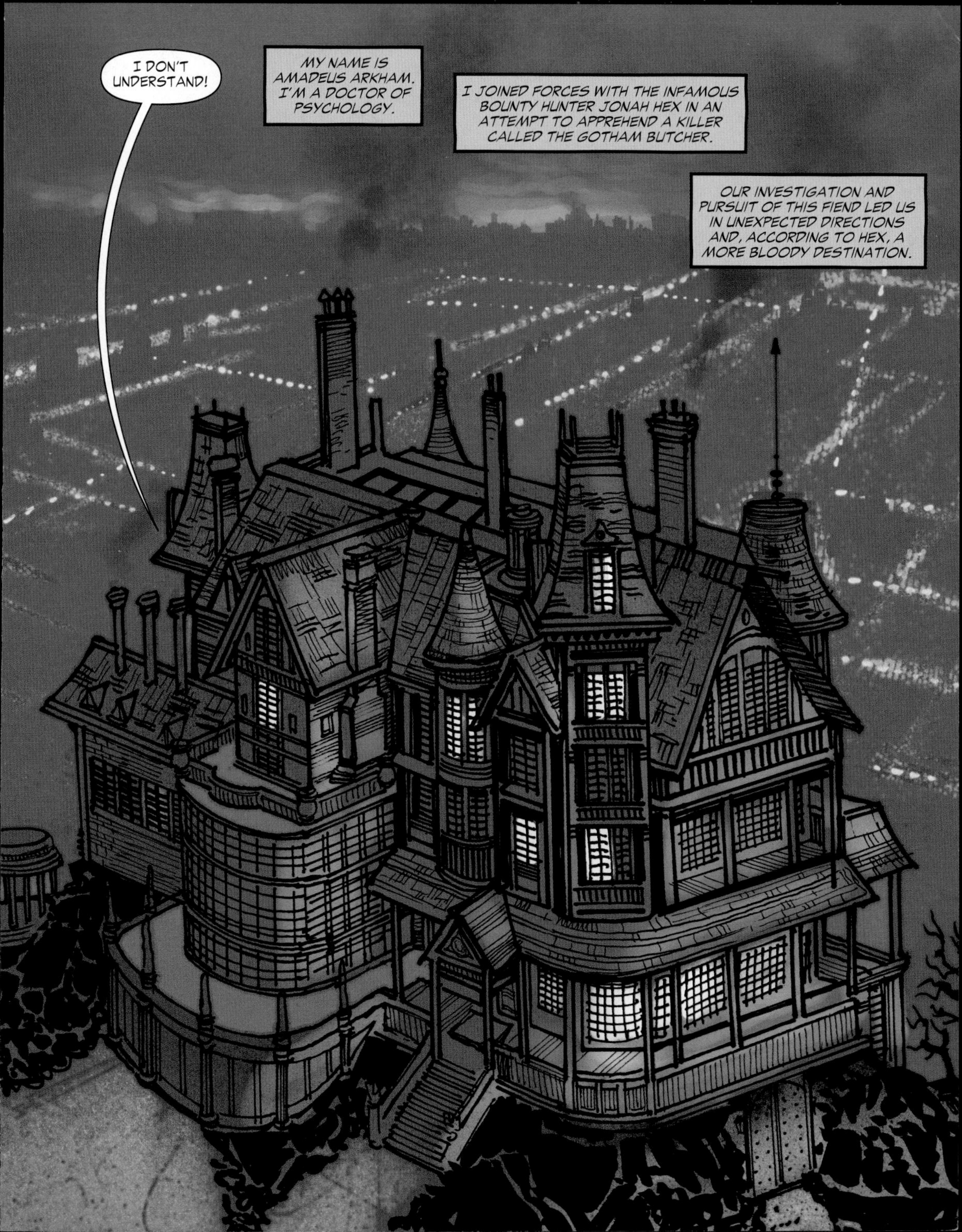
I DON'T UNDERSTAND!
MY NAME IS AMADEUS ARKHAM. I'M A DOCTOR OF PSYCHOLOGY.
I JOINED FORCES WITH THE INFAMOUS BOUNTY HUNTER JONAH HEX IN AN ATTEMPT TO APPREHEND A KILLER CALLED THE GOTHAM BUTCHER.
OUR INVESTIGATION AND PURSUIT OF THIS FIEND LED US IN UNEXPECTED DIRECTIONS AND, ACCORDING TO HEX, A MORE BLOODY DESTINATION.

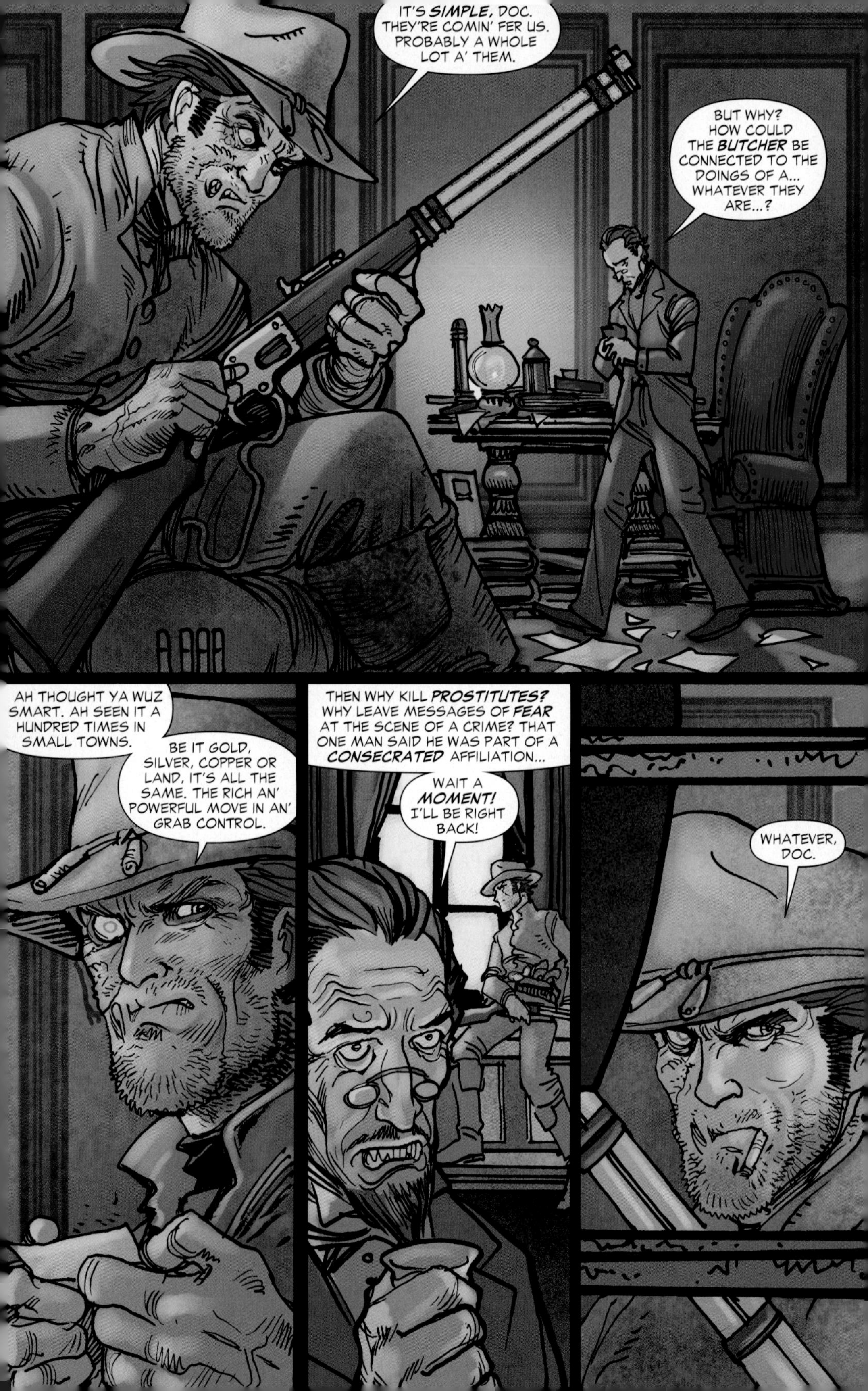
IT'S SIMPLE, DOC. THEY'RE COMIN' FER US. PROBABLY A WHOLE LOT A' THEM.
BUT WHY? HOW COULD THE BUTCHER BE CONNECTED TO THE DOINGS OF A... WHATEVER THEY ARE...?
AH THOUGHT YA WUZ SMART. AH SEEN IT A HUNDRED TIMES IN SMALL TOWNS.
BE IT GOLD, SILVER, COPPER OR LAND, IT'S ALL THE SAME. THE RICH AN' POWERFUL MOVE IN AN' GRAB CONTROL.
THEN WHY KILL PROSTITUTES? WHY LEAVE MESSAGES OF FEAR AT THE SCENE OF A CRIME? THAT ONE MAN SAID HE WAS PART OF A CONSECRATED AFFILIATION...
WAIT A MOMENT! I'LL BE RIGHT BACK!
WHATEVER, DOC.

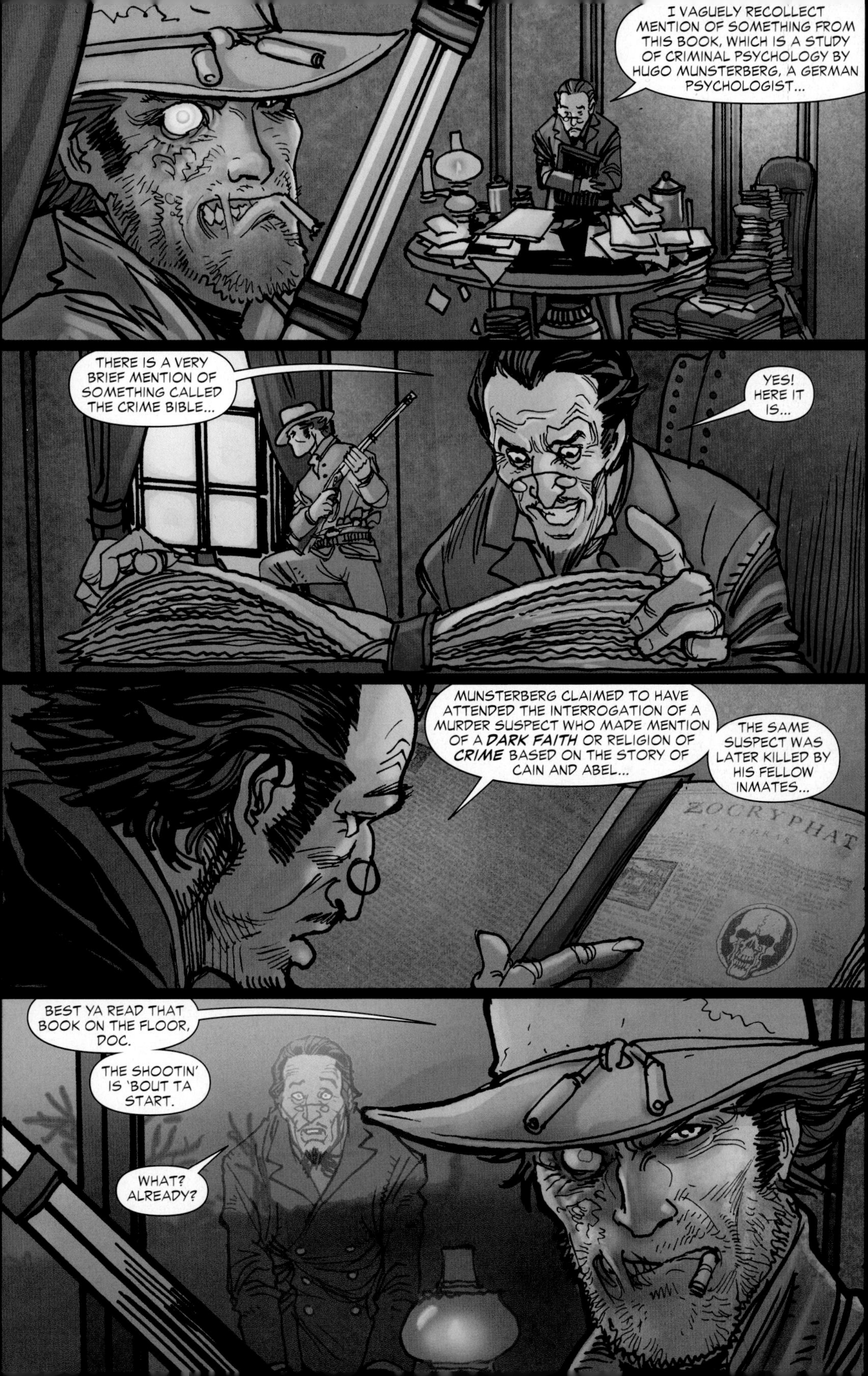
I VAGUELY RECOLLECT MENTION OF SOMETHING FROM THIS BOOK, WHICH IS A STUDY OF CRIMINAL PSYCHOLOGY BY HUGO MUNSTERBERG, A GERMAN PSYCHOLOGIST...
THERE IS A VERY BRIEF MENTION OF SOMETHING CALLED THE CRIME BIBLE...
YES! HERE IT IS...
MUNSTERBERG CLAIMED TO HAVE ATTENDED THE INTERROGATION OF A MURDER SUSPECT WHO MADE MENTION OF A *DARK FAITH* OR RELIGION OF *CRIME* BASED ON THE STORY OF CAIN AND ABEL...
THE SAME SUSPECT WAS LATER KILLED BY HIS FELLOW INMATES...
ZOCRYPHAT
BEST YA READ THAT BOOK ON THE FLOOR, DOC.
THE SHOOTIN' IS 'BOUT TA START.
WHAT? ALREADY?

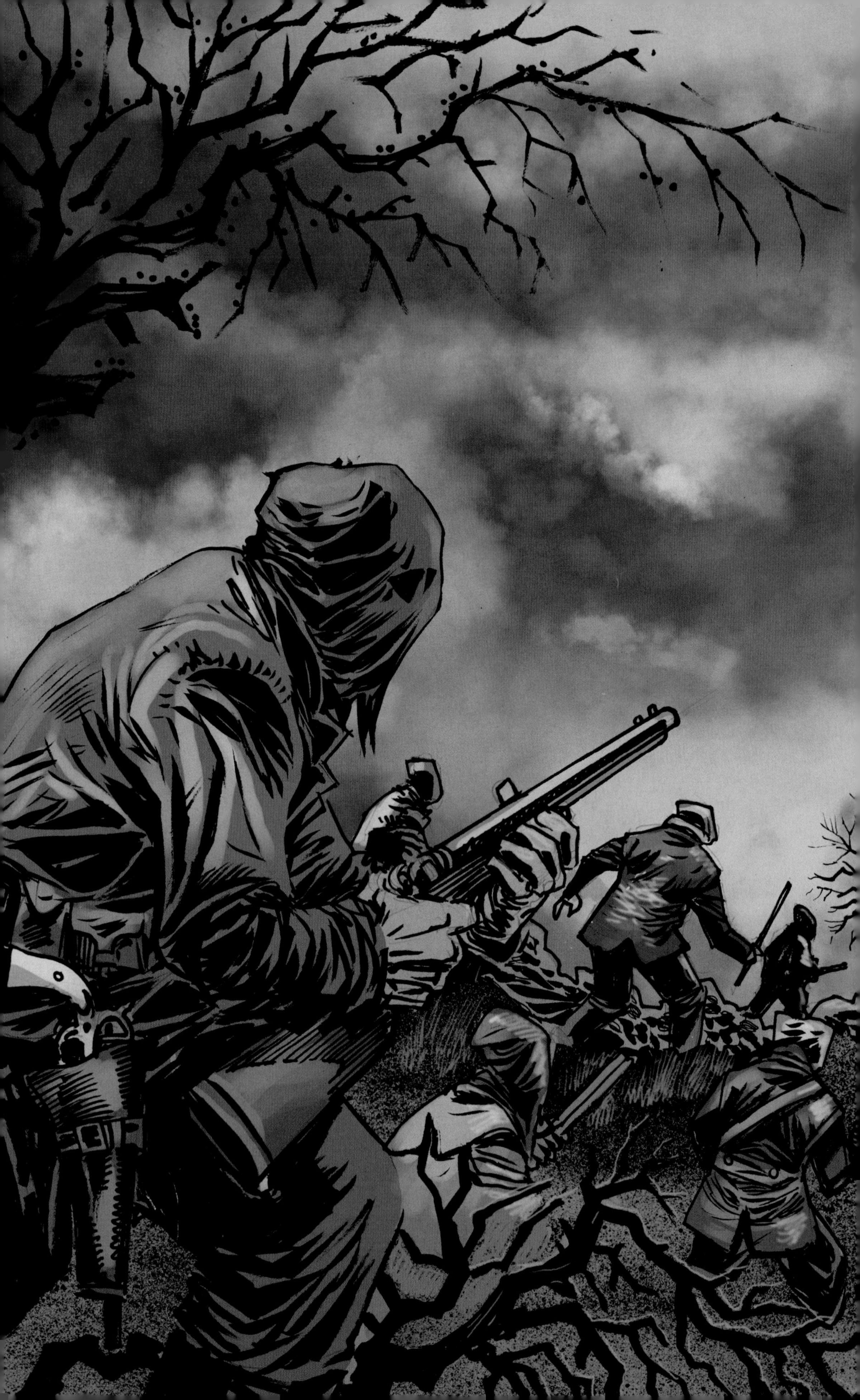

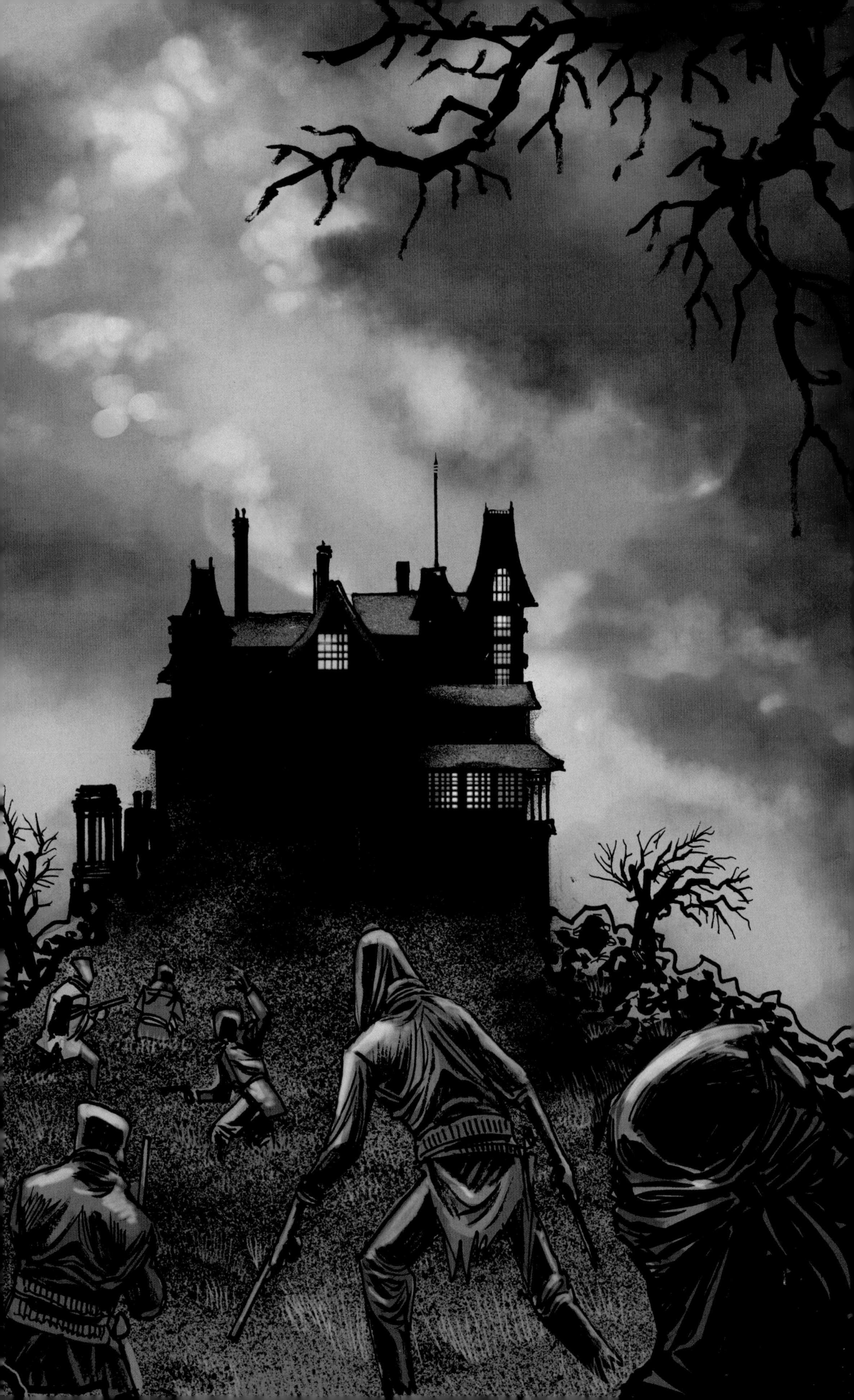

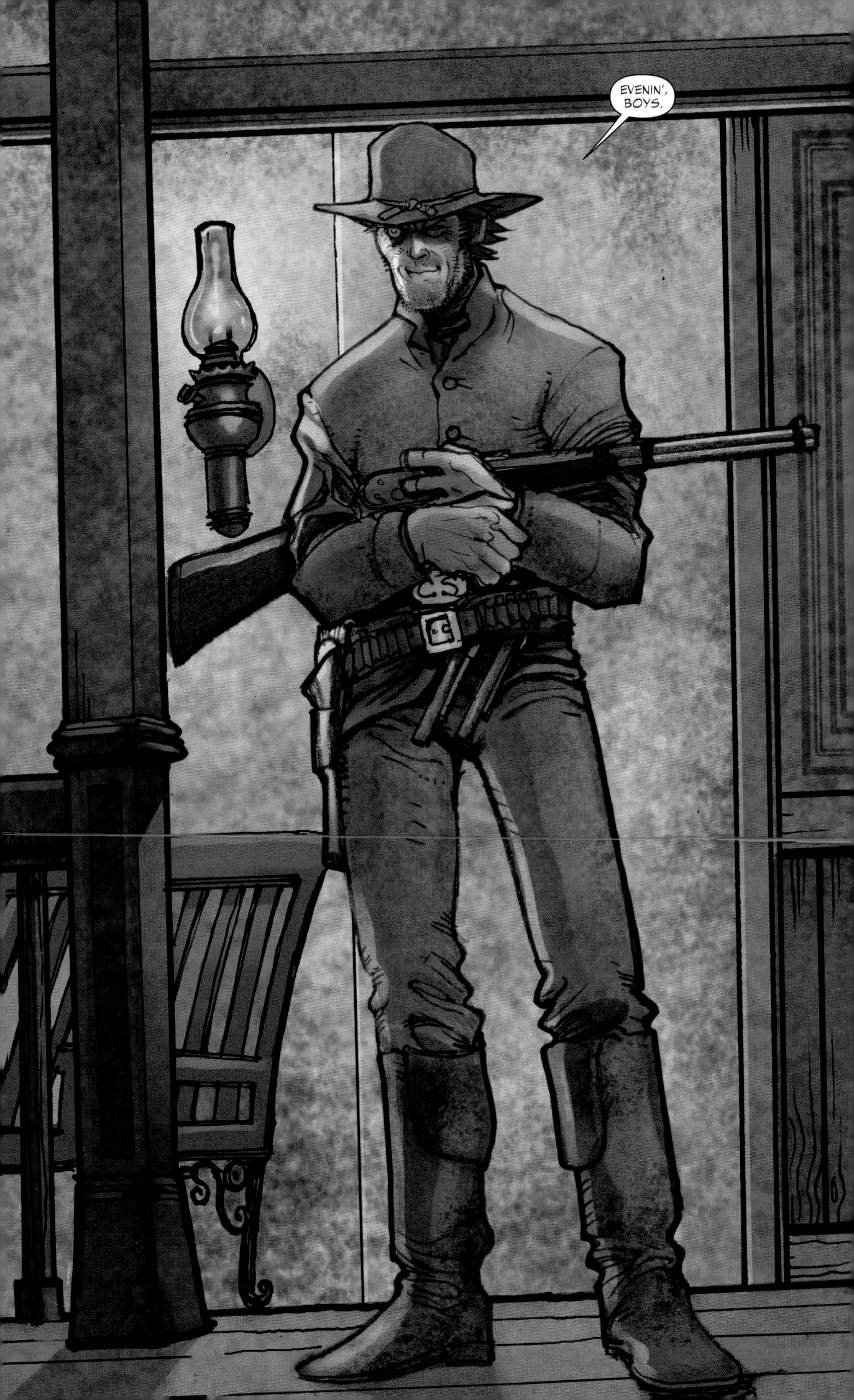
EVENIN', BOYS.

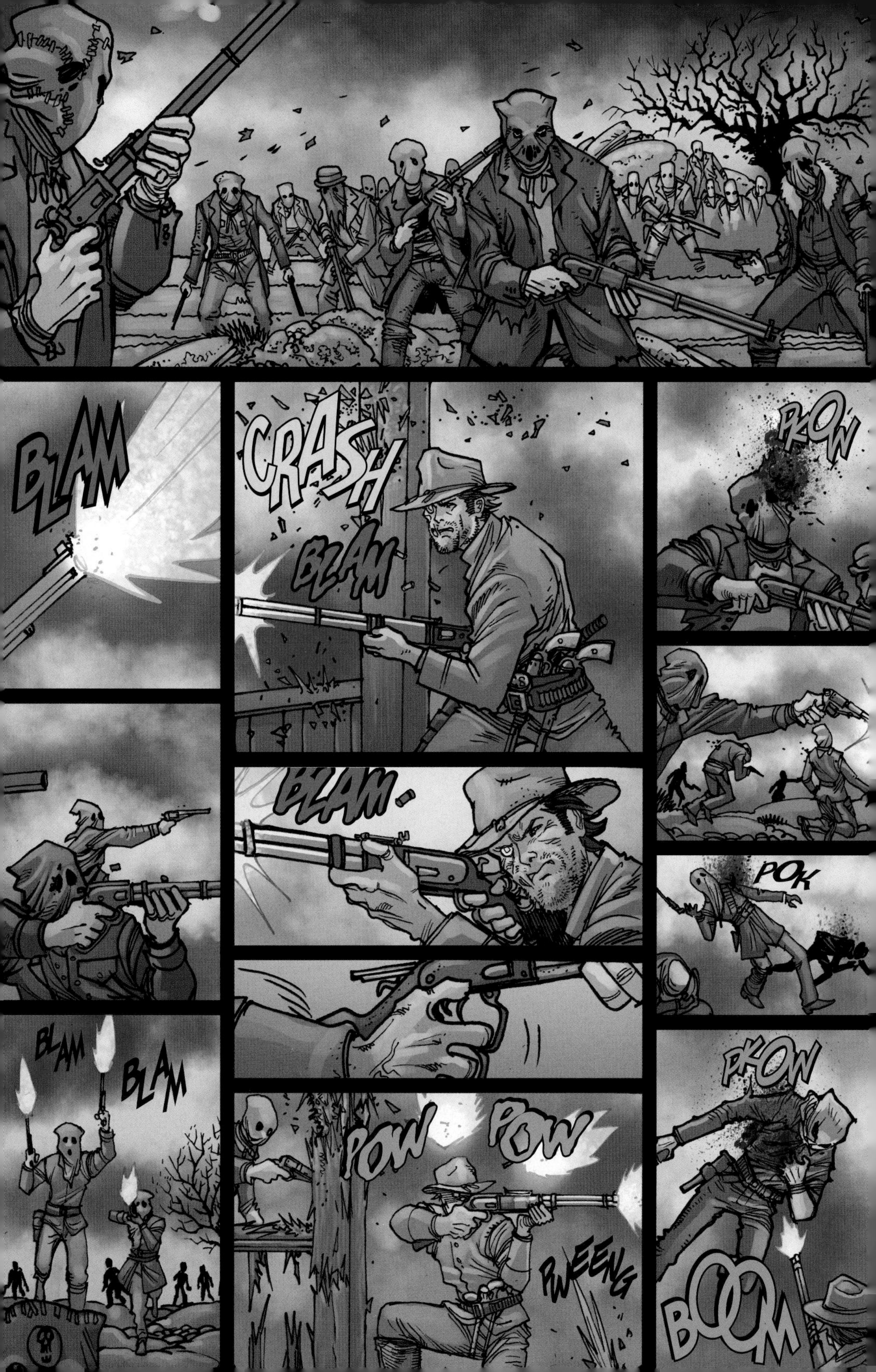
BLAM
CRASH
BLAM
PKOW
BLAM
POK
BLAM
BLAM
POW
POW
PKOW
PWEENG
BOOM

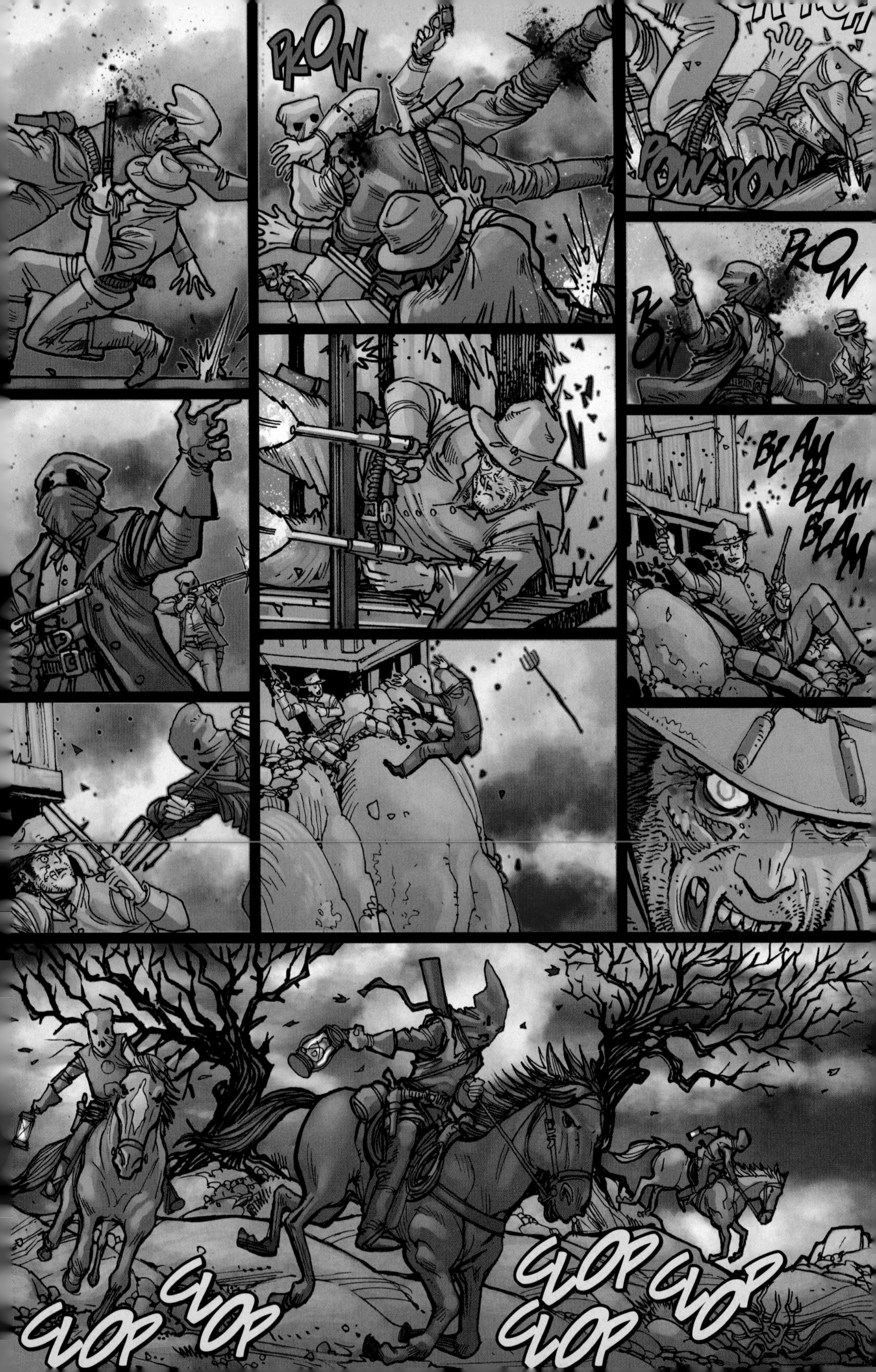
PKOW
POW POW
PKOW
PKOW
BLAM
BLAM
BLAM
CLOP
CLOP
CLOP
CLOP
CLOP

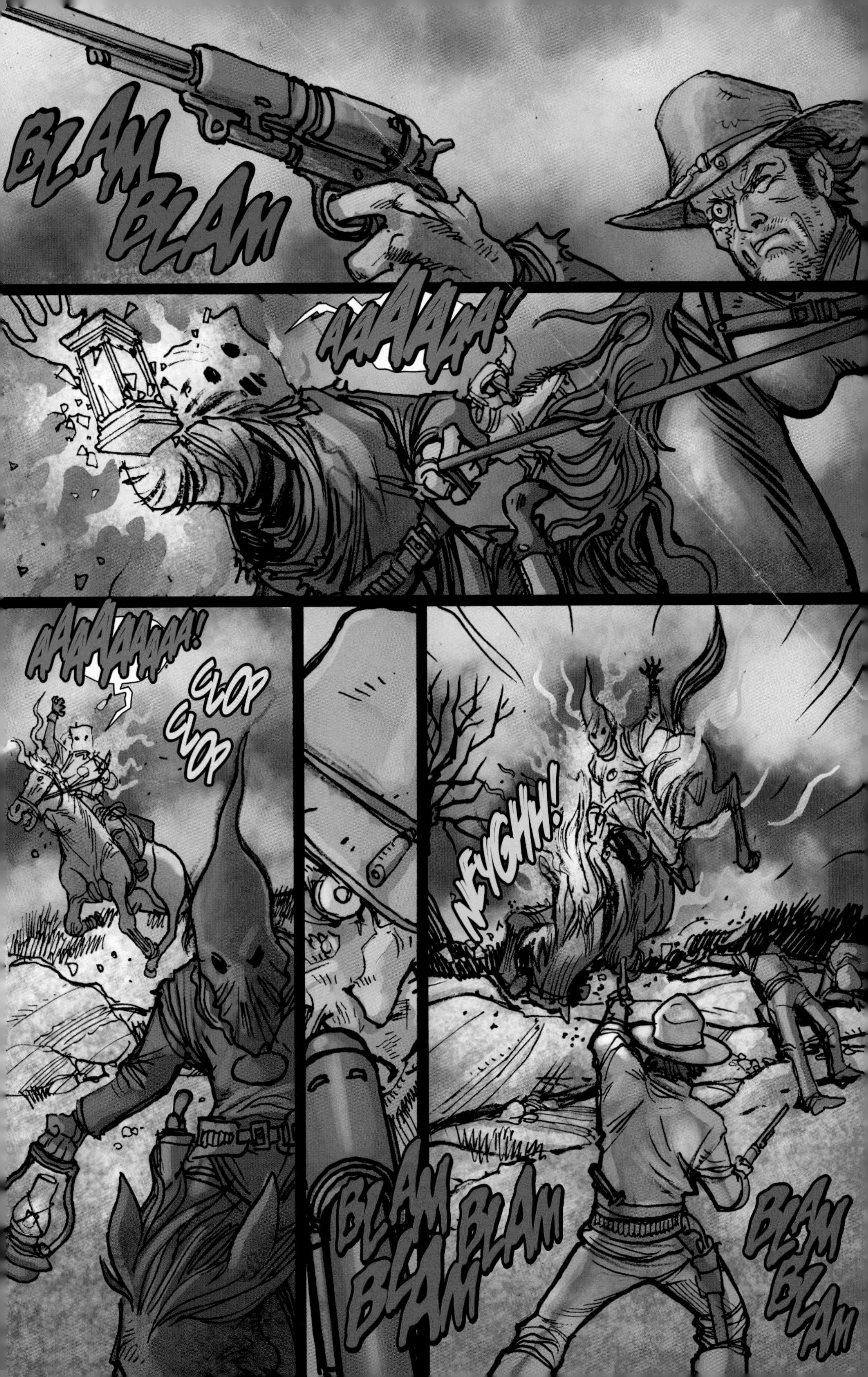
BLAM
BLAM
AAAAAAA!
AAAAAAAA!
CLOP
CLOP
NEYGHH!
BLAM
BLAM
BLAM
BLAM
BLAM

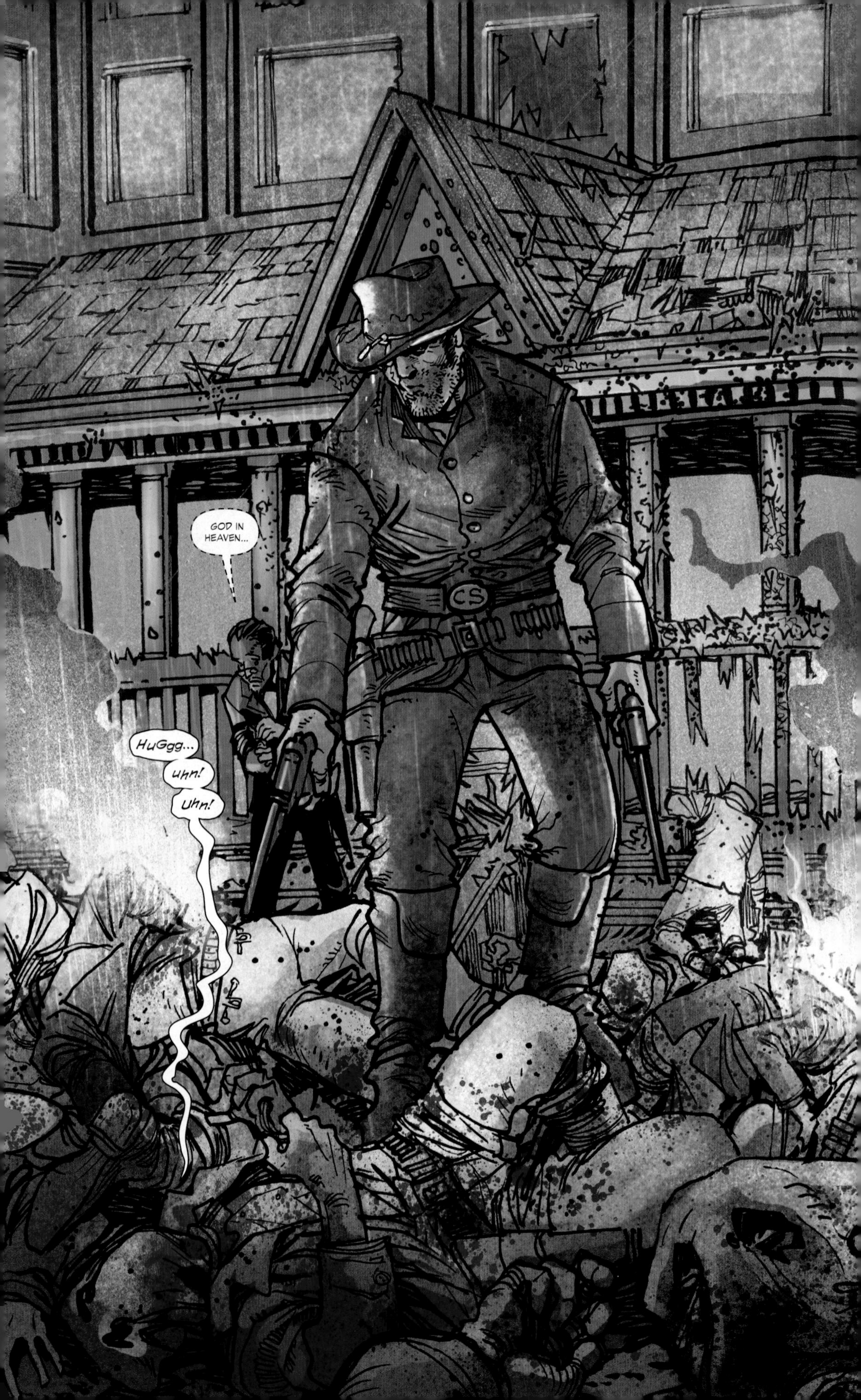
GOD IN HEAVEN...
HuGgg...
uhn!
Uhn!

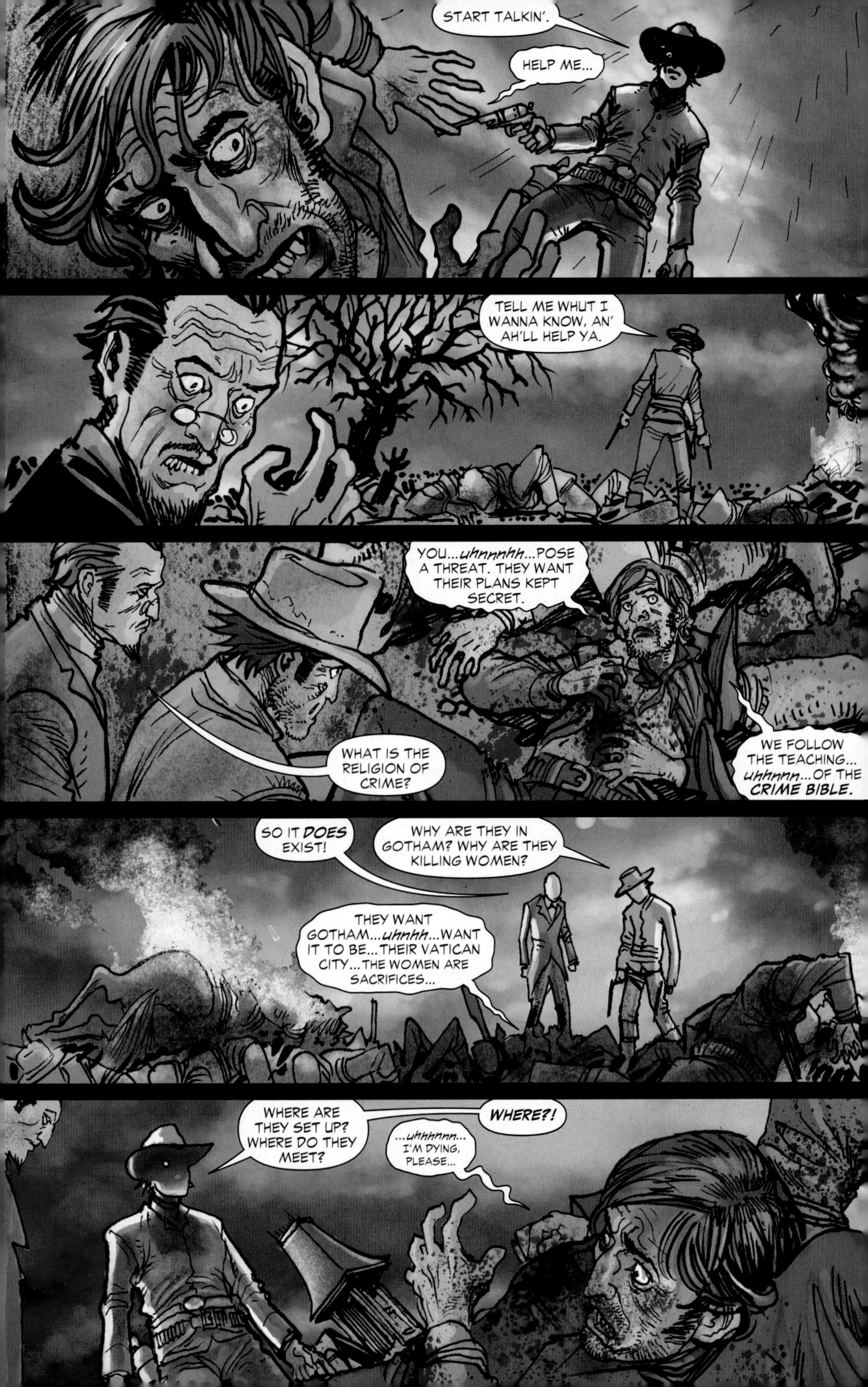
START TALKIN'.
HELP ME...
TELL ME WHUT I WANNA KNOW, AN' AH'LL HELP YA.
YOU...*uhnnnhh*...POSE A THREAT. THEY WANT THEIR PLANS KEPT SECRET.
WHAT IS THE RELIGION OF CRIME?
WE FOLLOW THE TEACHING... *uhhnnn*...OF THE ***CRIME BIBLE***.
SO IT ***DOES*** EXIST!
WHY ARE THEY IN GOTHAM? WHY ARE THEY KILLING WOMEN?
THEY WANT GOTHAM...*uhnhh*...WANT IT TO BE...THEIR VATICAN CITY...THE WOMEN ARE SACRIFICES...
WHERE ARE THEY SET UP? WHERE DO THEY MEET?
***WHERE?!***
...*uhhhnnn*... I'M DYING, PLEASE...

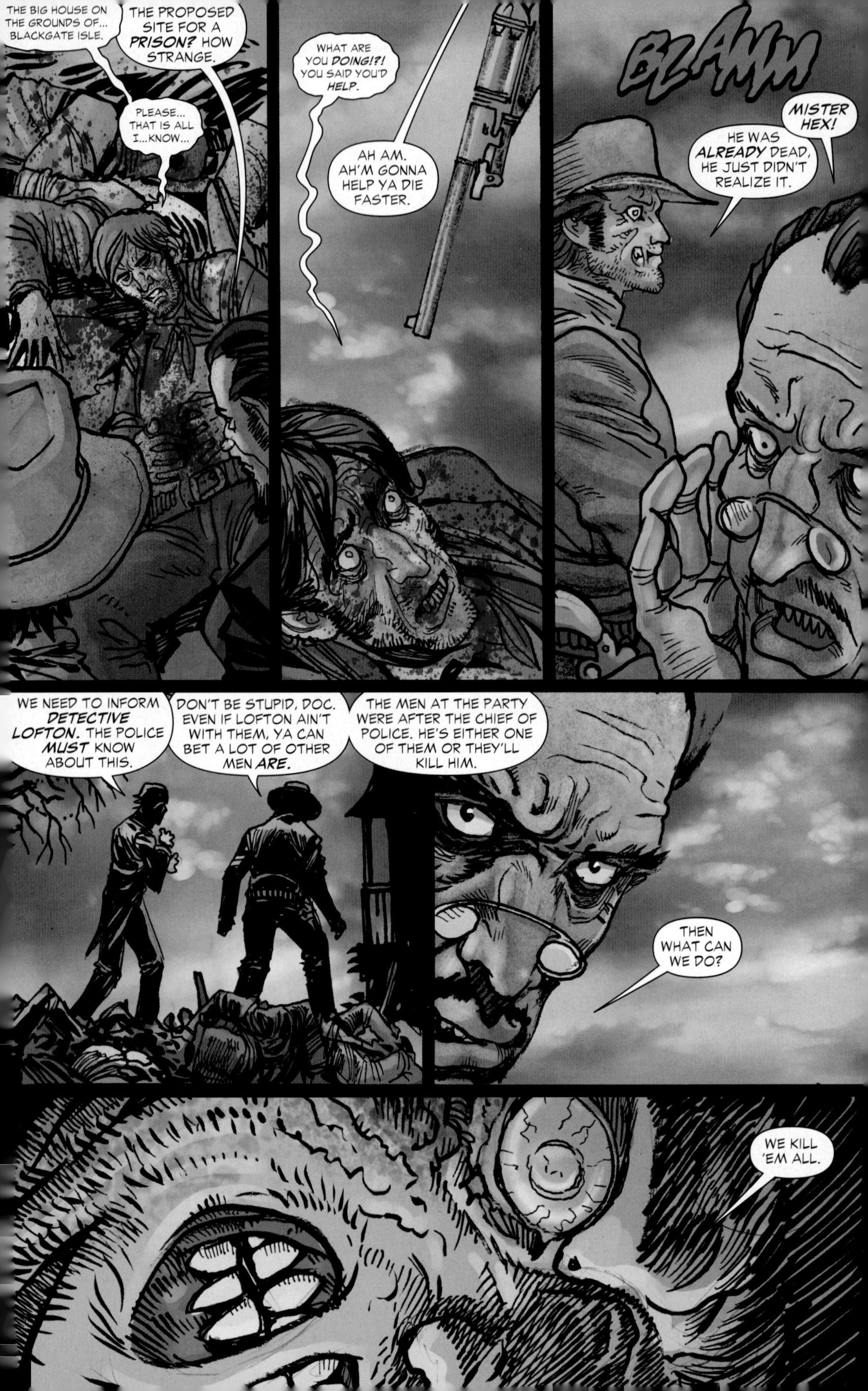
THE BIG HOUSE ON THE GROUNDS OF... BLACKGATE ISLE.
THE PROPOSED SITE FOR A PRISON? HOW STRANGE.
PLEASE... THAT IS ALL I...KNOW...
WHAT ARE YOU DOING!?! YOU SAID YOU'D HELP.
AH AM. AH'M GONNA HELP YA DIE FASTER.
BLAMM
MISTER HEX!
HE WAS ALREADY DEAD, HE JUST DIDN'T REALIZE IT.
WE NEED TO INFORM DETECTIVE LOFTON. THE POLICE MUST KNOW ABOUT THIS.
DON'T BE STUPID, DOC. EVEN IF LOFTON AIN'T WITH THEM, YA CAN BET A LOT OF OTHER MEN ARE.
THE MEN AT THE PARTY WERE AFTER THE CHIEF OF POLICE. HE'S EITHER ONE OF THEM OR THEY'LL KILL HIM.
THEN WHAT CAN WE DO?
WE KILL 'EM ALL.

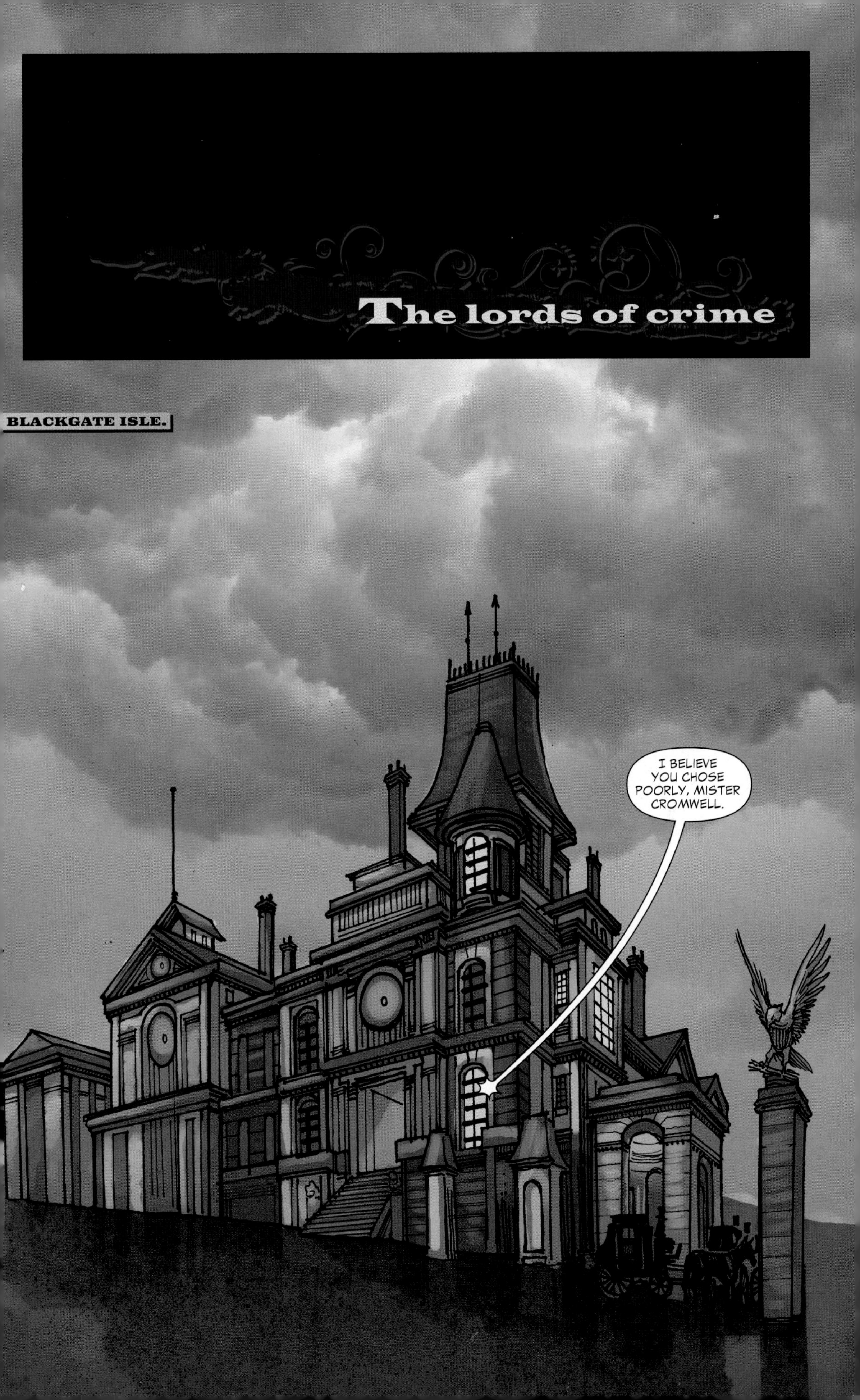
The lords of crime
BLACKGATE ISLE.
I BELIEVE YOU CHOSE POORLY, MISTER CROMWELL.

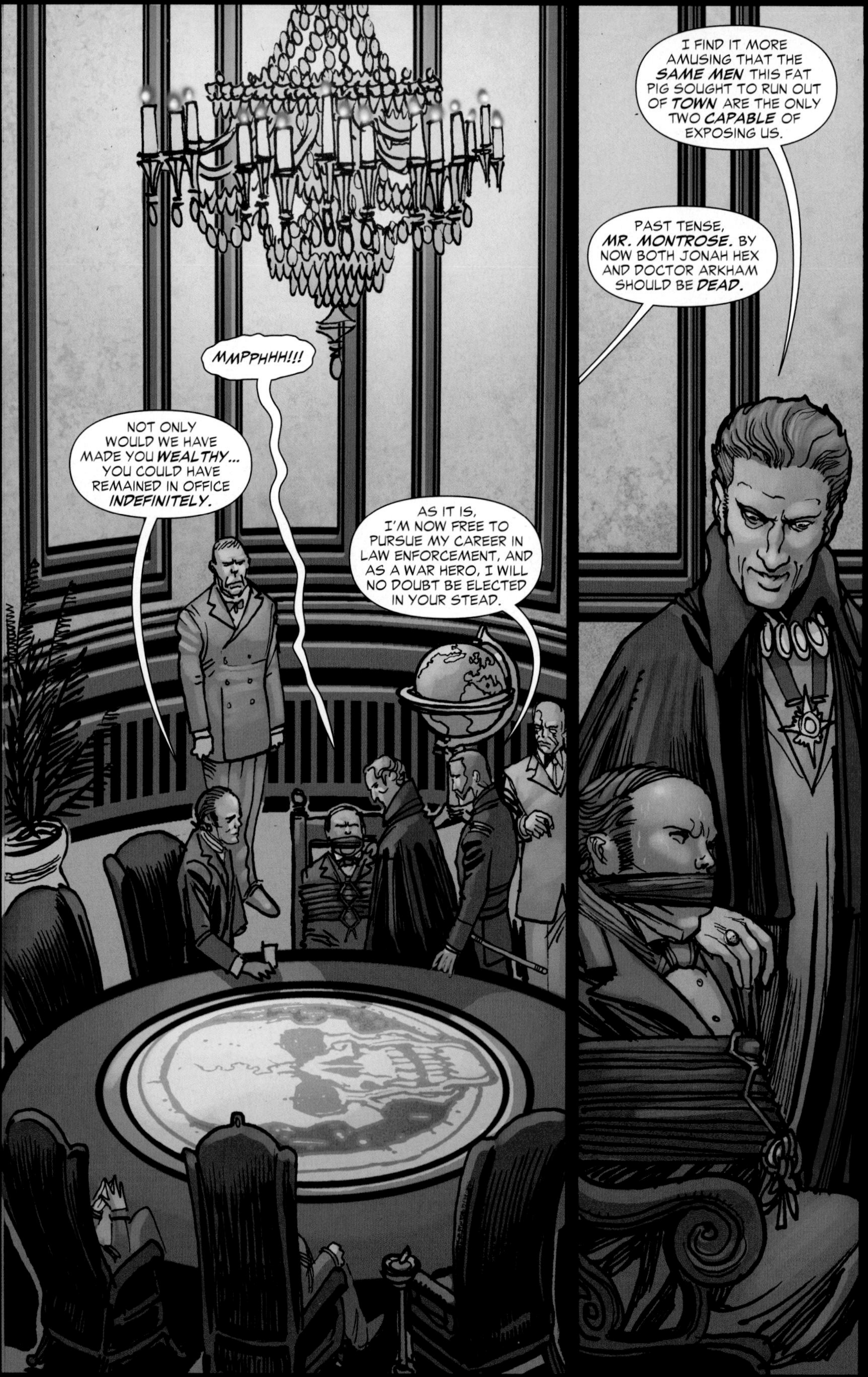
NOT ONLY WOULD WE HAVE MADE YOU WEALTHY... YOU COULD HAVE REMAINED IN OFFICE INDEFINITELY.
MMPPHHH!!!
AS IT IS, I'M NOW FREE TO PURSUE MY CAREER IN LAW ENFORCEMENT, AND AS A WAR HERO, I WILL NO DOUBT BE ELECTED IN YOUR STEAD.
I FIND IT MORE AMUSING THAT THE SAME MEN THIS FAT PIG SOUGHT TO RUN OUT OF TOWN ARE THE ONLY TWO CAPABLE OF EXPOSING US.
PAST TENSE, MR. MONTROSE. BY NOW BOTH JONAH HEX AND DOCTOR ARKHAM SHOULD BE DEAD.

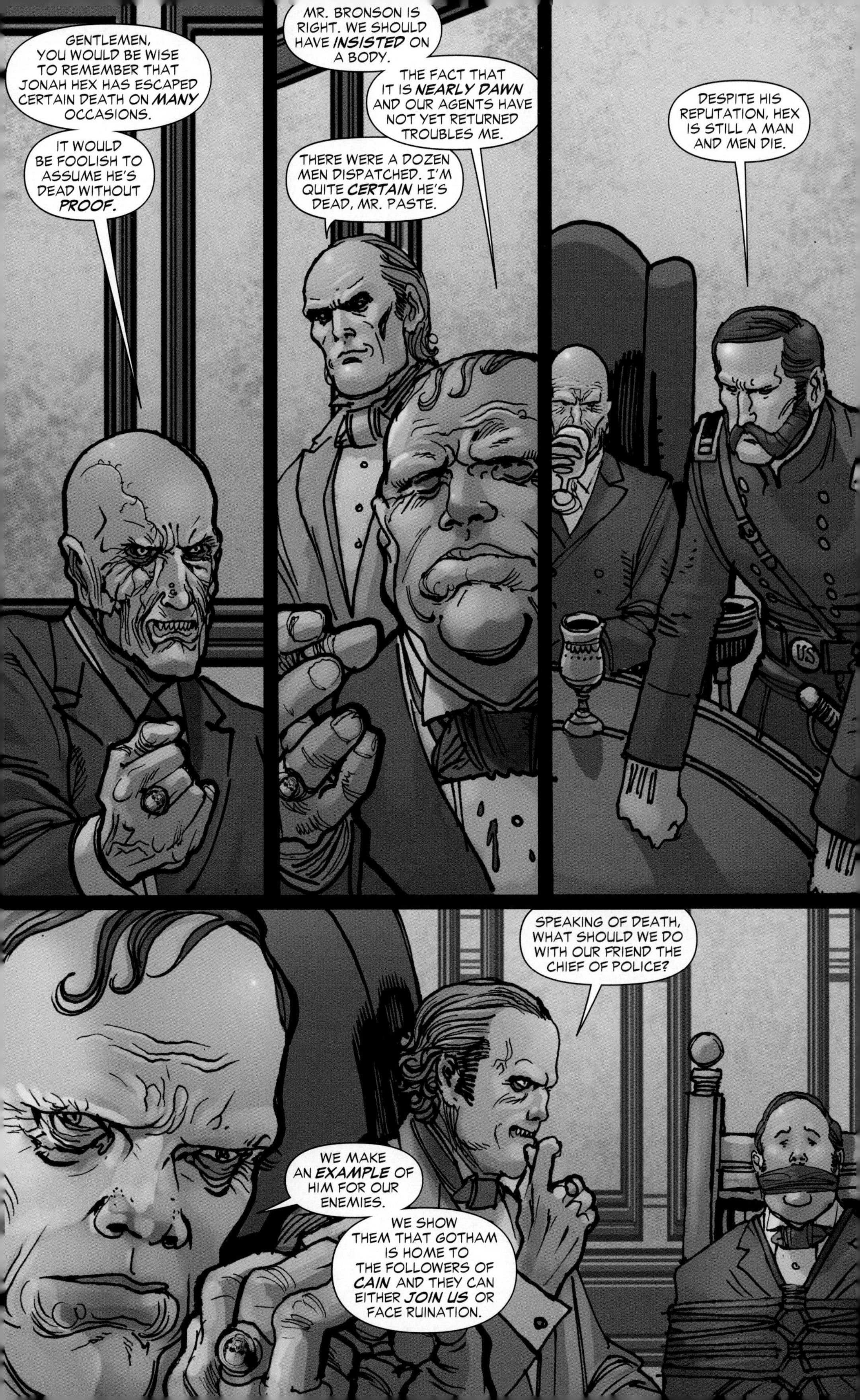
GENTLEMEN, YOU WOULD BE WISE TO REMEMBER THAT JONAH HEX HAS ESCAPED CERTAIN DEATH ON MANY OCCASIONS.
IT WOULD BE FOOLISH TO ASSUME HE'S DEAD WITHOUT PROOF.
MR. BRONSON IS RIGHT. WE SHOULD HAVE INSISTED ON A BODY.
THE FACT THAT IT IS NEARLY DAWN AND OUR AGENTS HAVE NOT YET RETURNED TROUBLES ME.
THERE WERE A DOZEN MEN DISPATCHED. I'M QUITE CERTAIN HE'S DEAD, MR. PASTE.
DESPITE HIS REPUTATION, HEX IS STILL A MAN AND MEN DIE.
SPEAKING OF DEATH, WHAT SHOULD WE DO WITH OUR FRIEND THE CHIEF OF POLICE?
WE MAKE AN EXAMPLE OF HIM FOR OUR ENEMIES.
WE SHOW THEM THAT GOTHAM IS HOME TO THE FOLLOWERS OF CAIN AND THEY CAN EITHER JOIN US OR FACE RUINATION.

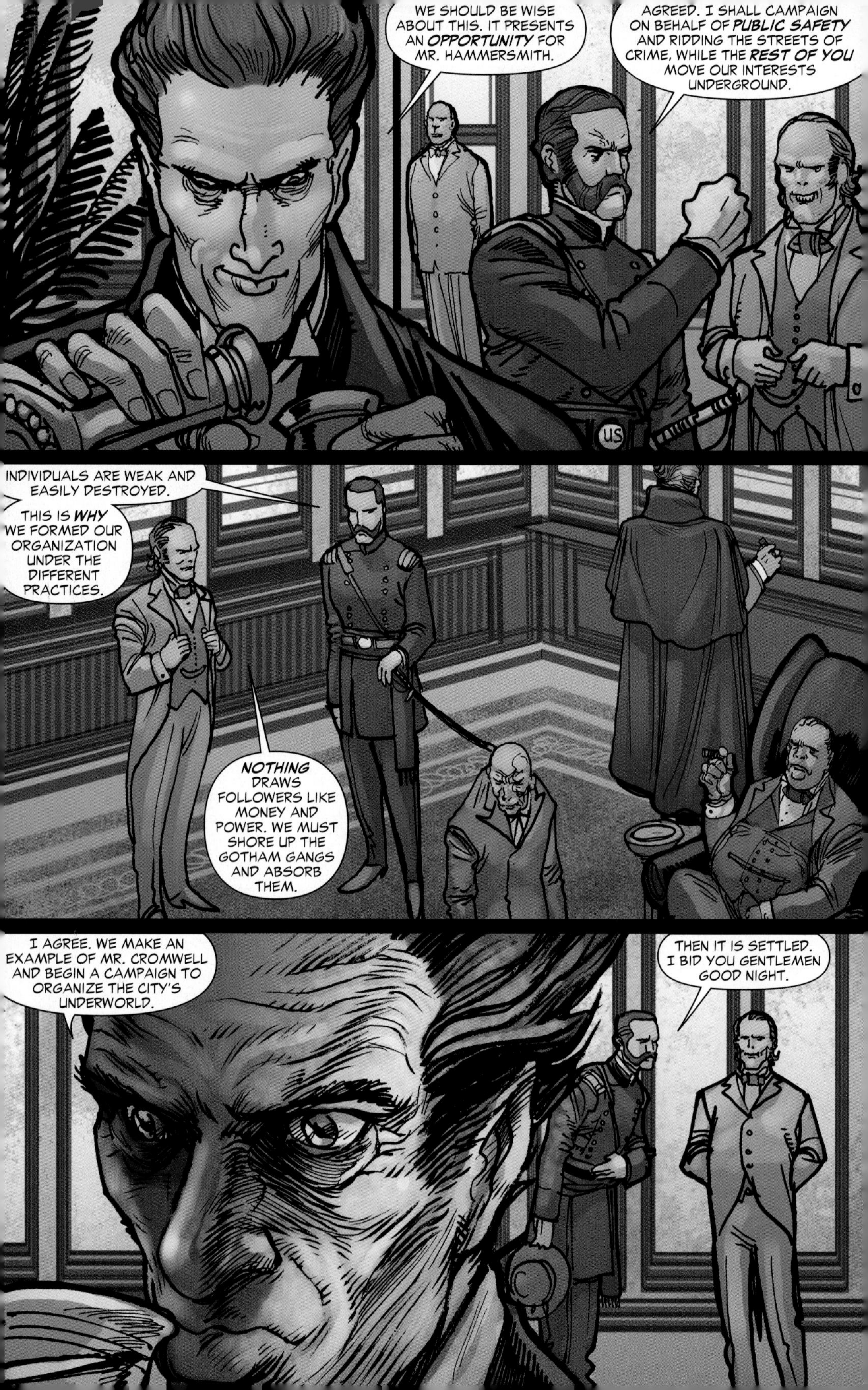
WE SHOULD BE WISE ABOUT THIS. IT PRESENTS AN *OPPORTUNITY* FOR MR. HAMMERSMITH.
AGREED. I SHALL CAMPAIGN ON BEHALF OF *PUBLIC SAFETY* AND RIDDING THE STREETS OF CRIME, WHILE THE *REST OF YOU* MOVE OUR INTERESTS UNDERGROUND.
US
INDIVIDUALS ARE WEAK AND EASILY DESTROYED.
THIS IS *WHY* WE FORMED OUR ORGANIZATION UNDER THE DIFFERENT PRACTICES.
*NOTHING* DRAWS FOLLOWERS LIKE MONEY AND POWER. WE MUST SHORE UP THE GOTHAM GANGS AND ABSORB THEM.
I AGREE. WE MAKE AN EXAMPLE OF MR. CROMWELL AND BEGIN A CAMPAIGN TO ORGANIZE THE CITY'S UNDERWORLD.
THEN IT IS SETTLED. I BID YOU GENTLEMEN GOOD NIGHT.

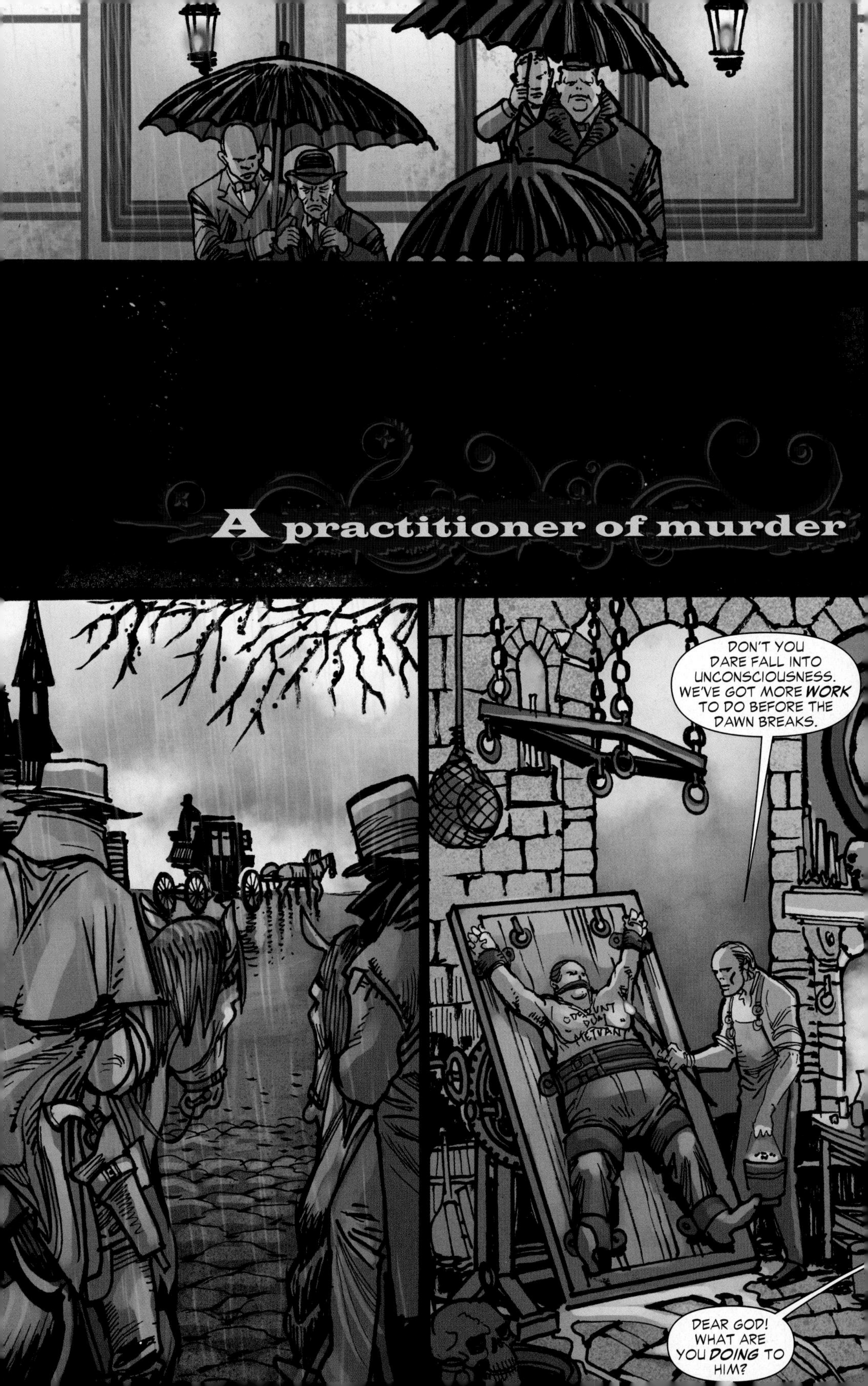
A practitioner of murder
DON'T YOU DARE FALL INTO UNCONSCIOUSNESS. WE'VE GOT MORE WORK TO DO BEFORE THE DAWN BREAKS.
DEAR GOD! WHAT ARE YOU DOING TO HIM?

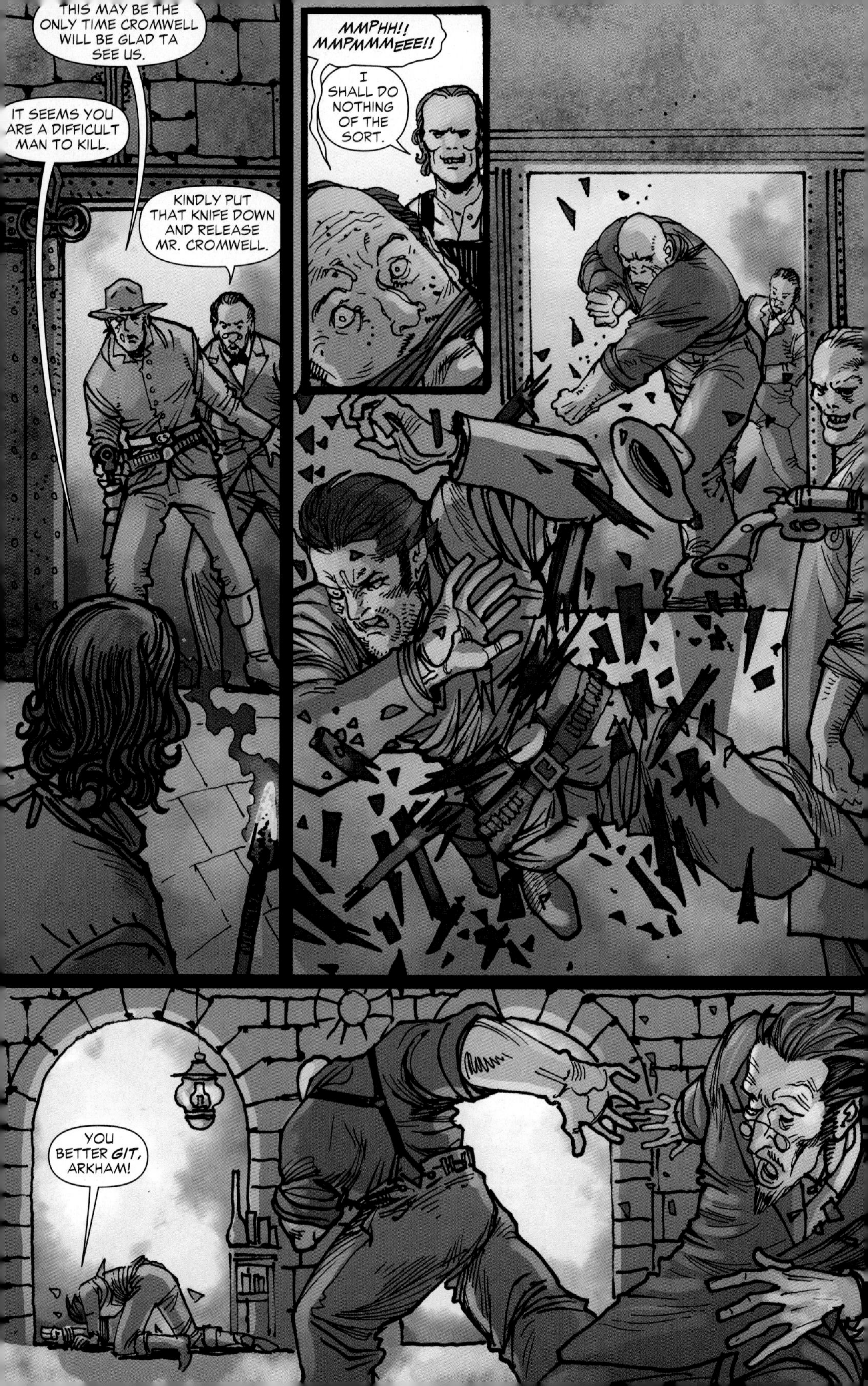
THIS MAY BE THE ONLY TIME CROMWELL WILL BE GLAD TA SEE US.
IT SEEMS YOU ARE A DIFFICULT MAN TO KILL.
KINDLY PUT THAT KNIFE DOWN AND RELEASE MR. CROMWELL.
MMPHH!! MMPMMMEEE!!
I SHALL DO NOTHING OF THE SORT.
YOU BETTER GIT, ARKHAM!

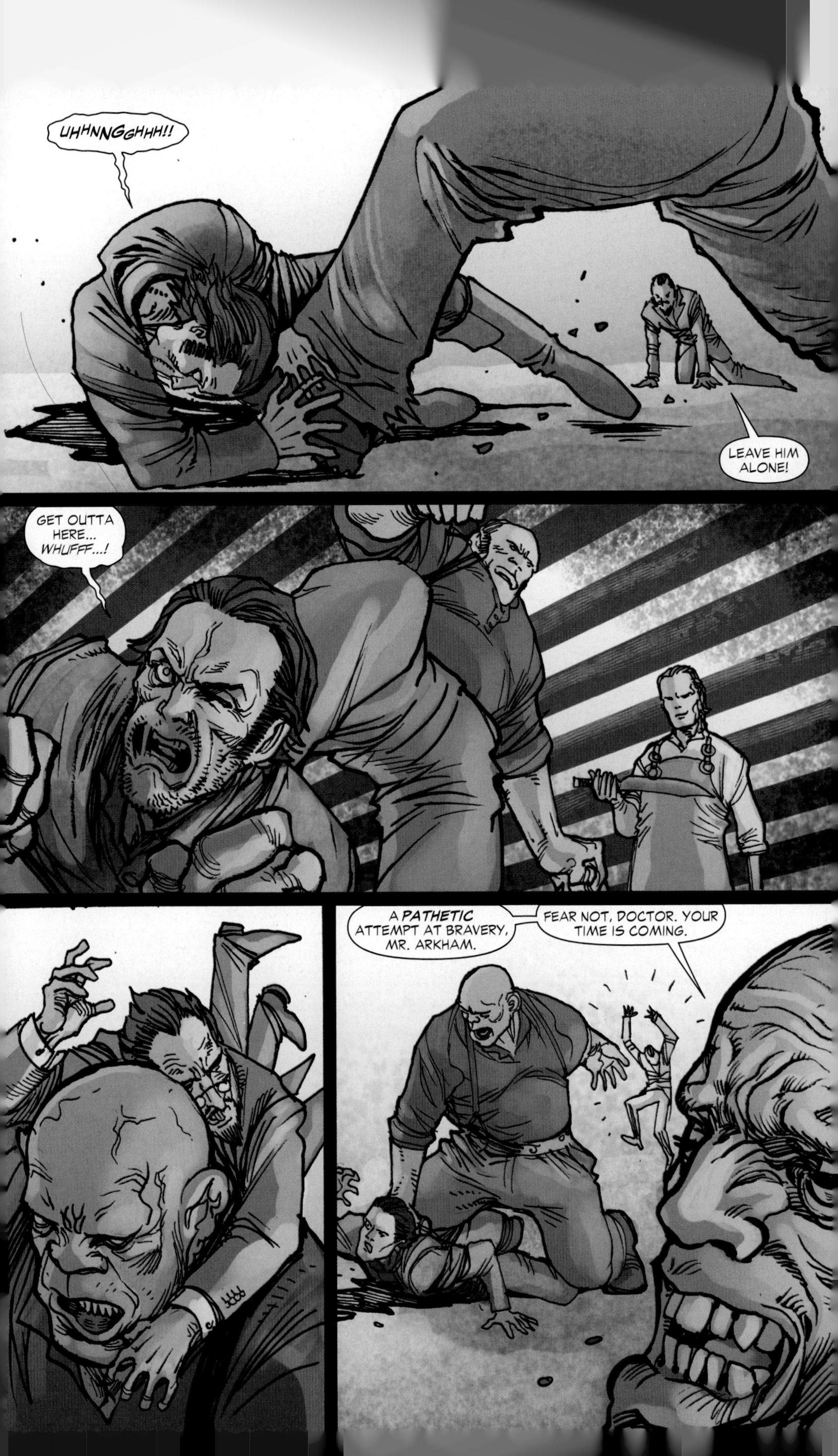

UHHNNGGHHH!!
LEAVE HIM ALONE!
GET OUTTA HERE... WHUFFF...!
A PATHETIC ATTEMPT AT BRAVERY, MR. ARKHAM.
FEAR NOT, DOCTOR. YOUR TIME IS COMING.

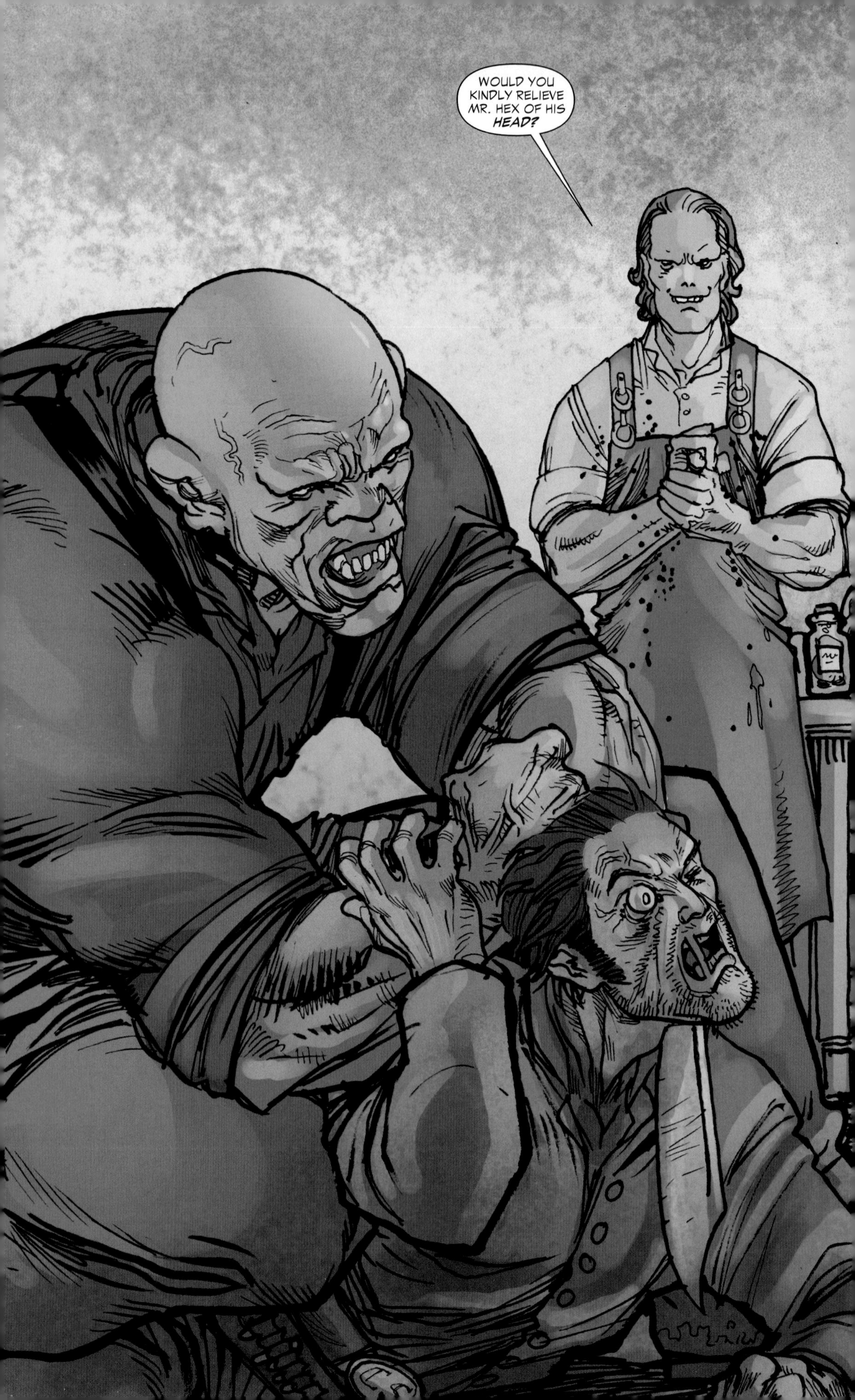
WOULD YOU KINDLY RELIEVE MR. HEX OF HIS HEAD?

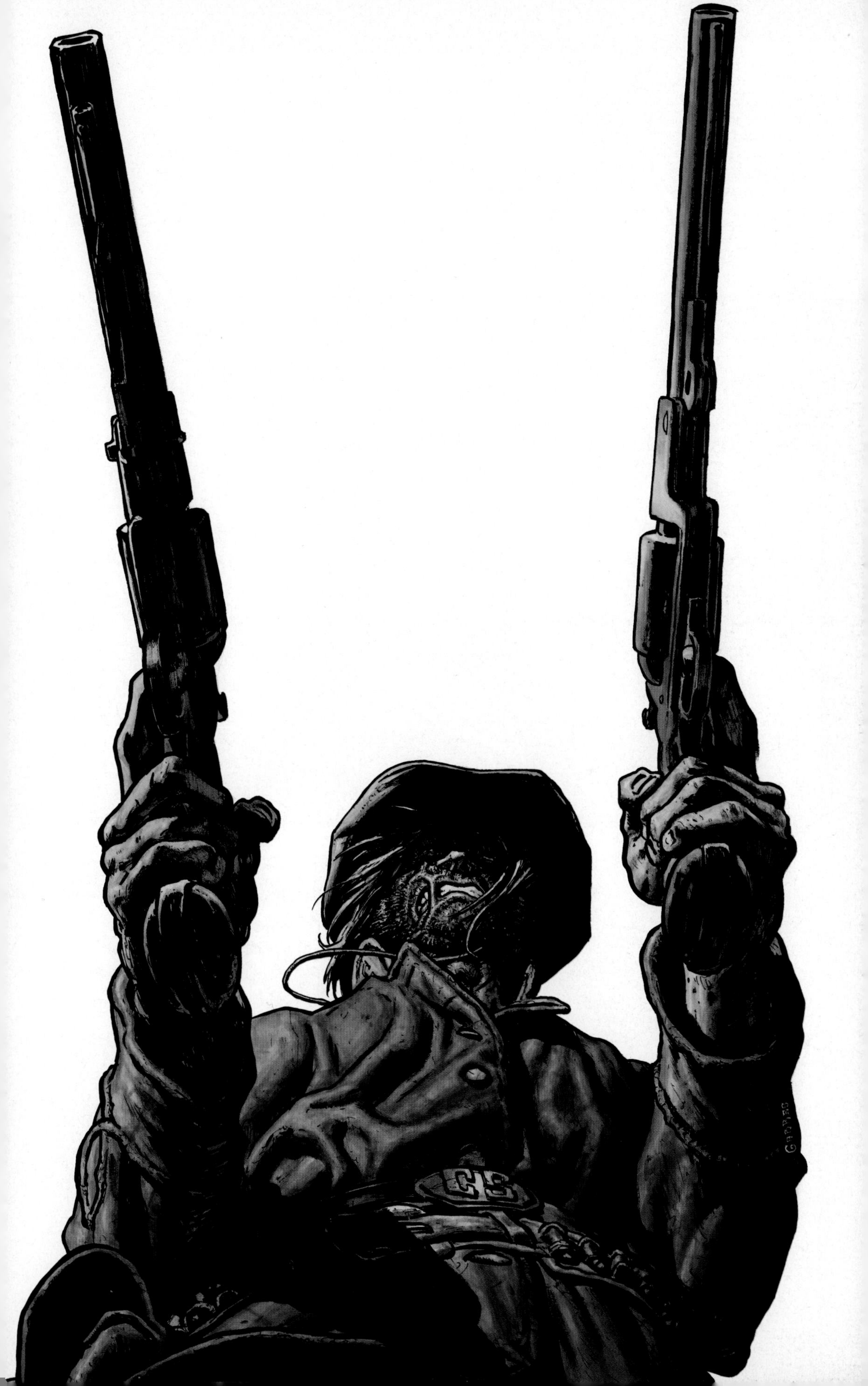

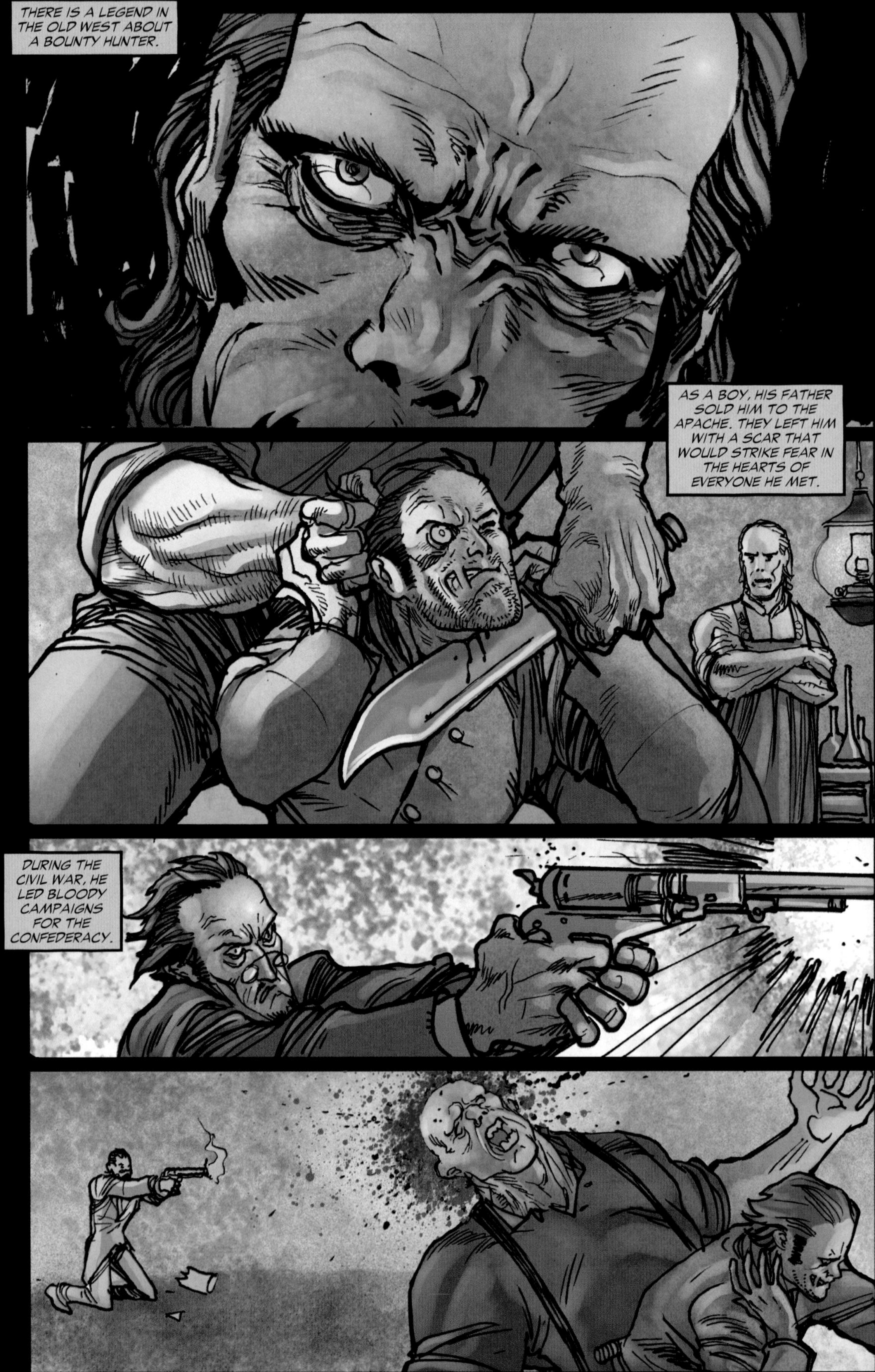
THERE IS A LEGEND IN THE OLD WEST ABOUT A BOUNTY HUNTER.
AS A BOY, HIS FATHER SOLD HIM TO THE APACHE. THEY LEFT HIM WITH A SCAR THAT WOULD STRIKE FEAR IN THE HEARTS OF EVERYONE HE MET.
DURING THE CIVIL WAR, HE LED BLOODY CAMPAIGNS FOR THE CONFEDERACY.

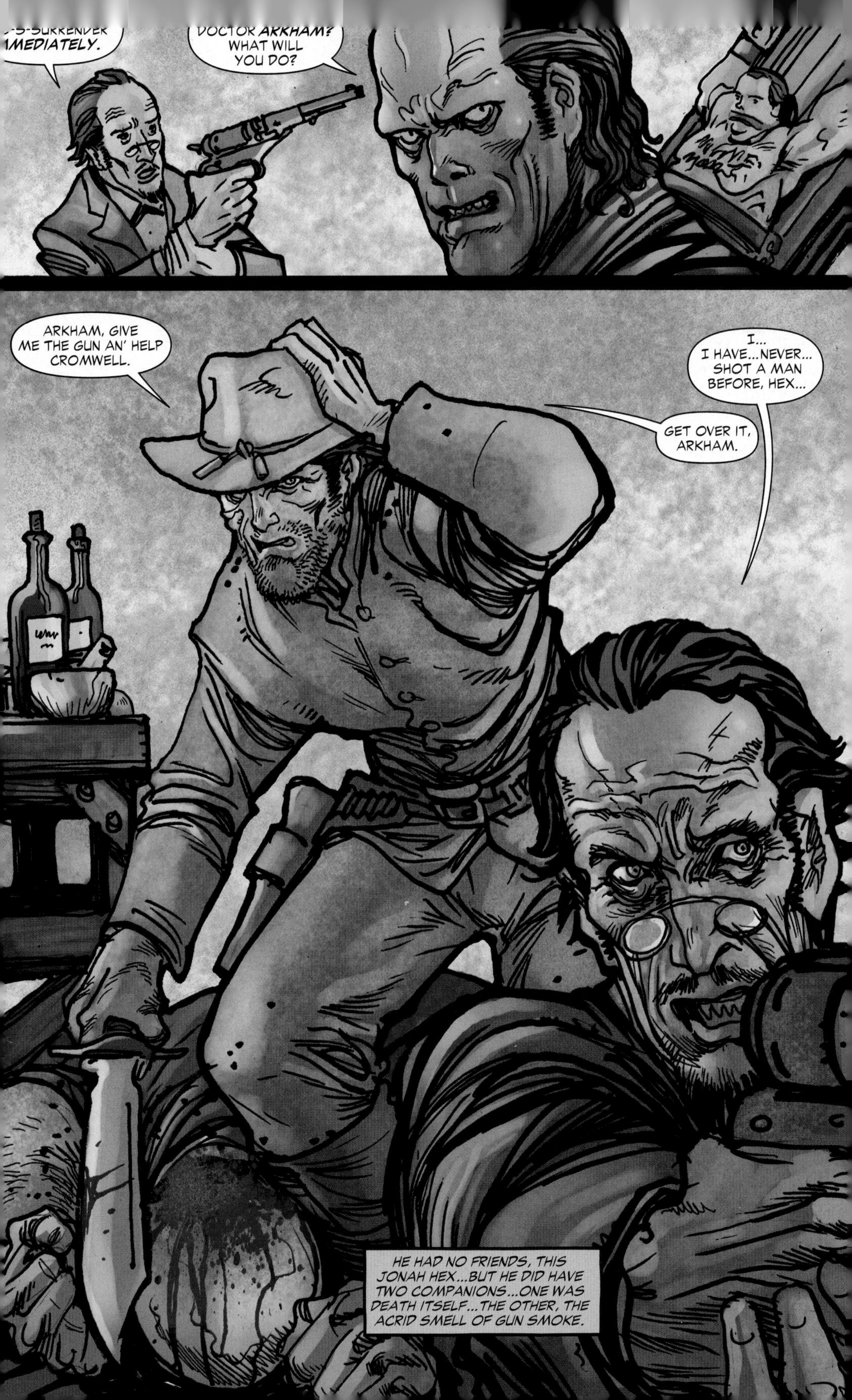

S-S-SURRENDER IMMEDIATELY.
DOCTOR ARKHAM? WHAT WILL YOU DO?
ARKHAM, GIVE ME THE GUN AN' HELP CROMWELL.
I... I HAVE...NEVER... SHOT A MAN BEFORE, HEX...
GET OVER IT, ARKHAM.
HE HAD NO FRIENDS, THIS JONAH HEX...BUT HE DID HAVE TWO COMPANIONS...ONE WAS DEATH ITSELF...THE OTHER, THE ACRID SMELL OF GUN SMOKE.

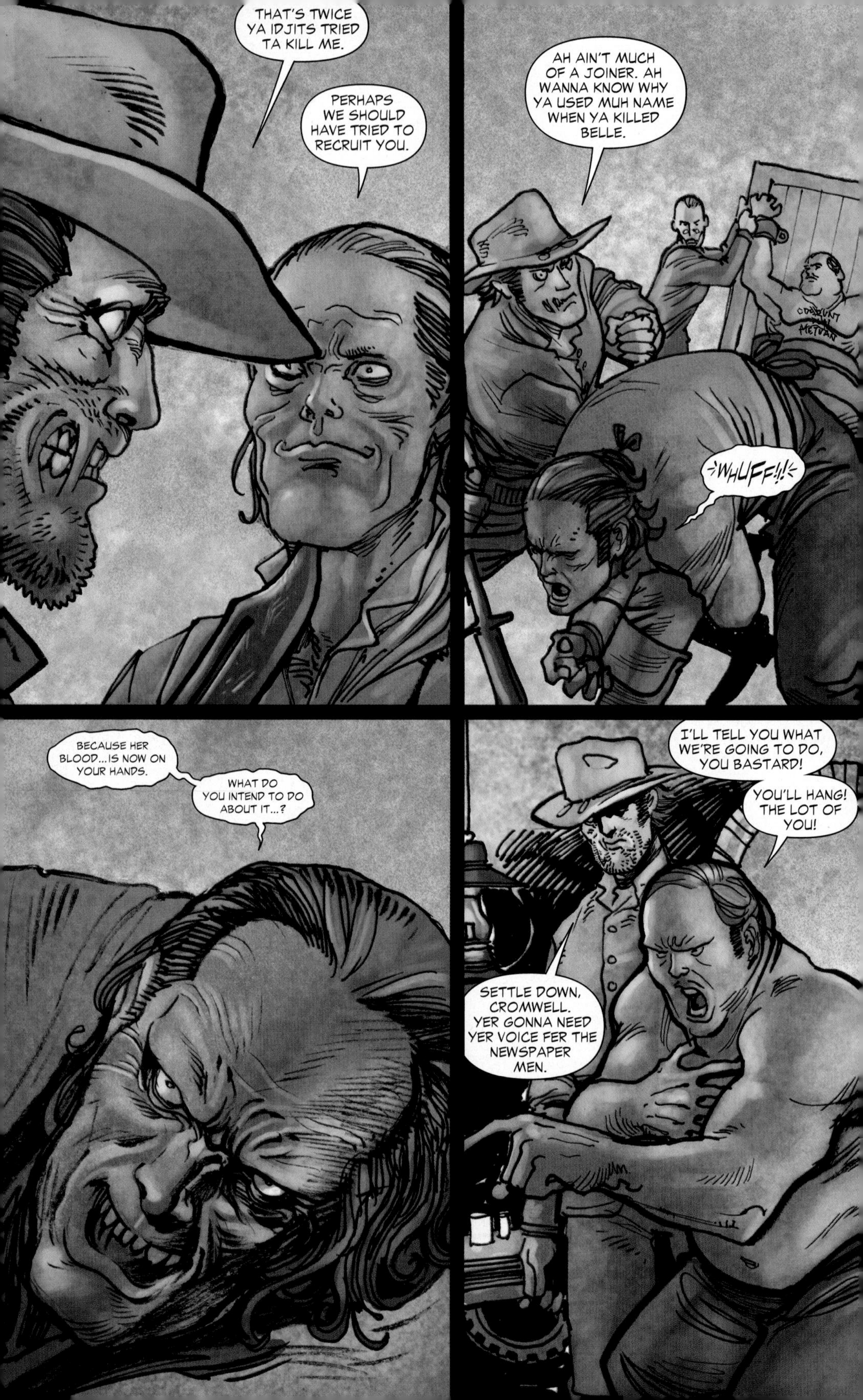
THAT'S TWICE YA IDJITS TRIED TA KILL ME.
PERHAPS WE SHOULD HAVE TRIED TO RECRUIT YOU.
AH AIN'T MUCH OF A JOINER. AH WANNA KNOW WHY YA USED MUH NAME WHEN YA KILLED BELLE.
WHUFF!!!
BECAUSE HER BLOOD...IS NOW ON YOUR HANDS.
WHAT DO YOU INTEND TO DO ABOUT IT...?
I'LL TELL YOU WHAT WE'RE GOING TO DO, YOU BASTARD!
YOU'LL HANG! THE LOT OF YOU!
SETTLE DOWN, CROMWELL. YER GONNA NEED YER VOICE FER THE NEWSPAPER MEN.

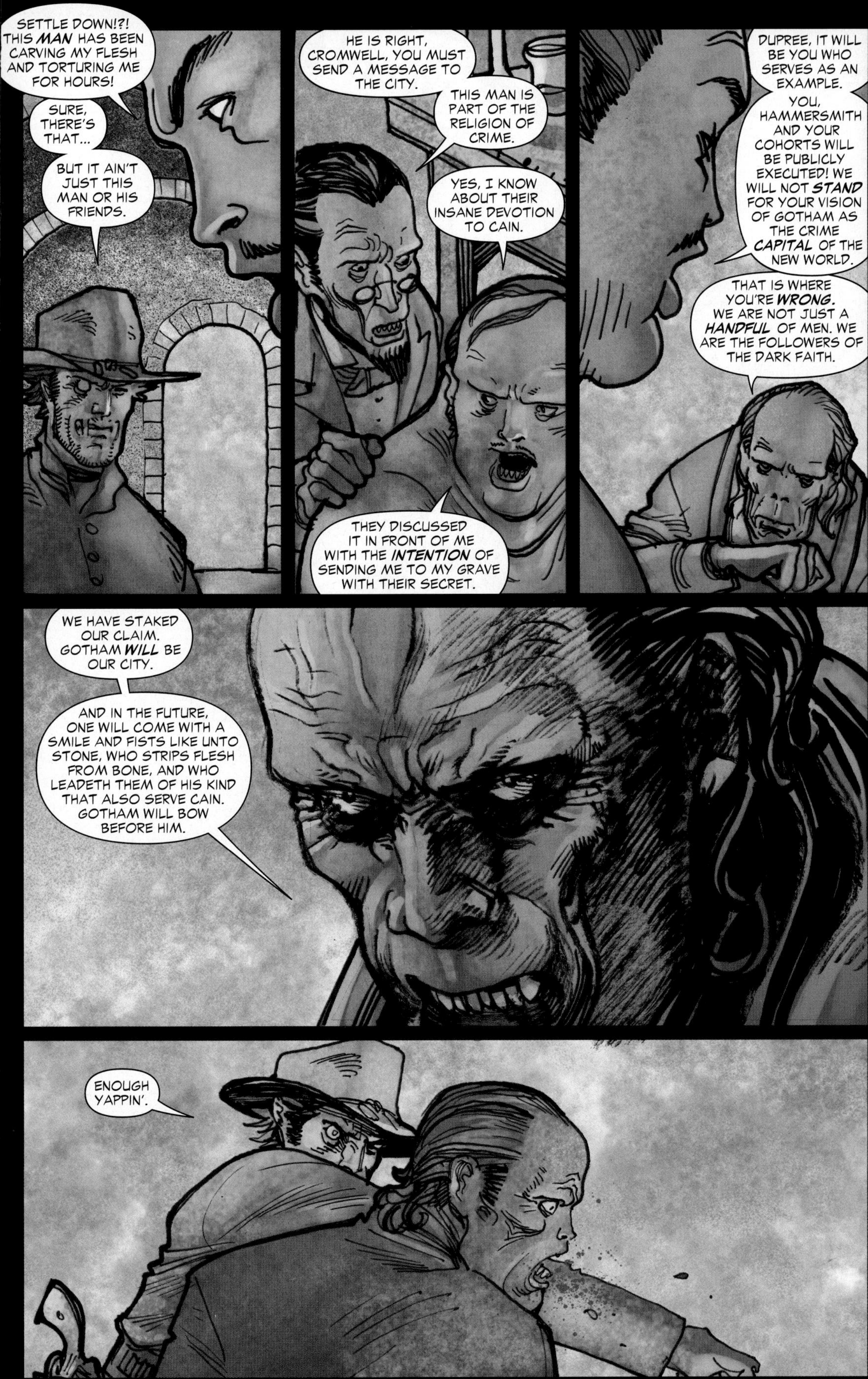
SETTLE DOWN!?! THIS MAN HAS BEEN CARVING MY FLESH AND TORTURING ME FOR HOURS!
SURE, THERE'S THAT...
BUT IT AIN'T JUST THIS MAN OR HIS FRIENDS.
HE IS RIGHT, CROMWELL, YOU MUST SEND A MESSAGE TO THE CITY.
THIS MAN IS PART OF THE RELIGION OF CRIME.
YES, I KNOW ABOUT THEIR INSANE DEVOTION TO CAIN.
THEY DISCUSSED IT IN FRONT OF ME WITH THE INTENTION OF SENDING ME TO MY GRAVE WITH THEIR SECRET.
DUPREE, IT WILL BE YOU WHO SERVES AS AN EXAMPLE.
YOU, HAMMERSMITH AND YOUR COHORTS WILL BE PUBLICLY EXECUTED! WE WILL NOT STAND FOR YOUR VISION OF GOTHAM AS THE CRIME CAPITAL OF THE NEW WORLD.
THAT IS WHERE YOU'RE WRONG. WE ARE NOT JUST A HANDFUL OF MEN. WE ARE THE FOLLOWERS OF THE DARK FAITH.
WE HAVE STAKED OUR CLAIM. GOTHAM WILL BE OUR CITY.
AND IN THE FUTURE, ONE WILL COME WITH A SMILE AND FISTS LIKE UNTO STONE, WHO STRIPS FLESH FROM BONE, AND WHO LEADETH THEM OF HIS KIND THAT ALSO SERVE CAIN. GOTHAM WILL BOW BEFORE HIM.
ENOUGH YAPPIN'.

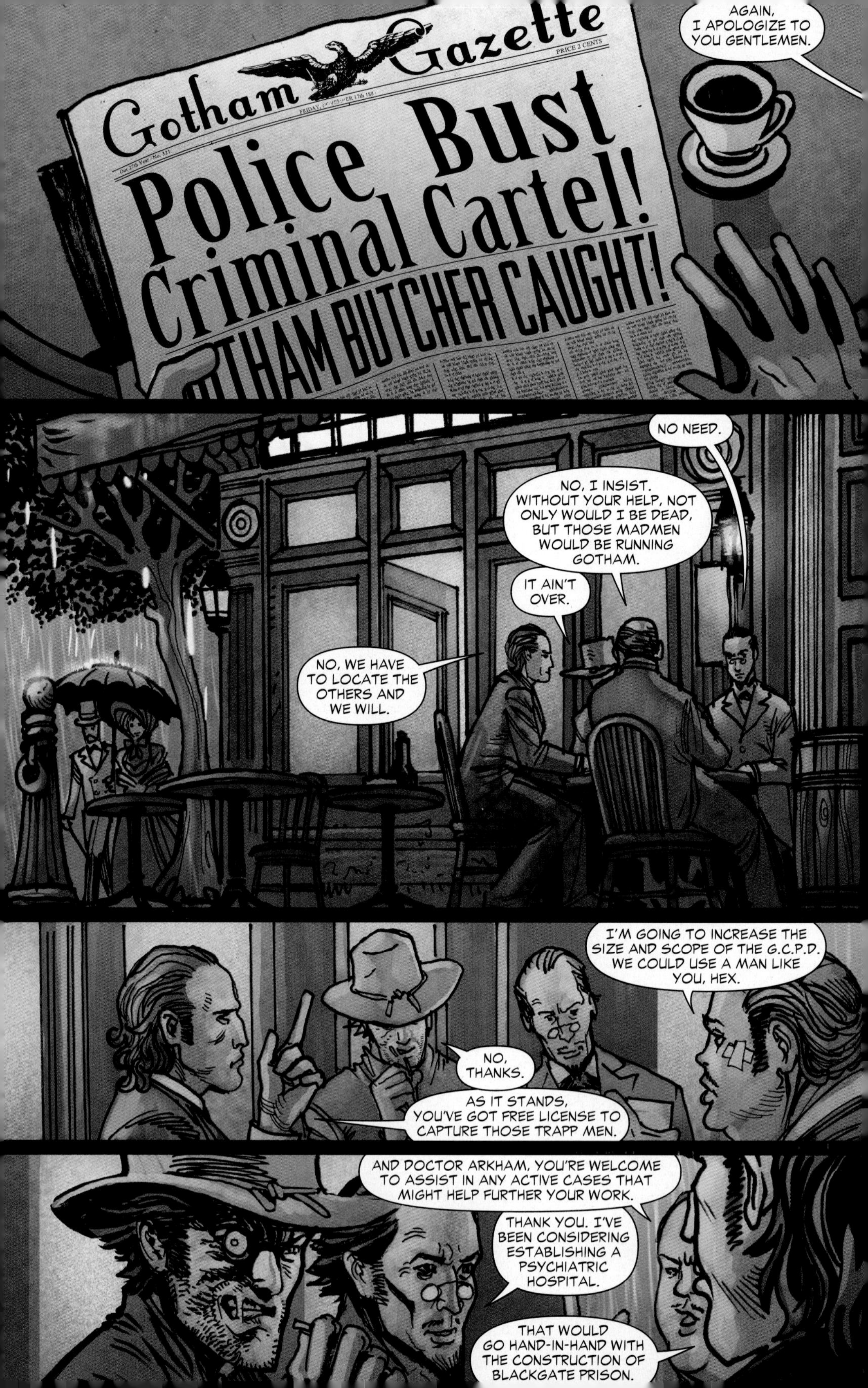
Gotham Gazette
PRICE 2 CENTS
Police Bust Criminal Cartel!
THAM BUTCHER CAUGHT!
AGAIN, I APOLOGIZE TO YOU GENTLEMEN.
NO NEED.
NO, I INSIST. WITHOUT YOUR HELP, NOT ONLY WOULD I BE DEAD, BUT THOSE MADMEN WOULD BE RUNNING GOTHAM.
IT AIN'T OVER.
NO, WE HAVE TO LOCATE THE OTHERS AND WE WILL.
I'M GOING TO INCREASE THE SIZE AND SCOPE OF THE G.C.P.D. WE COULD USE A MAN LIKE YOU, HEX.
NO, THANKS.
AS IT STANDS, YOU'VE GOT FREE LICENSE TO CAPTURE THOSE TRAPP MEN.
AND DOCTOR ARKHAM, YOU'RE WELCOME TO ASSIST IN ANY ACTIVE CASES THAT MIGHT HELP FURTHER YOUR WORK.
THANK YOU. I'VE BEEN CONSIDERING ESTABLISHING A PSYCHIATRIC HOSPITAL.
THAT WOULD GO HAND-IN-HAND WITH THE CONSTRUCTION OF BLACKGATE PRISON.

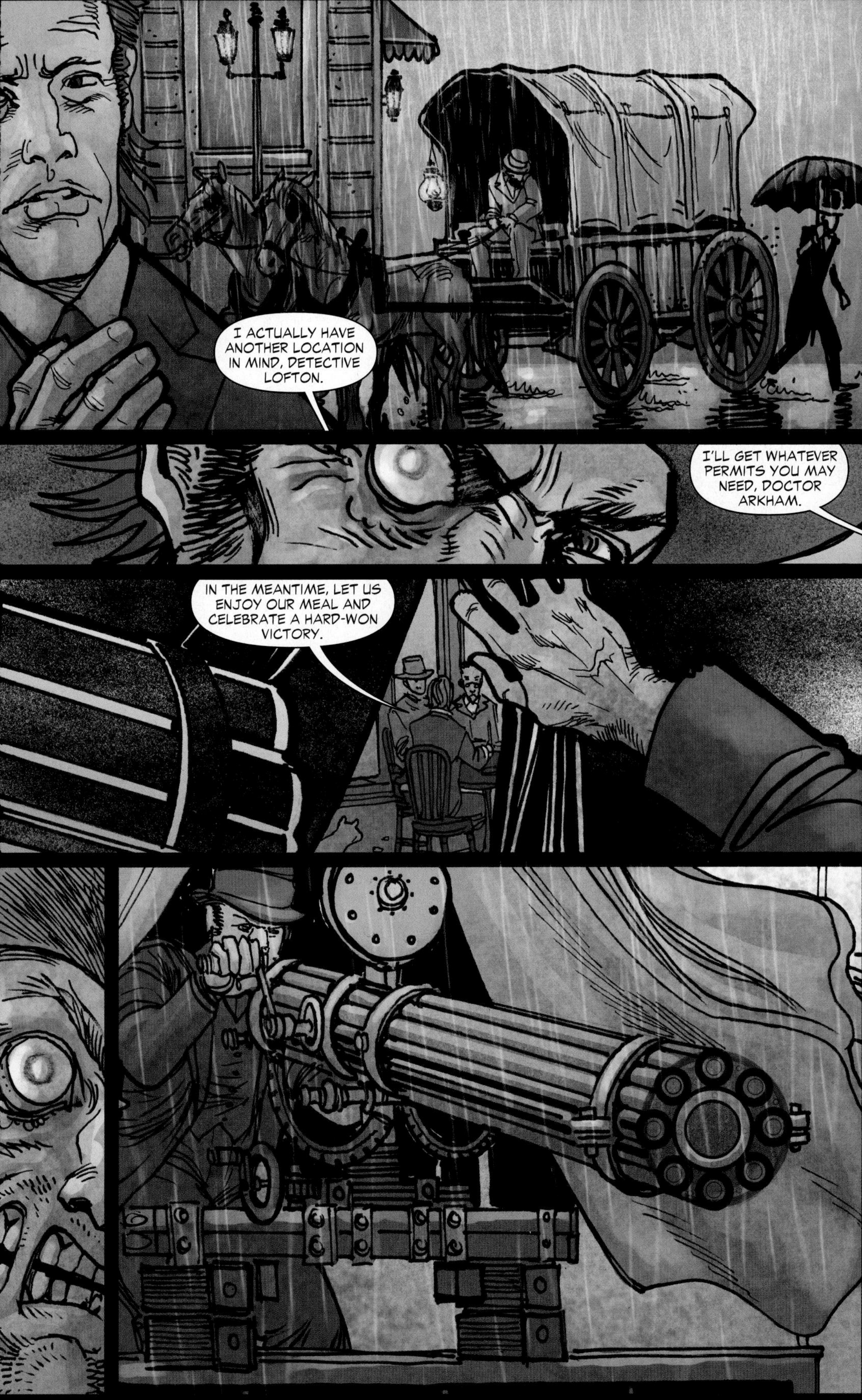
I ACTUALLY HAVE ANOTHER LOCATION IN MIND, DETECTIVE LOFTON.
I'LL GET WHATEVER PERMITS YOU MAY NEED, DOCTOR ARKHAM.
IN THE MEANTIME, LET US ENJOY OUR MEAL AND CELEBRATE A HARD-WON VICTORY.

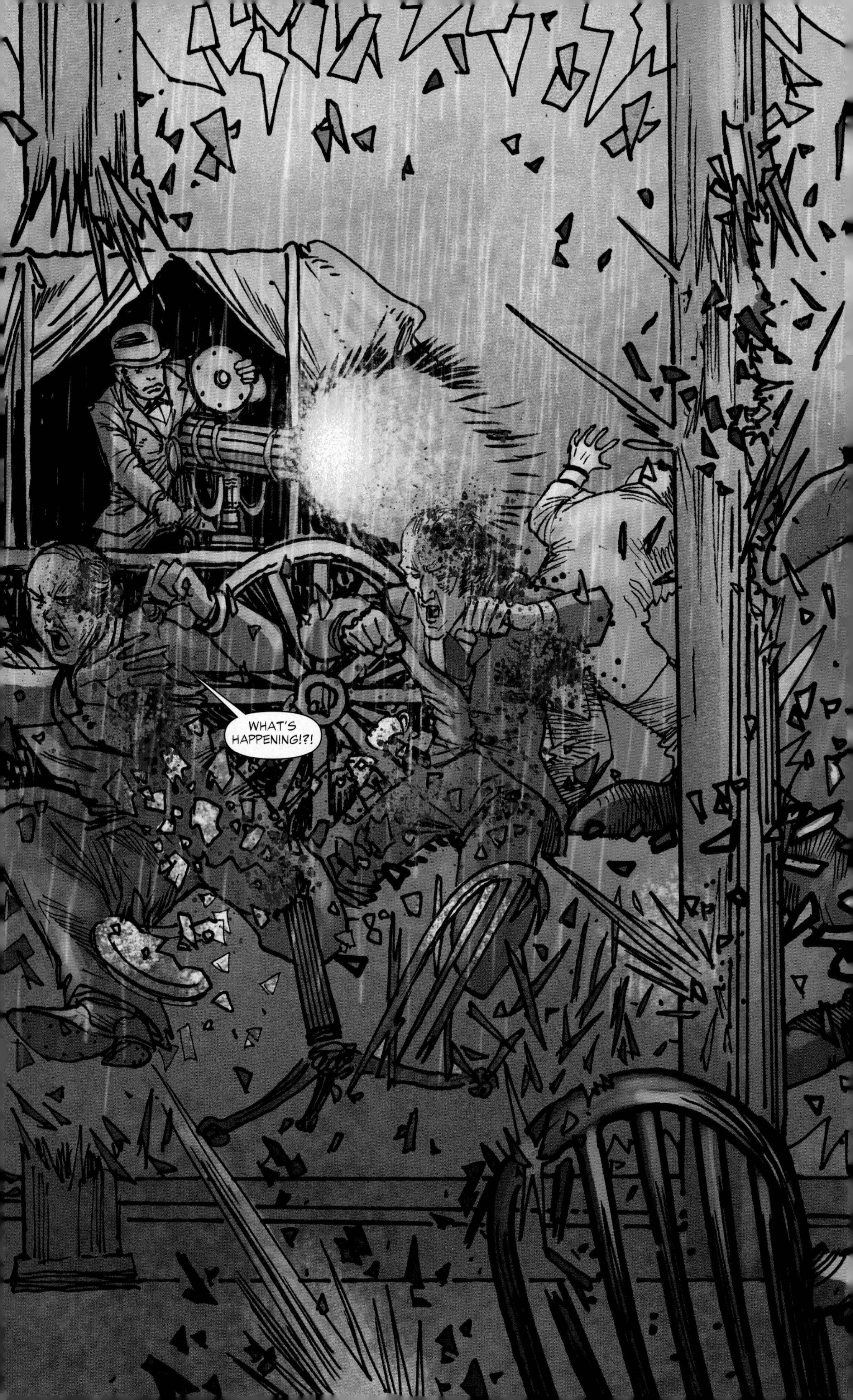
WHAT'S HAPPENING!?!

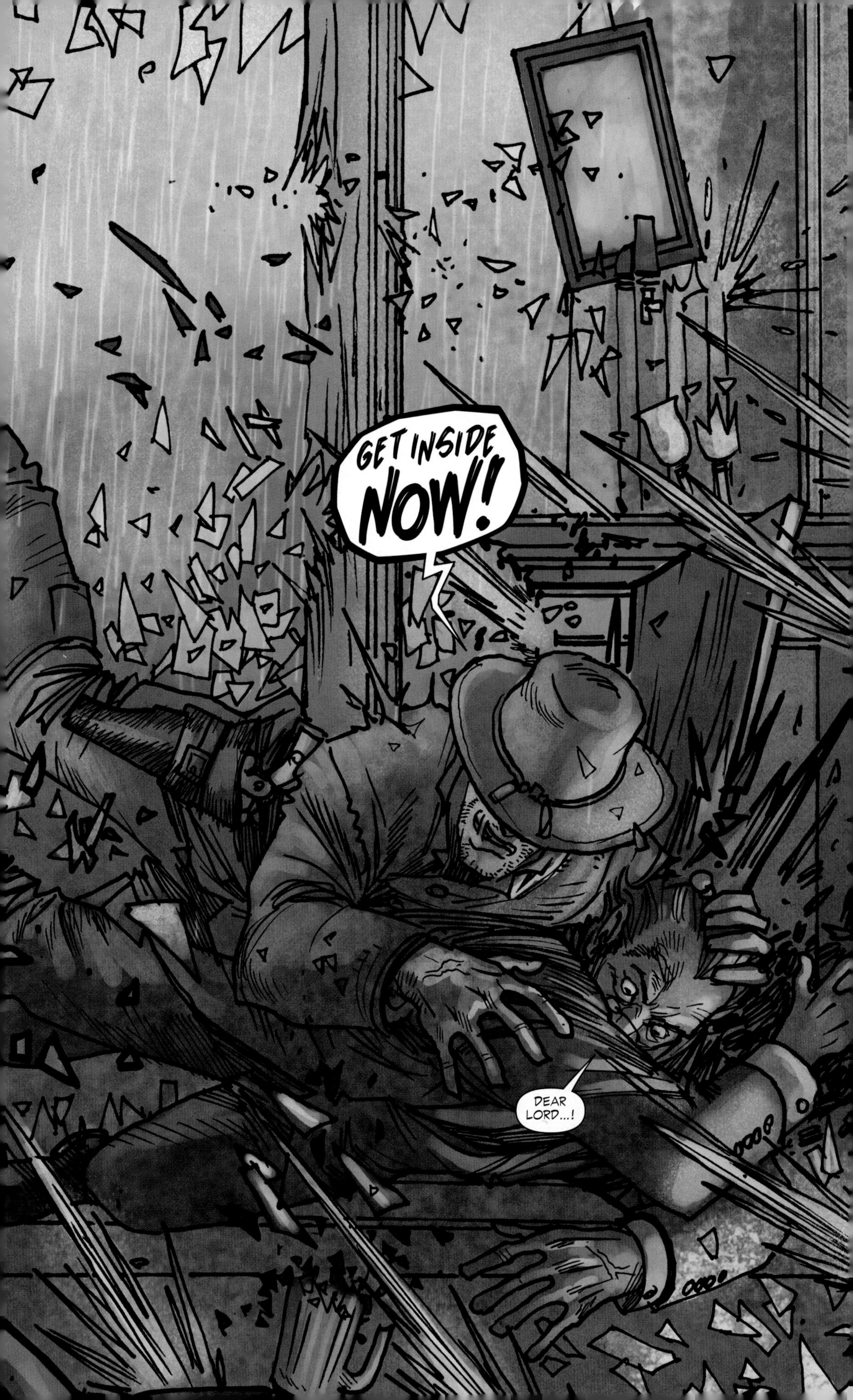
GET INSIDE NOW!
DEAR LORD...!

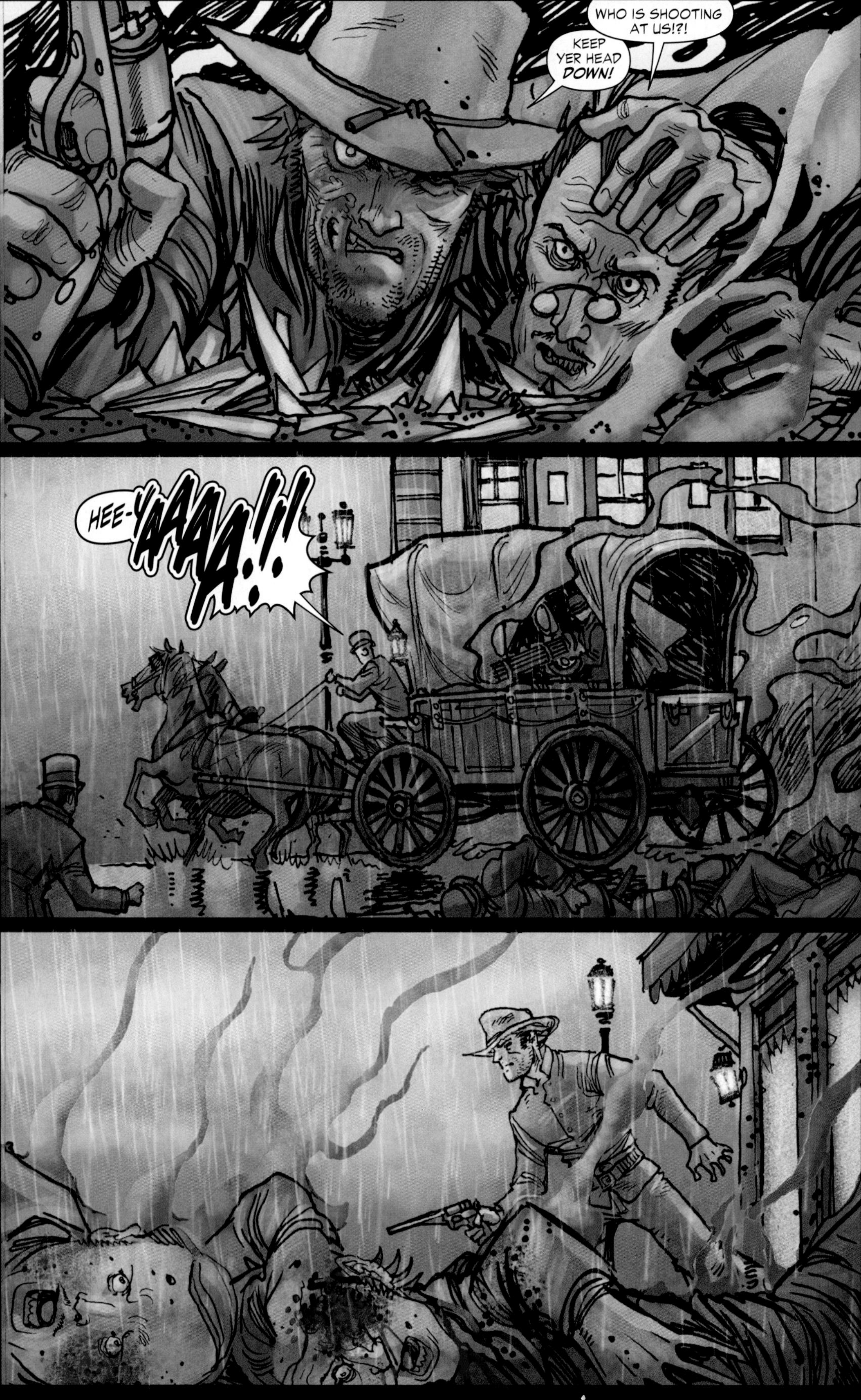
WHO IS SHOOTING AT US!?!
KEEP YER HEAD DOWN!
HEE-YAAAA!!!

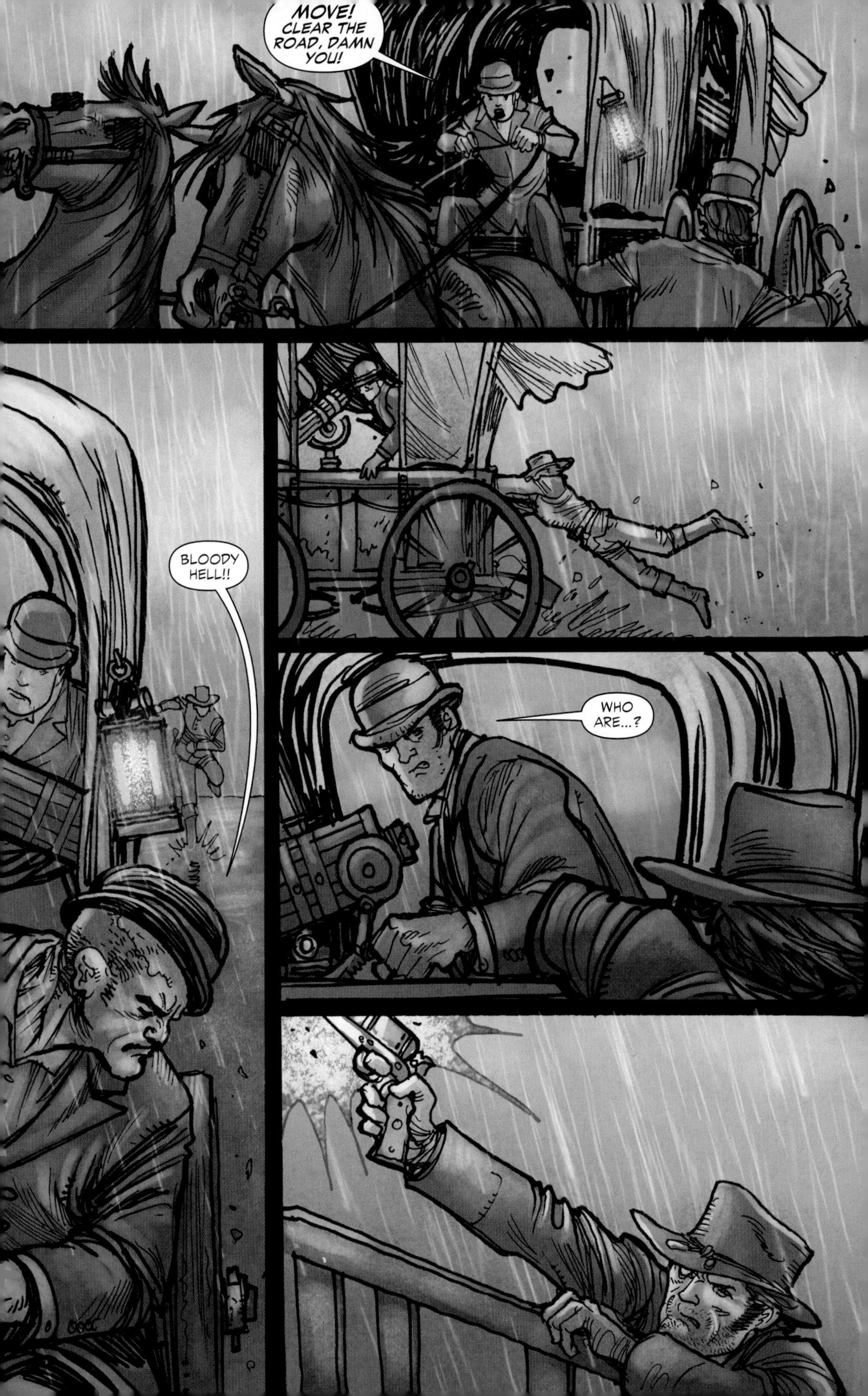
MOVE! CLEAR THE ROAD, DAMN YOU!
BLOODY HELL!!
WHO ARE...?

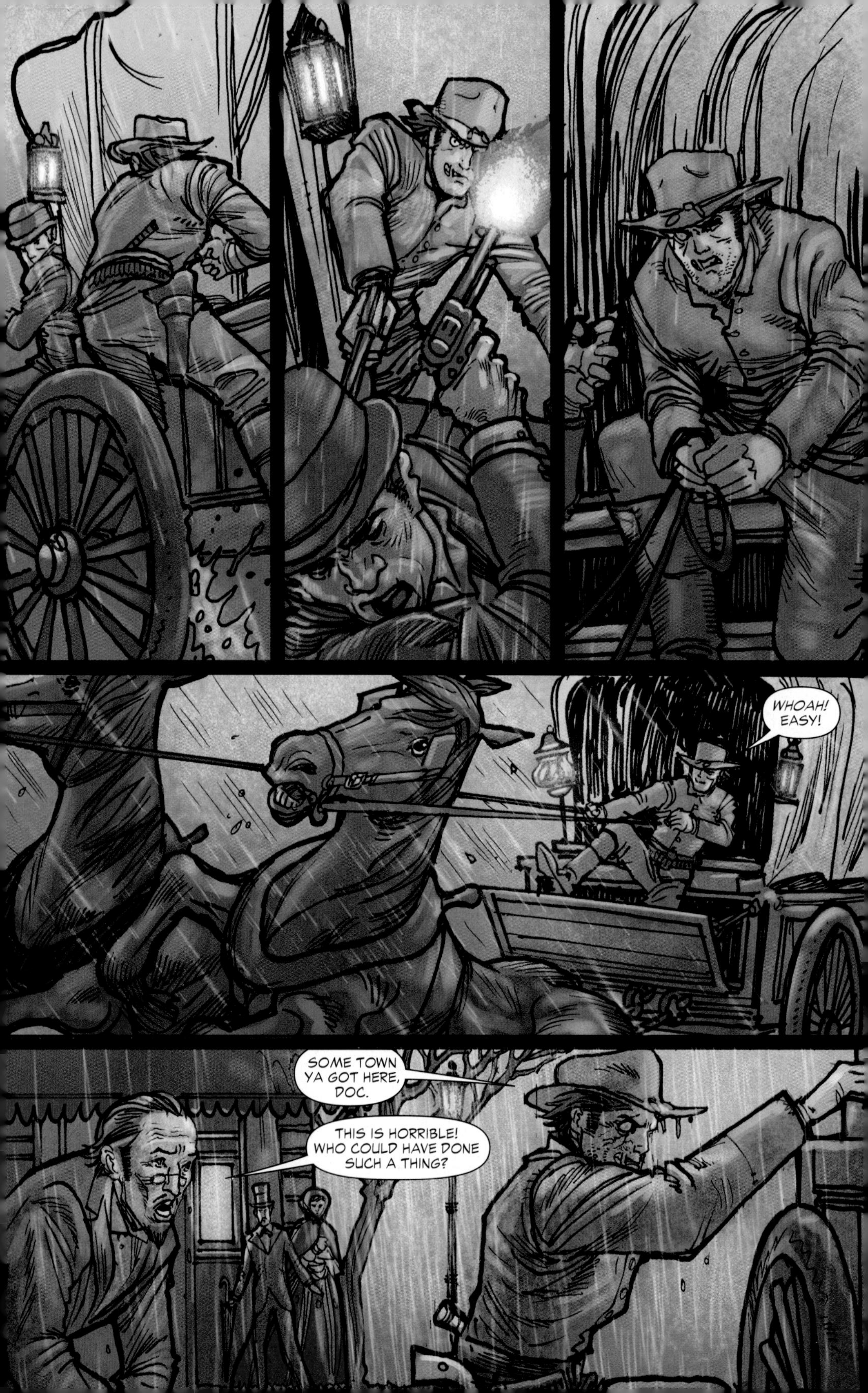
WHOAH! EASY!
SOME TOWN YA GOT HERE, DOC.
THIS IS HORRIBLE! WHO COULD HAVE DONE SUCH A THING?

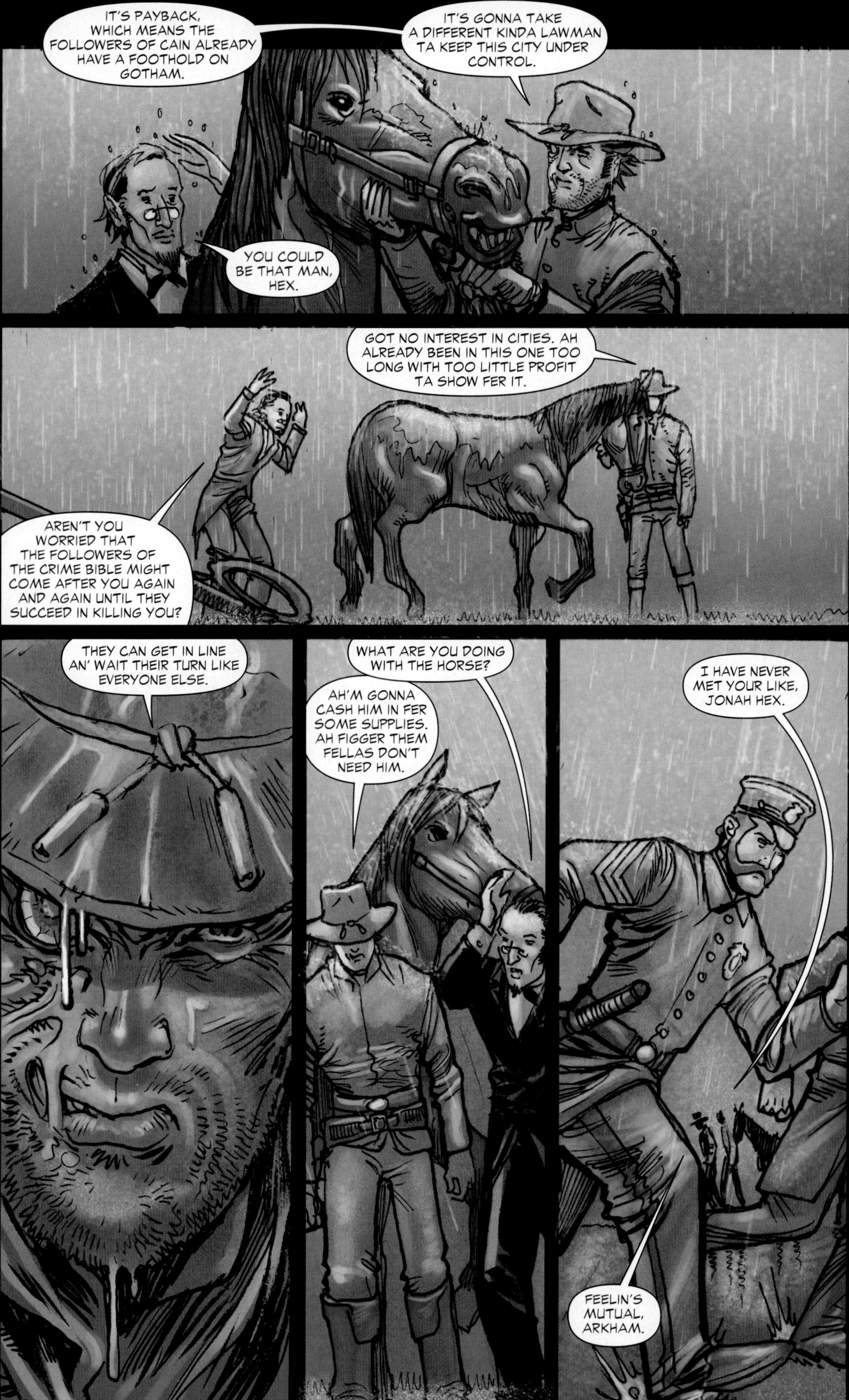
IT'S PAYBACK, WHICH MEANS THE FOLLOWERS OF CAIN ALREADY HAVE A FOOTHOLD ON GOTHAM.
IT'S GONNA TAKE A DIFFERENT KINDA LAWMAN TA KEEP THIS CITY UNDER CONTROL.
YOU COULD BE THAT MAN, HEX.
GOT NO INTEREST IN CITIES. AH ALREADY BEEN IN THIS ONE TOO LONG WITH TOO LITTLE PROFIT TA SHOW FER IT.
AREN'T YOU WORRIED THAT THE FOLLOWERS OF THE CRIME BIBLE MIGHT COME AFTER YOU AGAIN AND AGAIN UNTIL THEY SUCCEED IN KILLING YOU?
THEY CAN GET IN LINE AN' WAIT THEIR TURN LIKE EVERYONE ELSE.
WHAT ARE YOU DOING WITH THE HORSE?
AH'M GONNA CASH HIM IN FER SOME SUPPLIES. AH FIGGER THEM FELLAS DON'T NEED HIM.
I HAVE NEVER MET YOUR LIKE, JONAH HEX.
FEELIN'S MUTUAL, ARKHAM.

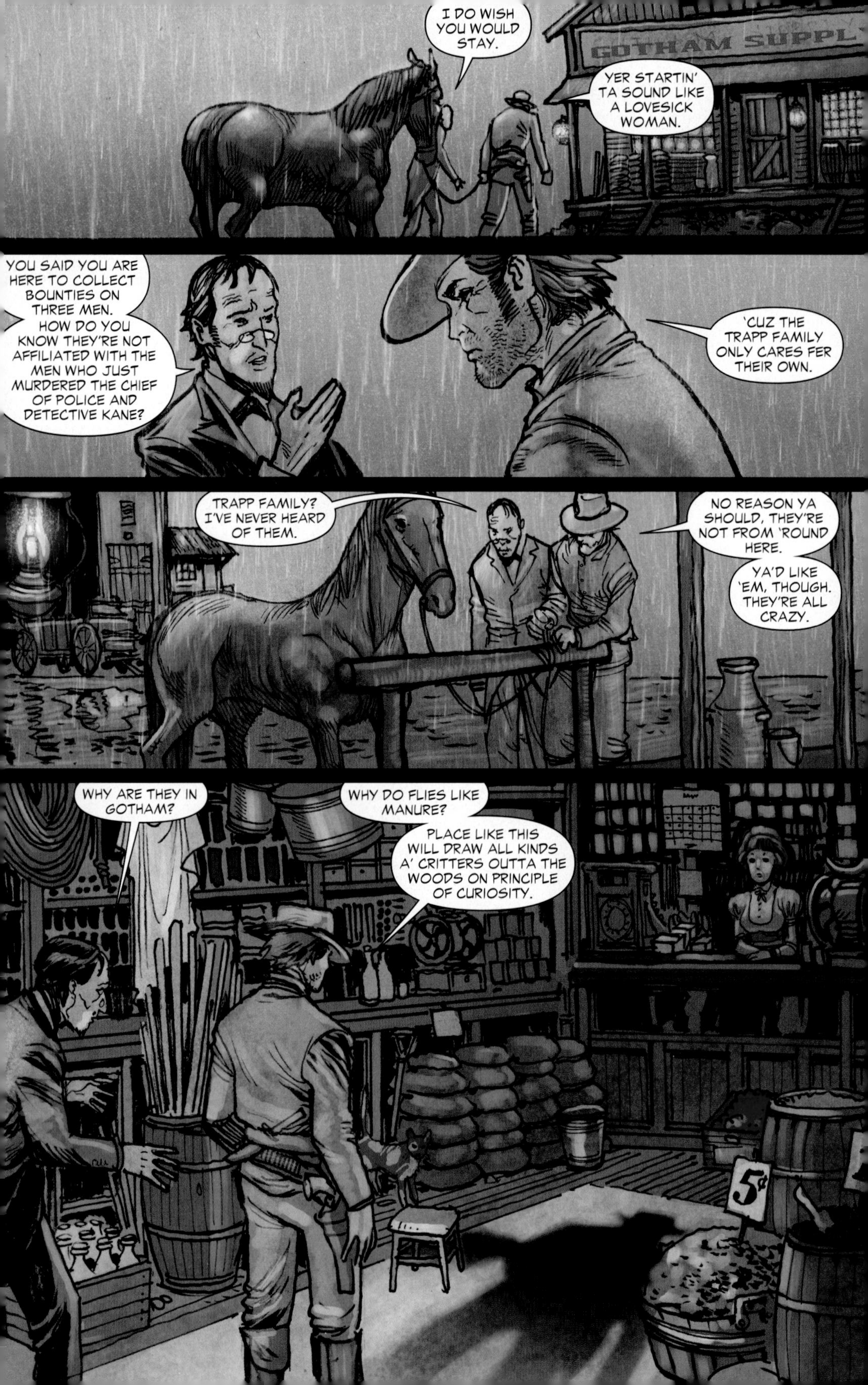
I DO WISH YOU WOULD STAY.
GOTHAM SUPPL
YER STARTIN' TA SOUND LIKE A LOVESICK WOMAN.
YOU SAID YOU ARE HERE TO COLLECT BOUNTIES ON THREE MEN. HOW DO YOU KNOW THEY'RE NOT AFFILIATED WITH THE MEN WHO JUST MURDERED THE CHIEF OF POLICE AND DETECTIVE KANE?
'CUZ THE TRAPP FAMILY ONLY CARES FER THEIR OWN.
TRAPP FAMILY? I'VE NEVER HEARD OF THEM.
NO REASON YA SHOULD, THEY'RE NOT FROM 'ROUND HERE.
YA'D LIKE 'EM, THOUGH. THEY'RE ALL CRAZY.
WHY ARE THEY IN GOTHAM?
WHY DO FLIES LIKE MANURE?
PLACE LIKE THIS WILL DRAW ALL KINDS A' CRITTERS OUTTA THE WOODS ON PRINCIPLE OF CURIOSITY.
5¢

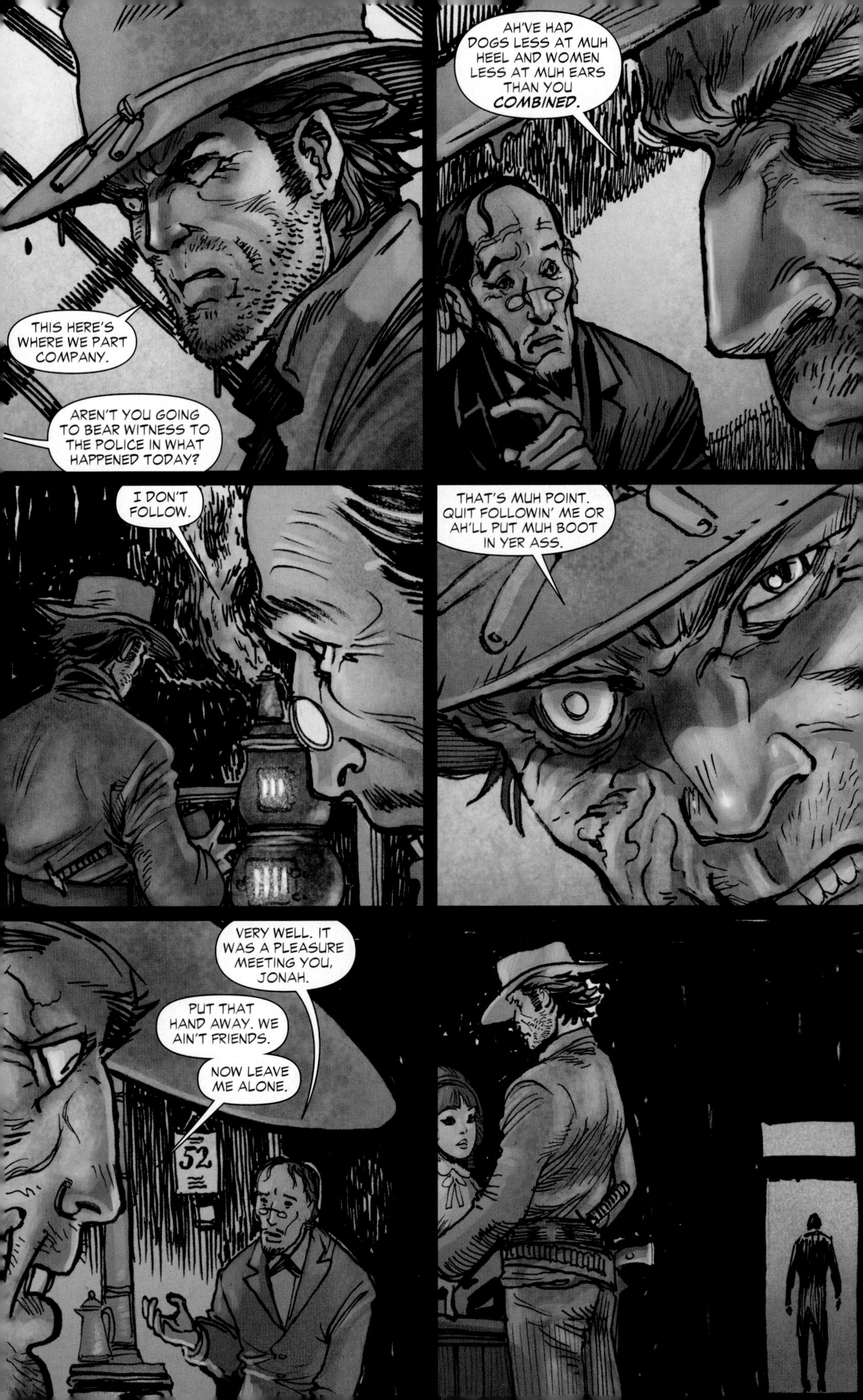
THIS HERE'S WHERE WE PART COMPANY.
AREN'T YOU GOING TO BEAR WITNESS TO THE POLICE IN WHAT HAPPENED TODAY?
AH'VE HAD DOGS LESS AT MUH HEEL AND WOMEN LESS AT MUH EARS THAN YOU COMBINED.
I DON'T FOLLOW.
THAT'S MUH POINT. QUIT FOLLOWIN' ME OR AH'LL PUT MUH BOOT IN YER ASS.
VERY WELL. IT WAS A PLEASURE MEETING YOU, JONAH.
PUT THAT HAND AWAY. WE AIN'T FRIENDS.
NOW LEAVE ME ALONE.
52

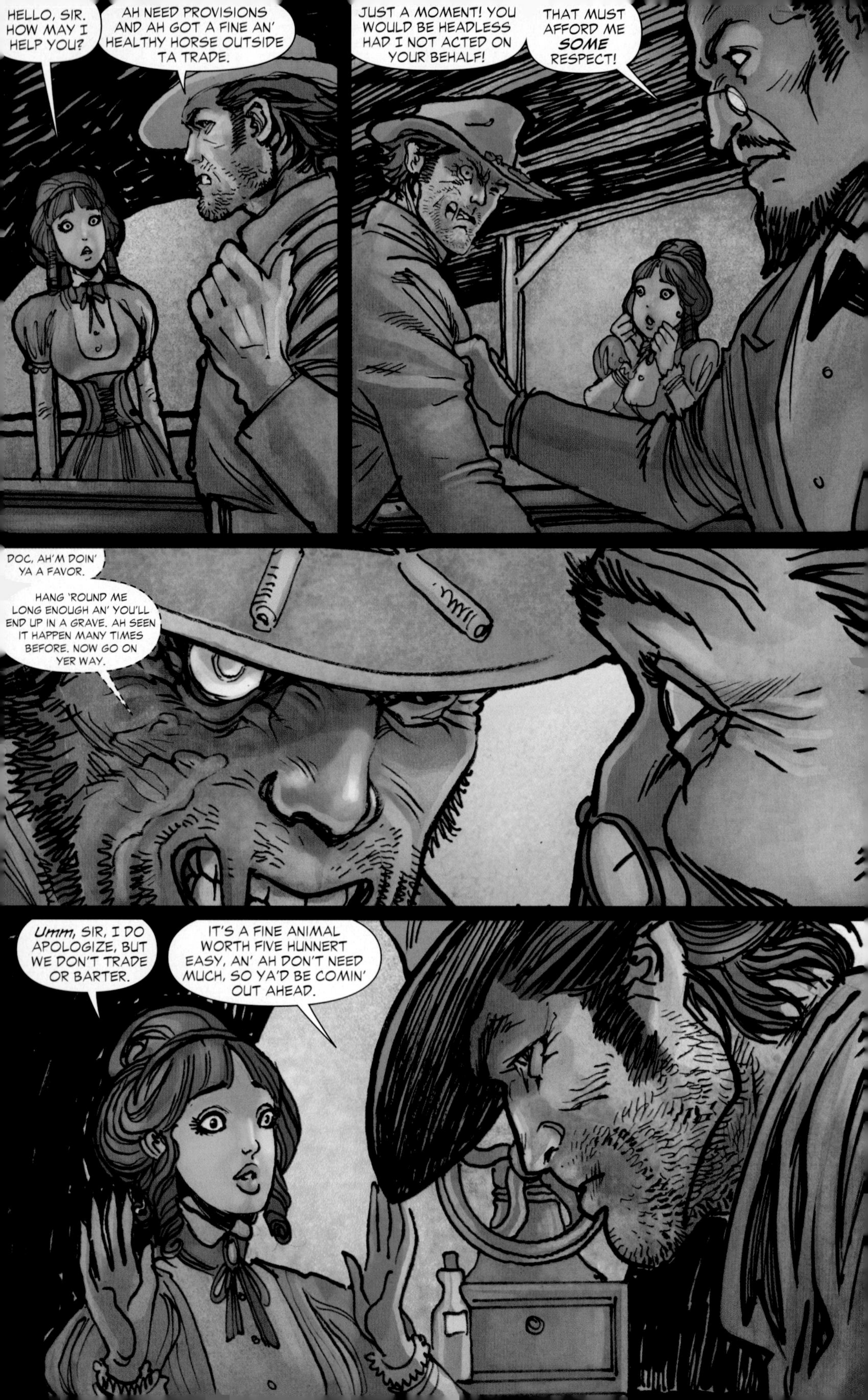
HELLO, SIR. HOW MAY I HELP YOU?
AH NEED PROVISIONS AND AH GOT A FINE AN' HEALTHY HORSE OUTSIDE TA TRADE.
JUST A MOMENT! YOU WOULD BE HEADLESS HAD I NOT ACTED ON YOUR BEHALF!
THAT MUST AFFORD ME *SOME* RESPECT!
DOC, AH'M DOIN' YA A FAVOR.
HANG 'ROUND ME LONG ENOUGH AN' YOU'LL END UP IN A GRAVE. AH SEEN IT HAPPEN MANY TIMES BEFORE. NOW GO ON YER WAY.
*Umm*, SIR, I DO APOLOGIZE, BUT WE DON'T TRADE OR BARTER.
IT'S A FINE ANIMAL WORTH FIVE HUNNERT EASY, AN' AH DON'T NEED MUCH, SO YA'D BE COMIN' OUT AHEAD.

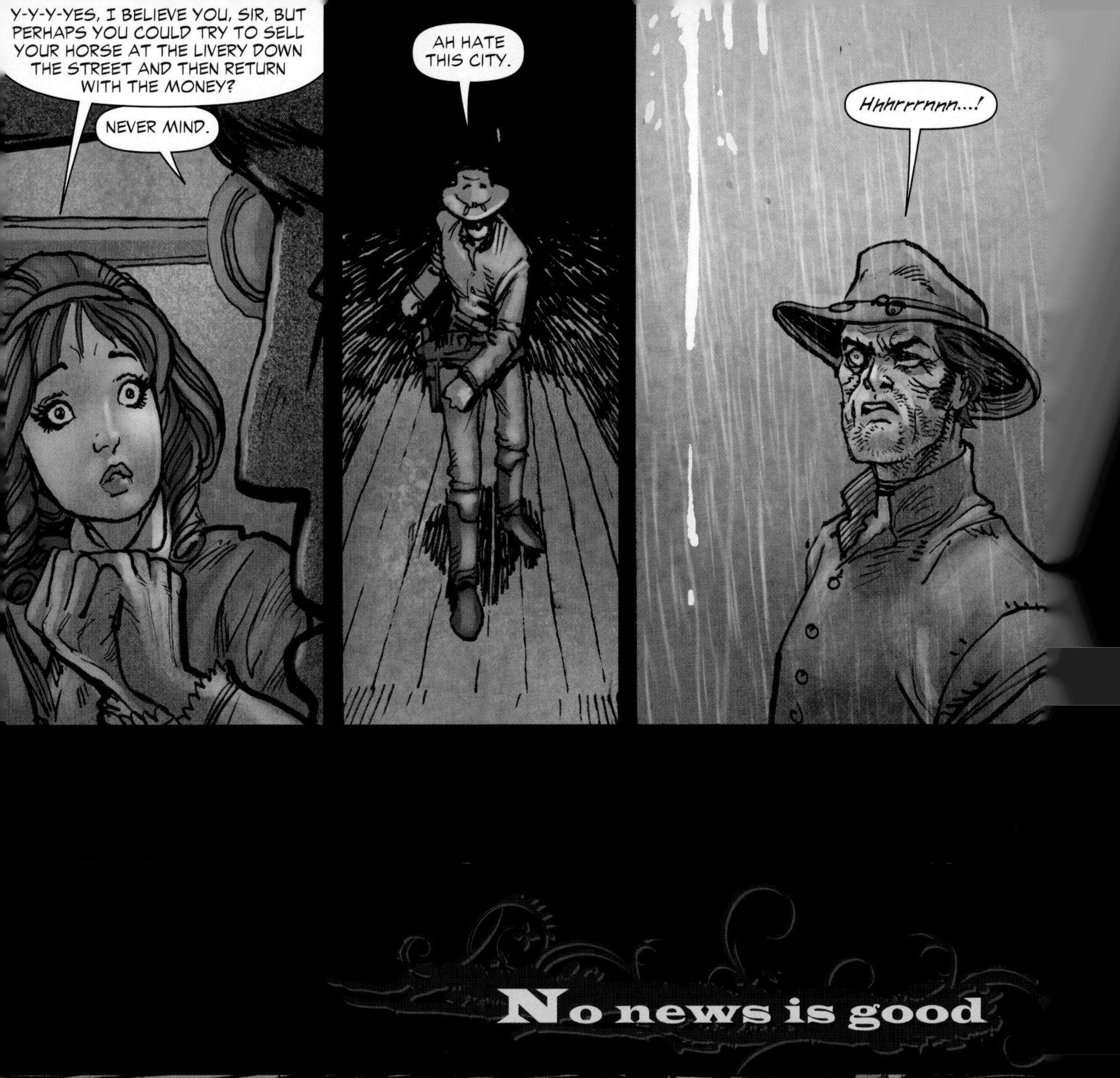
Y-Y-Y-YES, I BELIEVE YOU, SIR, BUT PERHAPS YOU COULD TRY TO SELL YOUR HORSE AT THE LIVERY DOWN THE STREET AND THEN RETURN WITH THE MONEY?
NEVER MIND.
AH HATE THIS CITY.
Hhhrrrnnn...!

# No news is good

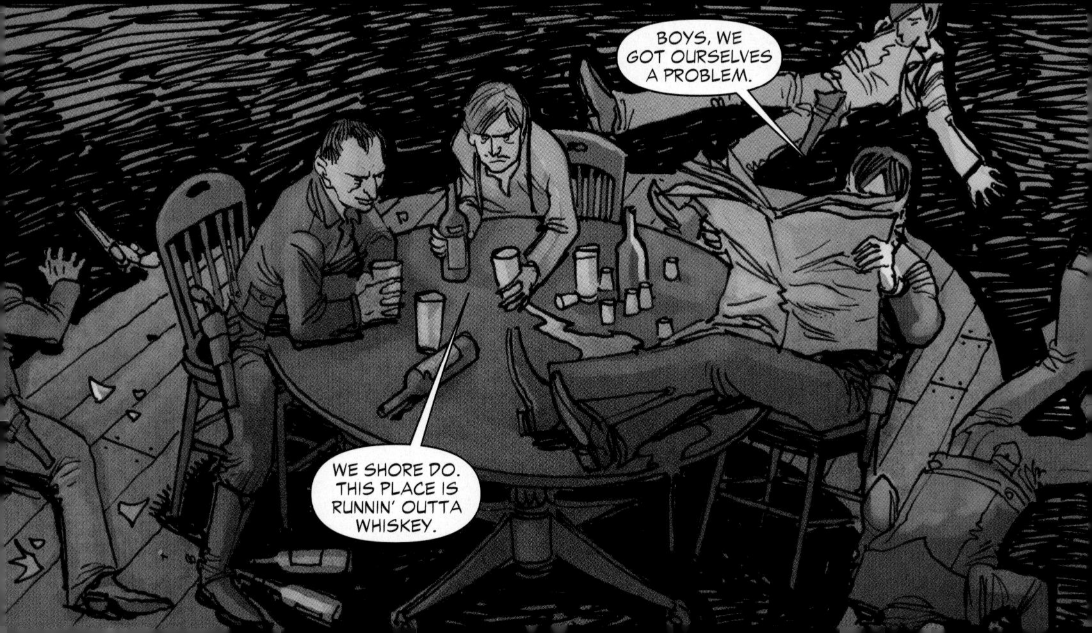
BOYS, WE GOT OURSELVES A PROBLEM.
WE SHORE DO. THIS PLACE IS RUNNIN' OUTTA WHISKEY.

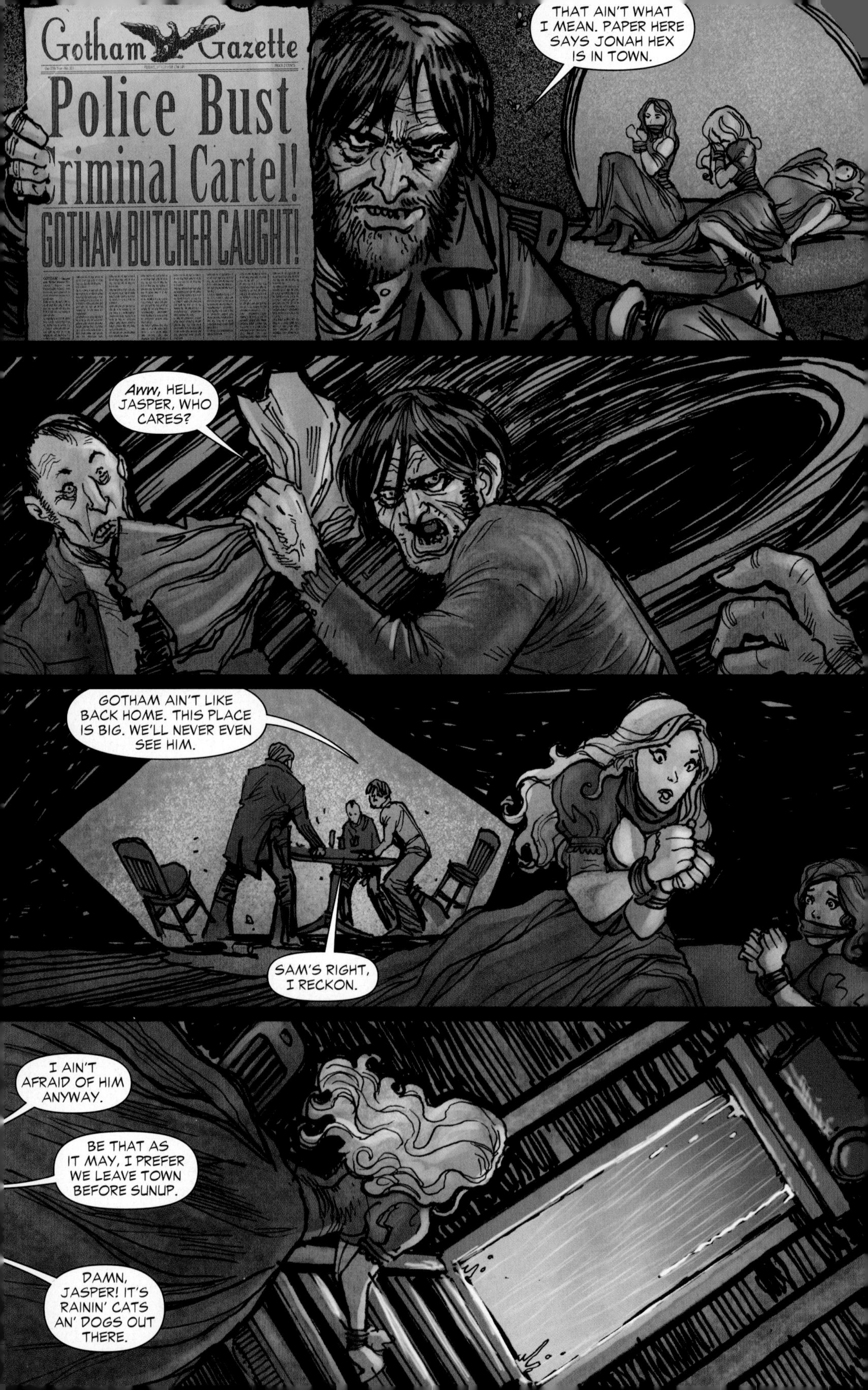
Gotham Gazette
Police Bust Criminal Cartel!
GOTHAM BUTCHER CAUGHT!
THAT AIN'T WHAT I MEAN. PAPER HERE SAYS JONAH HEX IS IN TOWN.
*Aww,* HELL, JASPER, WHO CARES?
GOTHAM AIN'T LIKE BACK HOME. THIS PLACE IS BIG. WE'LL NEVER EVEN SEE HIM.
SAM'S RIGHT, I RECKON.
I AIN'T AFRAID OF HIM ANYWAY.
BE THAT AS IT MAY, I PREFER WE LEAVE TOWN BEFORE SUNUP.
DAMN, JASPER! IT'S RAININ' CATS AN' DOGS OUT THERE.

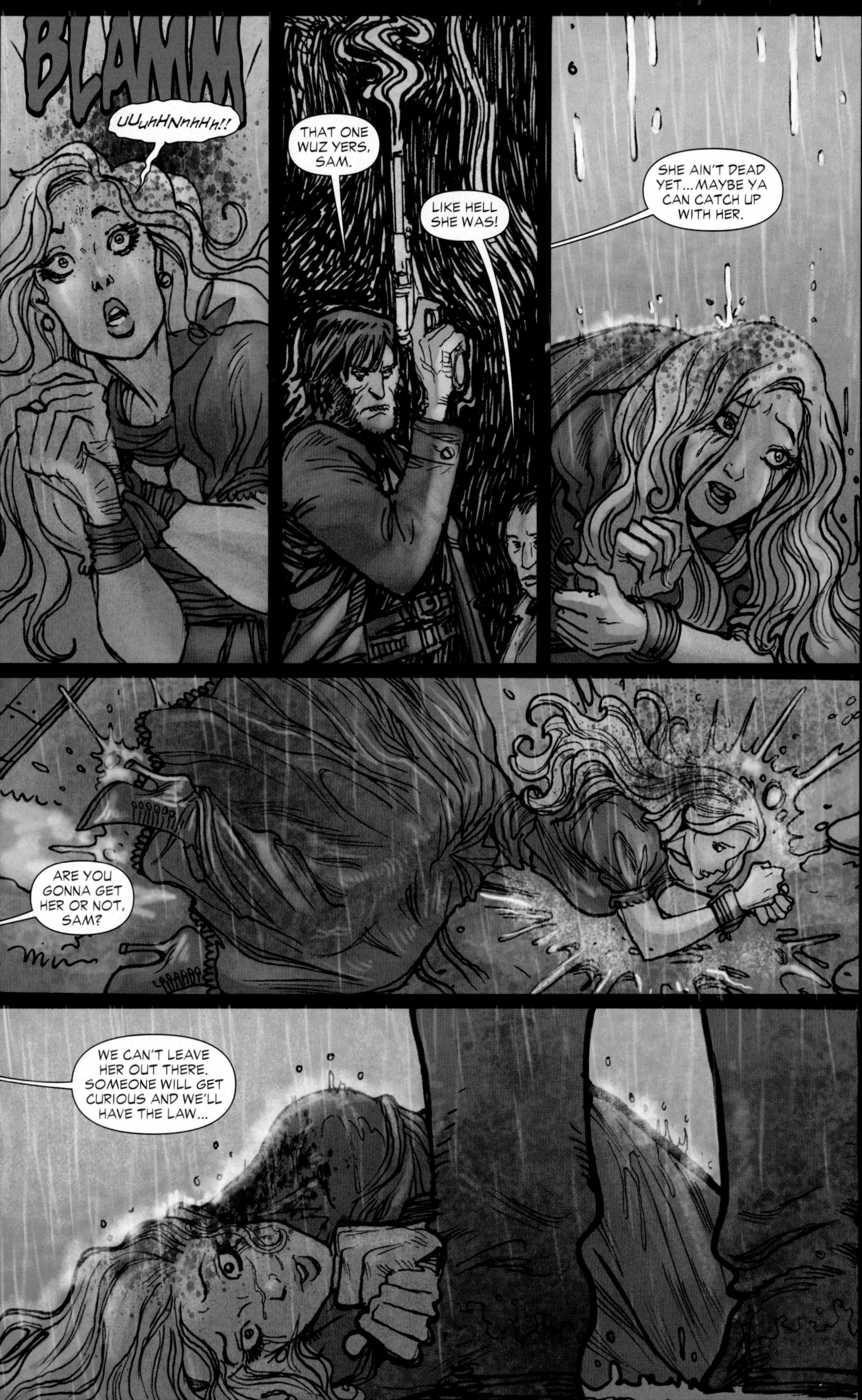
BLAMM
UUuhHNnhHh!!
THAT ONE WUZ YERS, SAM.
LIKE HELL SHE WAS!
SHE AIN'T DEAD YET...MAYBE YA CAN CATCH UP WITH HER.
ARE YOU GONNA GET HER OR NOT, SAM?
WE CAN'T LEAVE HER OUT THERE. SOMEONE WILL GET CURIOUS AND WE'LL HAVE THE LAW...

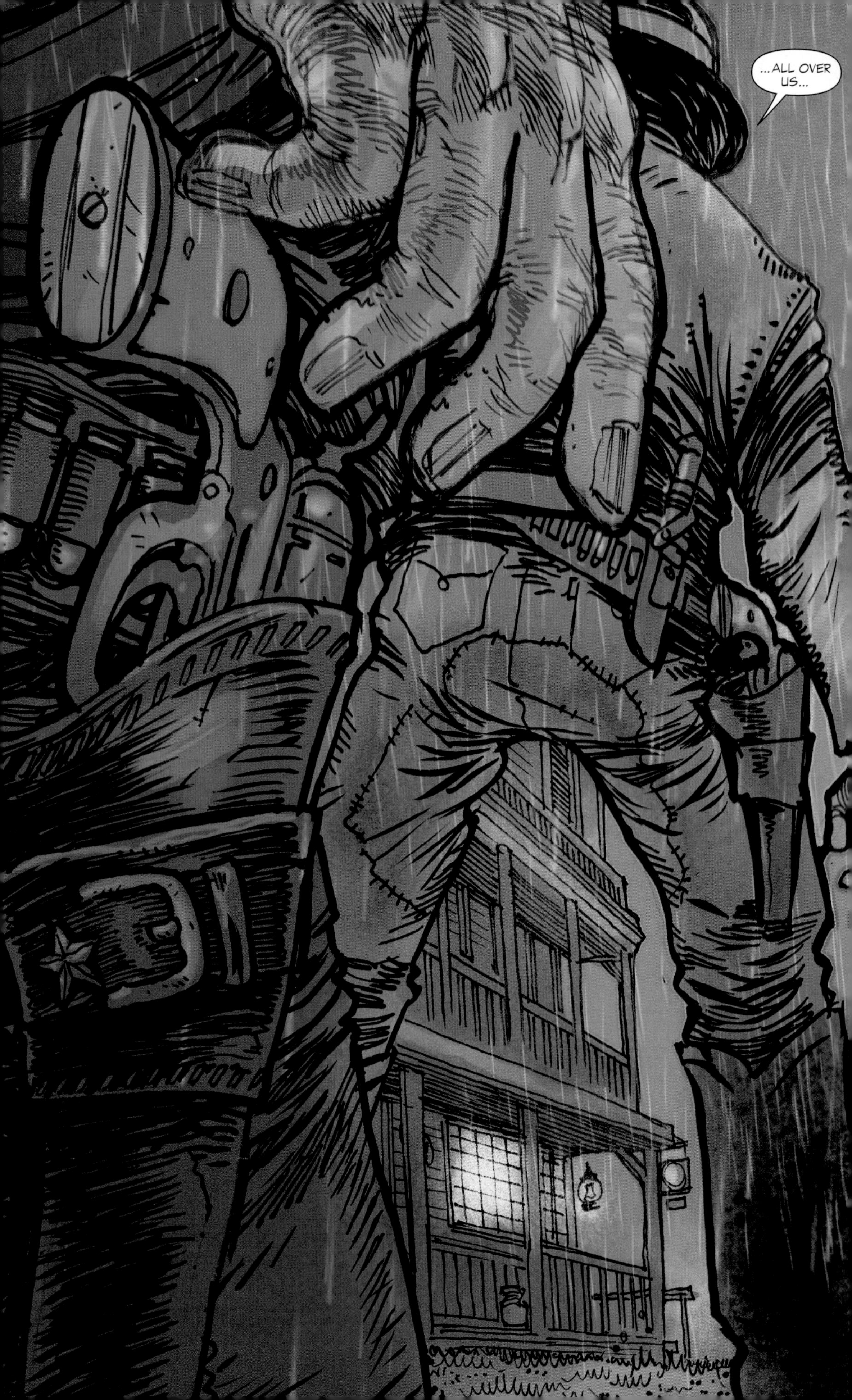
...ALL OVER US...

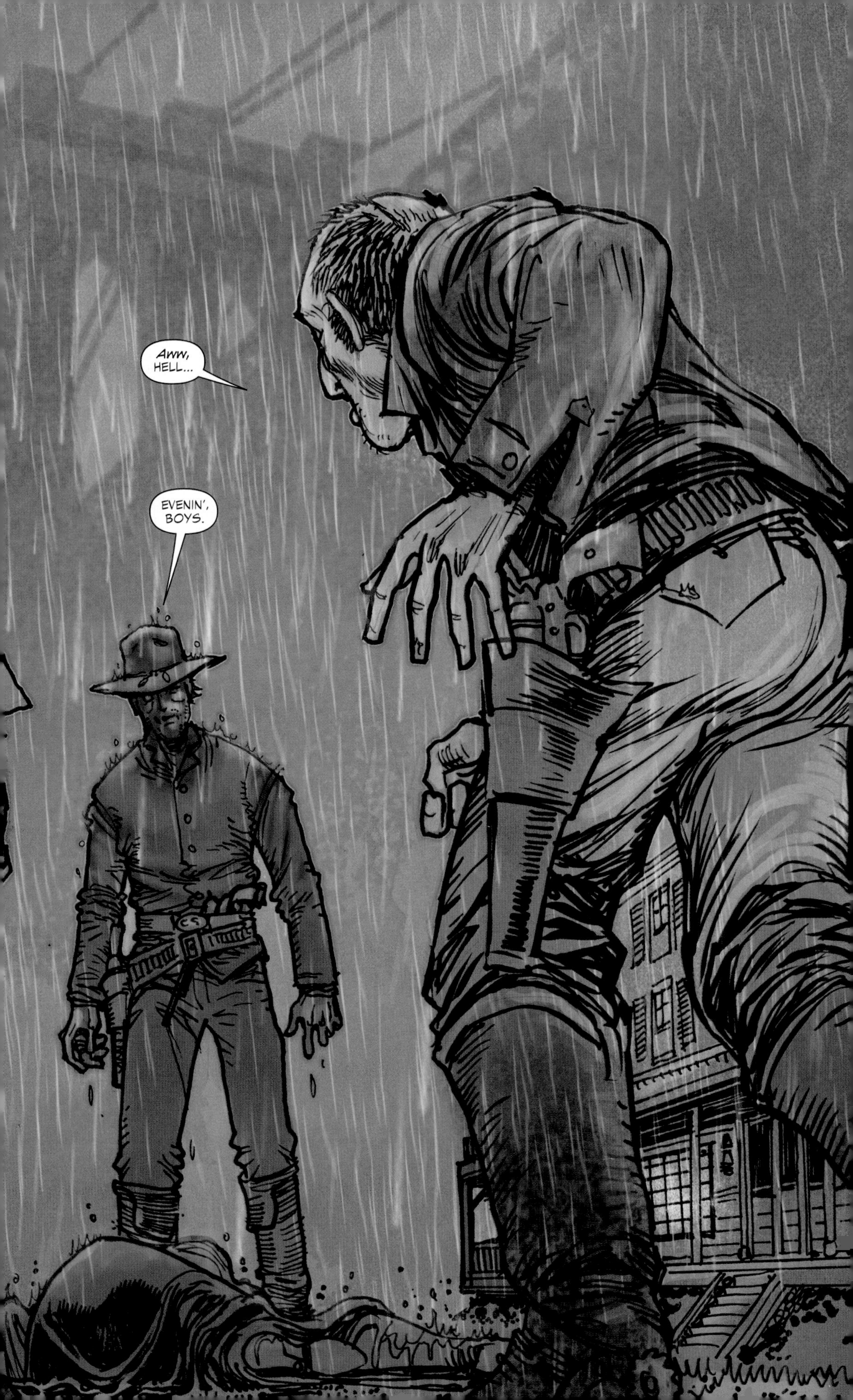
AWW, HELL...
EVENIN', BOYS.

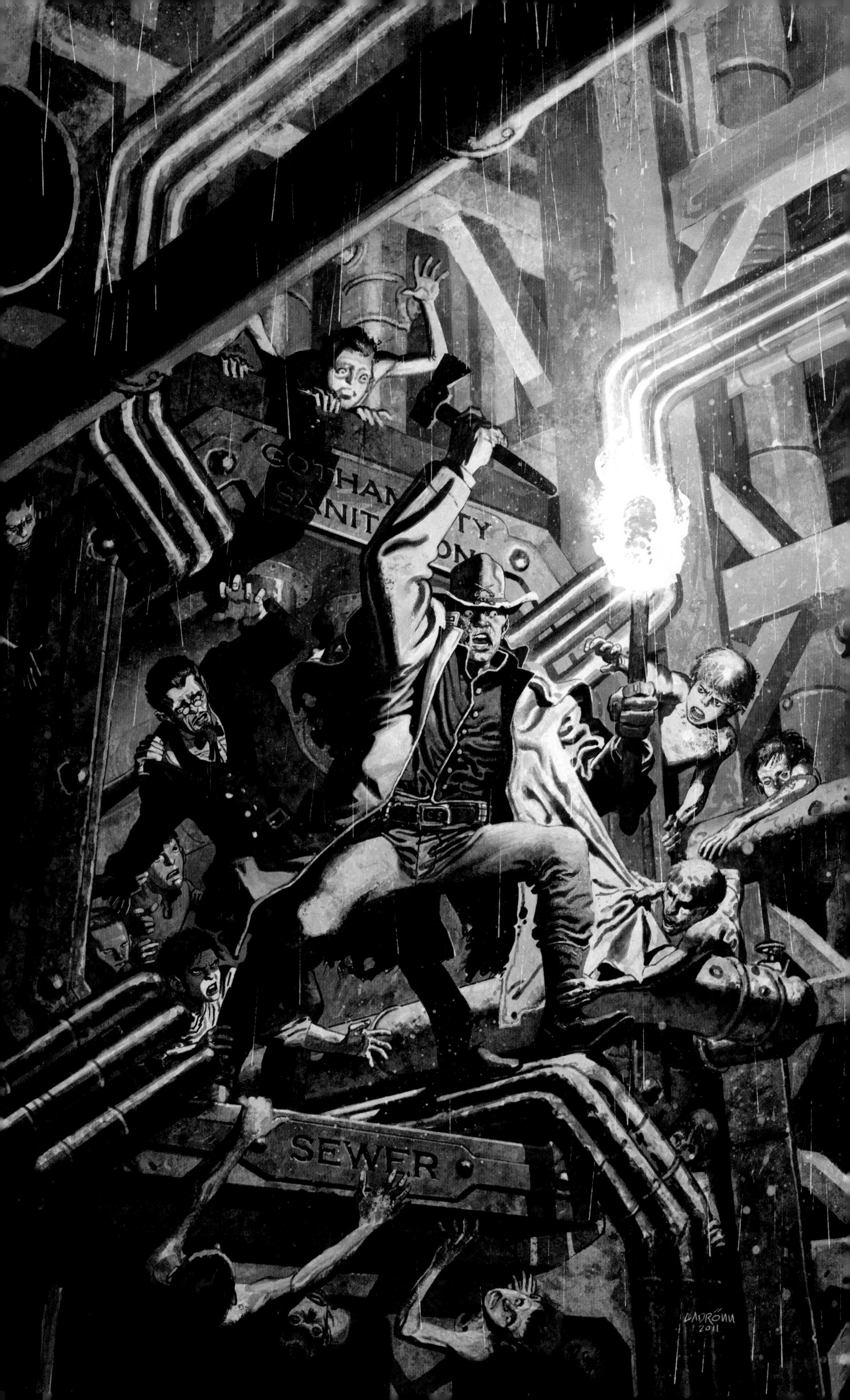
GOTHAM TY
SANIT ON
SEWER

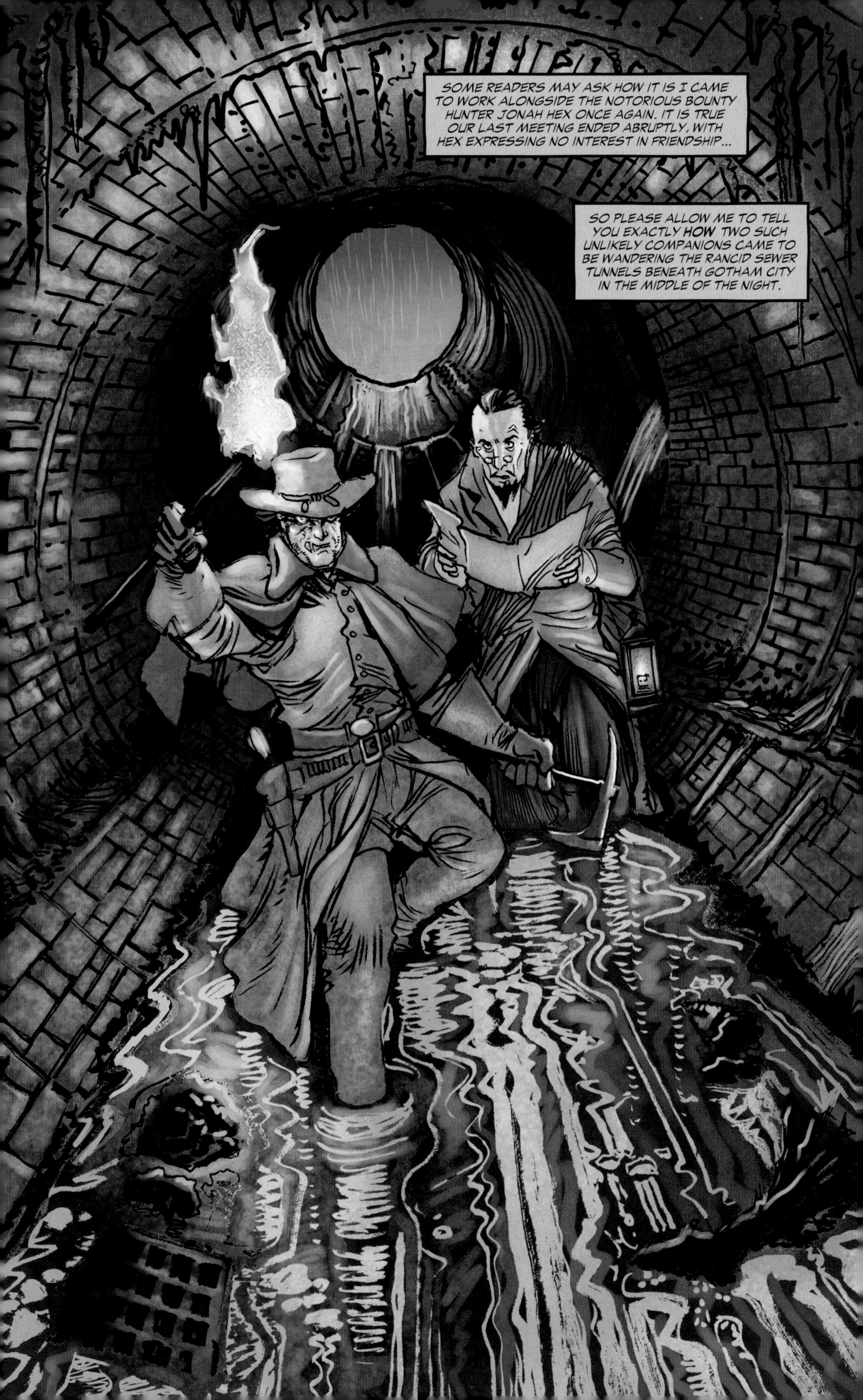
SOME READERS MAY ASK HOW IT IS I CAME TO WORK ALONGSIDE THE NOTORIOUS BOUNTY HUNTER JONAH HEX ONCE AGAIN. IT IS TRUE OUR LAST MEETING ENDED ABRUPTLY, WITH HEX EXPRESSING NO INTEREST IN FRIENDSHIP...
SO PLEASE ALLOW ME TO TELL YOU EXACTLY **HOW** TWO SUCH UNLIKELY COMPANIONS CAME TO BE WANDERING THE RANCID SEWER TUNNELS BENEATH GOTHAM CITY IN THE MIDDLE OF THE NIGHT.

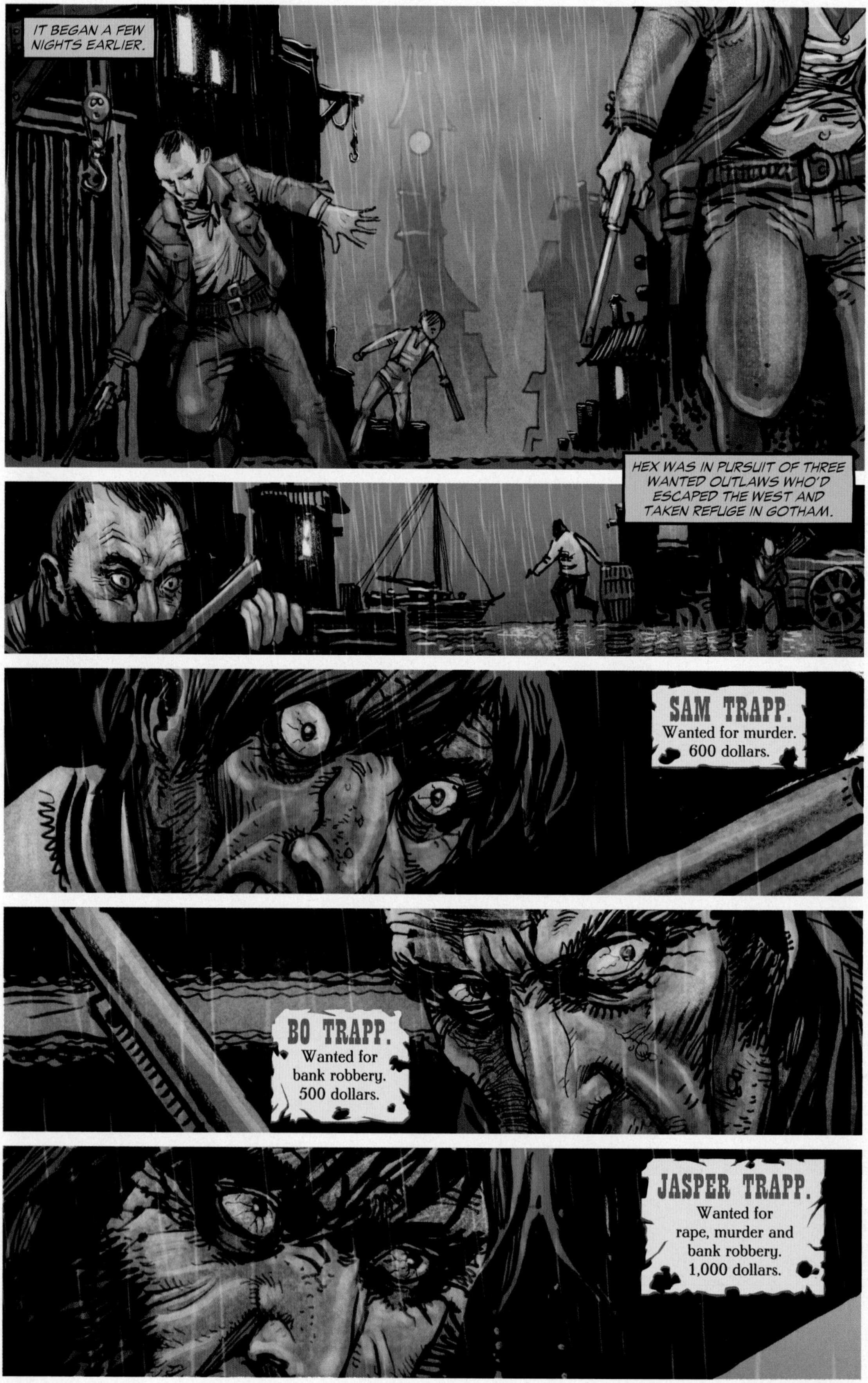
IT BEGAN A FEW NIGHTS EARLIER.
HEX WAS IN PURSUIT OF THREE WANTED OUTLAWS WHO'D ESCAPED THE WEST AND TAKEN REFUGE IN GOTHAM.
SAM TRAPP.
Wanted for murder.
600 dollars.
BO TRAPP.
Wanted for bank robbery.
500 dollars.
JASPER TRAPP.
Wanted for rape, murder and bank robbery.
1,000 dollars.

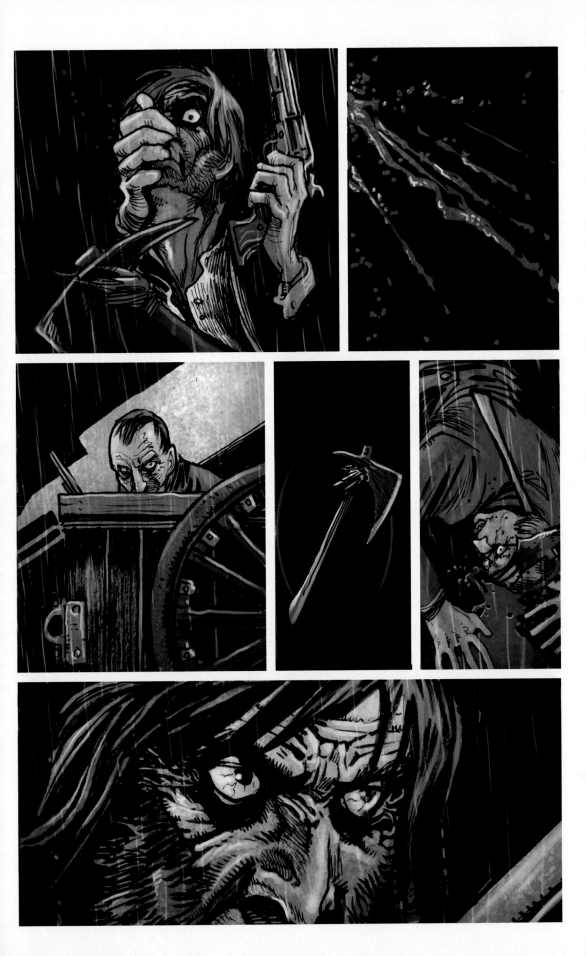

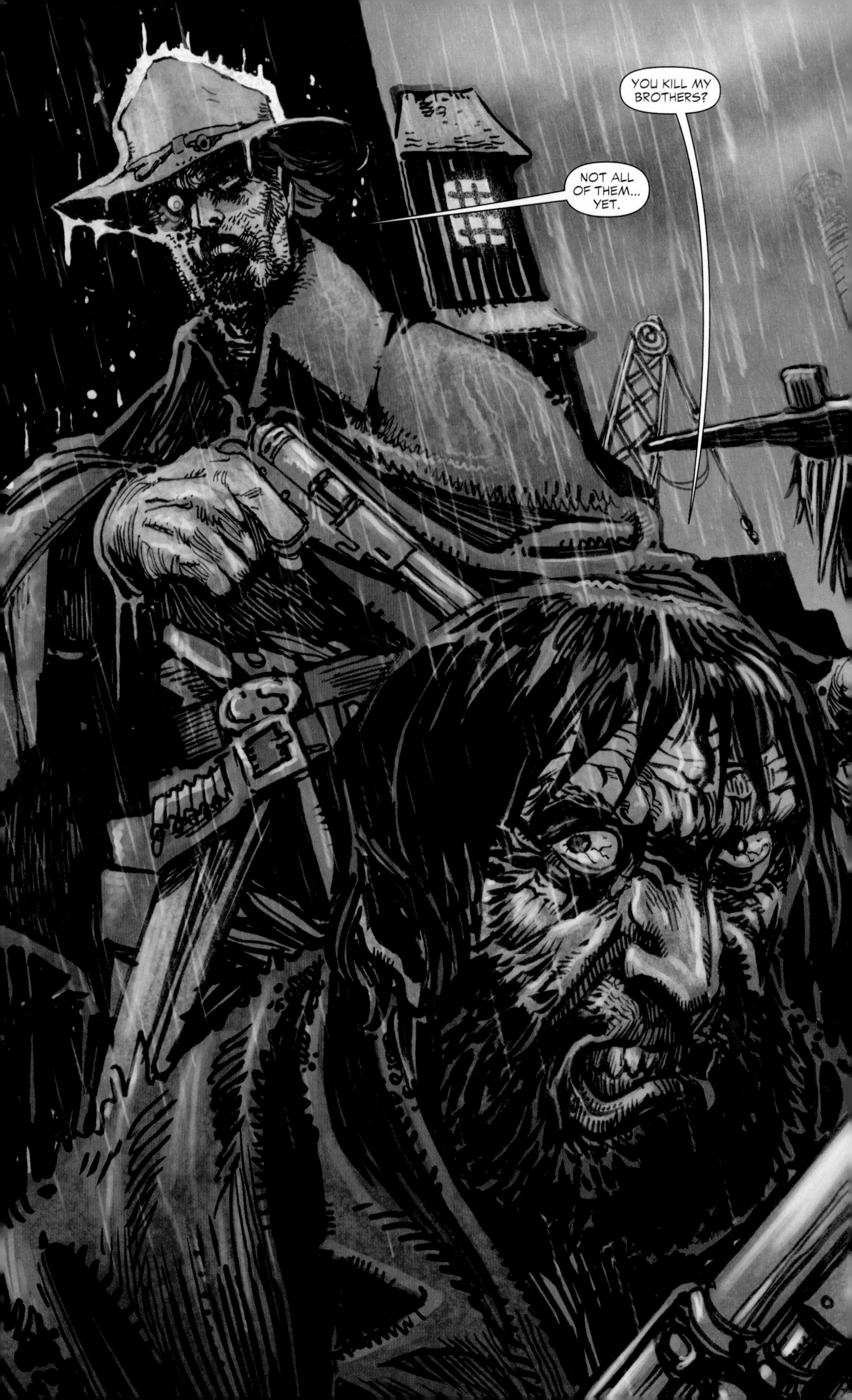
YOU KILL MY BROTHERS?
NOT ALL OF THEM... YET.

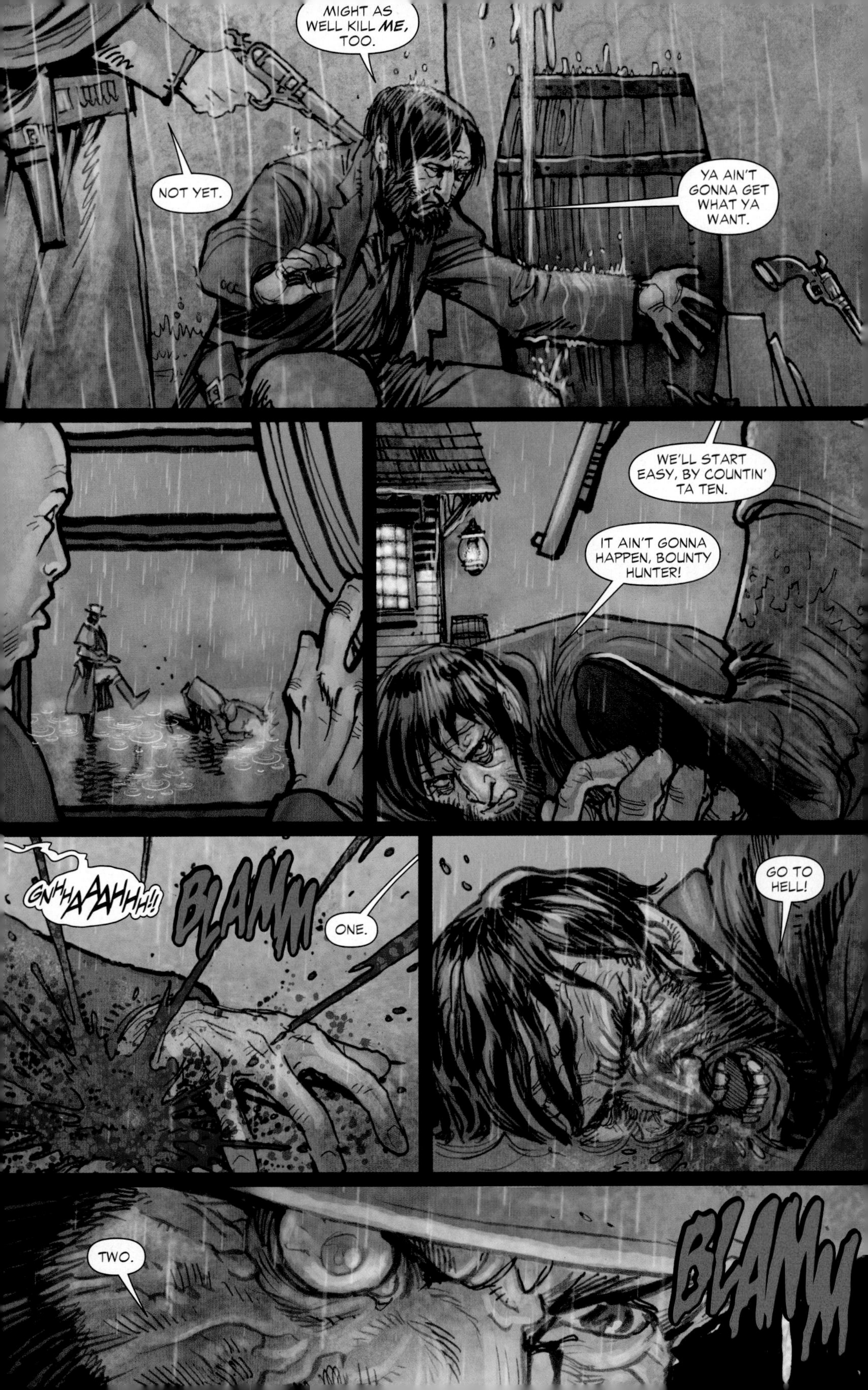
MIGHT AS WELL KILL *ME,* TOO.
NOT YET.
YA AIN'T GONNA GET WHAT YA WANT.
WE'LL START EASY, BY COUNTIN' TA TEN.
IT AIN'T GONNA HAPPEN, BOUNTY HUNTER!
GNHHAAAHHH!!
BLAMM
ONE.
GO TO HELL!
TWO.
BLAMM

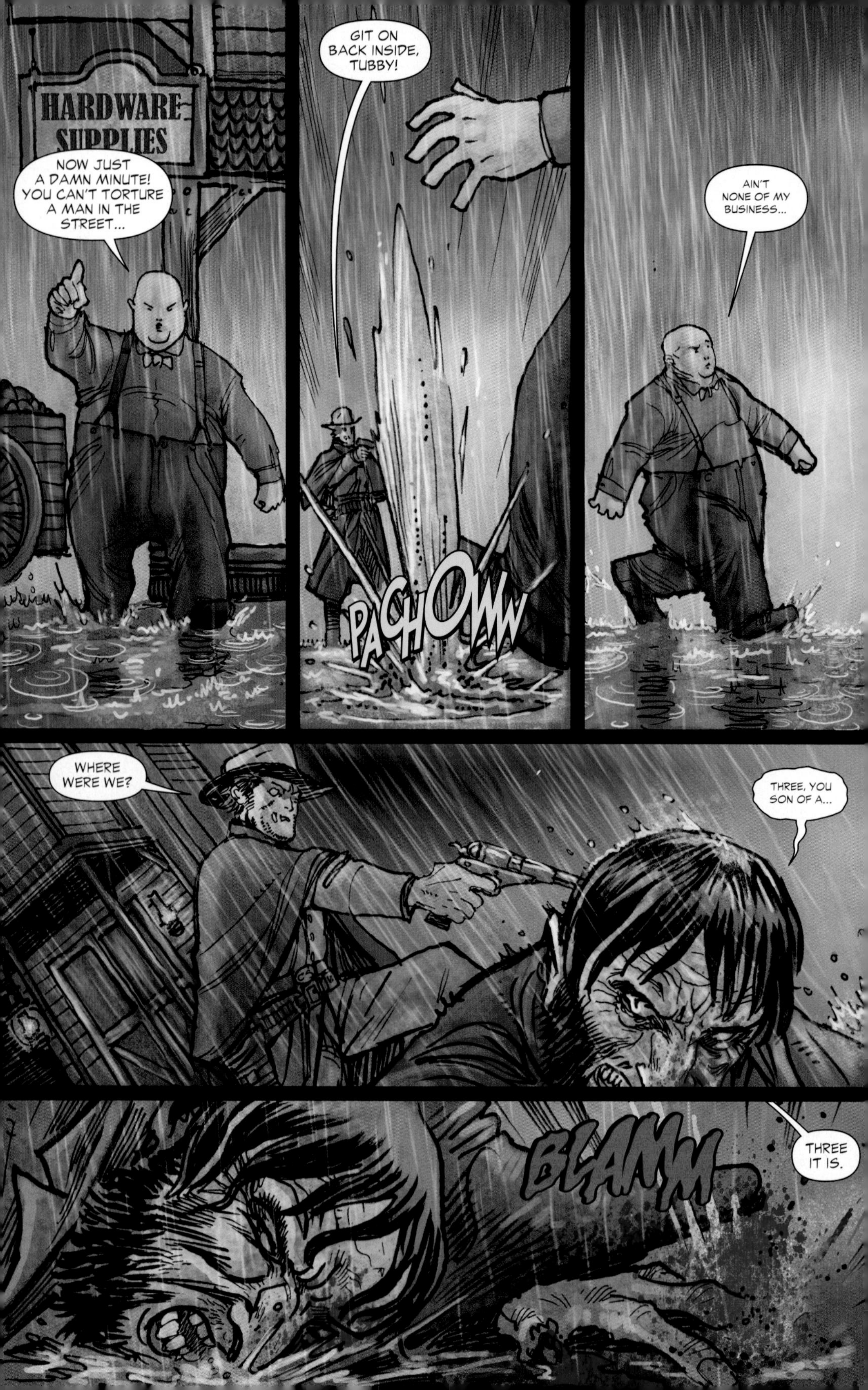
HARDWARE SUPPLIES
NOW JUST A DAMN MINUTE! YOU CAN'T TORTURE A MAN IN THE STREET...
GIT ON BACK INSIDE, TUBBY!
PACHOWW
AIN'T NONE OF MY BUSINESS...
WHERE WERE WE?
THREE, YOU SON OF A...
BLAMM
THREE IT IS.

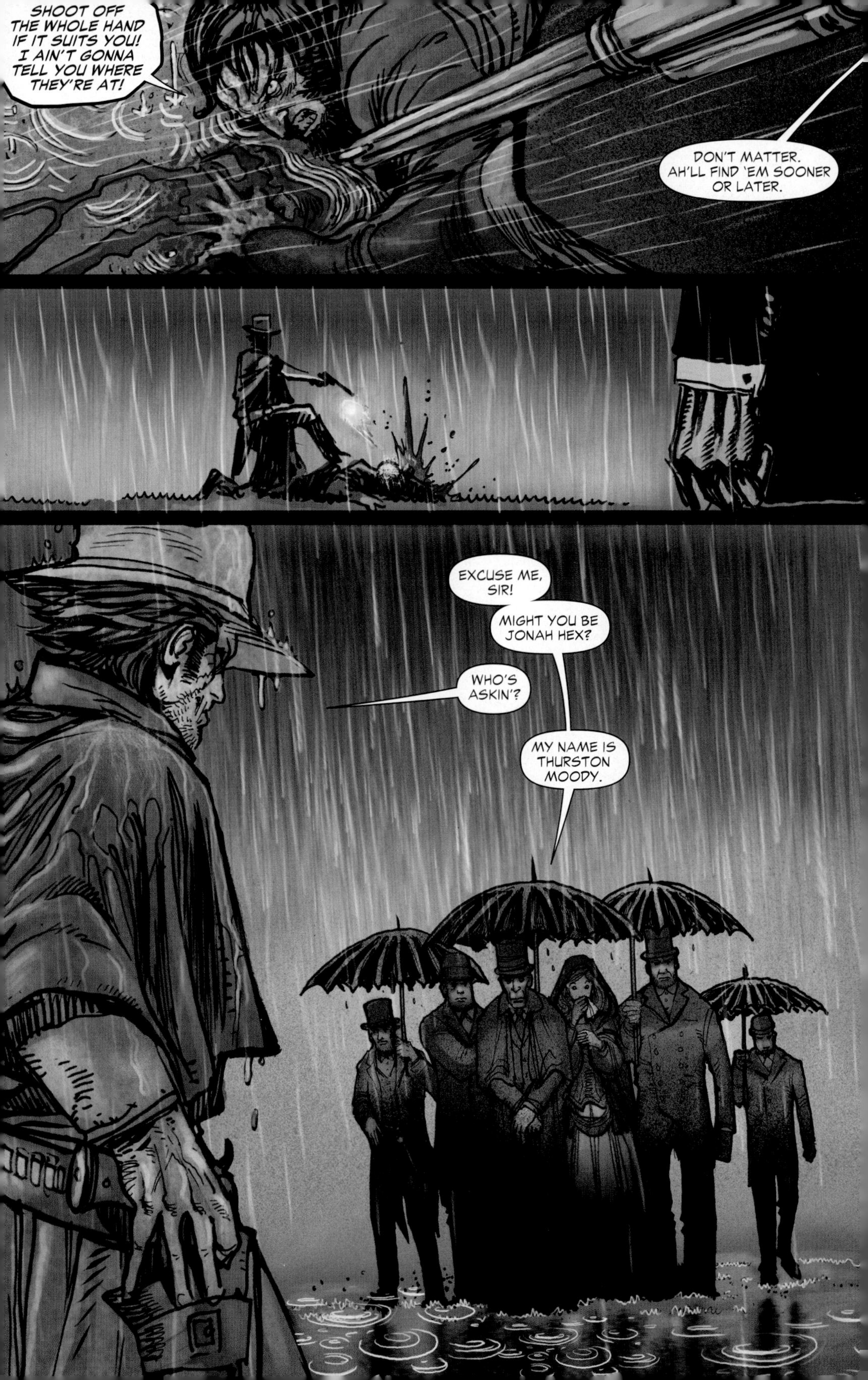

SHOOT OFF THE WHOLE HAND IF IT SUITS YOU! I AIN'T GONNA TELL YOU WHERE THEY'RE AT!
DON'T MATTER. AH'LL FIND 'EM SOONER OR LATER.
EXCUSE ME, SIR!
MIGHT YOU BE JONAH HEX?
WHO'S ASKIN'?
MY NAME IS THURSTON MOODY.

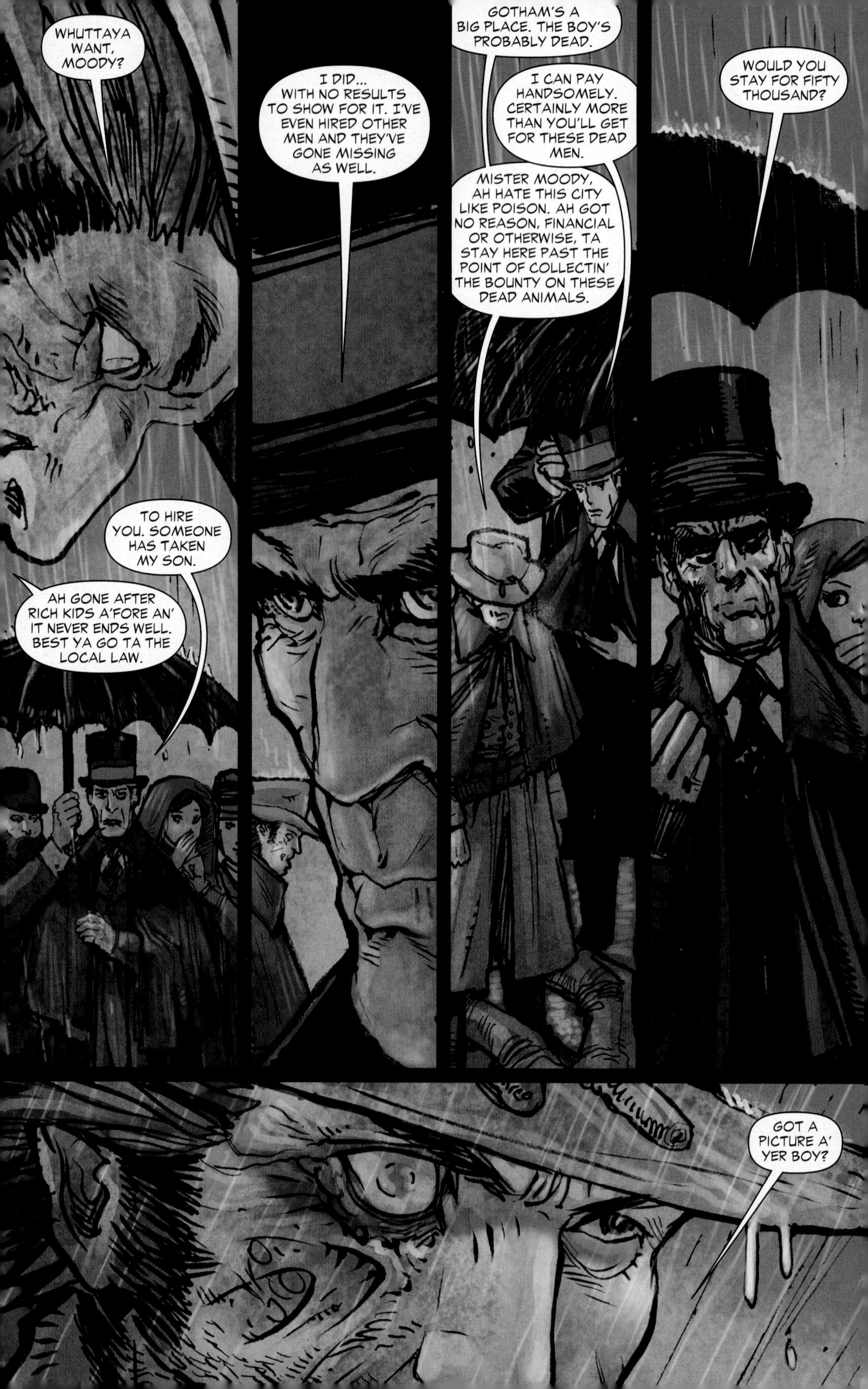
WHUTTAYA WANT, MOODY?
TO HIRE YOU. SOMEONE HAS TAKEN MY SON.
AH GONE AFTER RICH KIDS A'FORE AN' IT NEVER ENDS WELL. BEST YA GO TA THE LOCAL LAW.
I DID... WITH NO RESULTS TO SHOW FOR IT. I'VE EVEN HIRED OTHER MEN AND THEY'VE GONE MISSING AS WELL.
GOTHAM'S A BIG PLACE. THE BOY'S PROBABLY DEAD.
I CAN PAY HANDSOMELY. CERTAINLY MORE THAN YOU'LL GET FOR THESE DEAD MEN.
MISTER MOODY, AH HATE THIS CITY LIKE POISON. AH GOT NO REASON, FINANCIAL OR OTHERWISE, TA STAY HERE PAST THE POINT OF COLLECTIN' THE BOUNTY ON THESE DEAD ANIMALS.
WOULD YOU STAY FOR FIFTY THOUSAND?
GOT A PICTURE A' YER BOY?

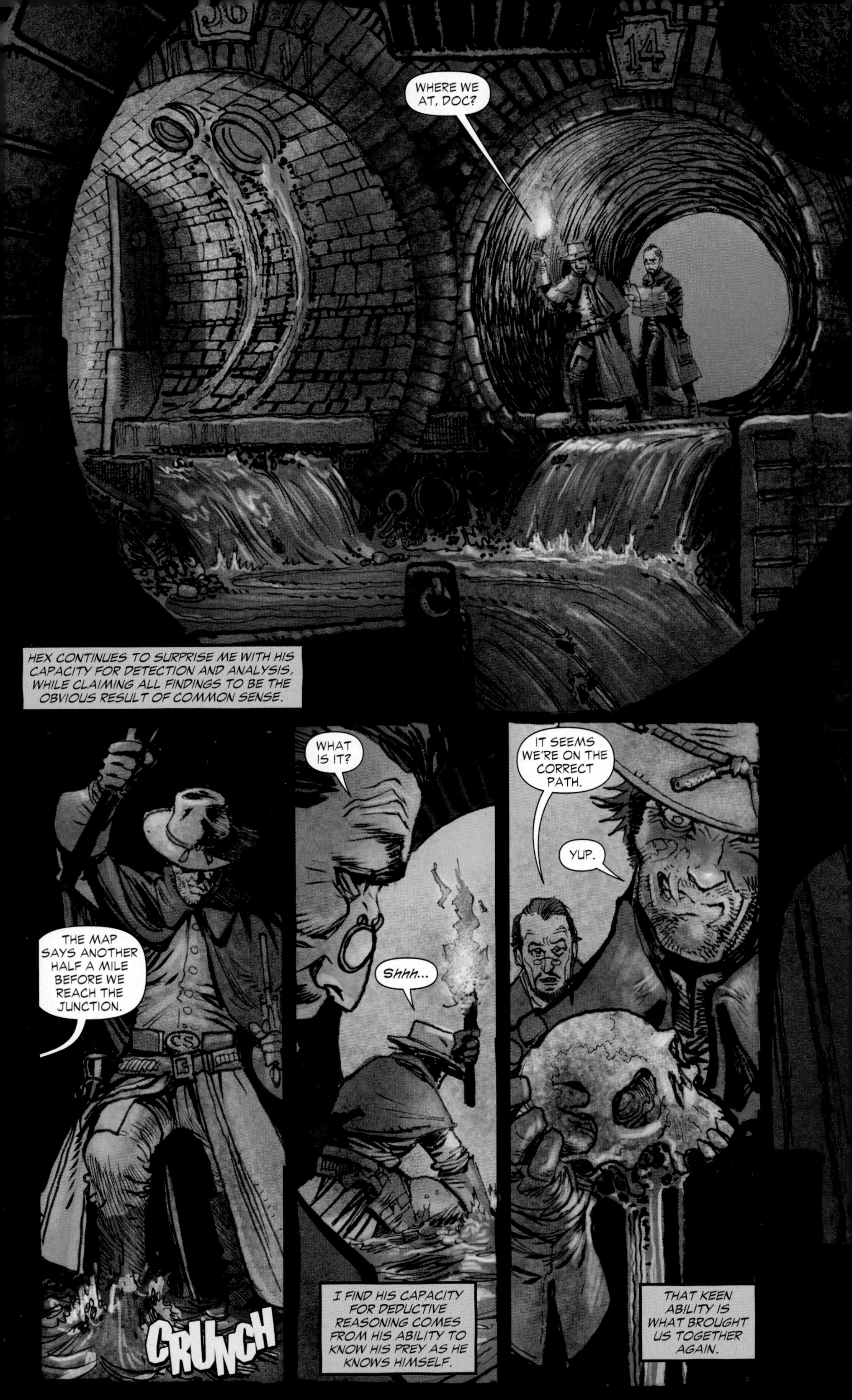

WHERE WE AT, DOC?
HEX CONTINUES TO SURPRISE ME WITH HIS CAPACITY FOR DETECTION AND ANALYSIS, WHILE CLAIMING ALL FINDINGS TO BE THE OBVIOUS RESULT OF COMMON SENSE.
THE MAP SAYS ANOTHER HALF A MILE BEFORE WE REACH THE JUNCTION.
CRUNCH
WHAT IS IT?
Shhh...
I FIND HIS CAPACITY FOR DEDUCTIVE REASONING COMES FROM HIS ABILITY TO KNOW HIS PREY AS HE KNOWS HIMSELF.
IT SEEMS WE'RE ON THE CORRECT PATH.
YUP.
THAT KEEN ABILITY IS WHAT BROUGHT US TOGETHER AGAIN.

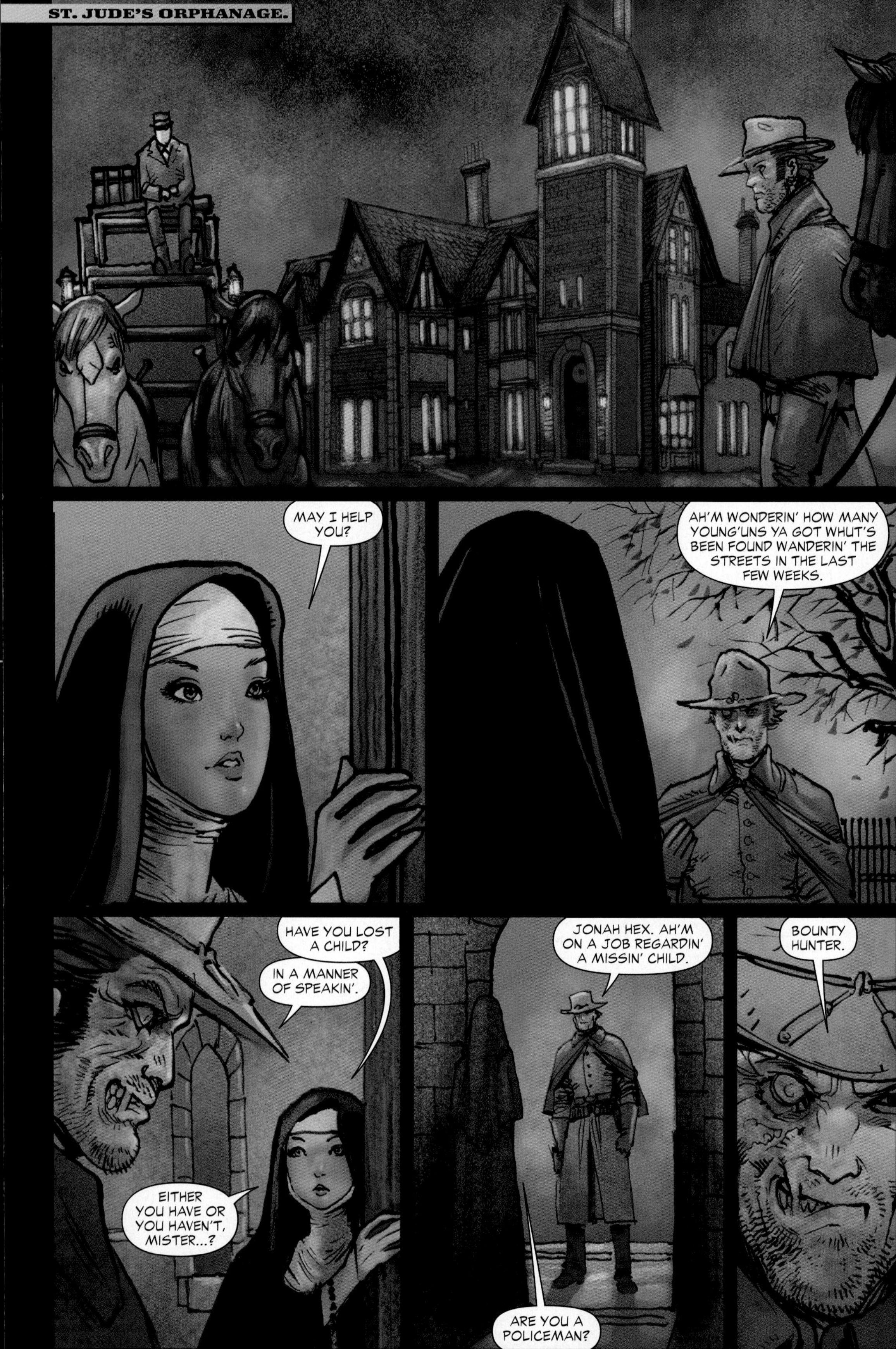
ST. JUDE'S ORPHANAGE.
MAY I HELP YOU?
AH'M WONDERIN' HOW MANY YOUNG'UNS YA GOT WHUT'S BEEN FOUND WANDERIN' THE STREETS IN THE LAST FEW WEEKS.
HAVE YOU LOST A CHILD?
IN A MANNER OF SPEAKIN'.
EITHER YOU HAVE OR YOU HAVEN'T, MISTER...?
JONAH HEX. AH'M ON A JOB REGARDIN' A MISSIN' CHILD.
ARE YOU A POLICEMAN?
BOUNTY HUNTER.

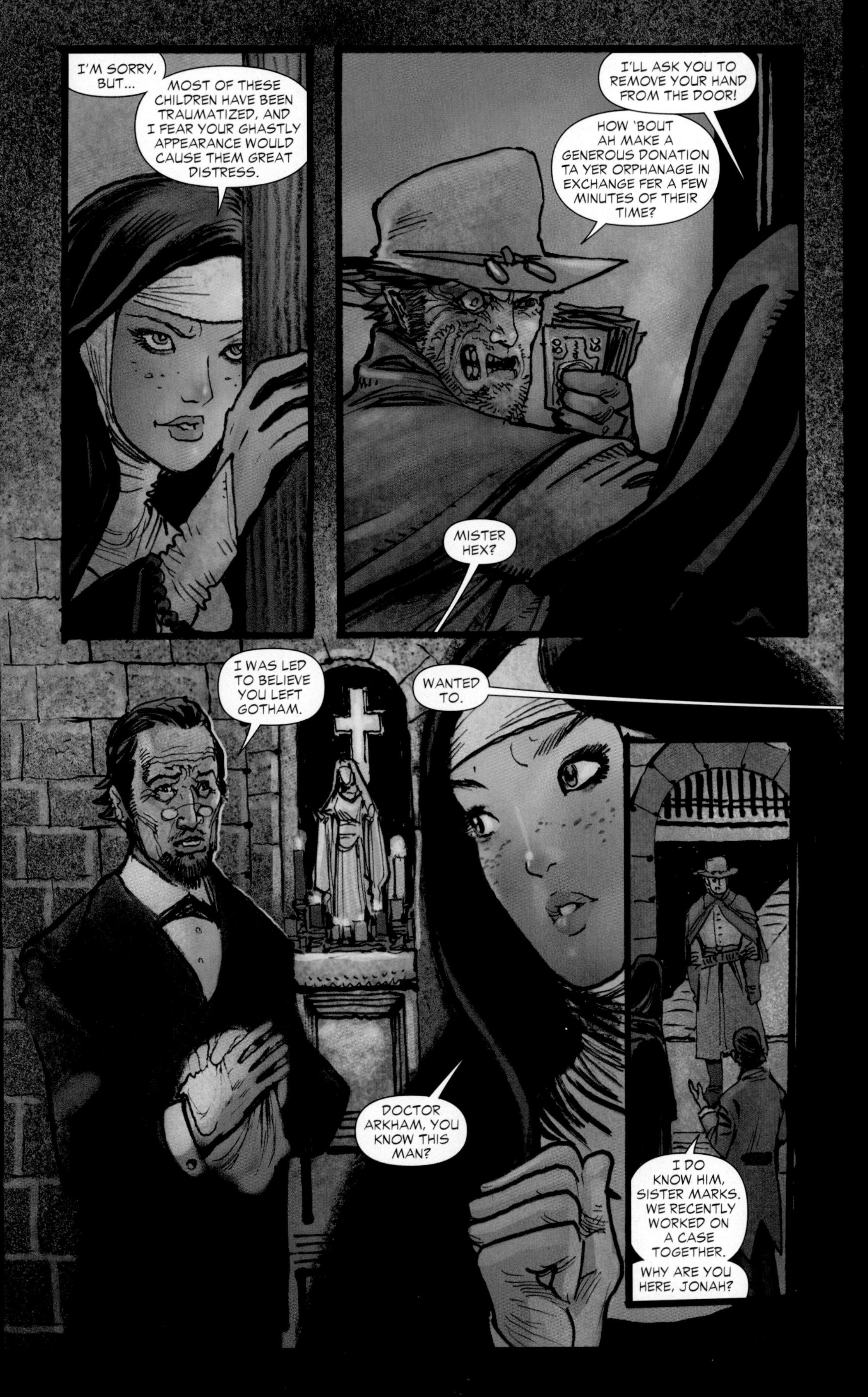
I'M SORRY, BUT...
MOST OF THESE CHILDREN HAVE BEEN TRAUMATIZED, AND I FEAR YOUR GHASTLY APPEARANCE WOULD CAUSE THEM GREAT DISTRESS.
I'LL ASK YOU TO REMOVE YOUR HAND FROM THE DOOR!
HOW 'BOUT AH MAKE A GENEROUS DONATION TA YER ORPHANAGE IN EXCHANGE FER A FEW MINUTES OF THEIR TIME?
MISTER HEX?
I WAS LED TO BELIEVE YOU LEFT GOTHAM.
WANTED TO.
DOCTOR ARKHAM, YOU KNOW THIS MAN?
I DO KNOW HIM, SISTER MARKS. WE RECENTLY WORKED ON A CASE TOGETHER.
WHY ARE YOU HERE, JONAH?

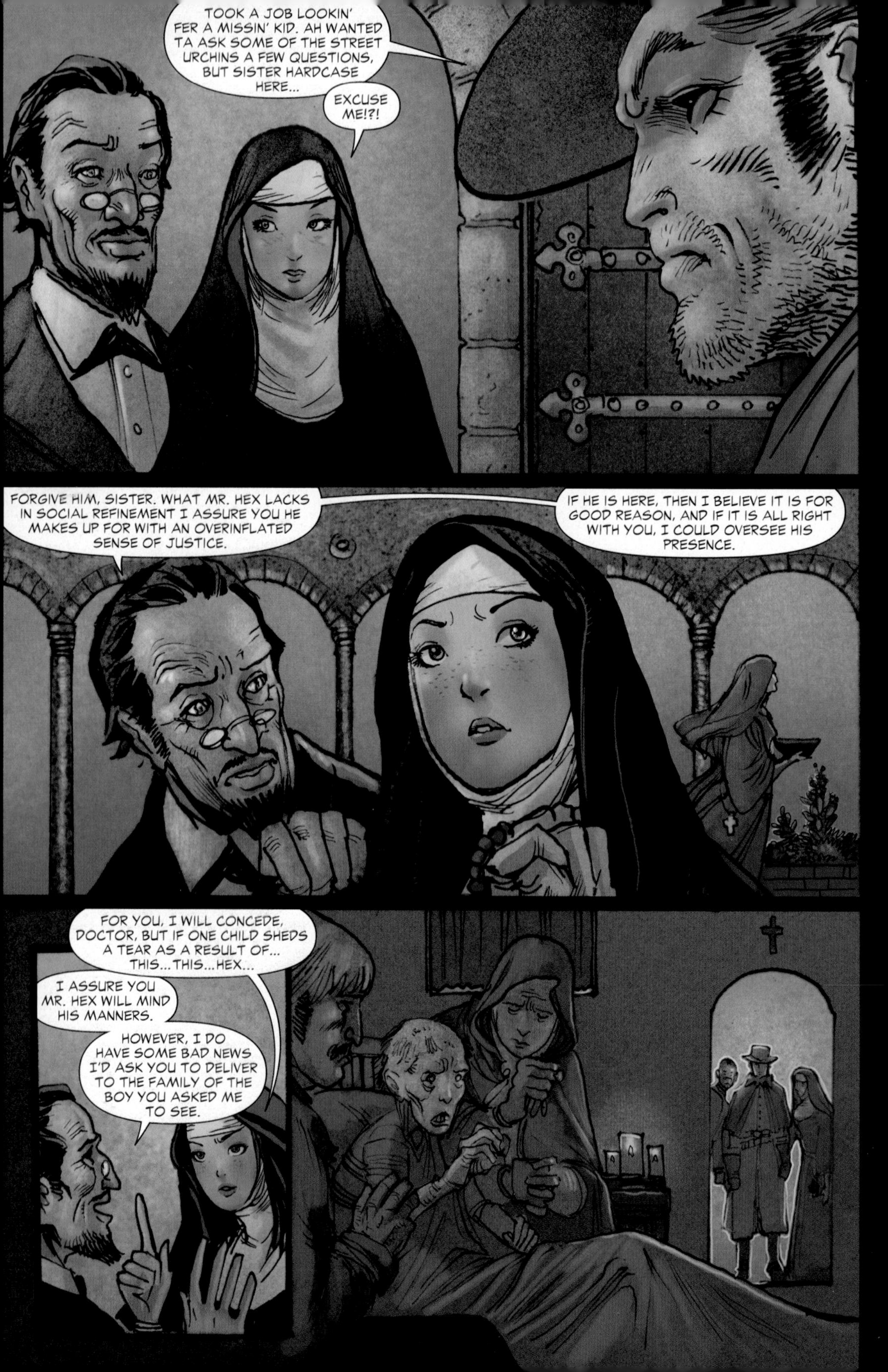
TOOK A JOB LOOKIN' FER A MISSIN' KID. AH WANTED TA ASK SOME OF THE STREET URCHINS A FEW QUESTIONS, BUT SISTER HARDCASE HERE...
EXCUSE ME!?!
FORGIVE HIM, SISTER. WHAT MR. HEX LACKS IN SOCIAL REFINEMENT I ASSURE YOU HE MAKES UP FOR WITH AN OVERINFLATED SENSE OF JUSTICE.
IF HE IS HERE, THEN I BELIEVE IT IS FOR GOOD REASON, AND IF IT IS ALL RIGHT WITH YOU, I COULD OVERSEE HIS PRESENCE.
FOR YOU, I WILL CONCEDE, DOCTOR, BUT IF ONE CHILD SHEDS A TEAR AS A RESULT OF... THIS...THIS...HEX...
I ASSURE YOU MR. HEX WILL MIND HIS MANNERS.
HOWEVER, I DO HAVE SOME BAD NEWS I'D ASK YOU TO DELIVER TO THE FAMILY OF THE BOY YOU ASKED ME TO SEE.

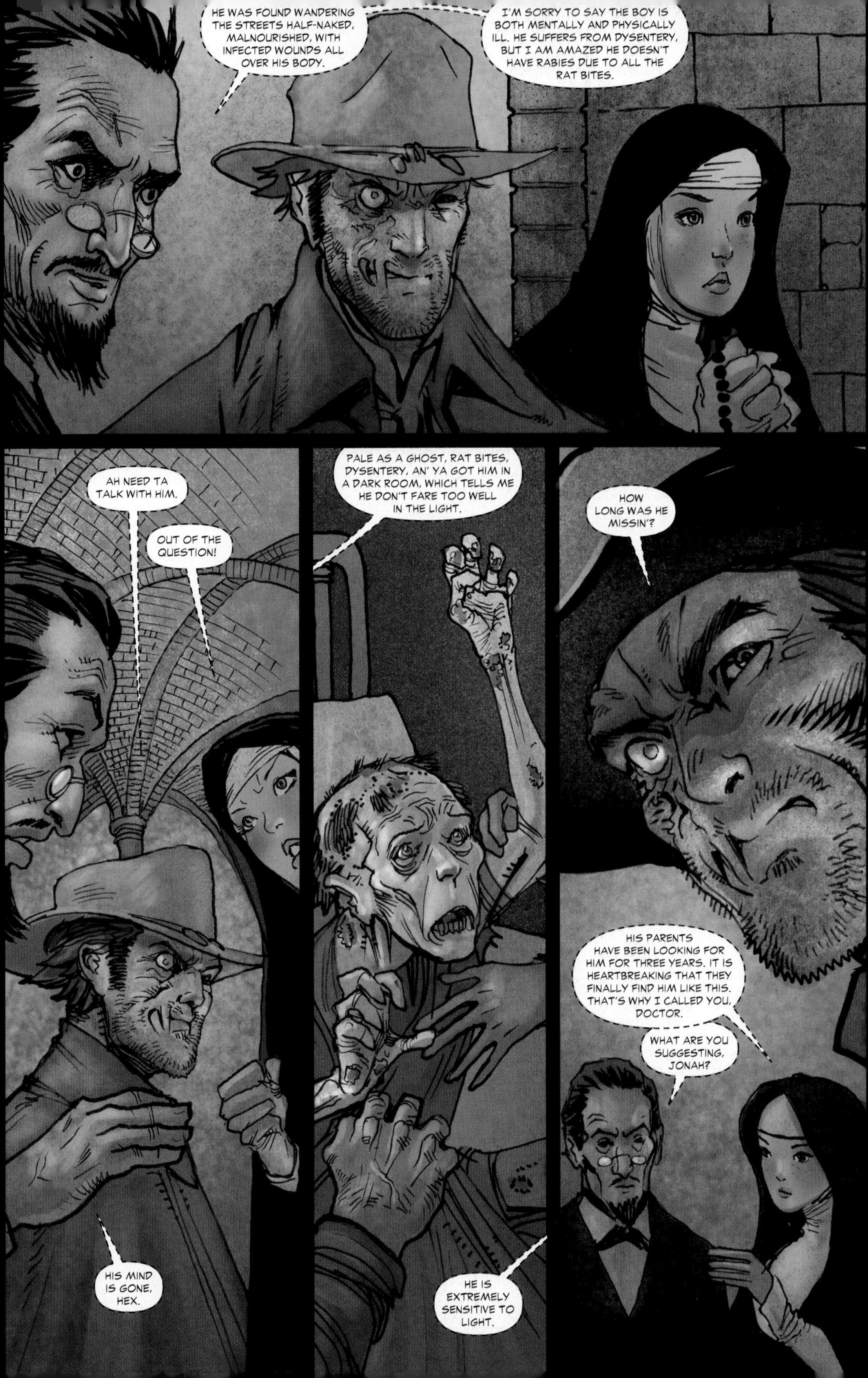
HE WAS FOUND WANDERING THE STREETS HALF-NAKED, MALNOURISHED, WITH INFECTED WOUNDS ALL OVER HIS BODY.
I'M SORRY TO SAY THE BOY IS BOTH MENTALLY AND PHYSICALLY ILL. HE SUFFERS FROM DYSENTERY, BUT I AM AMAZED HE DOESN'T HAVE RABIES DUE TO ALL THE RAT BITES.
AH NEED TA TALK WITH HIM.
OUT OF THE QUESTION!
HIS MIND IS GONE, HEX.
PALE AS A GHOST, RAT BITES, DYSENTERY, AN' YA GOT HIM IN A DARK ROOM, WHICH TELLS ME HE DON'T FARE TOO WELL IN THE LIGHT.
HE IS EXTREMELY SENSITIVE TO LIGHT.
HOW LONG WAS HE MISSIN'?
HIS PARENTS HAVE BEEN LOOKING FOR HIM FOR THREE YEARS. IT IS HEARTBREAKING THAT THEY FINALLY FIND HIM LIKE THIS. THAT'S WHY I CALLED YOU, DOCTOR.
WHAT ARE YOU SUGGESTING, JONAH?

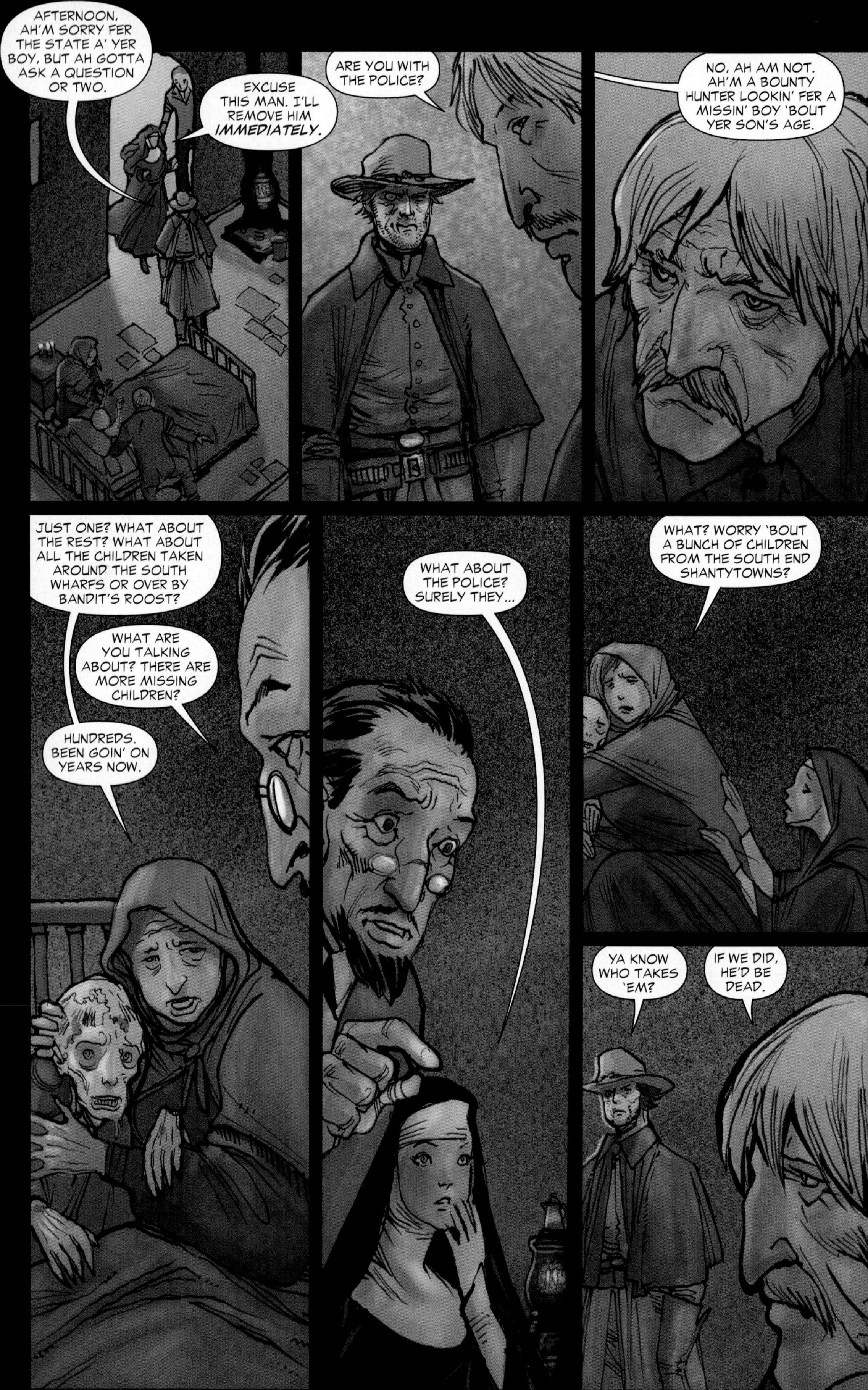
AFTERNOON, AH'M SORRY FER THE STATE A' YER BOY, BUT AH GOTTA ASK A QUESTION OR TWO.
EXCUSE THIS MAN. I'LL REMOVE HIM *IMMEDIATELY.*
ARE YOU WITH THE POLICE?
NO, AH AM NOT. AH'M A BOUNTY HUNTER LOOKIN' FER A MISSIN' BOY 'BOUT YER SON'S AGE.
JUST ONE? WHAT ABOUT THE REST? WHAT ABOUT ALL THE CHILDREN TAKEN AROUND THE SOUTH WHARFS OR OVER BY BANDIT'S ROOST?
WHAT ARE YOU TALKING ABOUT? THERE ARE MORE MISSING CHILDREN?
HUNDREDS. BEEN GOIN' ON YEARS NOW.
WHAT ABOUT THE POLICE? SURELY THEY...
WHAT? WORRY 'BOUT A BUNCH OF CHILDREN FROM THE SOUTH END SHANTYTOWNS?
YA KNOW WHO TAKES 'EM?
IF WE DID, HE'D BE DEAD.

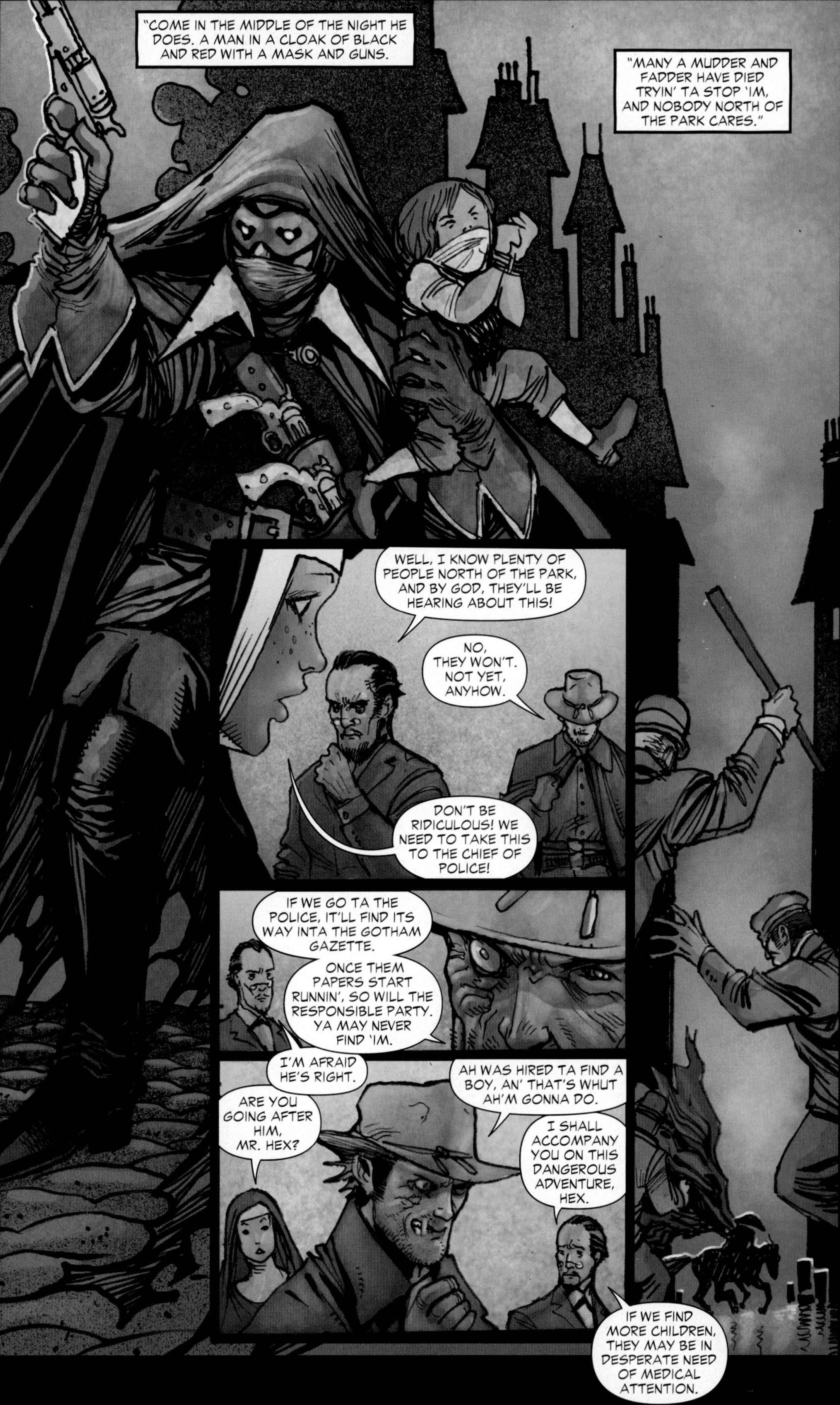
"COME IN THE MIDDLE OF THE NIGHT HE DOES. A MAN IN A CLOAK OF BLACK AND RED WITH A MASK AND GUNS.
"MANY A MUDDER AND FADDER HAVE DIED TRYIN' TA STOP 'IM, AND NOBODY NORTH OF THE PARK CARES."
WELL, I KNOW PLENTY OF PEOPLE NORTH OF THE PARK, AND BY GOD, THEY'LL BE HEARING ABOUT THIS!
NO, THEY WON'T. NOT YET, ANYHOW.
DON'T BE RIDICULOUS! WE NEED TO TAKE THIS TO THE CHIEF OF POLICE!
IF WE GO TA THE POLICE, IT'LL FIND ITS WAY INTA THE GOTHAM GAZETTE.
ONCE THEM PAPERS START RUNNIN', SO WILL THE RESPONSIBLE PARTY. YA MAY NEVER FIND 'IM.
I'M AFRAID HE'S RIGHT.
ARE YOU GOING AFTER HIM, MR. HEX?
AH WAS HIRED TA FIND A BOY, AN' THAT'S WHUT AH'M GONNA DO.
I SHALL ACCOMPANY YOU ON THIS DANGEROUS ADVENTURE, HEX.
IF WE FIND MORE CHILDREN, THEY MAY BE IN DESPERATE NEED OF MEDICAL ATTENTION.

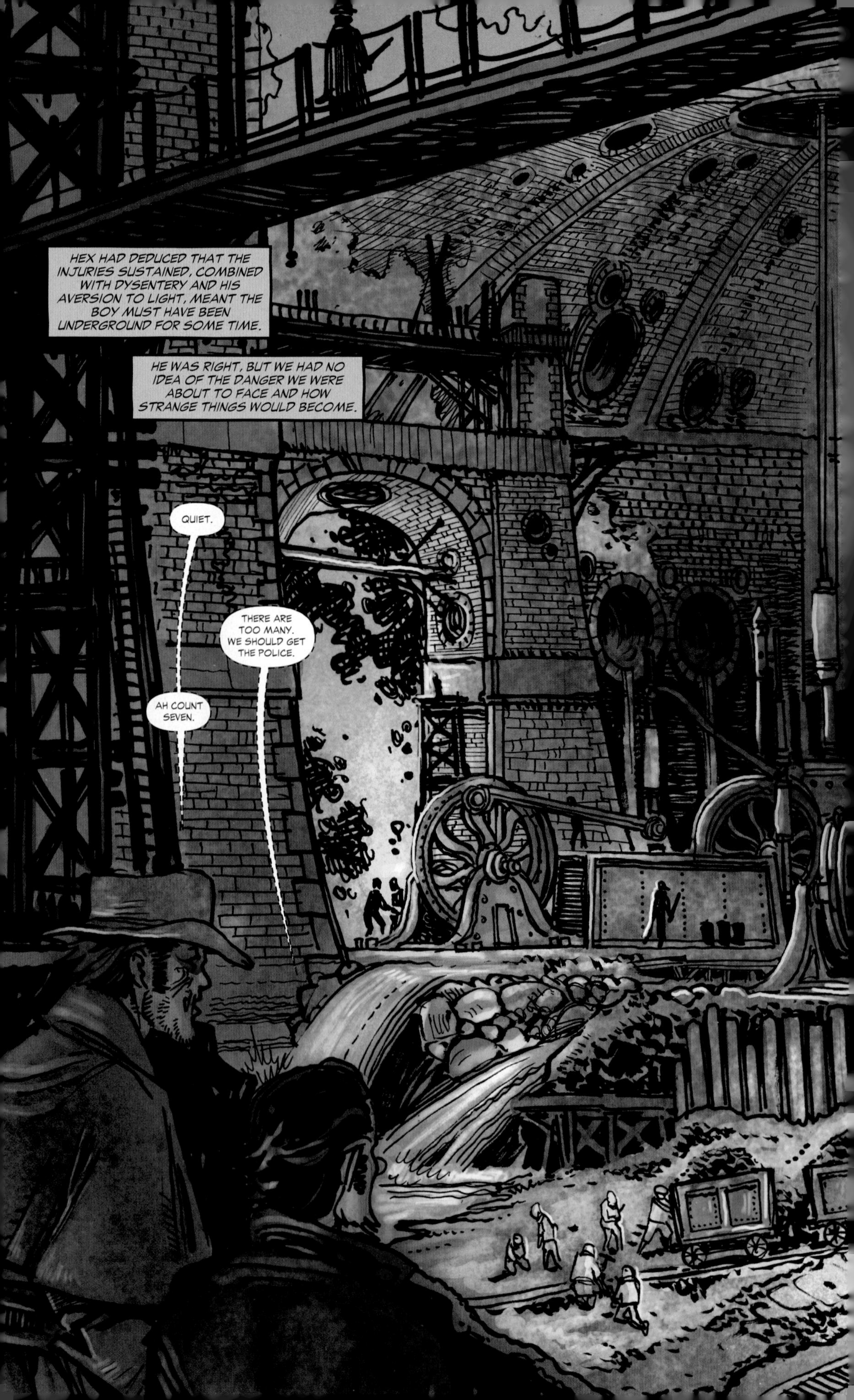
HEX HAD DEDUCED THAT THE INJURIES SUSTAINED, COMBINED WITH DYSENTERY AND HIS AVERSION TO LIGHT, MEANT THE BOY MUST HAVE BEEN UNDERGROUND FOR SOME TIME.
HE WAS RIGHT, BUT WE HAD NO IDEA OF THE DANGER WE WERE ABOUT TO FACE AND HOW STRANGE THINGS WOULD BECOME.
QUIET.
THERE ARE TOO MANY. WE SHOULD GET THE POLICE.
AH COUNT SEVEN.

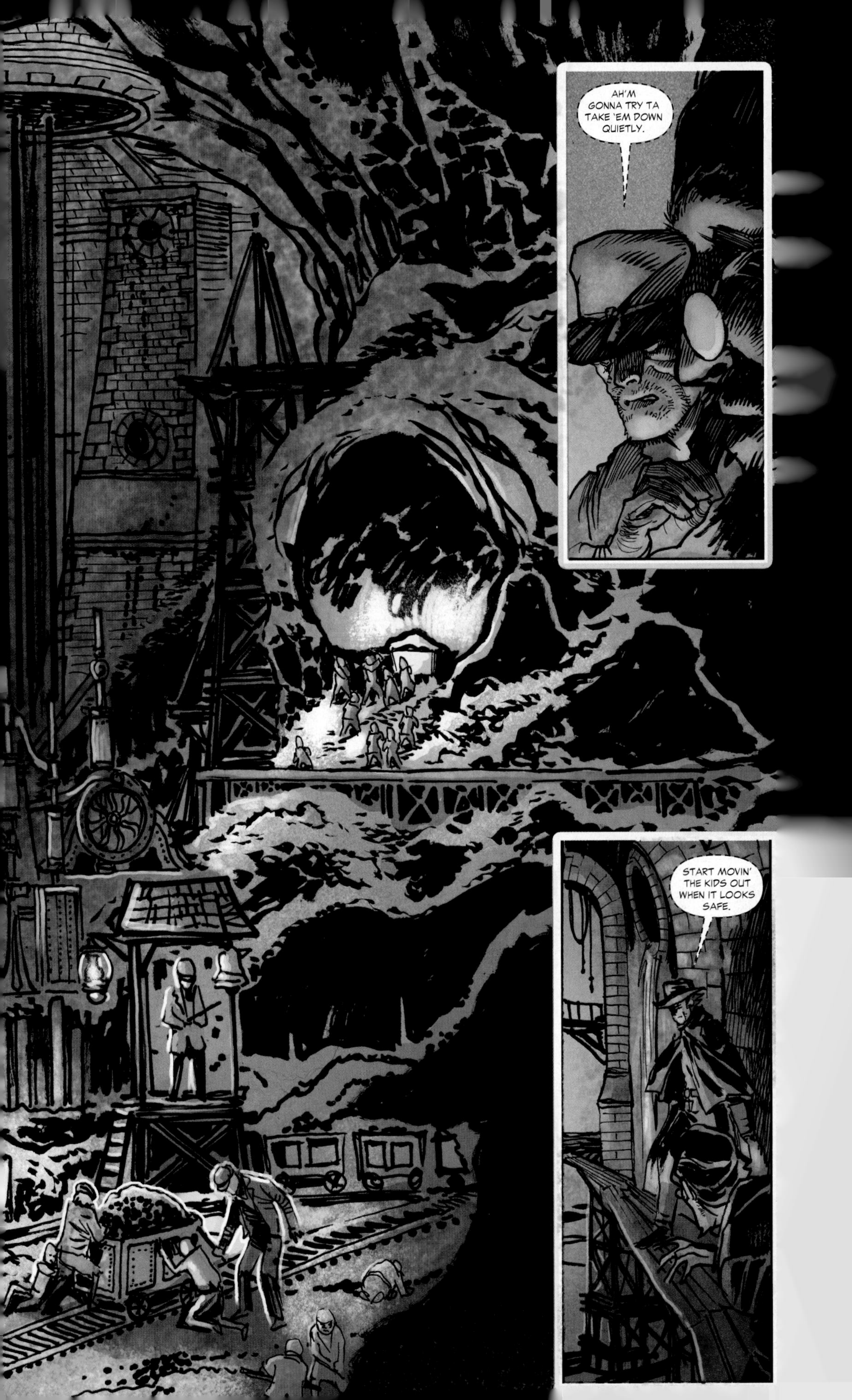
AH'M GONNA TRY TA TAKE 'EM DOWN QUIETLY.
START MOVIN' THE KIDS OUT WHEN IT LOOKS SAFE.

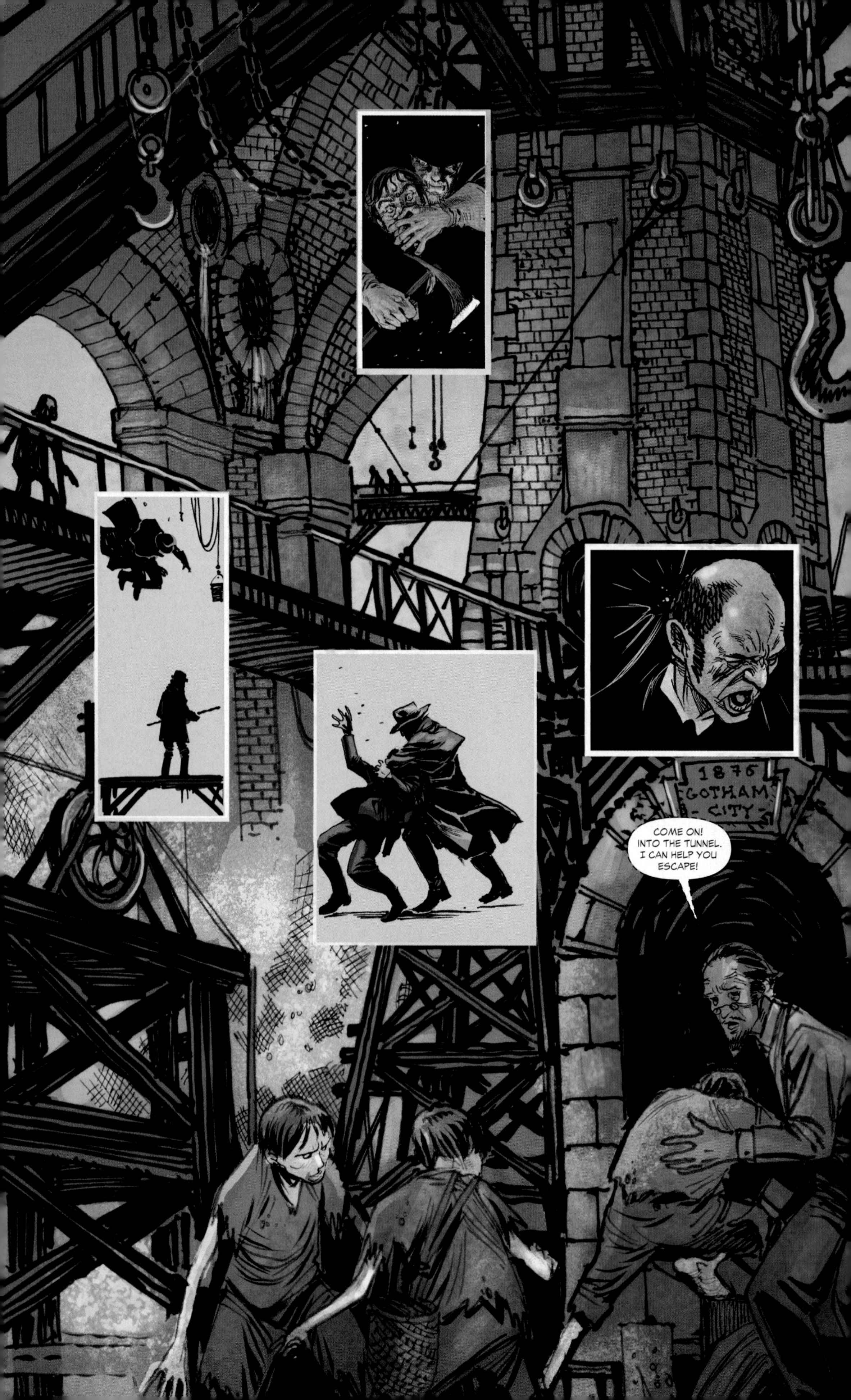
1876
GOTHAM
CITY
COME ON!
INTO THE TUNNEL.
I CAN HELP YOU
ESCAPE!

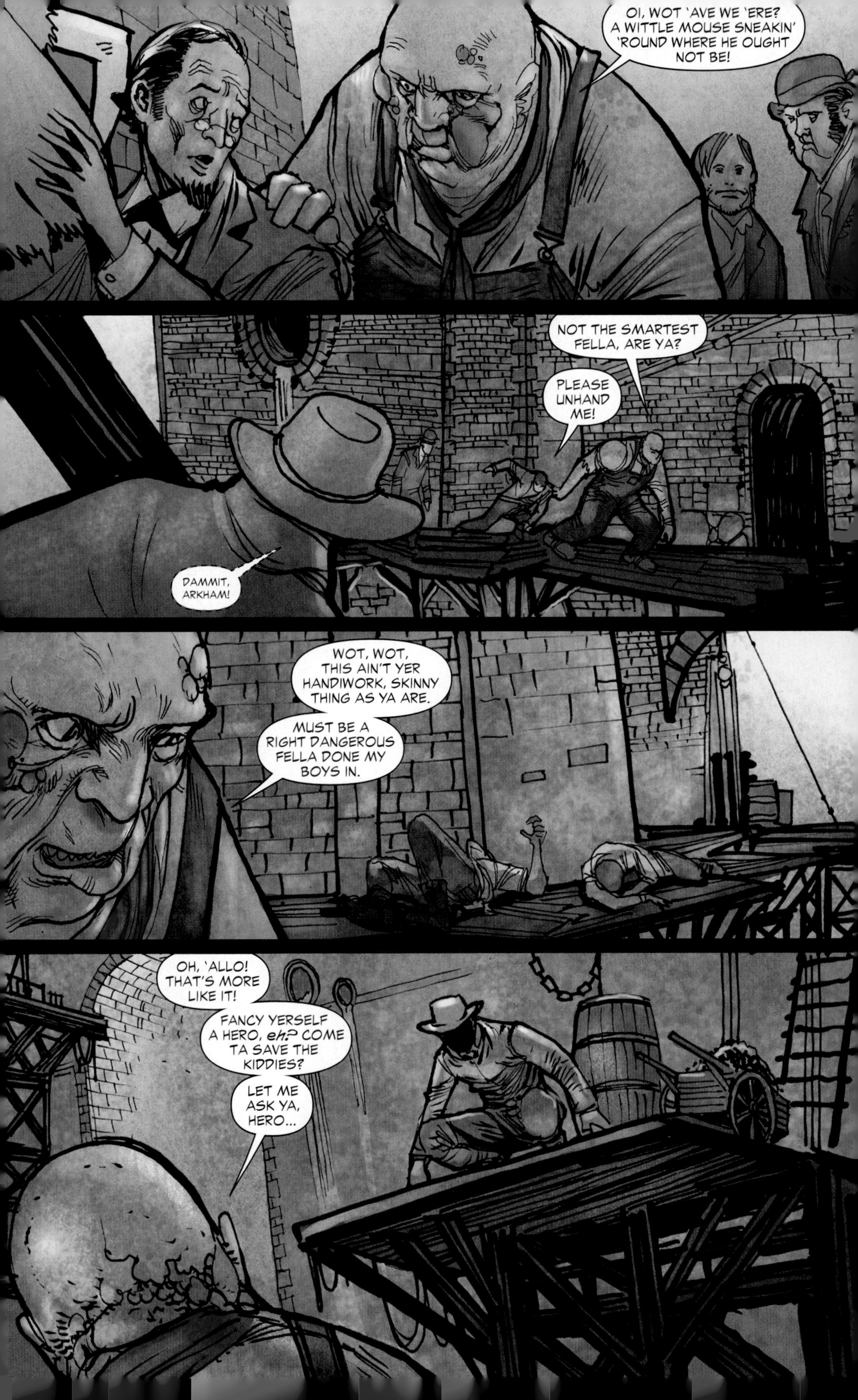
OI, WOT 'AVE WE 'ERE? A WITTLE MOUSE SNEAKIN' 'ROUND WHERE HE OUGHT NOT BE!
NOT THE SMARTEST FELLA, ARE YA?
PLEASE UNHAND ME!
DAMMIT, ARKHAM!
WOT, WOT, THIS AIN'T YER HANDIWORK, SKINNY THING AS YA ARE.
MUST BE A RIGHT DANGEROUS FELLA DONE MY BOYS IN.
OH, 'ALLO! THAT'S MORE LIKE IT!
FANCY YERSELF A HERO, *eh?* COME TA SAVE THE KIDDIES?
LET ME ASK YA, HERO...

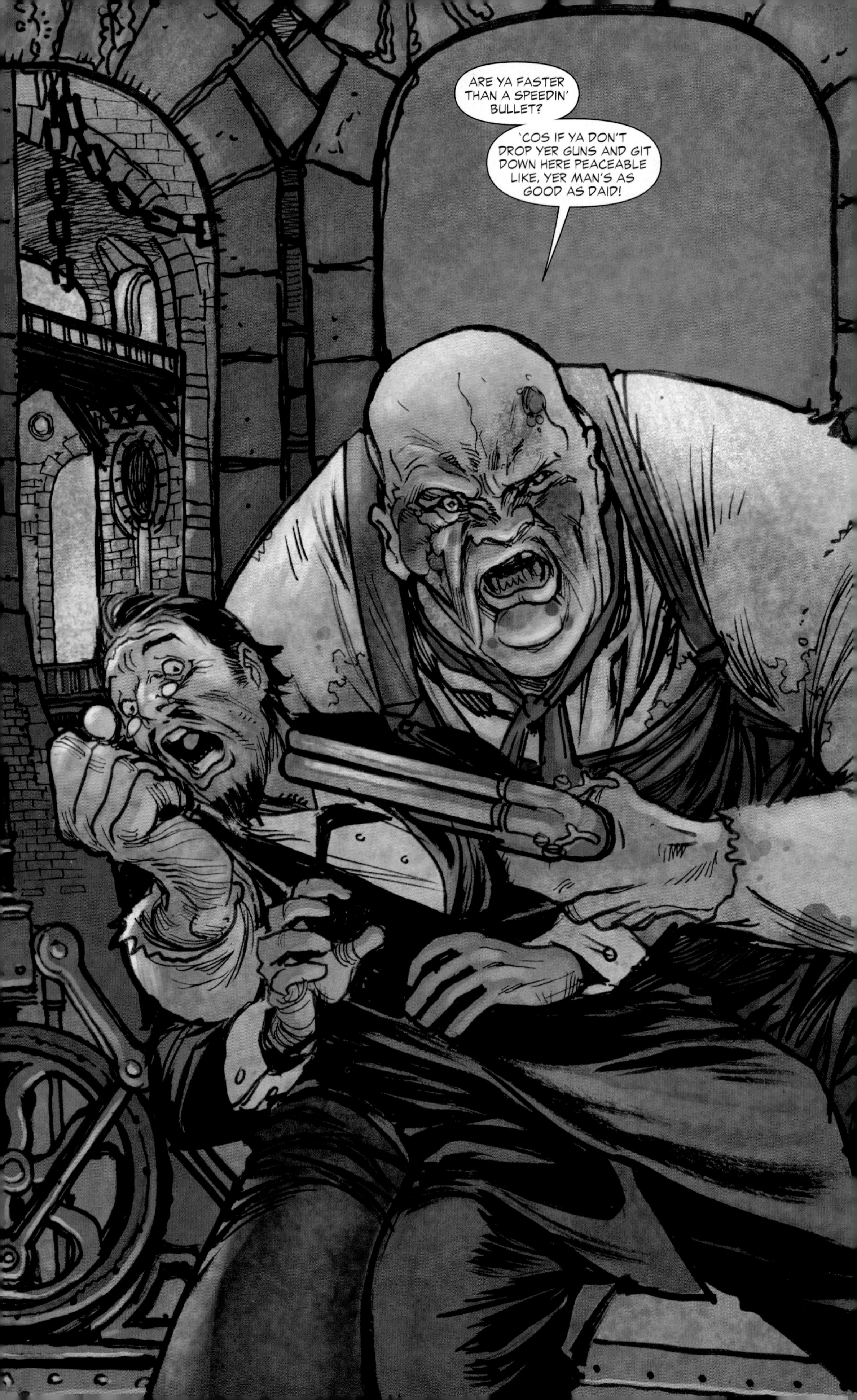
ARE YA FASTER THAN A SPEEDIN' BULLET?
'COS IF YA DON'T DROP YER GUNS AND GIT DOWN HERE PEACEABLE LIKE, YER MAN'S AS GOOD AS DAID!

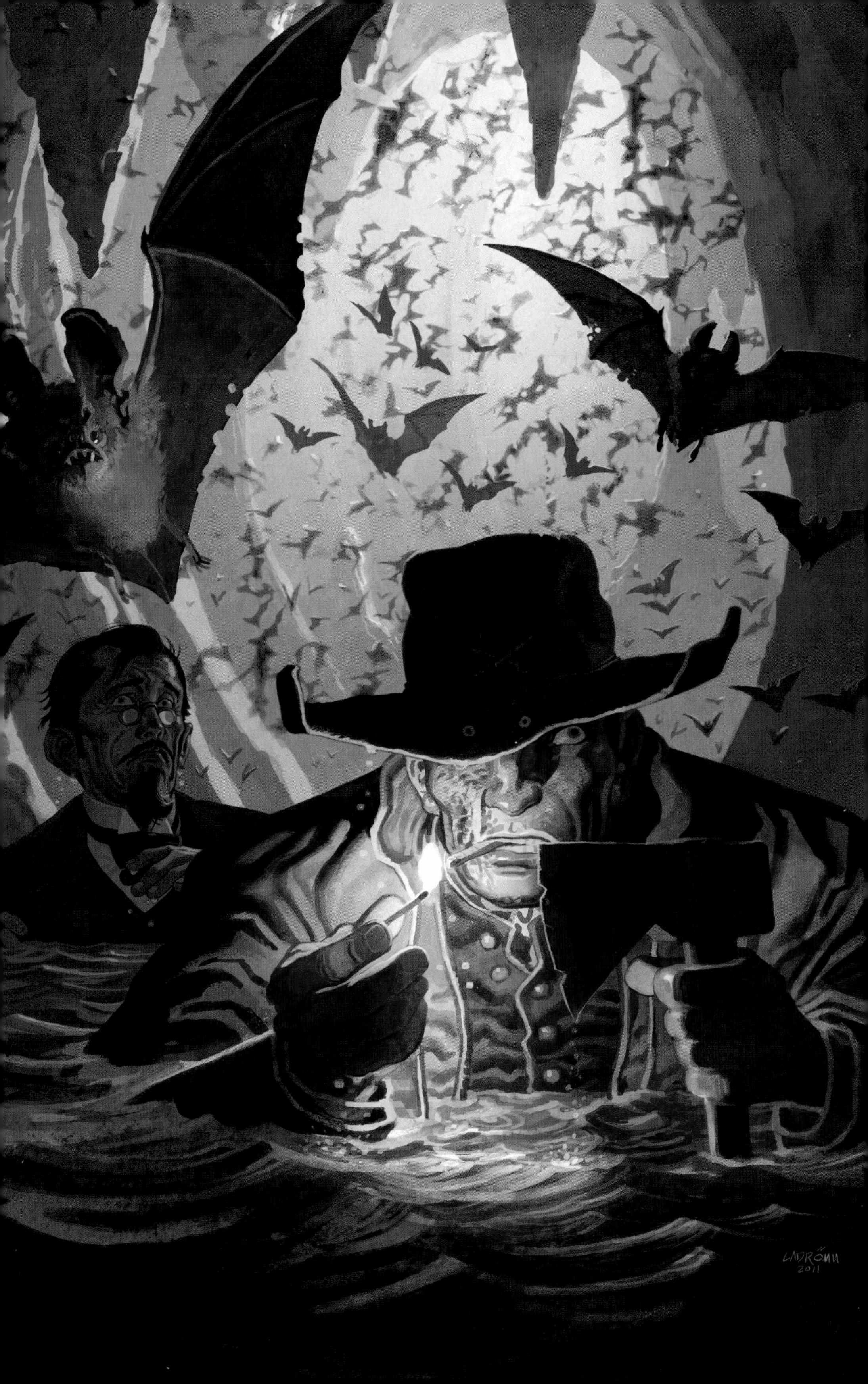
LADRÖNN
2011

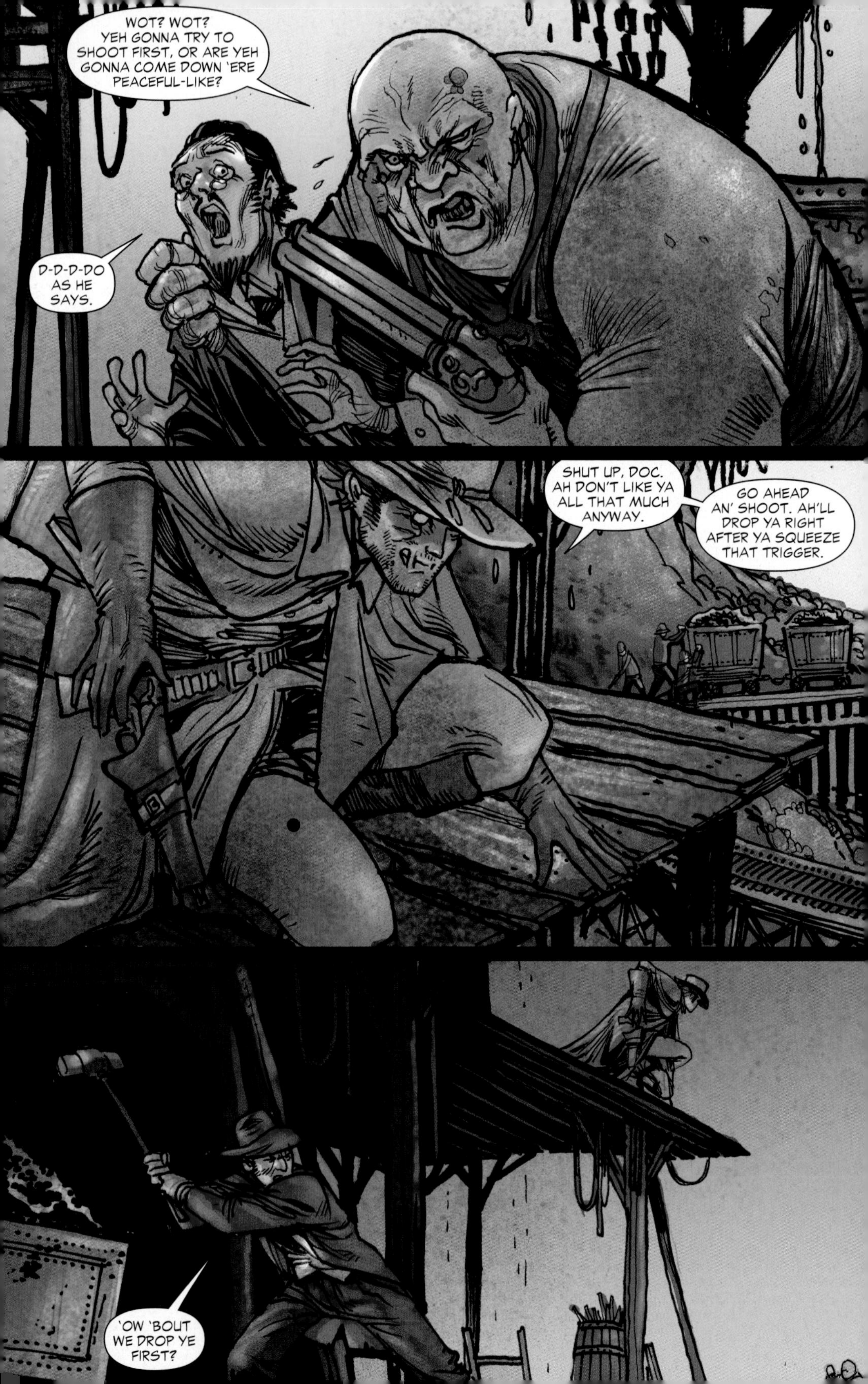
WOT? WOT? YEH GONNA TRY TO SHOOT FIRST, OR ARE YEH GONNA COME DOWN 'ERE PEACEFUL-LIKE?
D-D-D-DO AS HE SAYS.
SHUT UP, DOC. AH DON'T LIKE YA ALL THAT MUCH ANYWAY.
GO AHEAD AN' SHOOT. AH'LL DROP YA RIGHT AFTER YA SQUEEZE THAT TRIGGER.
'OW 'BOUT WE DROP YE FIRST?

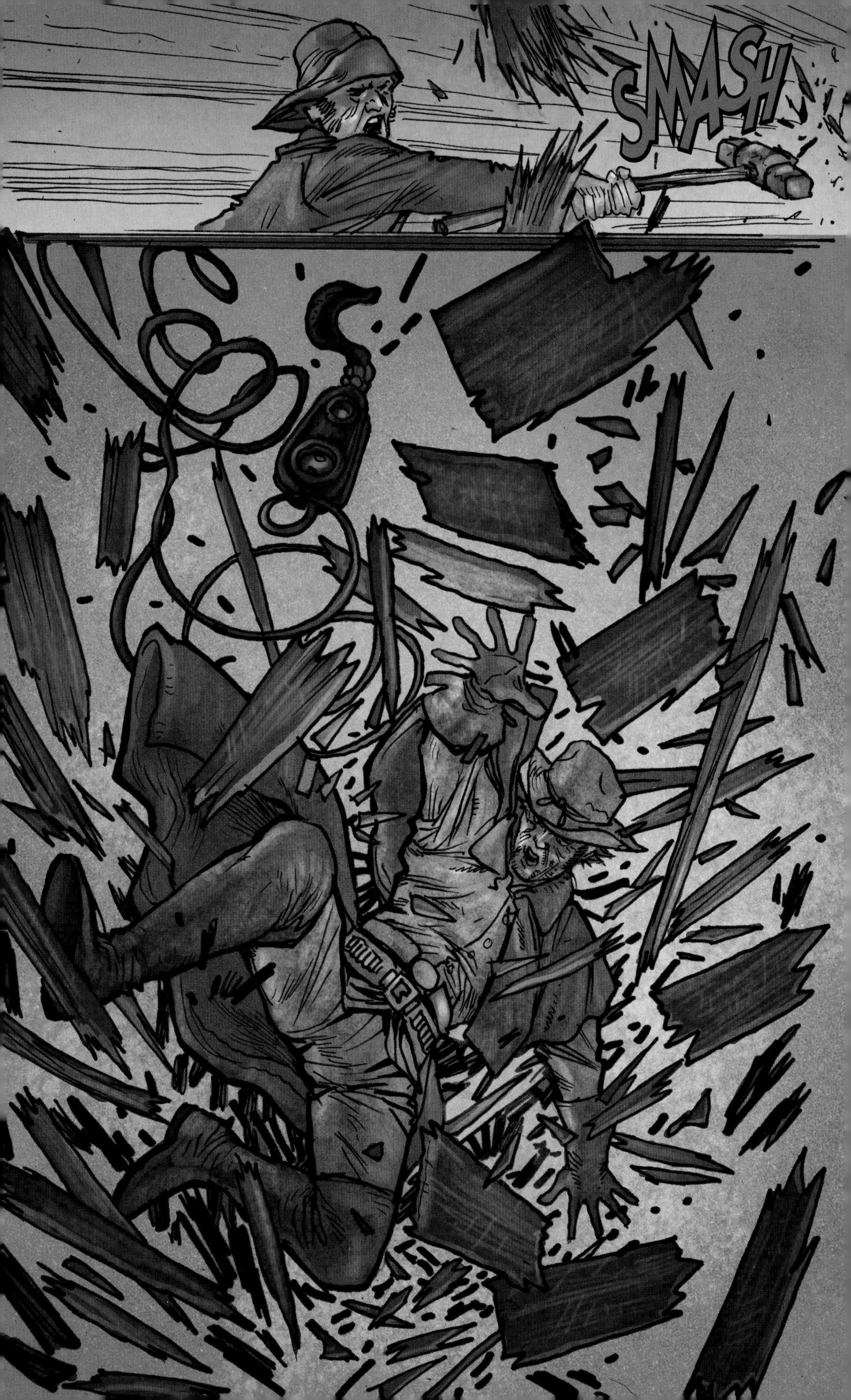
SMASH

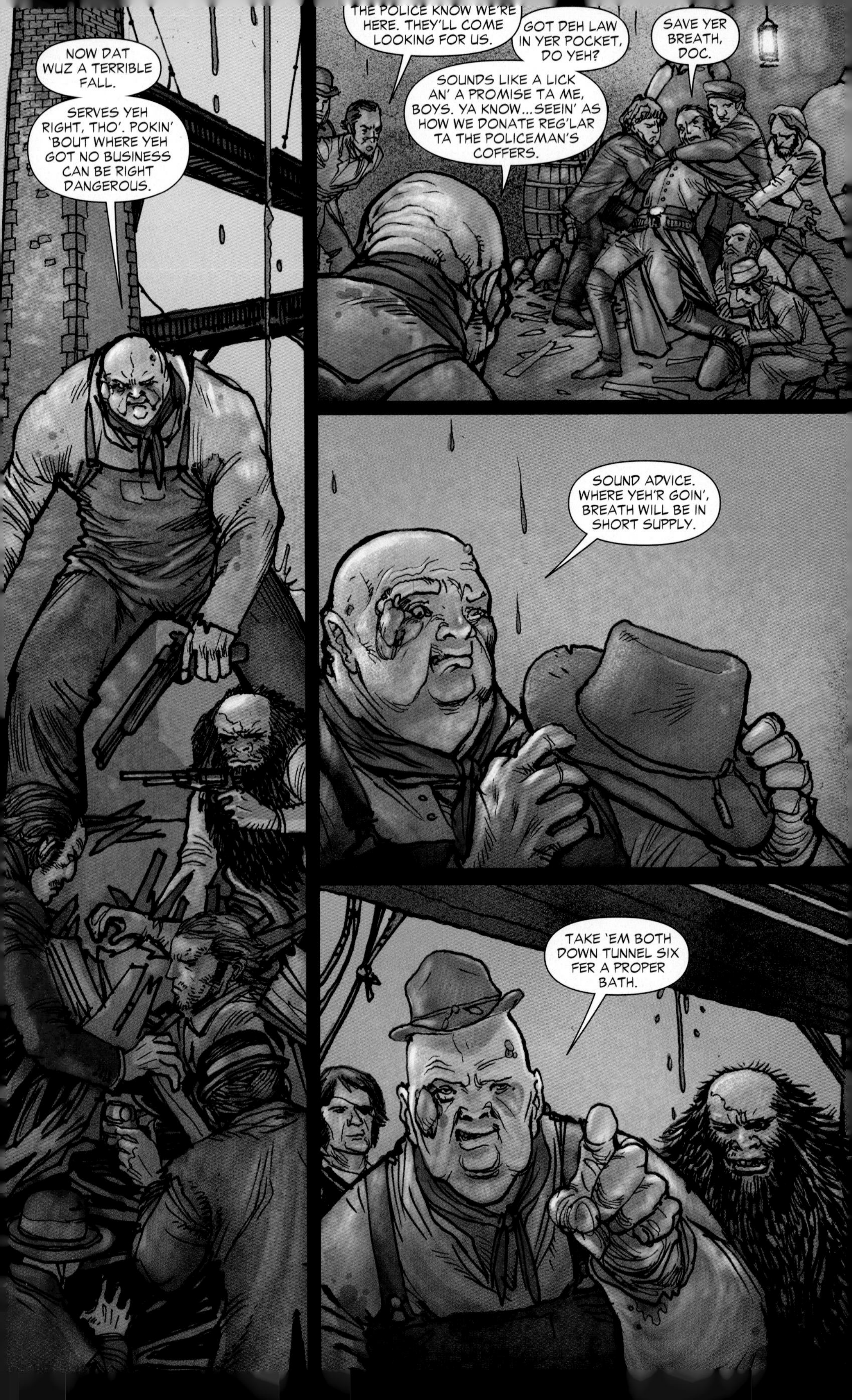
NOW DAT WUZ A TERRIBLE FALL.
SERVES YEH RIGHT, THO'. POKIN' 'BOUT WHERE YEH GOT NO BUSINESS CAN BE RIGHT DANGEROUS.
THE POLICE KNOW WE'RE HERE. THEY'LL COME LOOKING FOR US.
GOT DEH LAW IN YER POCKET, DO YEH?
SOUNDS LIKE A LICK AN' A PROMISE TA ME, BOYS. YA KNOW...SEEIN' AS HOW WE DONATE REG'LAR TA THE POLICEMAN'S COFFERS.
SAVE YER BREATH, DOC.
SOUND ADVICE. WHERE YEH'R GOIN', BREATH WILL BE IN SHORT SUPPLY.
TAKE 'EM BOTH DOWN TUNNEL SIX FER A PROPER BATH.

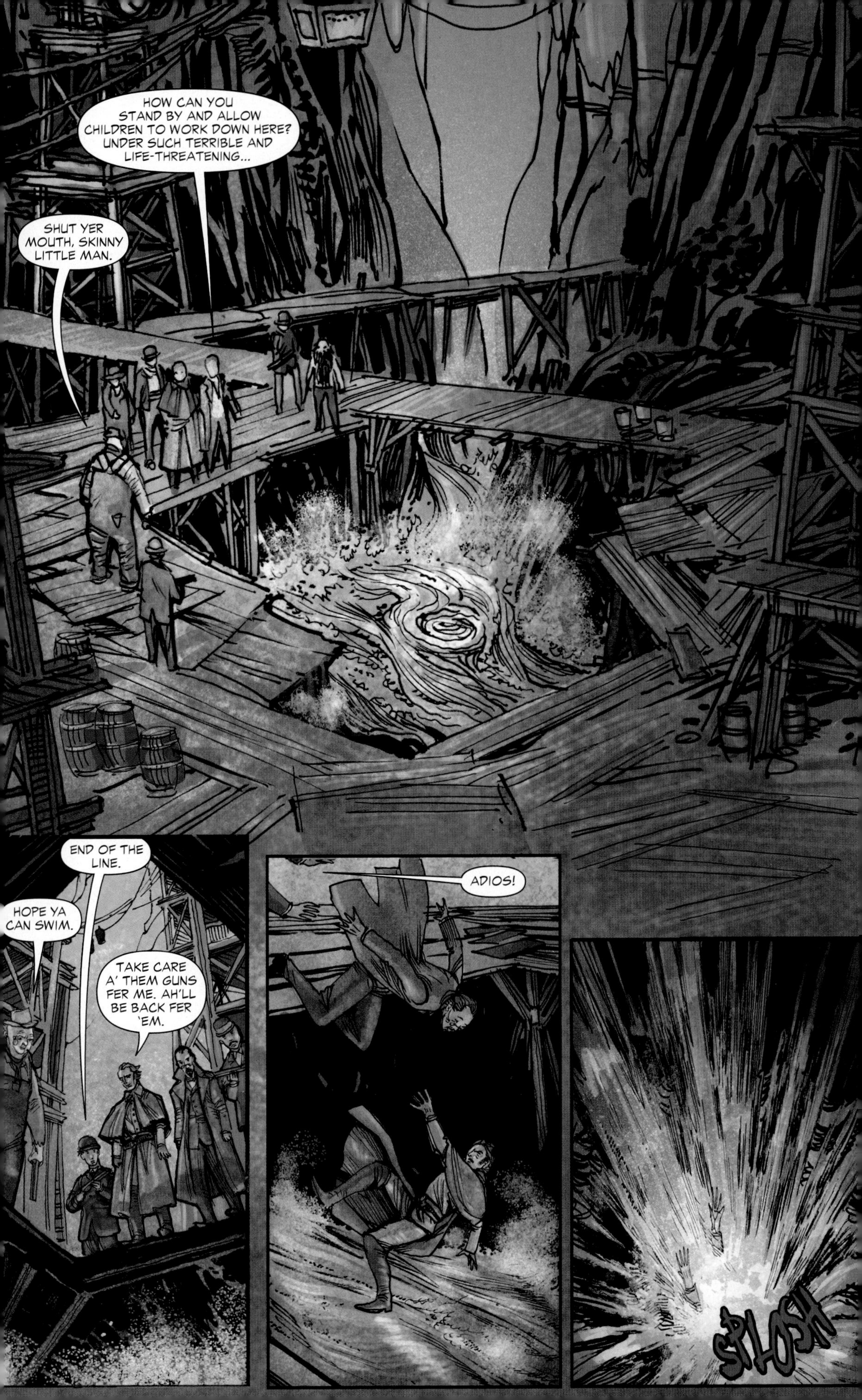
HOW CAN YOU STAND BY AND ALLOW CHILDREN TO WORK DOWN HERE? UNDER SUCH TERRIBLE AND LIFE-THREATENING...
SHUT YER MOUTH, SKINNY LITTLE MAN.
END OF THE LINE.
HOPE YA CAN SWIM.
TAKE CARE A' THEM GUNS FER ME. AH'LL BE BACK FER 'EM.
ADIOS!
SPLOSH

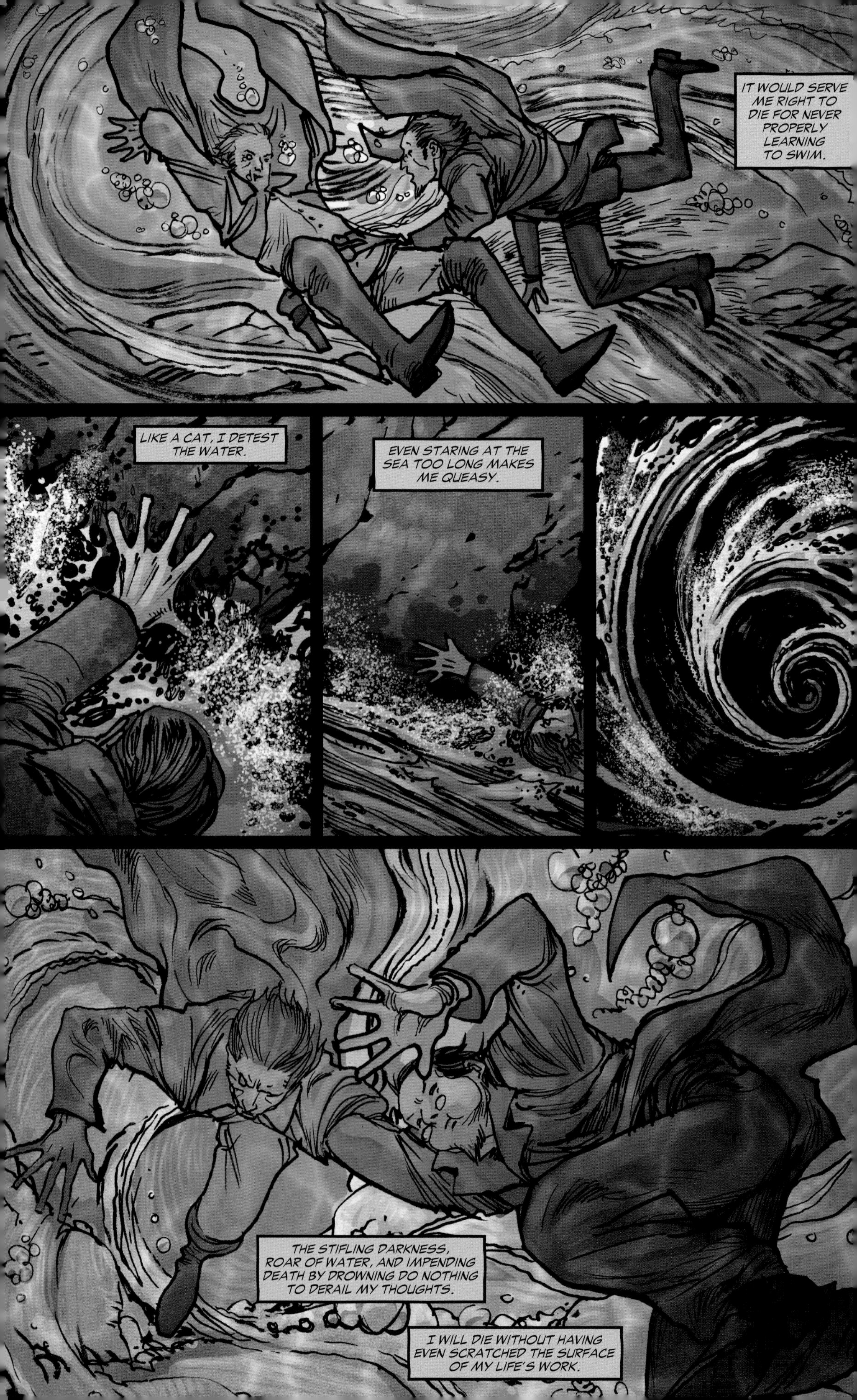
IT WOULD SERVE ME RIGHT TO DIE FOR NEVER PROPERLY LEARNING TO SWIM.
LIKE A CAT, I DETEST THE WATER.
EVEN STARING AT THE SEA TOO LONG MAKES ME QUEASY.
THE STIFLING DARKNESS, ROAR OF WATER, AND IMPENDING DEATH BY DROWNING DO NOTHING TO DERAIL MY THOUGHTS.
I WILL DIE WITHOUT HAVING EVEN SCRATCHED THE SURFACE OF MY LIFE'S WORK.

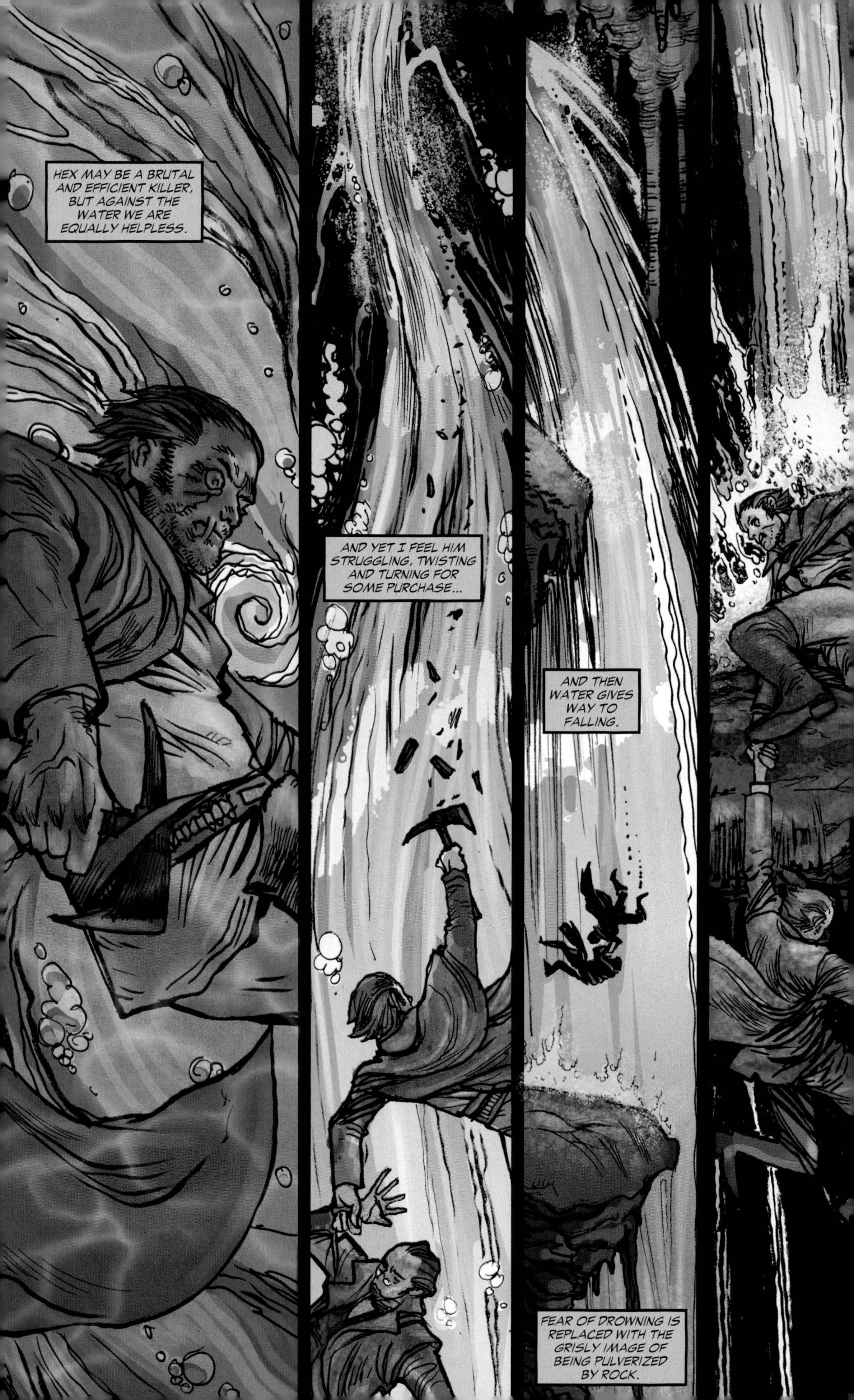
HEX MAY BE A BRUTAL AND EFFICIENT KILLER, BUT AGAINST THE WATER WE ARE EQUALLY HELPLESS.
AND YET I FEEL HIM STRUGGLING, TWISTING AND TURNING FOR SOME PURCHASE...
AND THEN WATER GIVES WAY TO FALLING.
FEAR OF DROWNING IS REPLACED WITH THE GRISLY IMAGE OF BEING PULVERIZED BY ROCK.

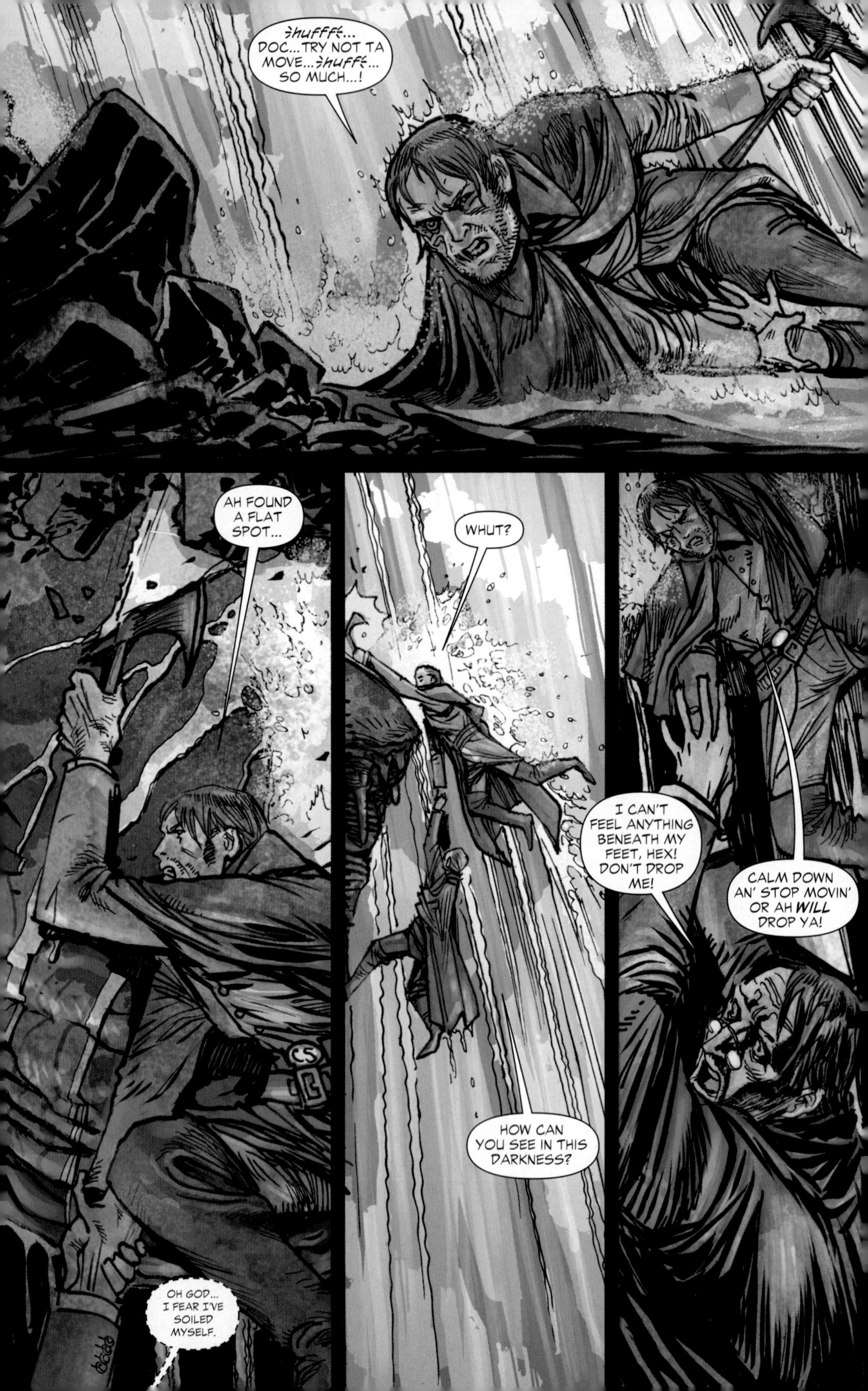

huffff... DOC...TRY NOT TA MOVE...huff... SO MUCH...!
AH FOUND A FLAT SPOT...
OH GOD... I FEAR I'VE SOILED MYSELF.
WHUT?
HOW CAN YOU SEE IN THIS DARKNESS?
I CAN'T FEEL ANYTHING BENEATH MY FEET, HEX! DON'T DROP ME!
CALM DOWN AN' STOP MOVIN' OR AH ***WILL*** DROP YA!

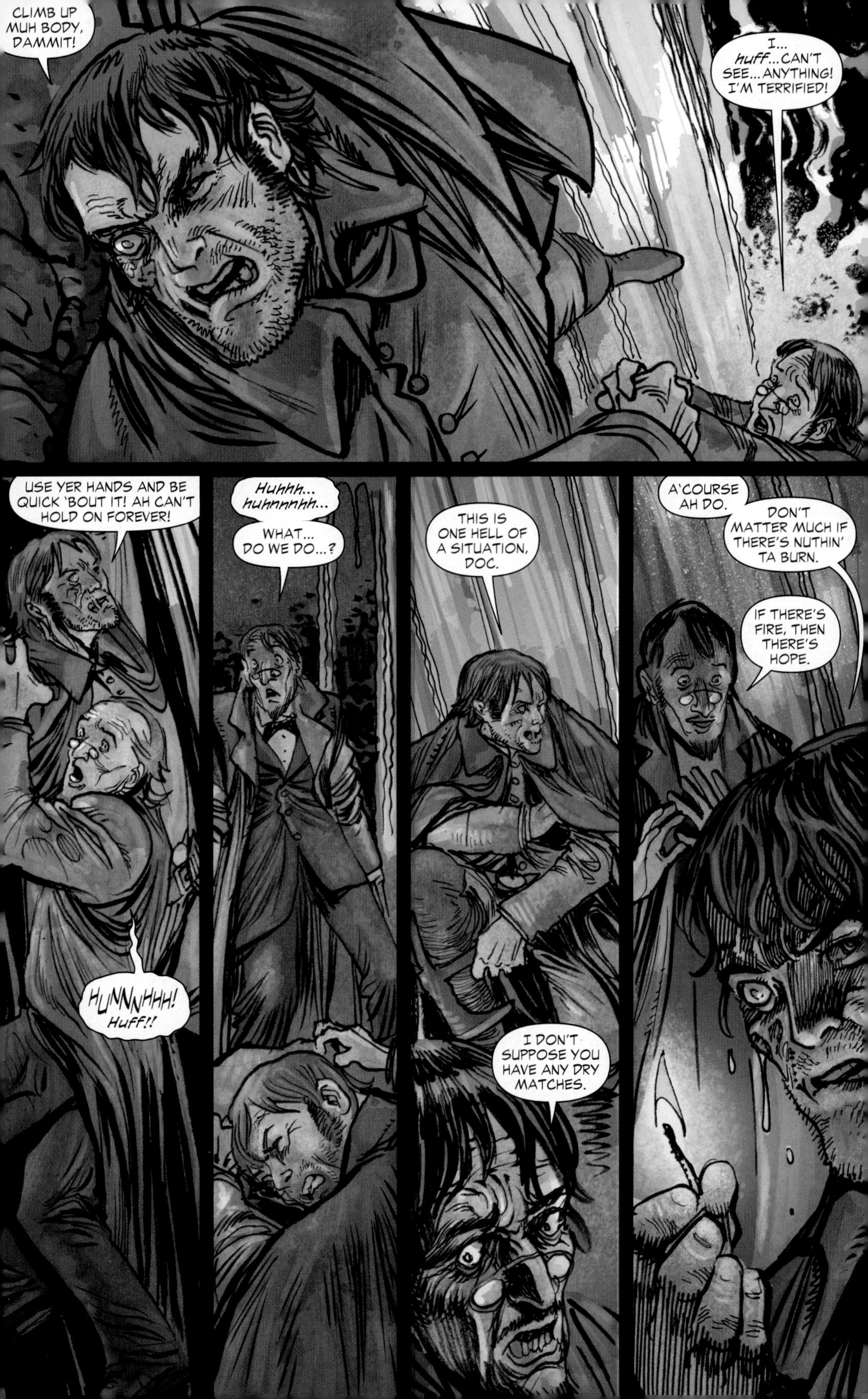
CLIMB UP MUH BODY, DAMMIT!
I... *huff*...CAN'T SEE...ANYTHING! I'M TERRIFIED!
USE YER HANDS AND BE QUICK 'BOUT IT! AH CAN'T HOLD ON FOREVER!
HUNNNHHH! *Huff!!*
*Huhhh... huhhnnhhh...*
WHAT... DO WE DO...?
THIS IS ONE HELL OF A SITUATION, DOC.
I DON'T SUPPOSE YOU HAVE ANY DRY MATCHES.
A'COURSE AH DO.
DON'T MATTER MUCH IF THERE'S NUTHIN' TA BURN.
IF THERE'S FIRE, THEN THERE'S HOPE.

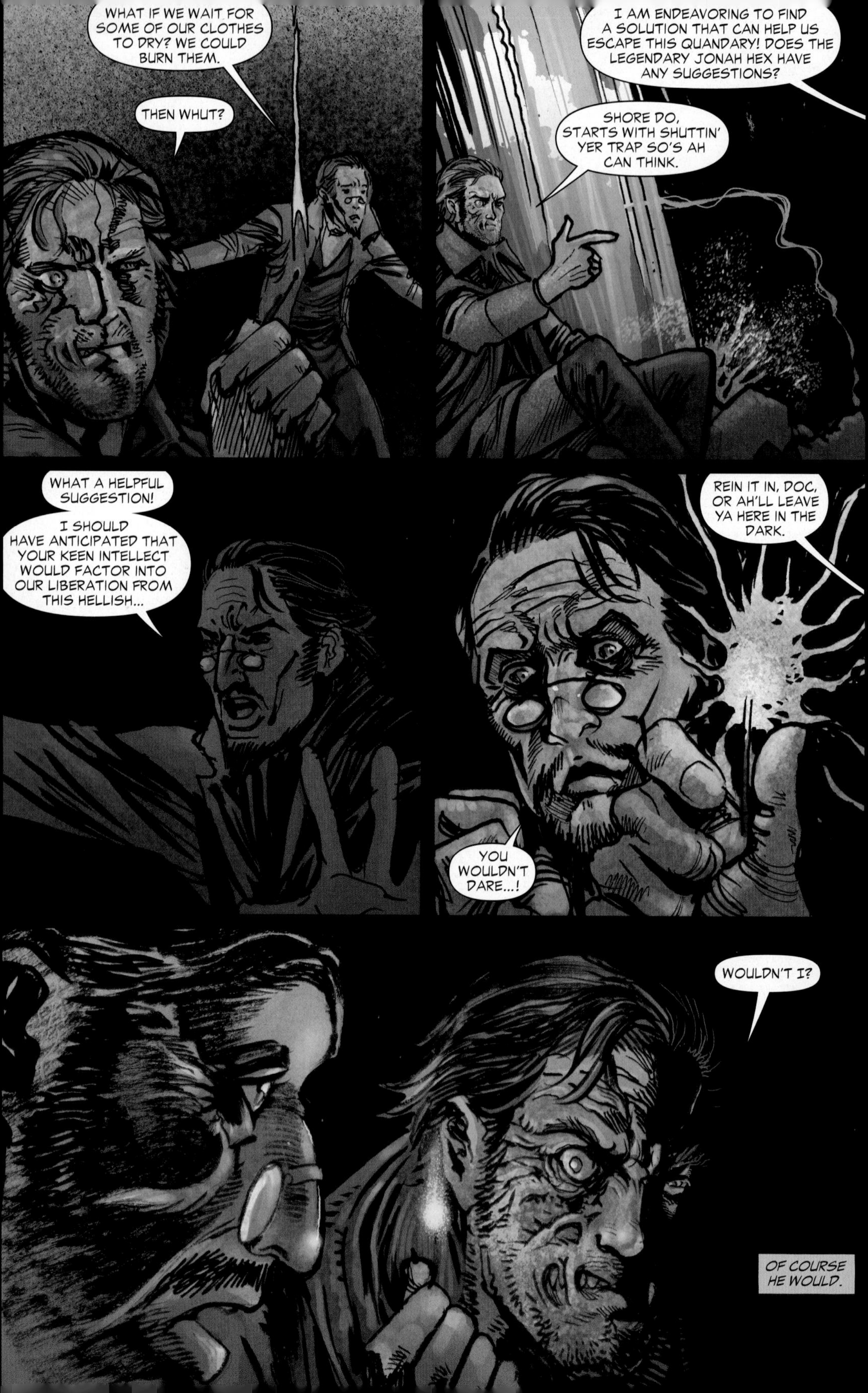
WHAT IF WE WAIT FOR SOME OF OUR CLOTHES TO DRY? WE COULD BURN THEM.
THEN WHUT?
I AM ENDEAVORING TO FIND A SOLUTION THAT CAN HELP US ESCAPE THIS QUANDARY! DOES THE LEGENDARY JONAH HEX HAVE ANY SUGGESTIONS?
SHORE DO, STARTS WITH SHUTTIN' YER TRAP SO'S AH CAN THINK.
WHAT A HELPFUL SUGGESTION!
I SHOULD HAVE ANTICIPATED THAT YOUR KEEN INTELLECT WOULD FACTOR INTO OUR LIBERATION FROM THIS HELLISH...
REIN IT IN, DOC, OR AH'LL LEAVE YA HERE IN THE DARK.
YOU WOULDN'T DARE...!
WOULDN'T I?
OF COURSE HE WOULD.

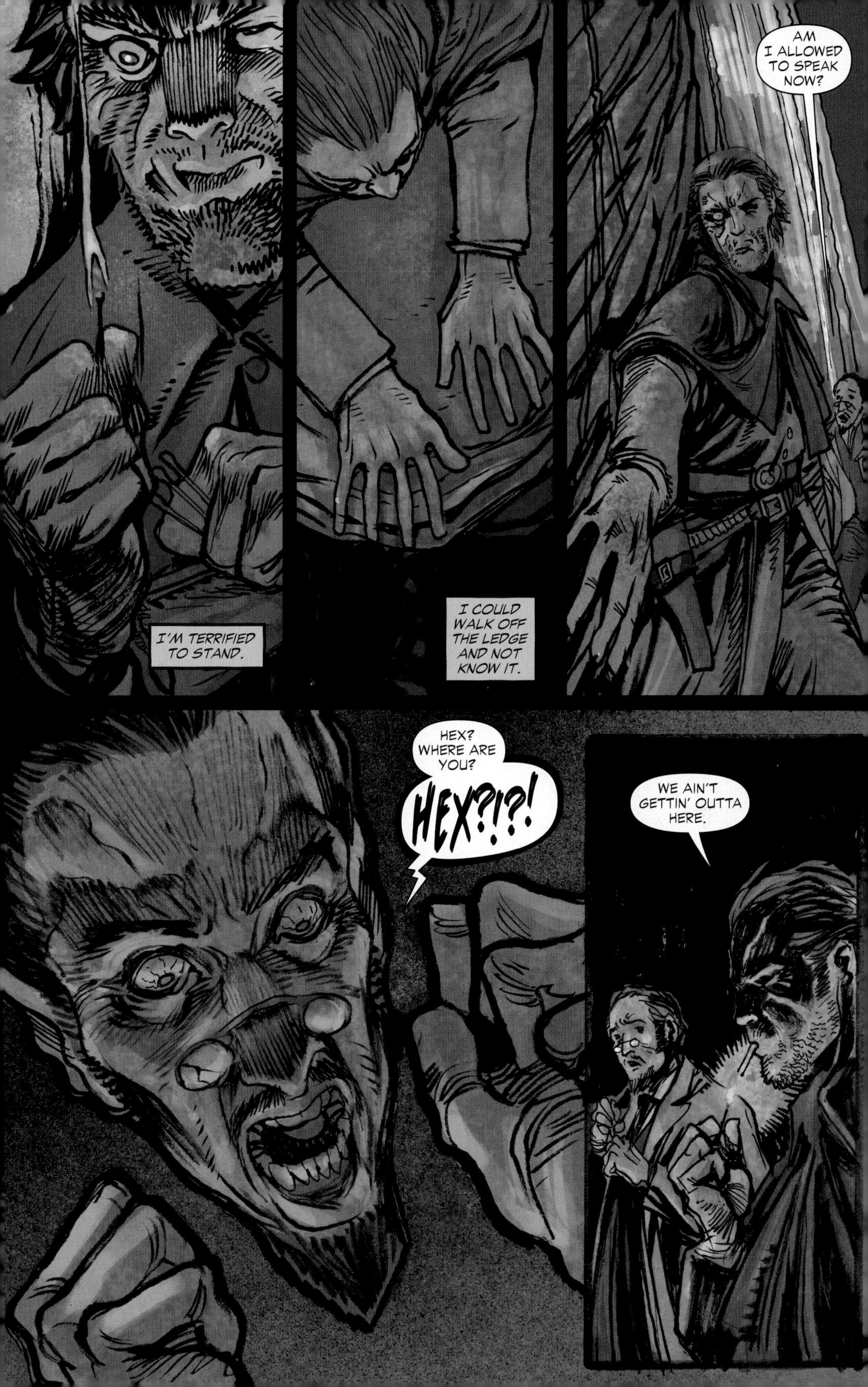
I'M TERRIFIED TO STAND.
I COULD WALK OFF THE LEDGE AND NOT KNOW IT.
AM I ALLOWED TO SPEAK NOW?
HEX? WHERE ARE YOU?
HEX?!?!
WE AIN'T GETTIN' OUTTA HERE.

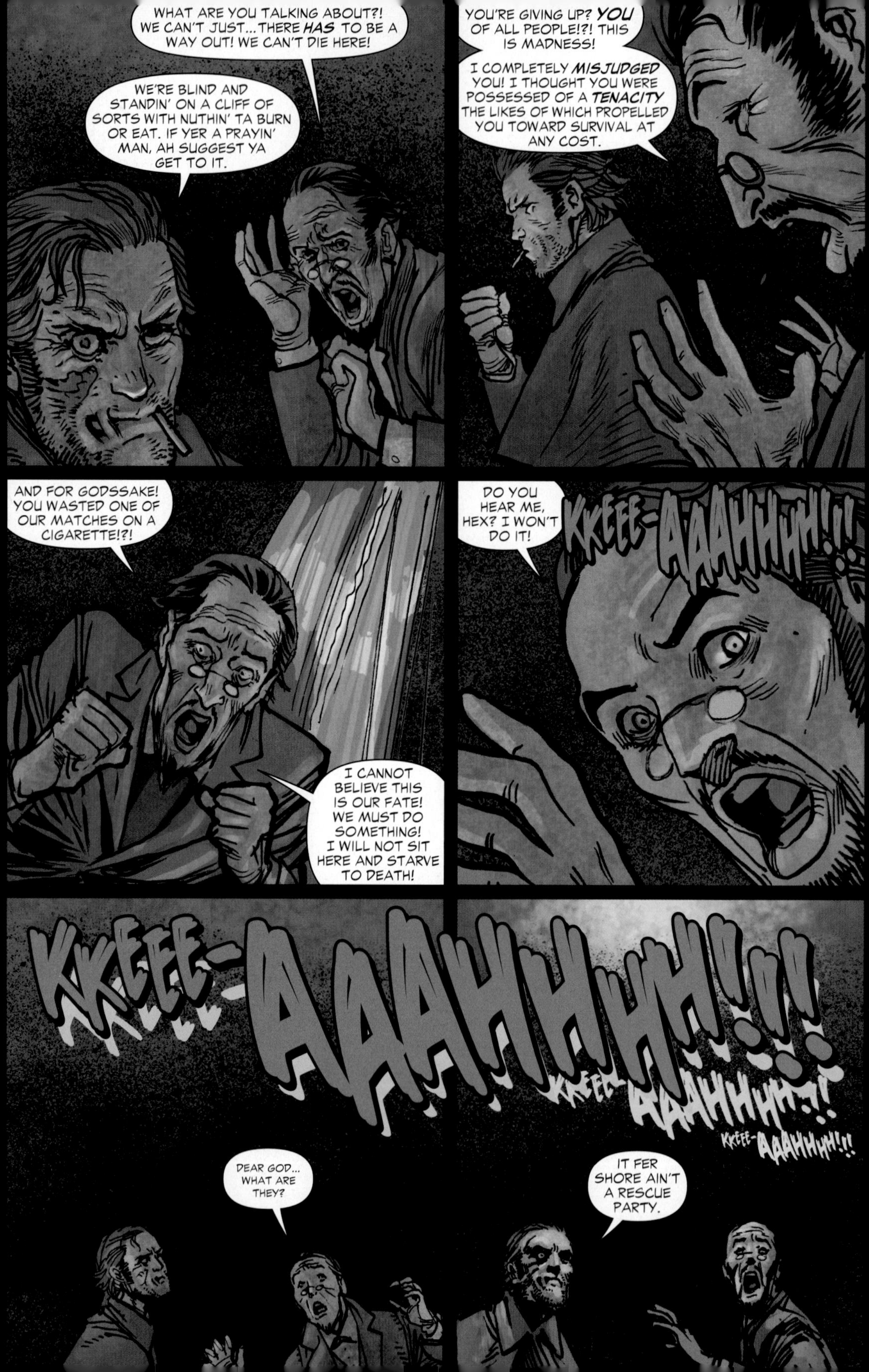
WHAT ARE YOU TALKING ABOUT?! WE CAN'T JUST...THERE HAS TO BE A WAY OUT! WE CAN'T DIE HERE!
WE'RE BLIND AND STANDIN' ON A CLIFF OF SORTS WITH NUTHIN' TA BURN OR EAT. IF YER A PRAYIN' MAN, AH SUGGEST YA GET TO IT.
YOU'RE GIVING UP? YOU OF ALL PEOPLE!?! THIS IS MADNESS!
I COMPLETELY MISJUDGED YOU! I THOUGHT YOU WERE POSSESSED OF A TENACITY THE LIKES OF WHICH PROPELLED YOU TOWARD SURVIVAL AT ANY COST.
AND FOR GODSSAKE! YOU WASTED ONE OF OUR MATCHES ON A CIGARETTE!?!
I CANNOT BELIEVE THIS IS OUR FATE! WE MUST DO SOMETHING! I WILL NOT SIT HERE AND STARVE TO DEATH!
DO YOU HEAR ME, HEX? I WON'T DO IT!
KKEEE-AAAHHHH!!!
KKEEE-AAAHHHH!!!
KKEEE-AAAHHHH!!!
KKEEE-AAAHHHH!!!
DEAR GOD... WHAT ARE THEY?
IT FER SHORE AIN'T A RESCUE PARTY.

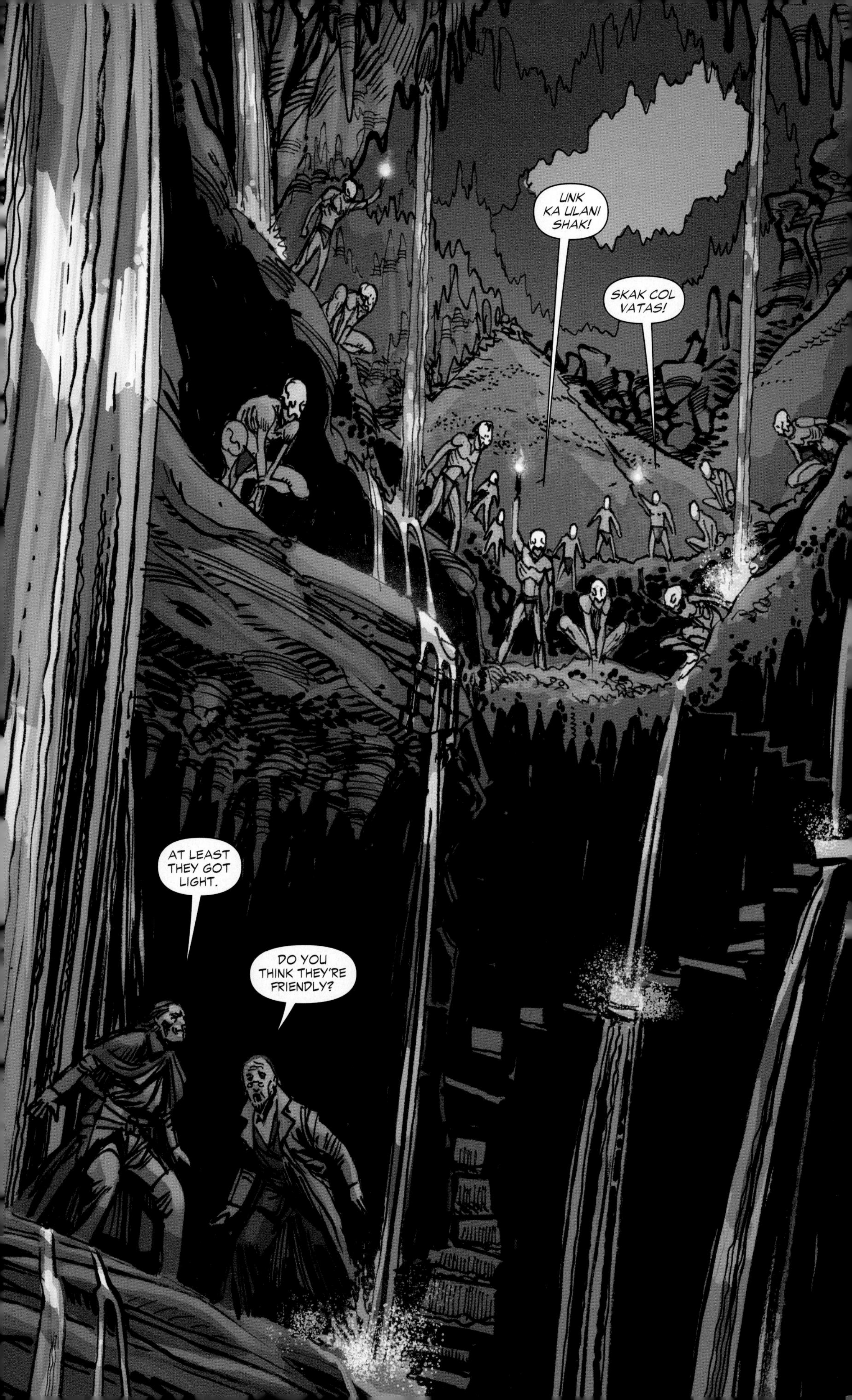
UNK KA ULANI SHAK!
SKAK COL VATAS!
AT LEAST THEY GOT LIGHT.
DO YOU THINK THEY'RE FRIENDLY?

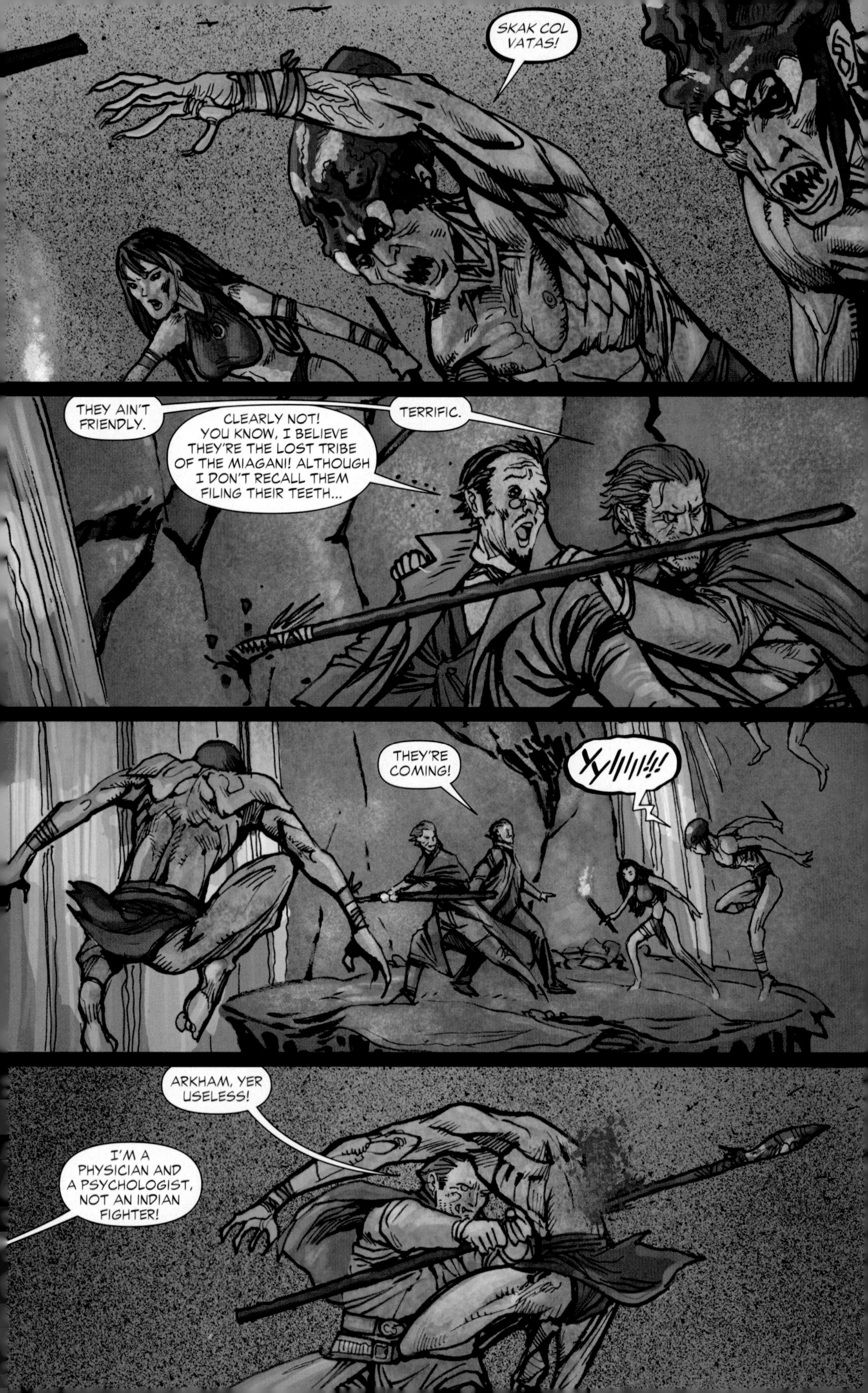
SKAK COL VATAS!
THEY AIN'T FRIENDLY.
CLEARLY NOT! YOU KNOW, I BELIEVE THEY'RE THE LOST TRIBE OF THE MIAGANI! ALTHOUGH I DON'T RECALL THEM FILING THEIR TEETH...
TERRIFIC.
THEY'RE COMING!
ARKHAM, YER USELESS!
I'M A PHYSICIAN AND A PSYCHOLOGIST, NOT AN INDIAN FIGHTER!

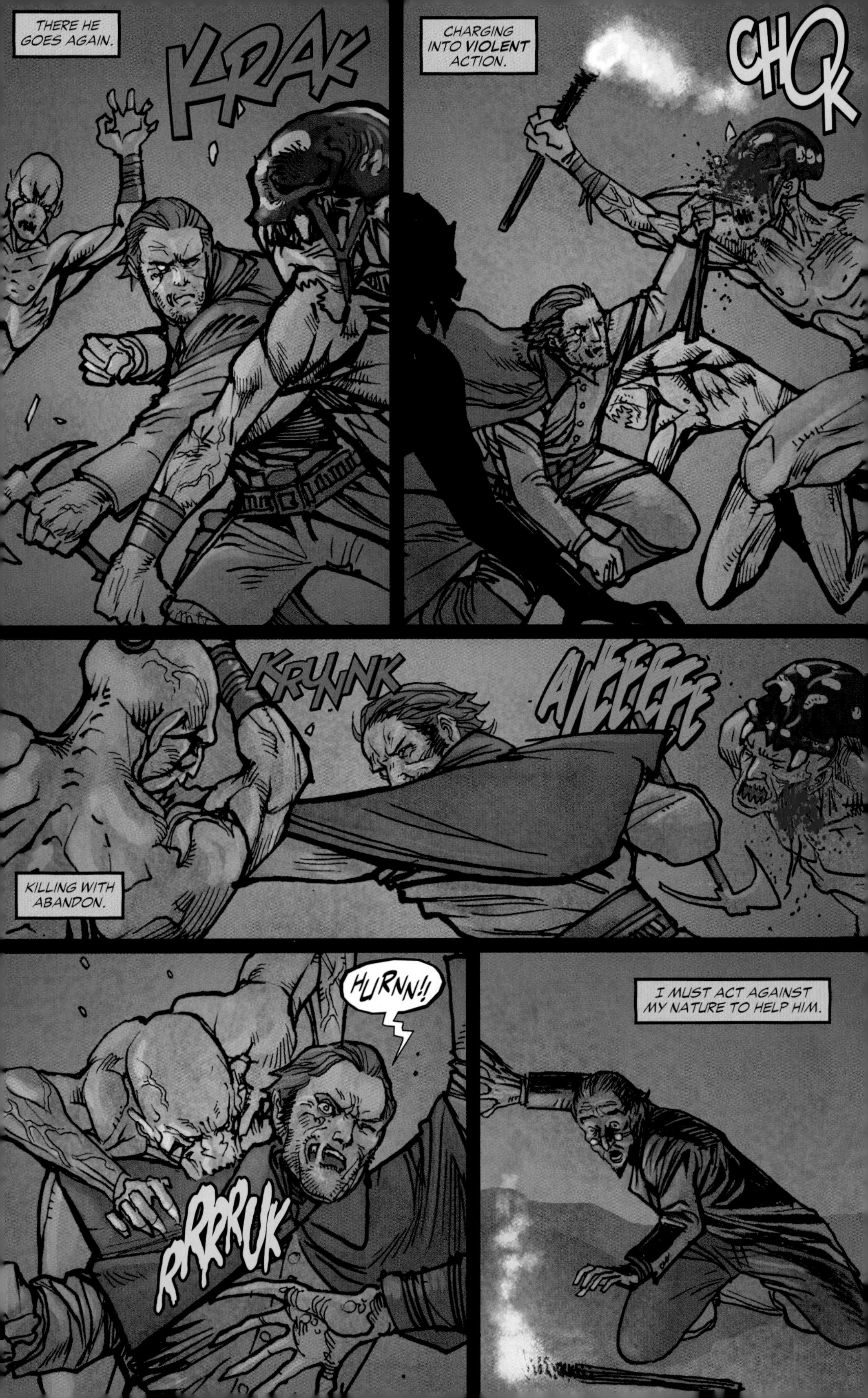
THERE HE GOES AGAIN.
KRAK
CHARGING INTO VIOLENT ACTION.
CHOK
KRUNNK
AIEEEEE
KILLING WITH ABANDON.
HURNN!!
RRRRRUK
I MUST ACT AGAINST MY NATURE TO HELP HIM.

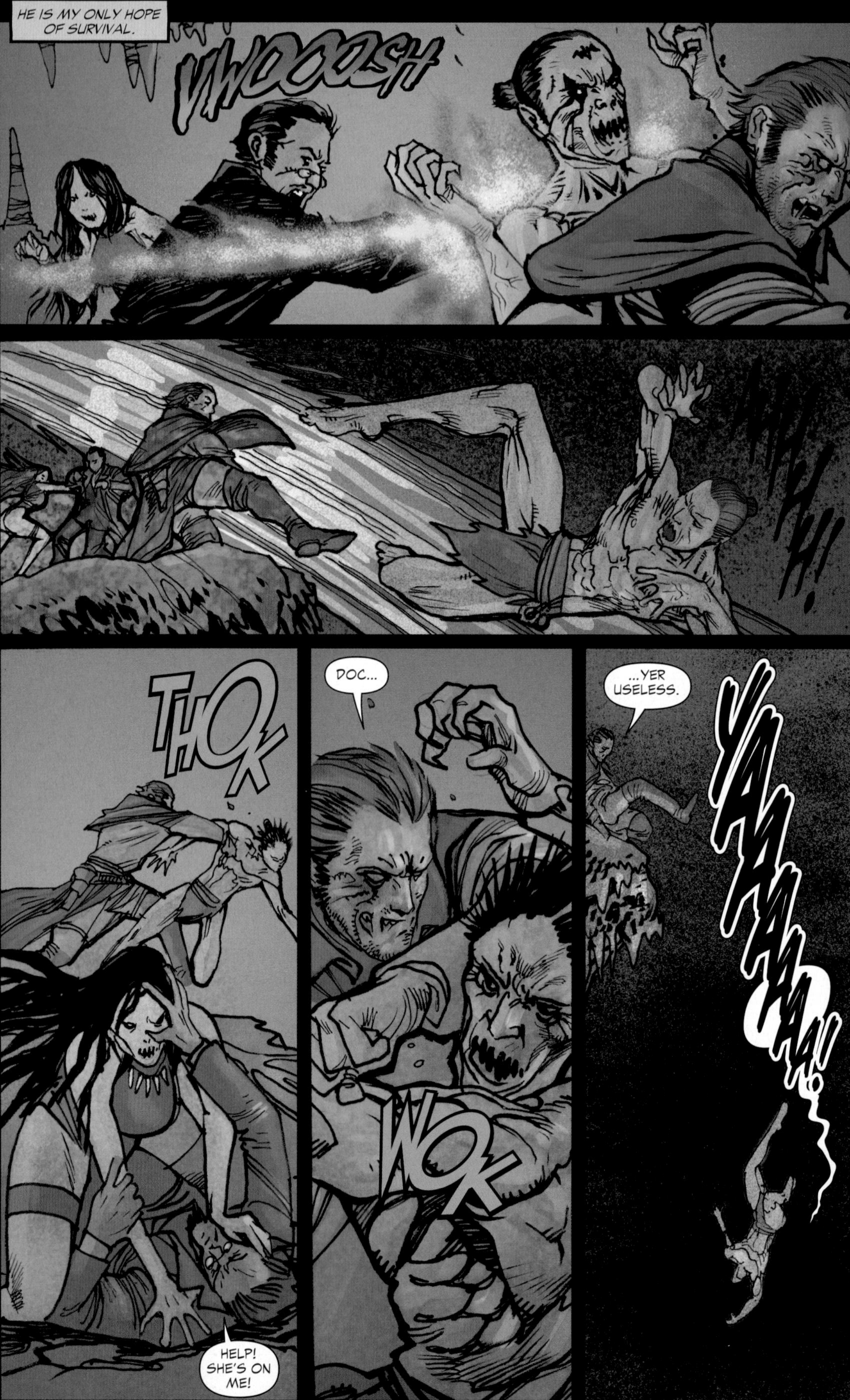
HE IS MY ONLY HOPE OF SURVIVAL.
VWOOOSH
THOK
HELP! SHE'S ON ME!
DOC...
WOK
...YER USELESS.

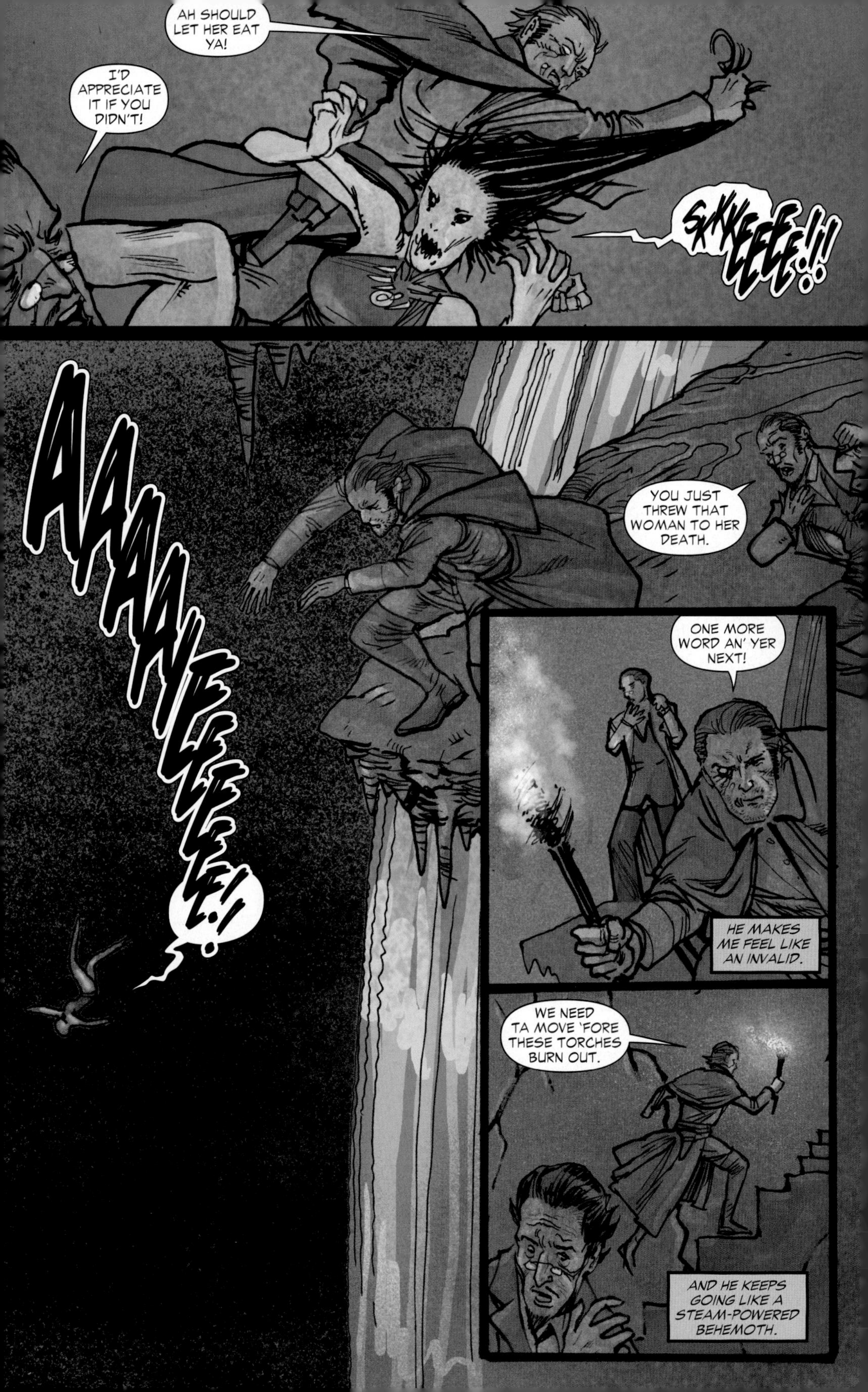
AH SHOULD LET HER EAT YA!
I'D APPRECIATE IT IF YOU DIDN'T!
SKKKEEEE!!!
AAAAAYEEEEEE!!
YOU JUST THREW THAT WOMAN TO HER DEATH.
ONE MORE WORD AN' YER NEXT!
HE MAKES ME FEEL LIKE AN INVALID.
WE NEED TA MOVE 'FORE THESE TORCHES BURN OUT.
AND HE KEEPS GOING LIKE A STEAM-POWERED BEHEMOTH.

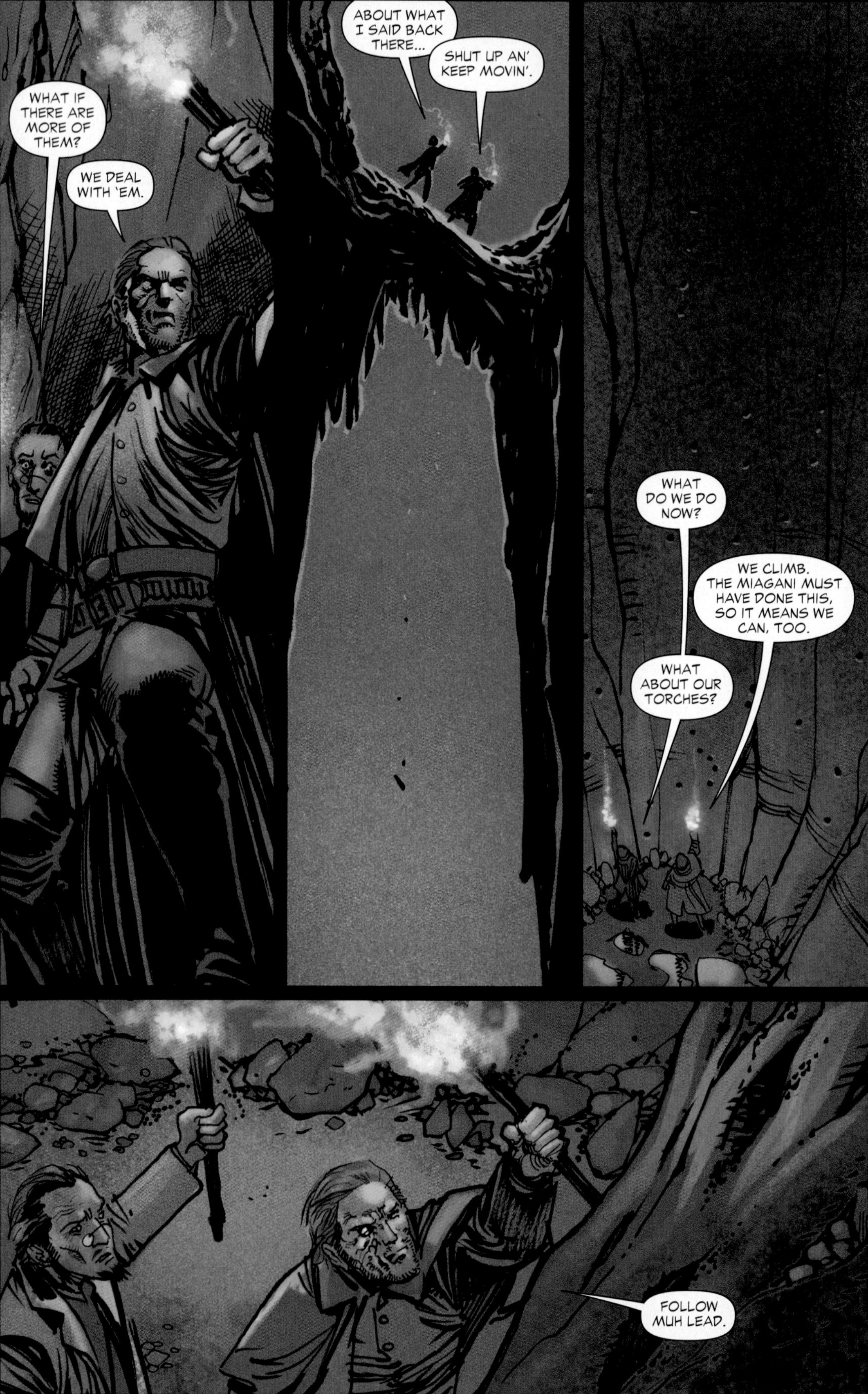
WHAT IF THERE ARE MORE OF THEM?
WE DEAL WITH 'EM.
ABOUT WHAT I SAID BACK THERE...
SHUT UP AN' KEEP MOVIN'.
WHAT DO WE DO NOW?
WE CLIMB. THE MIAGANI MUST HAVE DONE THIS, SO IT MEANS WE CAN, TOO.
WHAT ABOUT OUR TORCHES?
FOLLOW MUH LEAD.

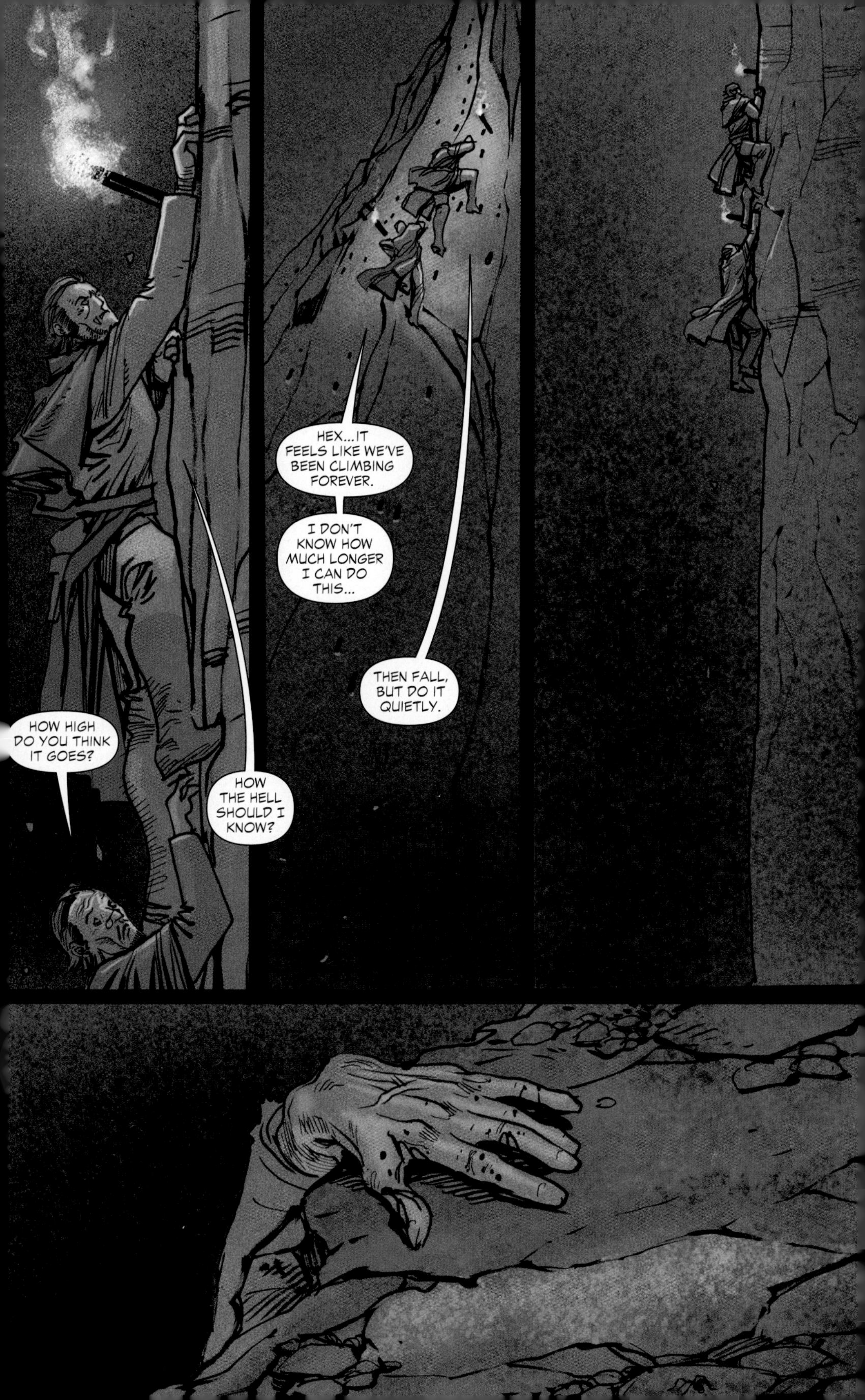
HOW HIGH DO YOU THINK IT GOES?
HOW THE HELL SHOULD I KNOW?
HEX...IT FEELS LIKE WE'VE BEEN CLIMBING FOREVER.
I DON'T KNOW HOW MUCH LONGER I CAN DO THIS...
THEN FALL, BUT DO IT QUIETLY.

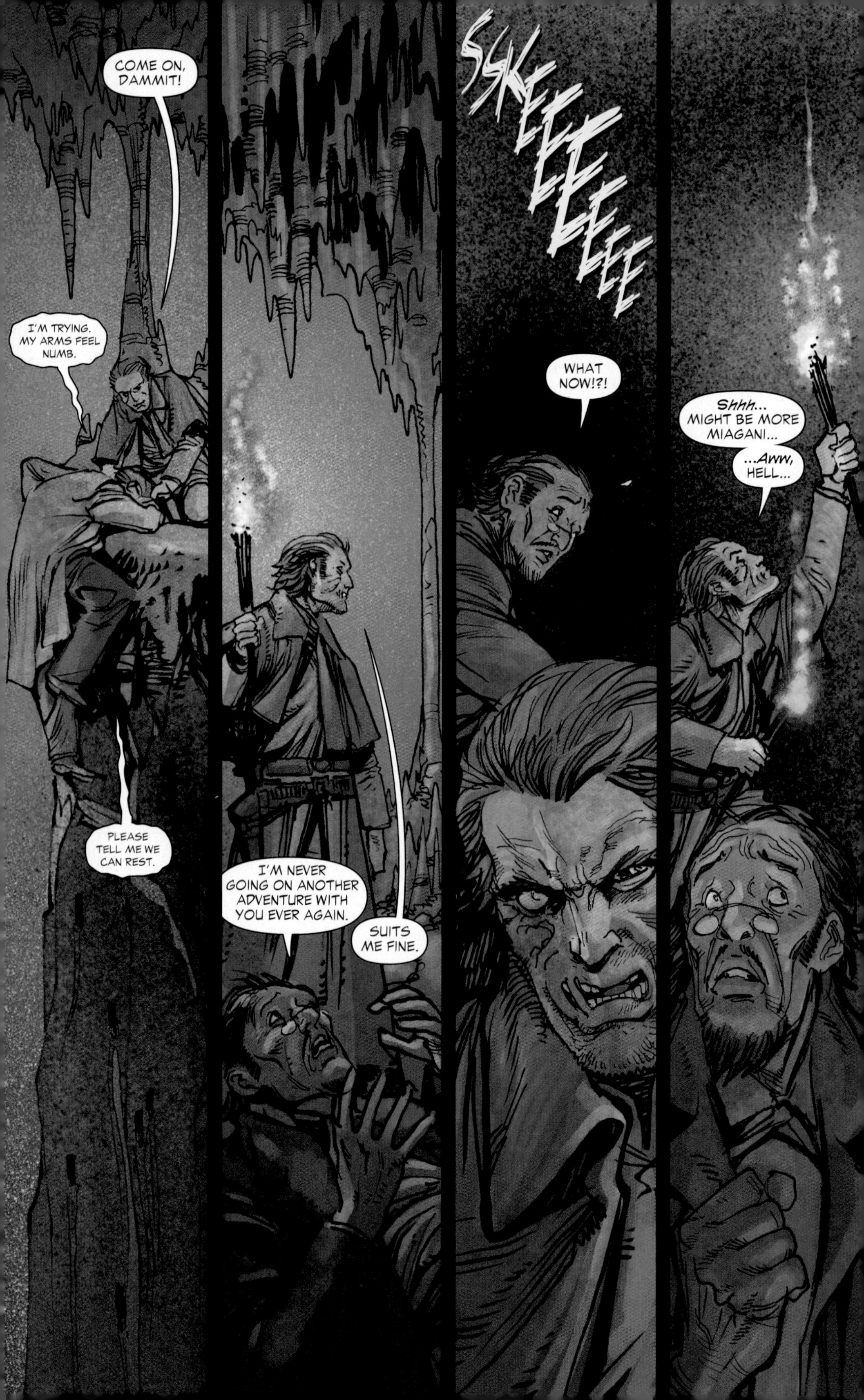
COME ON, DAMMIT!
I'M TRYING. MY ARMS FEEL NUMB.
PLEASE TELL ME WE CAN REST.
I'M NEVER GOING ON ANOTHER ADVENTURE WITH YOU EVER AGAIN.
SUITS ME FINE.
SSKEEEEEEEEE
WHAT NOW!?!
*Shhh*... MIGHT BE MORE MIAGANI...
...*Aww*, HELL...

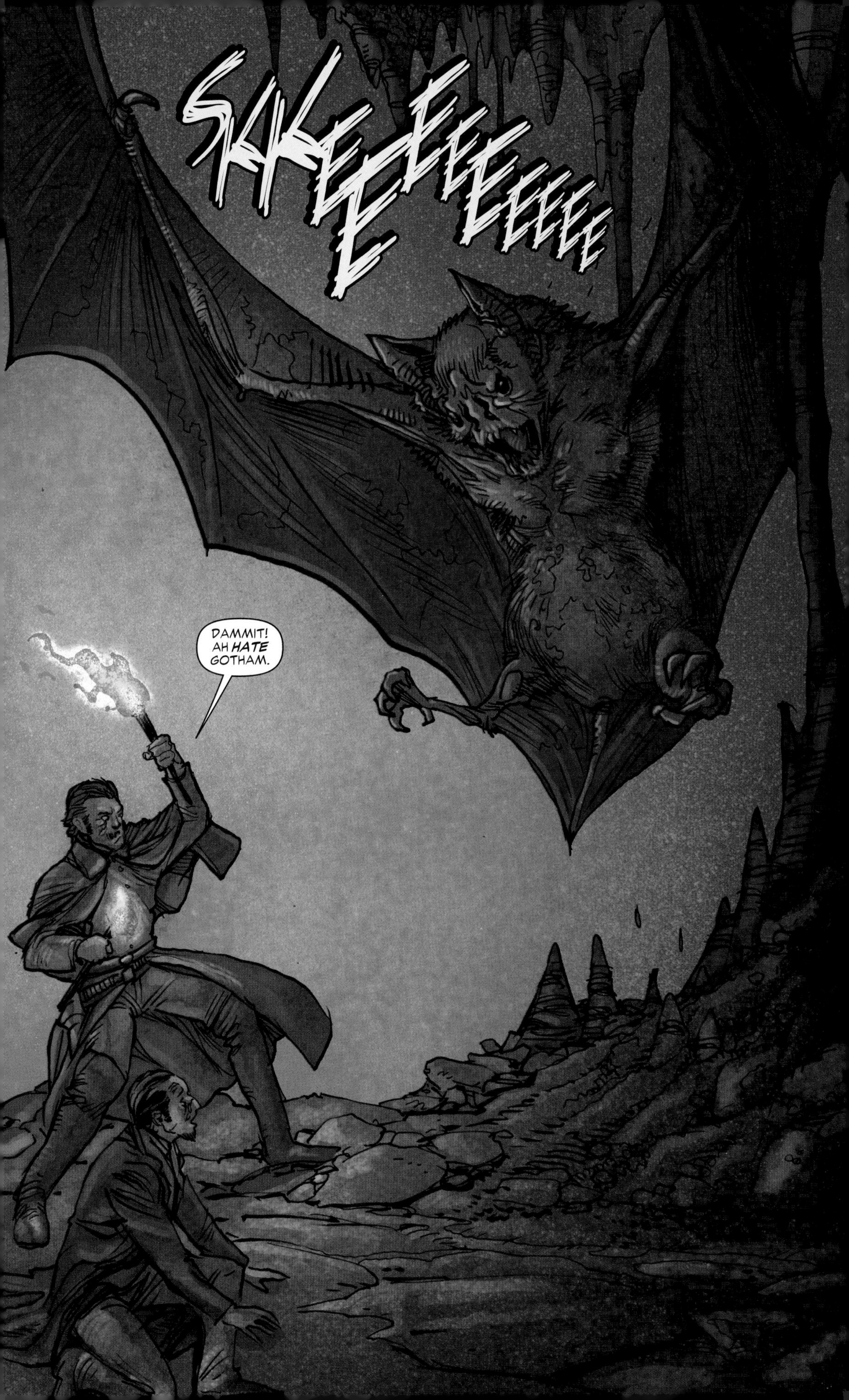
SKKEEEEEEEEEE
DAMMIT! AH HATE GOTHAM.

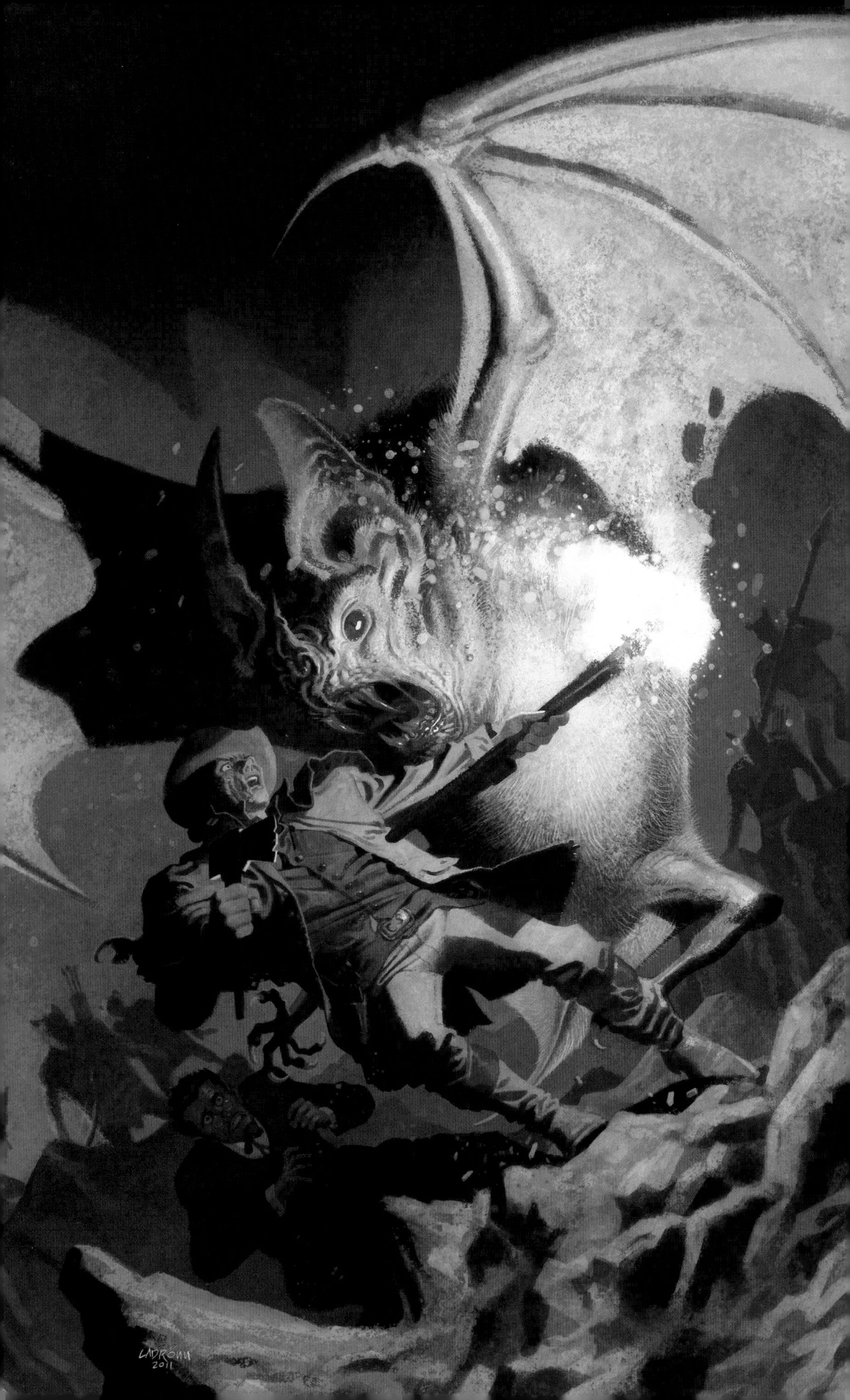
LADRONN
2011

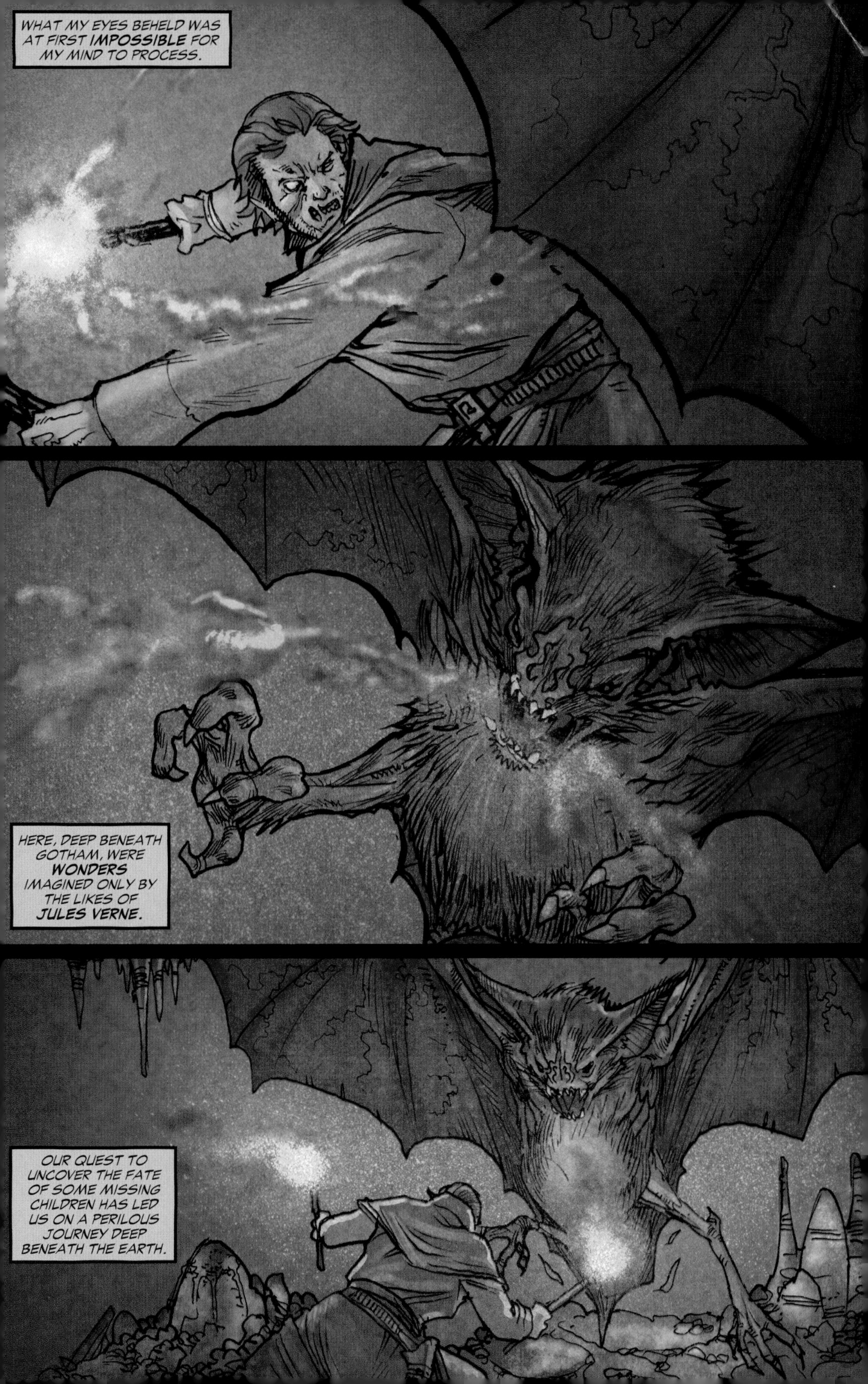
WHAT MY EYES BEHELD WAS AT FIRST IMPOSSIBLE FOR MY MIND TO PROCESS.
HERE, DEEP BENEATH GOTHAM, WERE WONDERS IMAGINED ONLY BY THE LIKES OF JULES VERNE.
OUR QUEST TO UNCOVER THE FATE OF SOME MISSING CHILDREN HAS LED US ON A PERILOUS JOURNEY DEEP BENEATH THE EARTH.

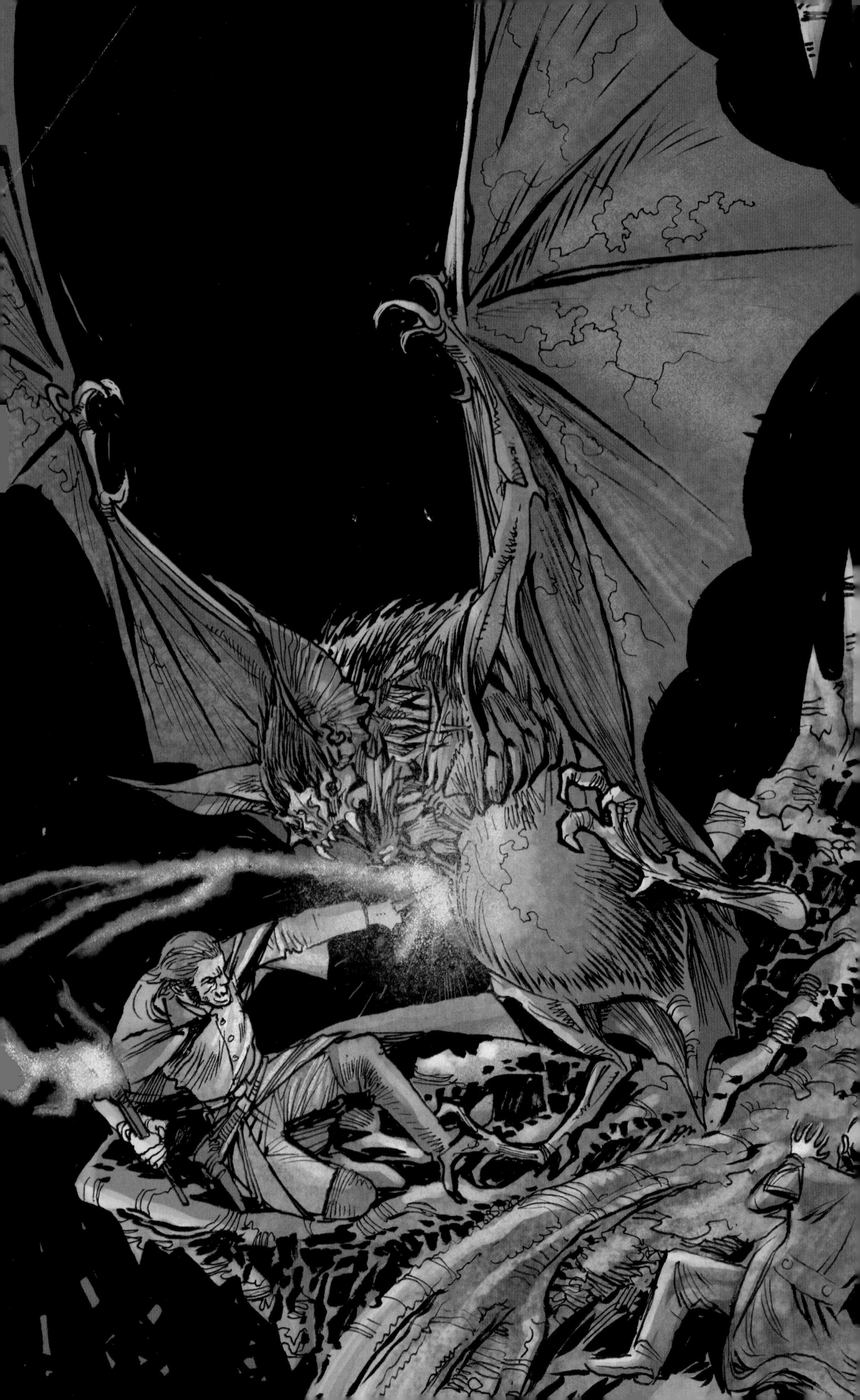

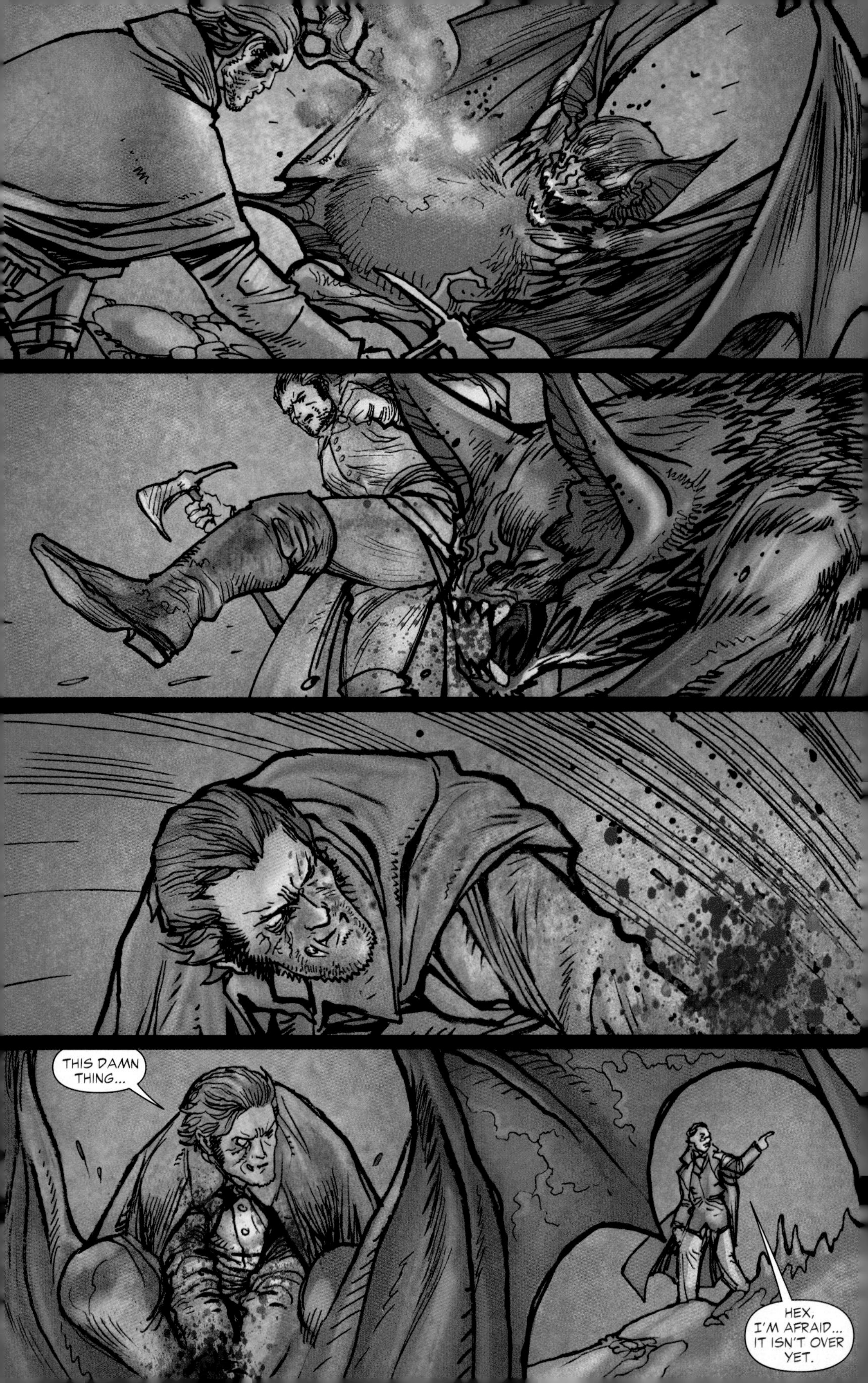
THIS DAMN THING...
HEX, I'M AFRAID... IT ISN'T OVER YET.

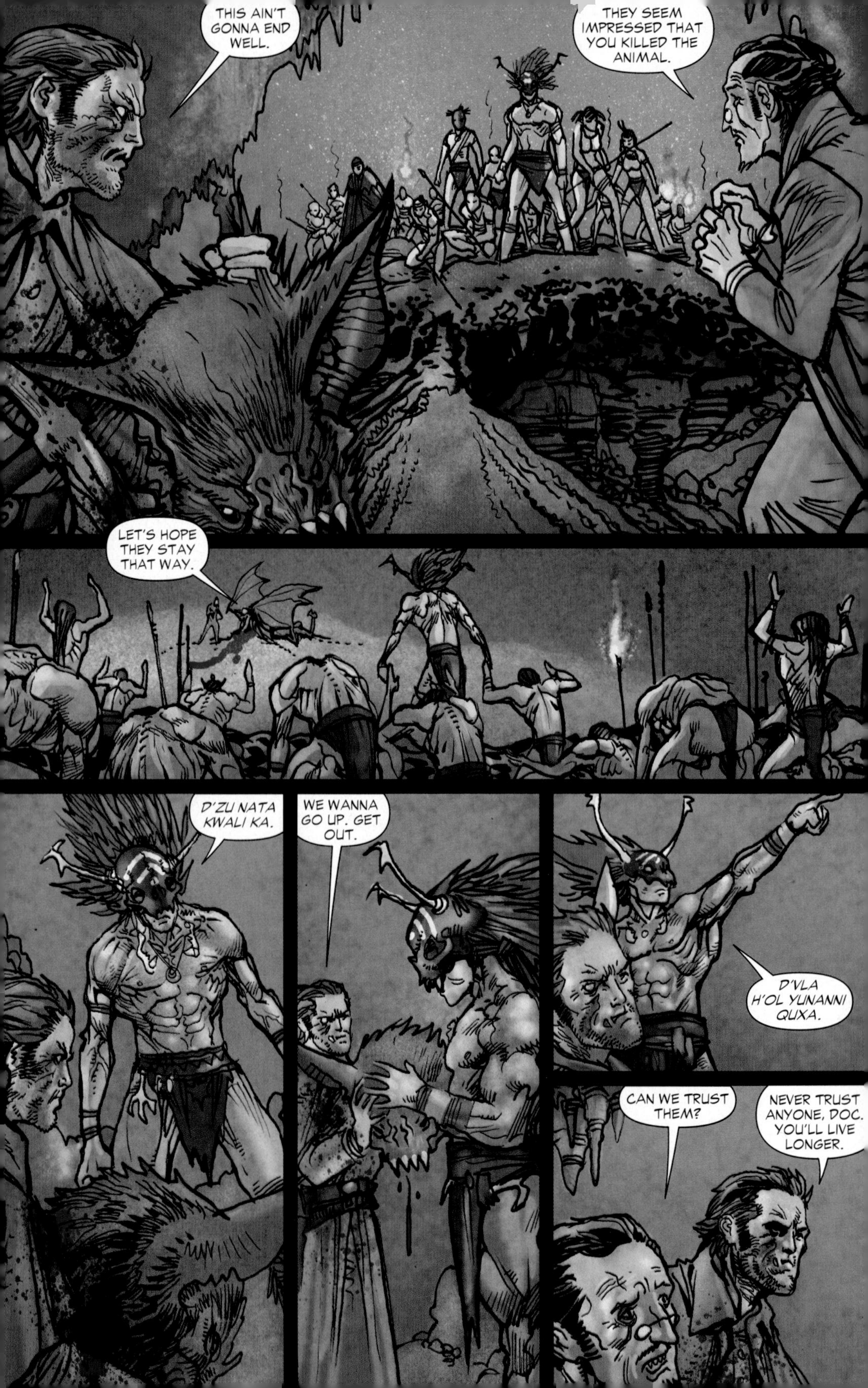
THIS AIN'T GONNA END WELL.
THEY SEEM IMPRESSED THAT YOU KILLED THE ANIMAL.
LET'S HOPE THEY STAY THAT WAY.
D'ZU NATA KWALI KA.
WE WANNA GO UP. GET OUT.
D'VLA H'OL YUNANNI QUXA.
CAN WE TRUST THEM?
NEVER TRUST ANYONE, DOC. YOU'LL LIVE LONGER.

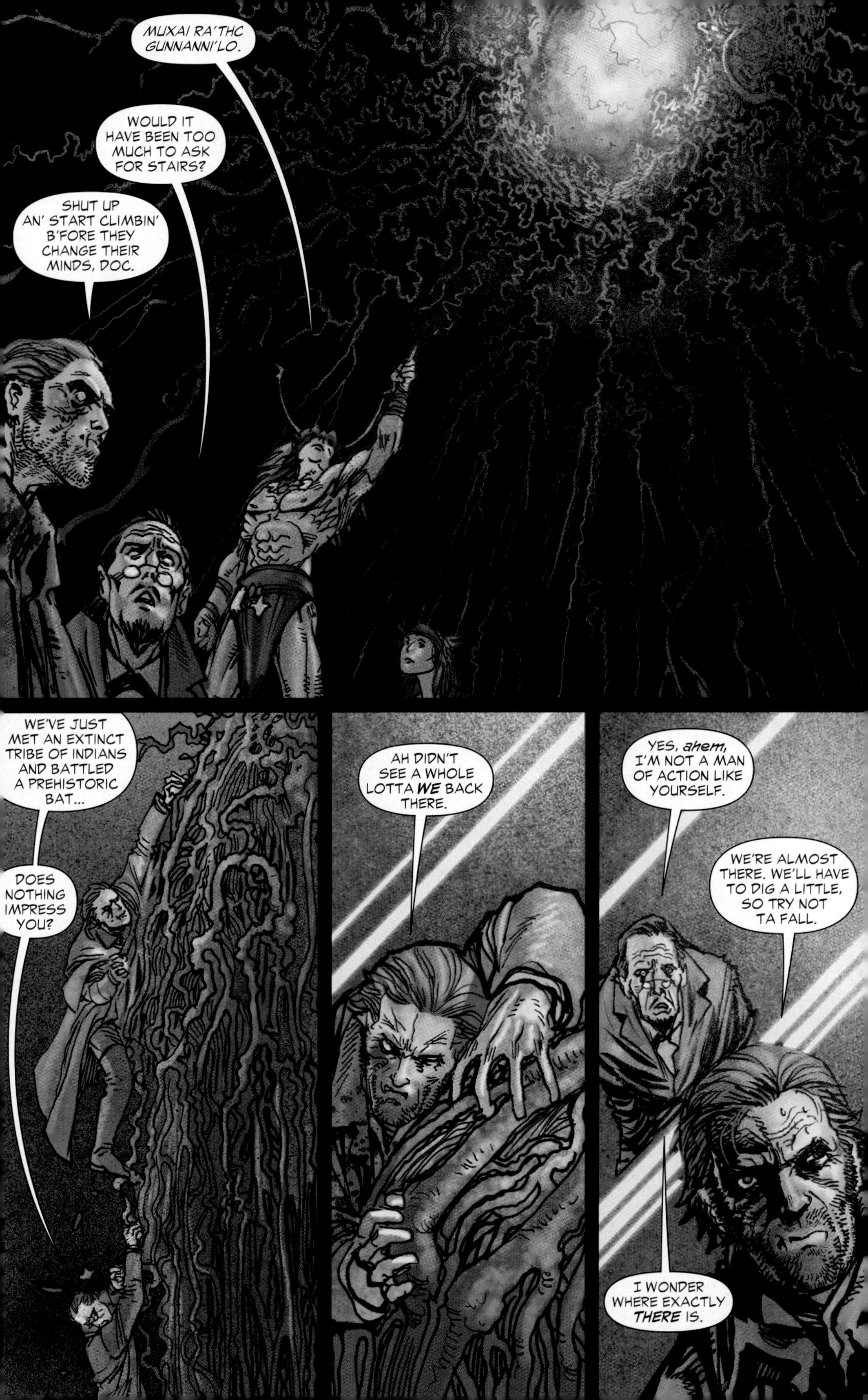
MUXAI RA'THC GUNNANNI'LO.
WOULD IT HAVE BEEN TOO MUCH TO ASK FOR STAIRS?
SHUT UP AN' START CLIMBIN' B'FORE THEY CHANGE THEIR MINDS, DOC.
WE'VE JUST MET AN EXTINCT TRIBE OF INDIANS AND BATTLED A PREHISTORIC BAT...
DOES NOTHING IMPRESS YOU?
AH DIDN'T SEE A WHOLE LOTTA *WE* BACK THERE.
YES, *ahem,* I'M NOT A MAN OF ACTION LIKE YOURSELF.
WE'RE ALMOST THERE. WE'LL HAVE TO DIG A LITTLE, SO TRY NOT TA FALL.
I WONDER WHERE EXACTLY *THERE* IS.

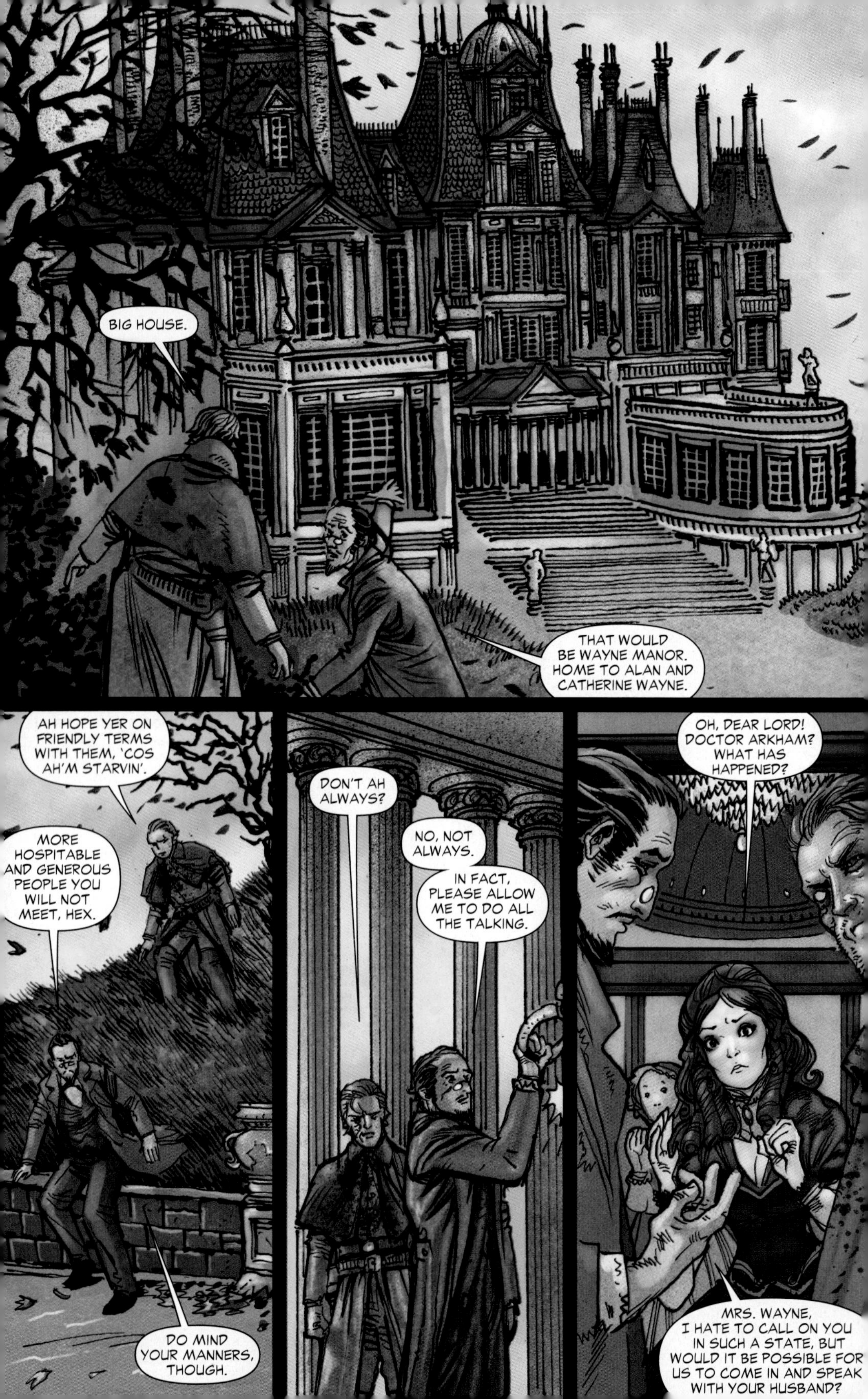
BIG HOUSE.
THAT WOULD BE WAYNE MANOR. HOME TO ALAN AND CATHERINE WAYNE.
AH HOPE YER ON FRIENDLY TERMS WITH THEM, 'COS AH'M STARVIN'.
MORE HOSPITABLE AND GENEROUS PEOPLE YOU WILL NOT MEET, HEX.
DO MIND YOUR MANNERS, THOUGH.
DON'T AH ALWAYS?
NO, NOT ALWAYS.
IN FACT, PLEASE ALLOW ME TO DO ALL THE TALKING.
OH, DEAR LORD! DOCTOR ARKHAM? WHAT HAS HAPPENED?
MRS. WAYNE, I HATE TO CALL ON YOU IN SUCH A STATE, BUT WOULD IT BE POSSIBLE FOR US TO COME IN AND SPEAK WITH YOUR HUSBAND?

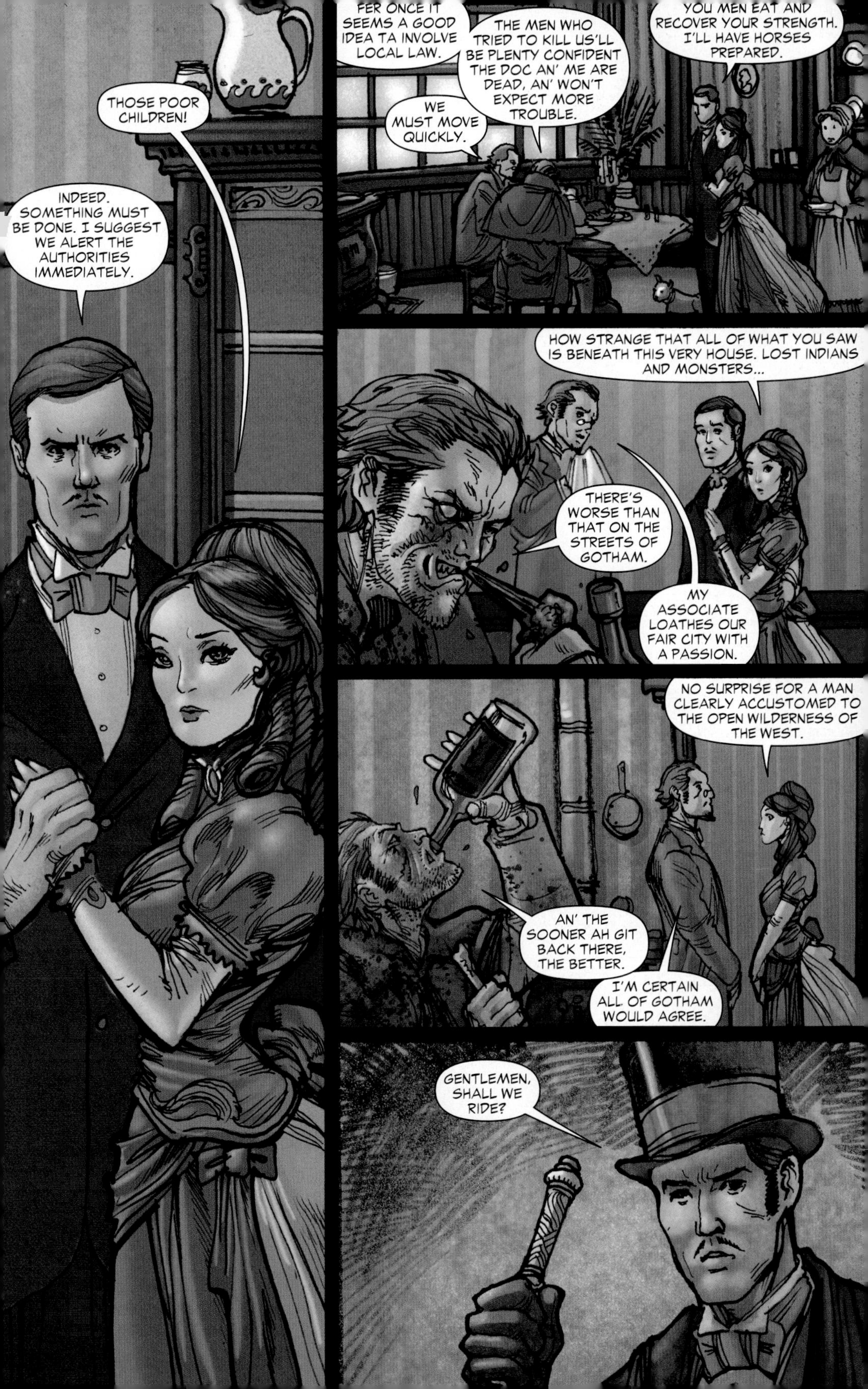
THOSE POOR CHILDREN!
INDEED. SOMETHING MUST BE DONE. I SUGGEST WE ALERT THE AUTHORITIES IMMEDIATELY.
FER ONCE IT SEEMS A GOOD IDEA TA INVOLVE LOCAL LAW.
THE MEN WHO TRIED TO KILL US'LL BE PLENTY CONFIDENT THE DOC AN' ME ARE DEAD, AN' WON'T EXPECT MORE TROUBLE.
WE MUST MOVE QUICKLY.
YOU MEN EAT AND RECOVER YOUR STRENGTH. I'LL HAVE HORSES PREPARED.
HOW STRANGE THAT ALL OF WHAT YOU SAW IS BENEATH THIS VERY HOUSE. LOST INDIANS AND MONSTERS...
THERE'S WORSE THAN THAT ON THE STREETS OF GOTHAM.
MY ASSOCIATE LOATHES OUR FAIR CITY WITH A PASSION.
NO SURPRISE FOR A MAN CLEARLY ACCUSTOMED TO THE OPEN WILDERNESS OF THE WEST.
AN' THE SOONER AH GIT BACK THERE, THE BETTER.
I'M CERTAIN ALL OF GOTHAM WOULD AGREE.
GENTLEMEN, SHALL WE RIDE?

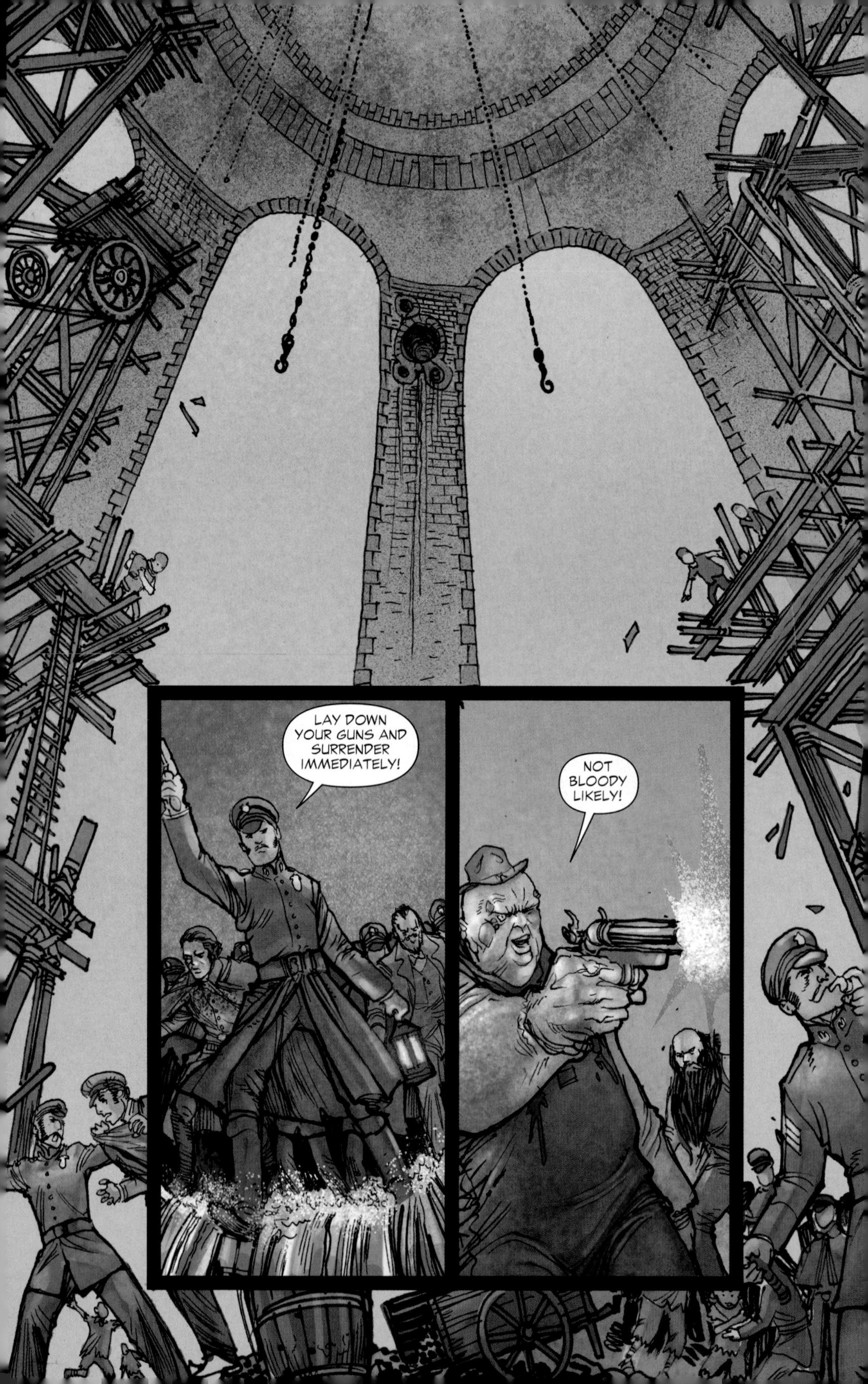
LAY DOWN YOUR GUNS AND SURRENDER IMMEDIATELY!
NOT BLOODY LIKELY!

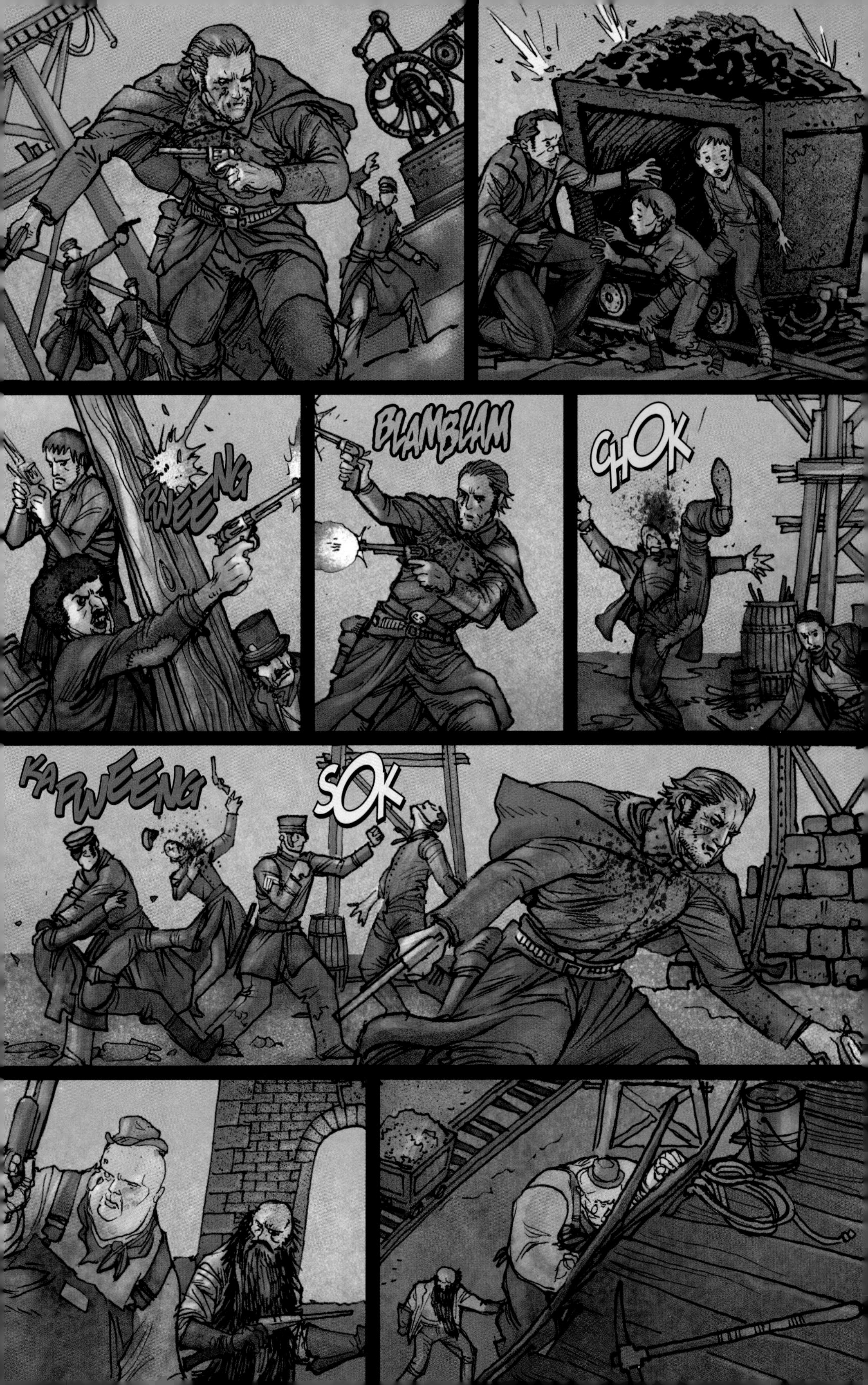
PWEENG
BLAMBLAM
CHOK
KAPWEENG
SOK

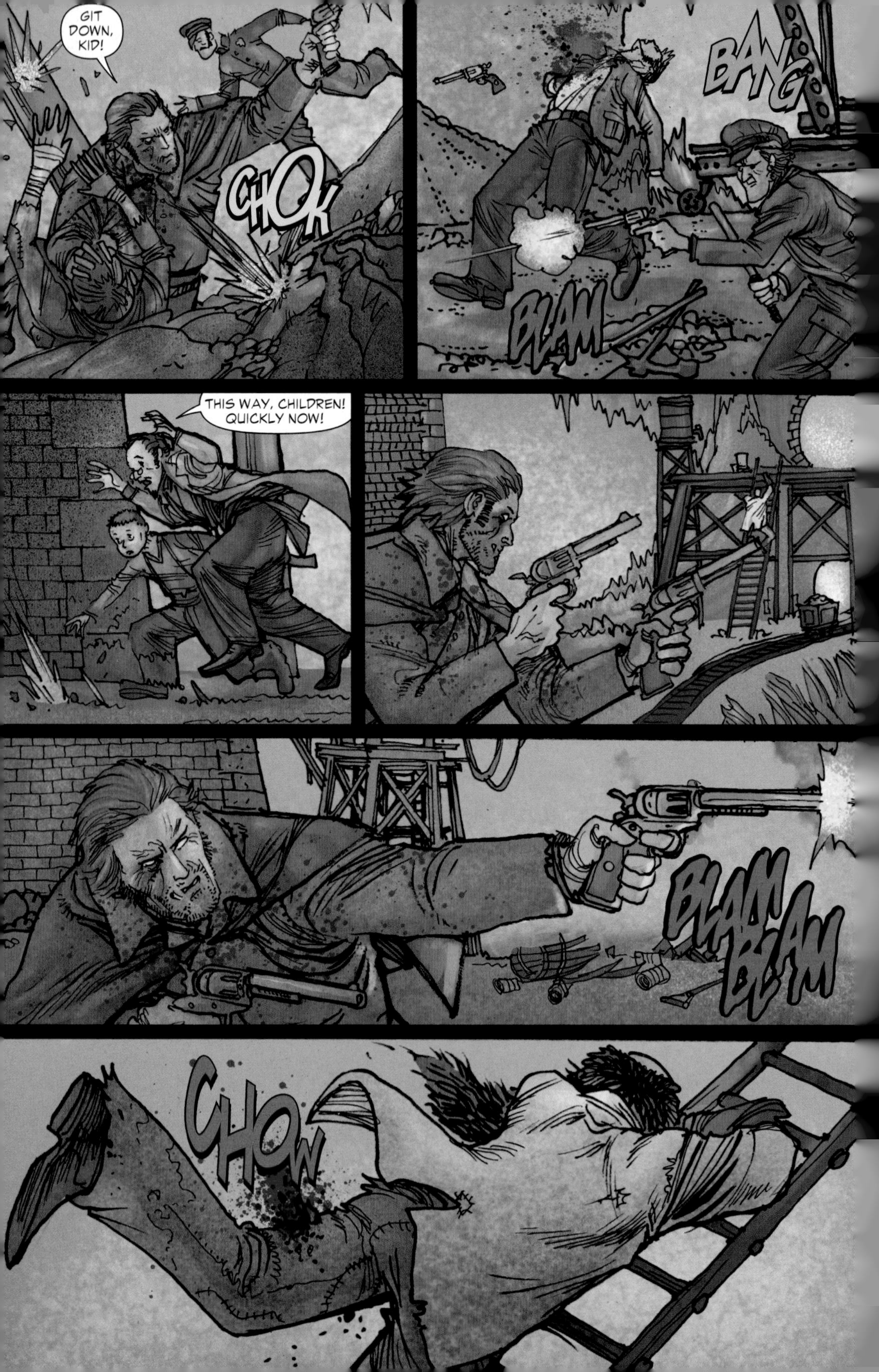
GIT DOWN, KID!
CHOK
BANG
BLAM
THIS WAY, CHILDREN! QUICKLY NOW!
BLAM
BLAM
CHOW

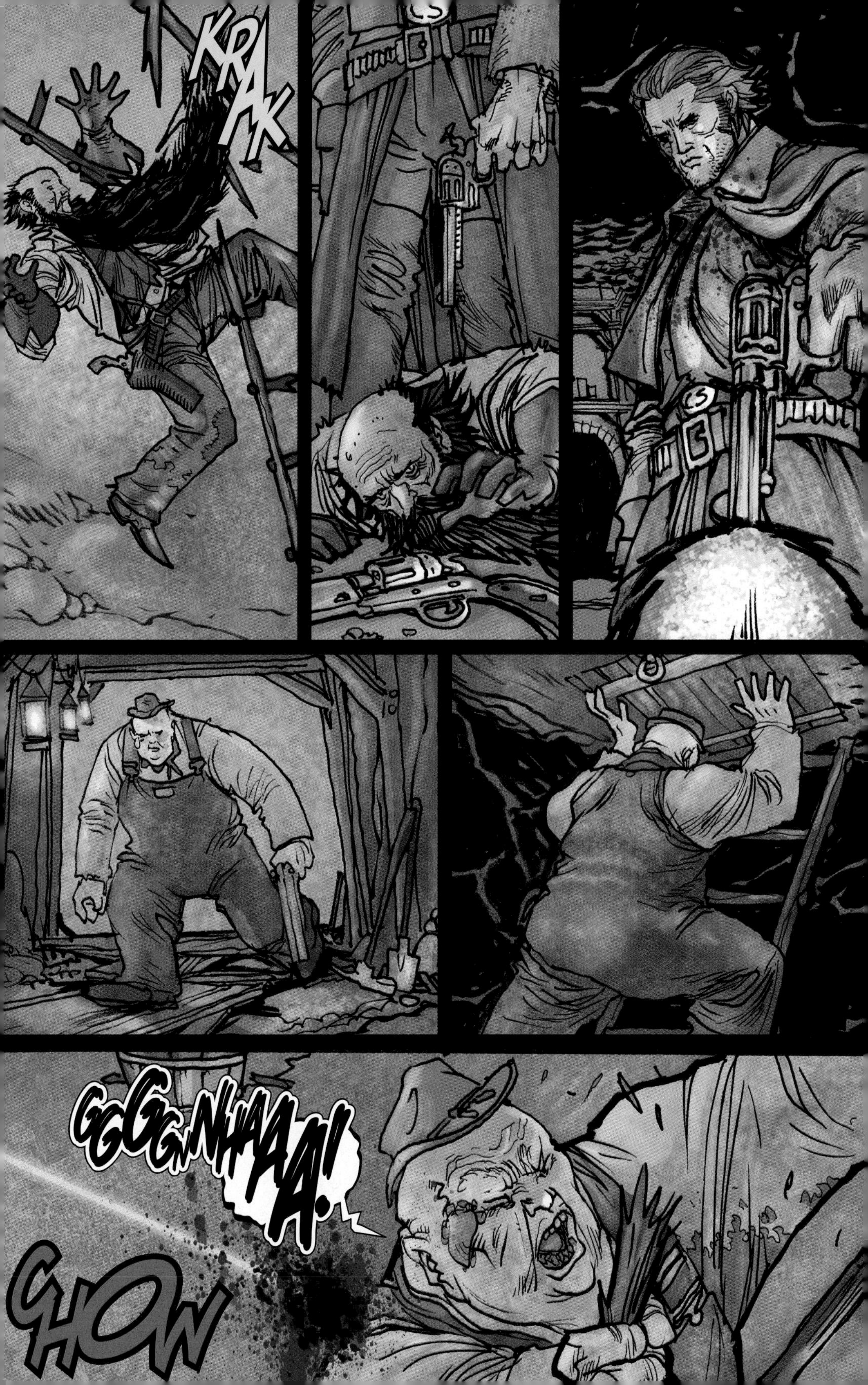
KRAK
GGGGNHAAAA!
CHOW

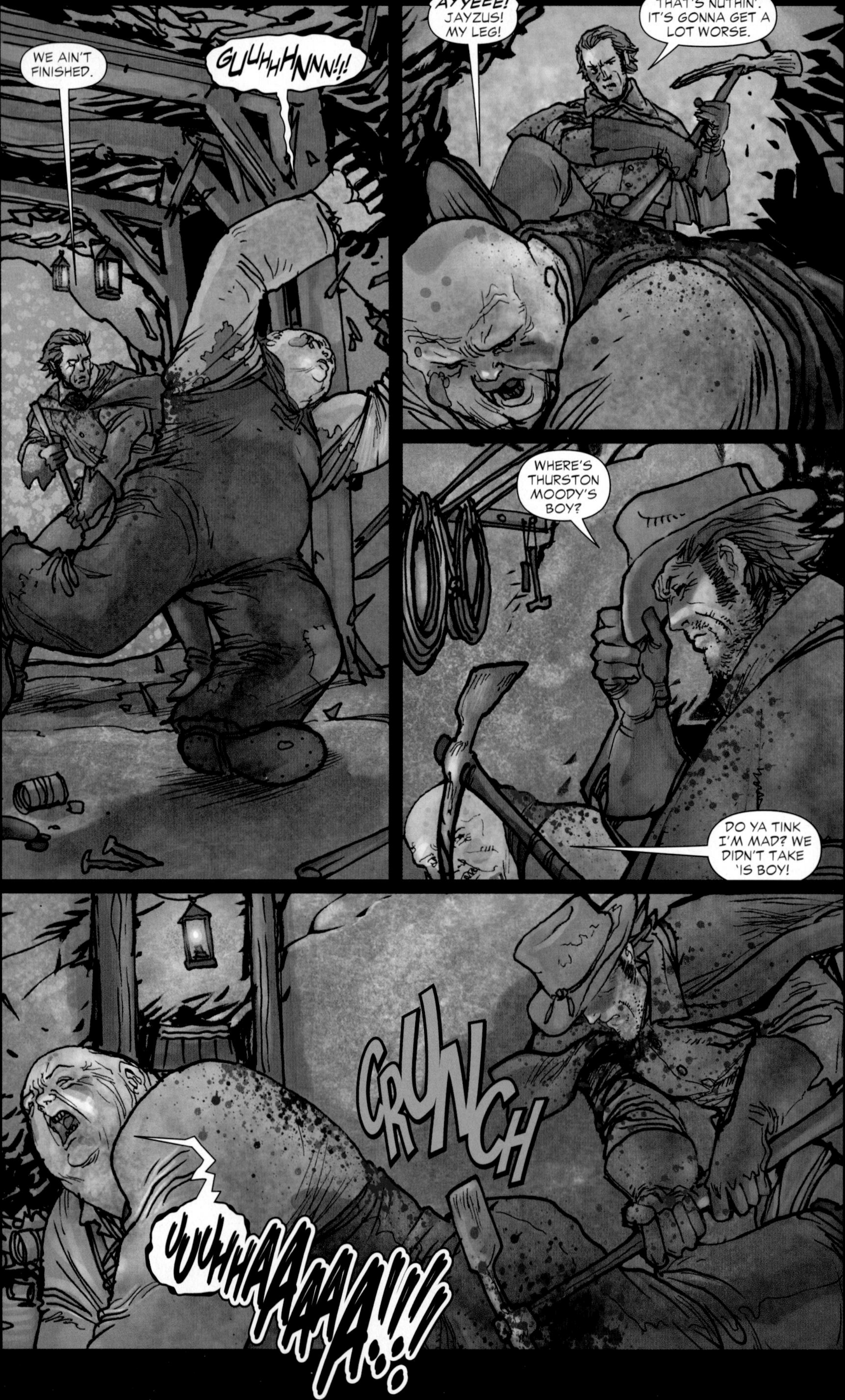
WE AIN'T FINISHED.
GUUHHHNNN!!!
AYYEEE! JAYZUS! MY LEG!
THAT'S NUTHIN'. IT'S GONNA GET A LOT WORSE.
WHERE'S THURSTON MOODY'S BOY?
DO YA TINK I'M MAD? WE DIDN'T TAKE 'IS BOY!
CRUNCH
UUUHHAAAAAAA!!!

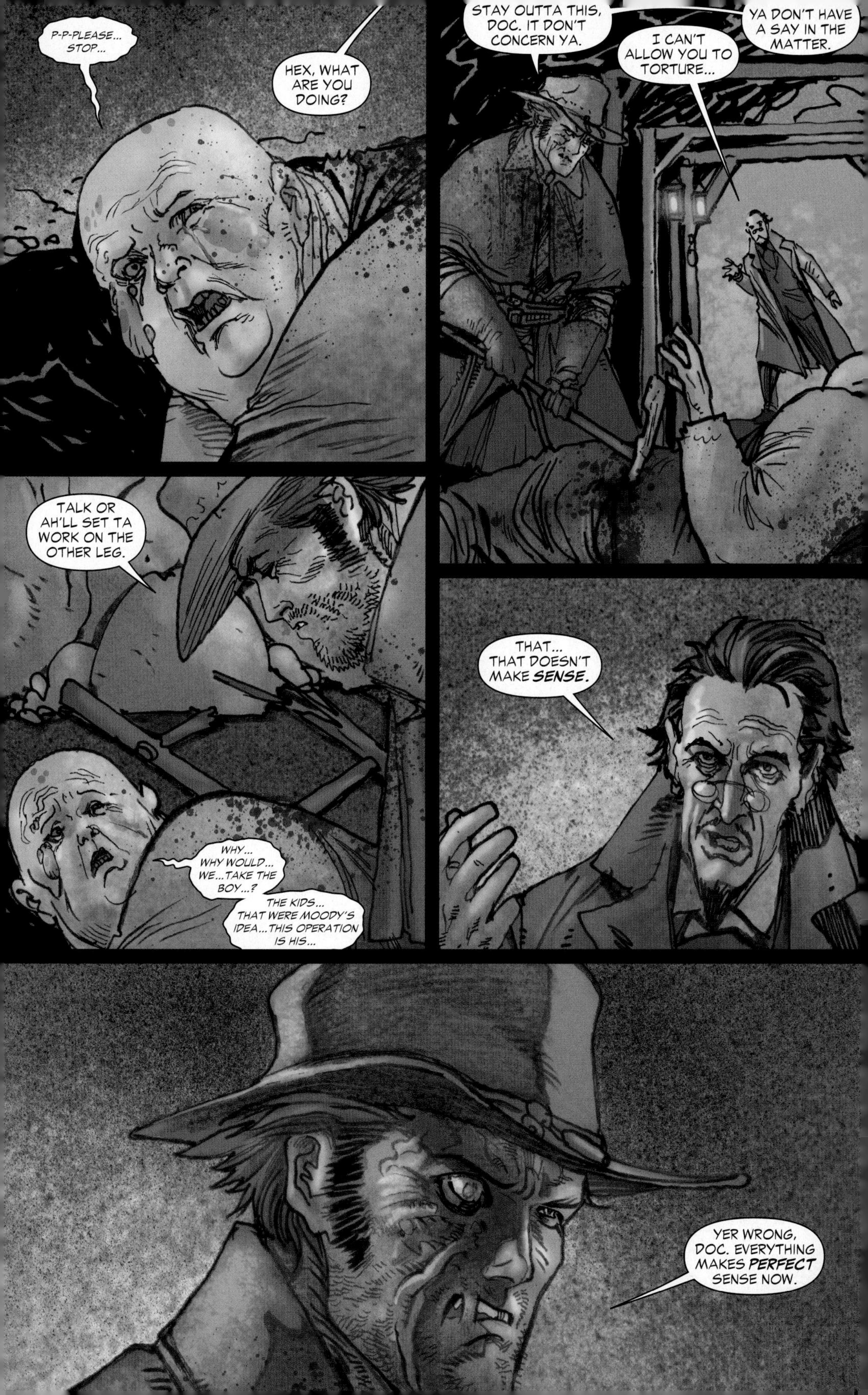
P-P-PLEASE... STOP...
HEX, WHAT ARE YOU DOING?
STAY OUTTA THIS, DOC. IT DON'T CONCERN YA.
I CAN'T ALLOW YOU TO TORTURE...
YA DON'T HAVE A SAY IN THE MATTER.
TALK OR AH'LL SET TA WORK ON THE OTHER LEG.
WHY... WHY WOULD... WE...TAKE THE BOY...?
THE KIDS... THAT WERE MOODY'S IDEA...THIS OPERATION IS HIS...
THAT... THAT DOESN'T MAKE SENSE.
YER WRONG, DOC. EVERYTHING MAKES PERFECT SENSE NOW.

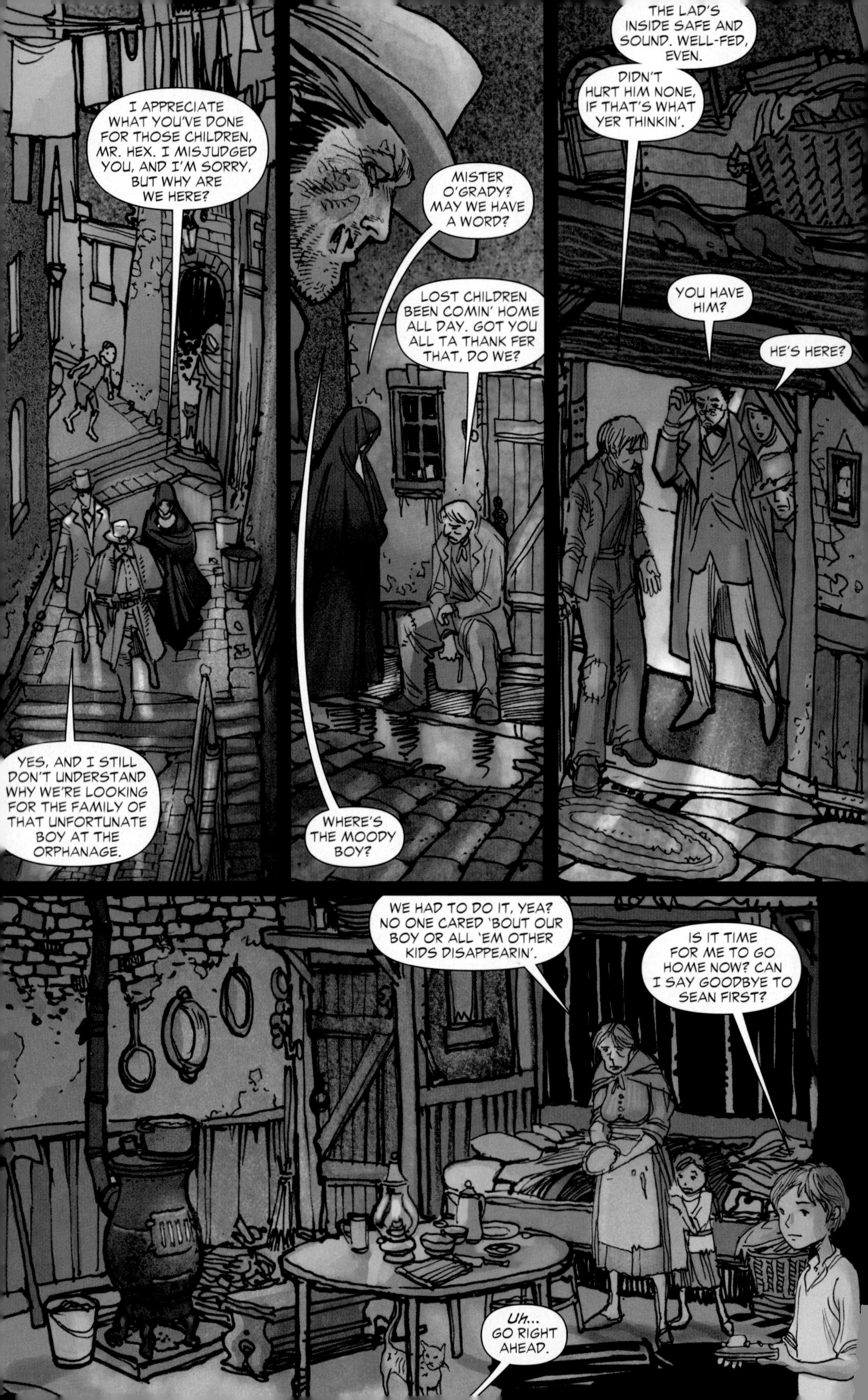
I APPRECIATE WHAT YOU'VE DONE FOR THOSE CHILDREN, MR. HEX. I MISJUDGED YOU, AND I'M SORRY, BUT WHY ARE WE HERE?
YES, AND I STILL DON'T UNDERSTAND WHY WE'RE LOOKING FOR THE FAMILY OF THAT UNFORTUNATE BOY AT THE ORPHANAGE.
MISTER O'GRADY? MAY WE HAVE A WORD?
LOST CHILDREN BEEN COMIN' HOME ALL DAY. GOT YOU ALL TA THANK FER THAT, DO WE?
WHERE'S THE MOODY BOY?
THE LAD'S INSIDE SAFE AND SOUND. WELL-FED, EVEN.
DIDN'T HURT HIM NONE, IF THAT'S WHAT YER THINKIN'.
YOU HAVE HIM?
HE'S HERE?
WE HAD TO DO IT, YEA? NO ONE CARED 'BOUT OUR BOY OR ALL 'EM OTHER KIDS DISAPPEARIN'.
IS IT TIME FOR ME TO GO HOME NOW? CAN I SAY GOODBYE TO SEAN FIRST?
*Uh...* GO RIGHT AHEAD.

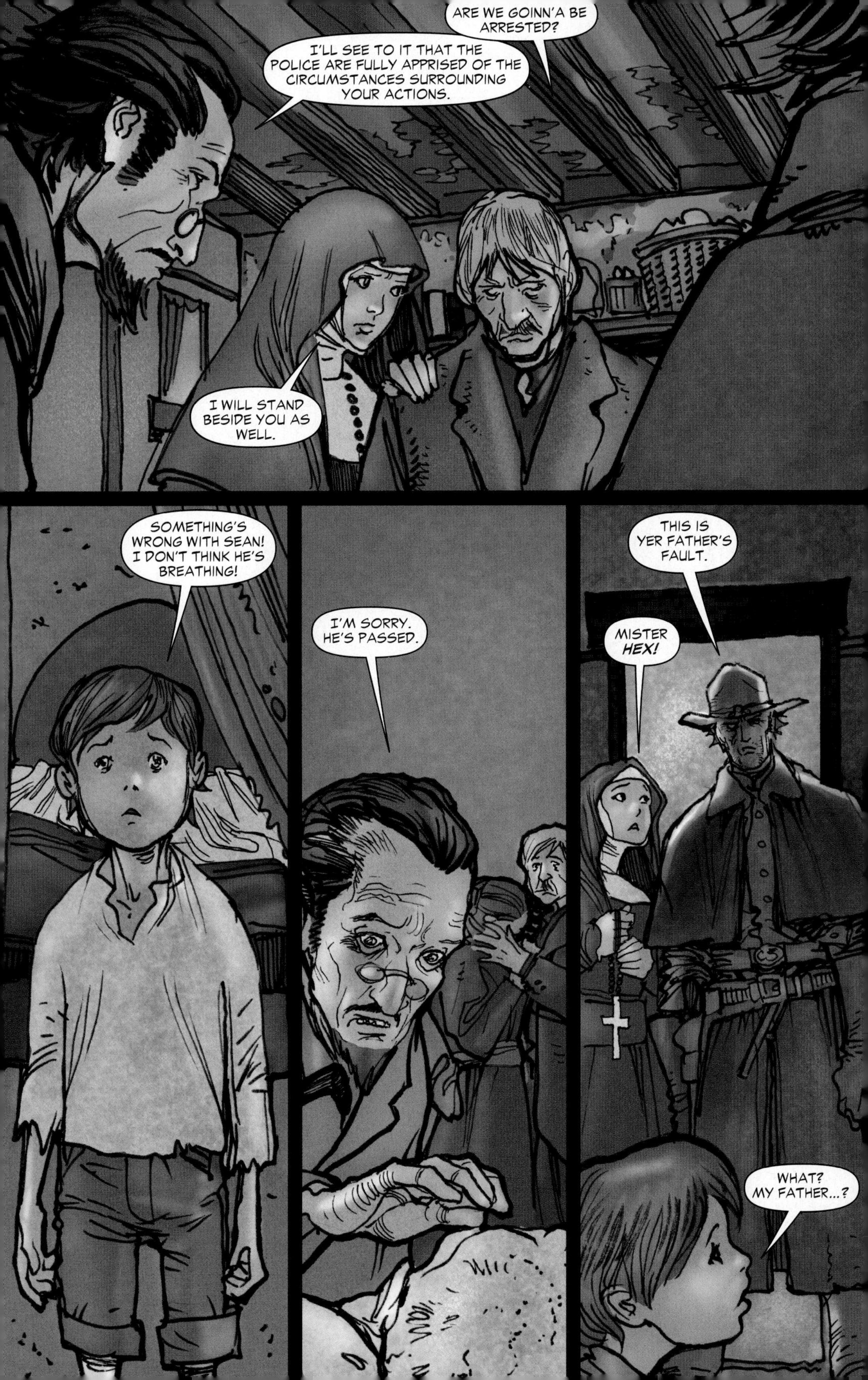
ARE WE GOINN'A BE ARRESTED?
I'LL SEE TO IT THAT THE POLICE ARE FULLY APPRISED OF THE CIRCUMSTANCES SURROUNDING YOUR ACTIONS.
I WILL STAND BESIDE YOU AS WELL.
SOMETHING'S WRONG WITH SEAN! I DON'T THINK HE'S BREATHING!
I'M SORRY. HE'S PASSED.
THIS IS YER FATHER'S FAULT.
MISTER HEX!
WHAT? MY FATHER...?

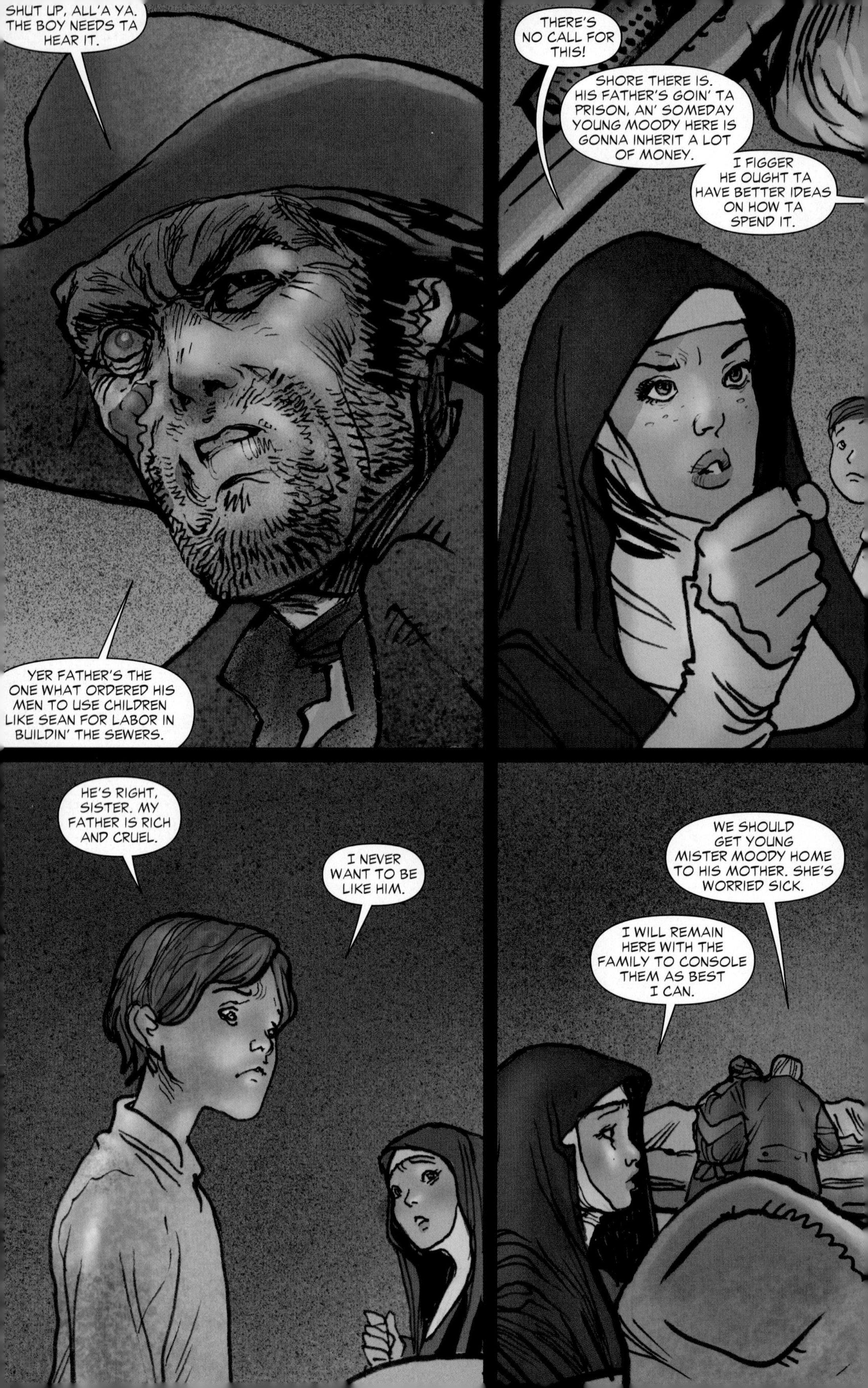
SHUT UP, ALL'A YA. THE BOY NEEDS TA HEAR IT.
YER FATHER'S THE ONE WHAT ORDERED HIS MEN TO USE CHILDREN LIKE SEAN FOR LABOR IN BUILDIN' THE SEWERS.
THERE'S NO CALL FOR THIS!
SHORE THERE IS. HIS FATHER'S GOIN' TA PRISON, AN' SOMEDAY YOUNG MOODY HERE IS GONNA INHERIT A LOT OF MONEY.
I FIGGER HE OUGHT TA HAVE BETTER IDEAS ON HOW TA SPEND IT.
HE'S RIGHT, SISTER. MY FATHER IS RICH AND CRUEL.
I NEVER WANT TO BE LIKE HIM.
WE SHOULD GET YOUNG MISTER MOODY HOME TO HIS MOTHER. SHE'S WORRIED SICK.
I WILL REMAIN HERE WITH THE FAMILY TO CONSOLE THEM AS BEST I CAN.

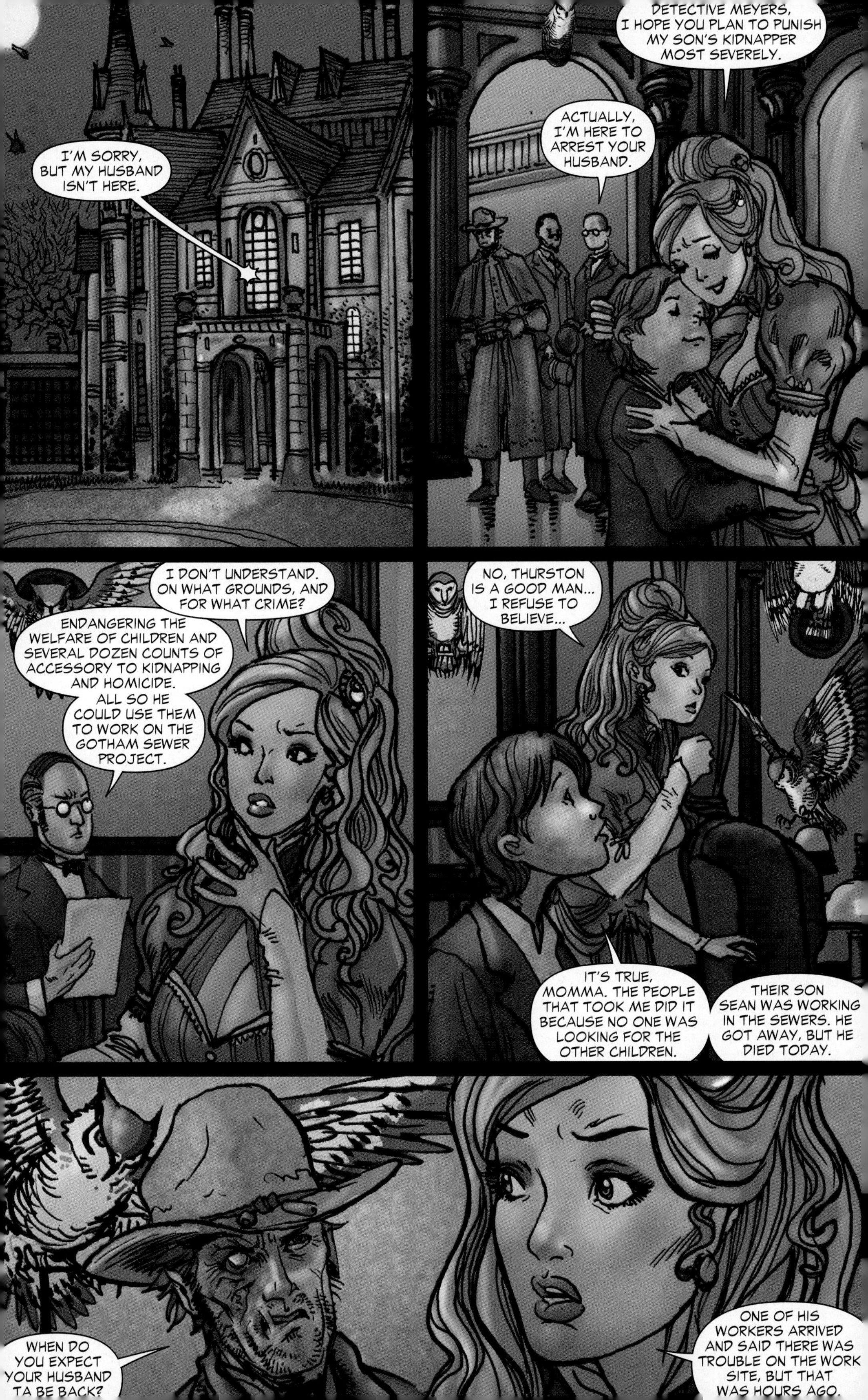
I'M SORRY, BUT MY HUSBAND ISN'T HERE.
DETECTIVE MEYERS, I HOPE YOU PLAN TO PUNISH MY SON'S KIDNAPPER MOST SEVERELY.
ACTUALLY, I'M HERE TO ARREST YOUR HUSBAND.
I DON'T UNDERSTAND. ON WHAT GROUNDS, AND FOR WHAT CRIME?
ENDANGERING THE WELFARE OF CHILDREN AND SEVERAL DOZEN COUNTS OF ACCESSORY TO KIDNAPPING AND HOMICIDE.
ALL SO HE COULD USE THEM TO WORK ON THE GOTHAM SEWER PROJECT.
NO, THURSTON IS A GOOD MAN... I REFUSE TO BELIEVE...
IT'S TRUE, MOMMA. THE PEOPLE THAT TOOK ME DID IT BECAUSE NO ONE WAS LOOKING FOR THE OTHER CHILDREN.
THEIR SON SEAN WAS WORKING IN THE SEWERS. HE GOT AWAY, BUT HE DIED TODAY.
WHEN DO YOU EXPECT YOUR HUSBAND TA BE BACK?
ONE OF HIS WORKERS ARRIVED AND SAID THERE WAS TROUBLE ON THE WORK SITE, BUT THAT WAS HOURS AGO.

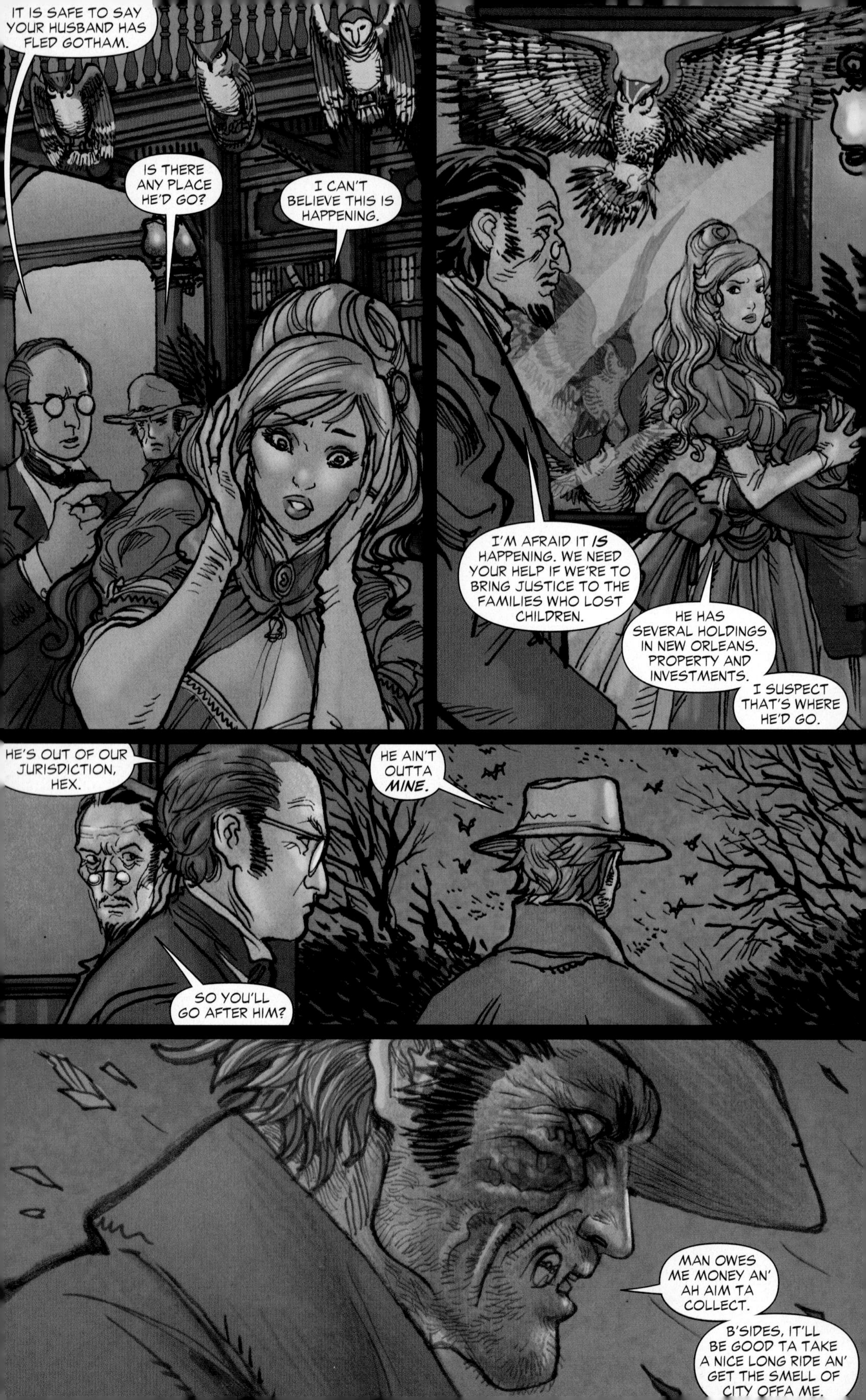
IT IS SAFE TO SAY YOUR HUSBAND HAS FLED GOTHAM.
IS THERE ANY PLACE HE'D GO?
I CAN'T BELIEVE THIS IS HAPPENING.
I'M AFRAID IT *IS* HAPPENING. WE NEED YOUR HELP IF WE'RE TO BRING JUSTICE TO THE FAMILIES WHO LOST CHILDREN.
HE HAS SEVERAL HOLDINGS IN NEW ORLEANS. PROPERTY AND INVESTMENTS.
I SUSPECT THAT'S WHERE HE'D GO.
HE'S OUT OF OUR JURISDICTION, HEX.
HE AIN'T OUTTA *MINE.*
SO YOU'LL GO AFTER HIM?
MAN OWES ME MONEY AN' AH AIM TA COLLECT.
B'SIDES, IT'LL BE GOOD TA TAKE A NICE LONG RIDE AN' GET THE SMELL OF CITY OFFA ME.

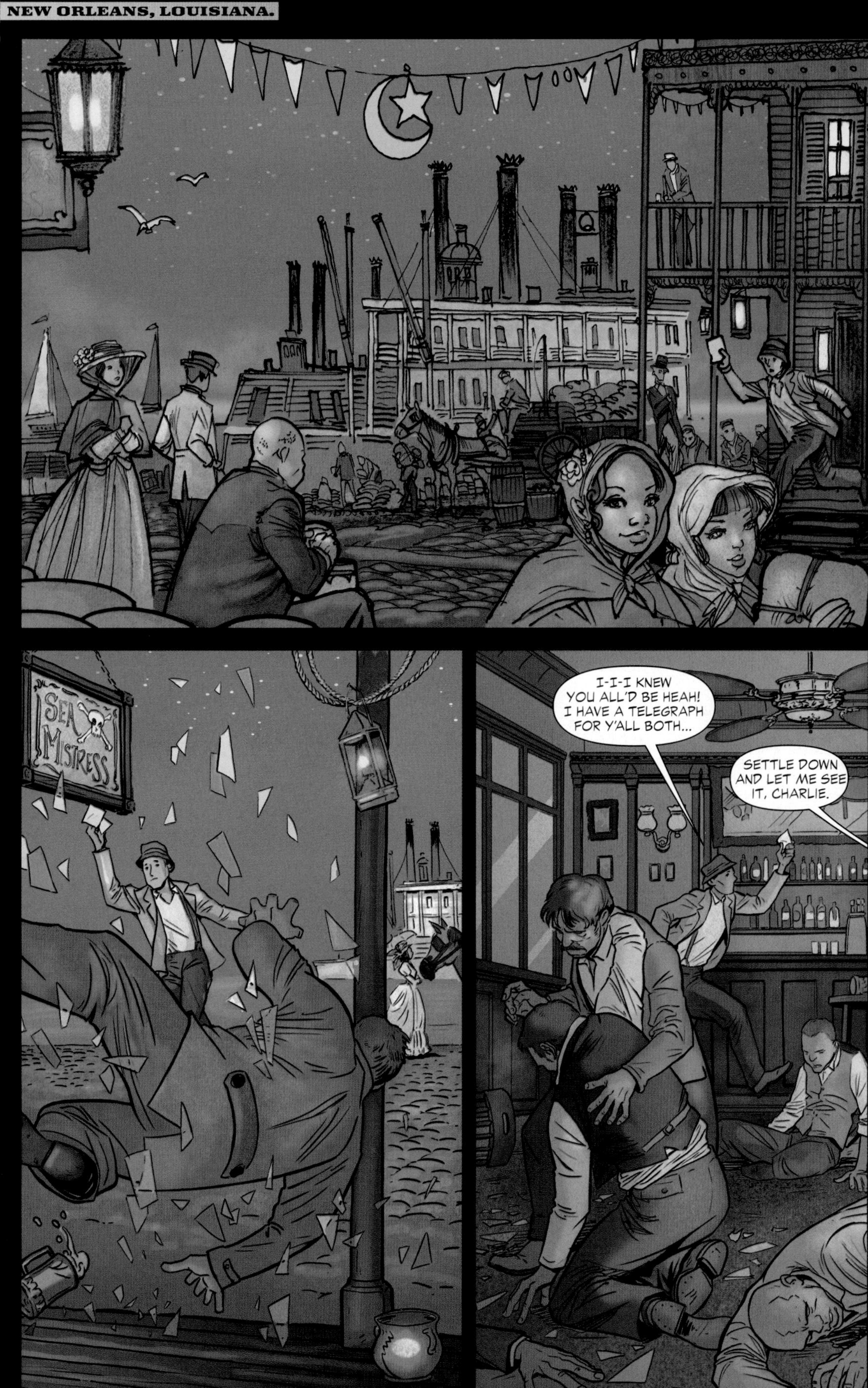
NEW ORLEANS, LOUISIANA.
SEA MISTRESS
I-I-I KNEW YOU ALL'D BE HEAH! I HAVE A TELEGRAPH FOR Y'ALL BOTH...
SETTLE DOWN AND LET ME SEE IT, CHARLIE.

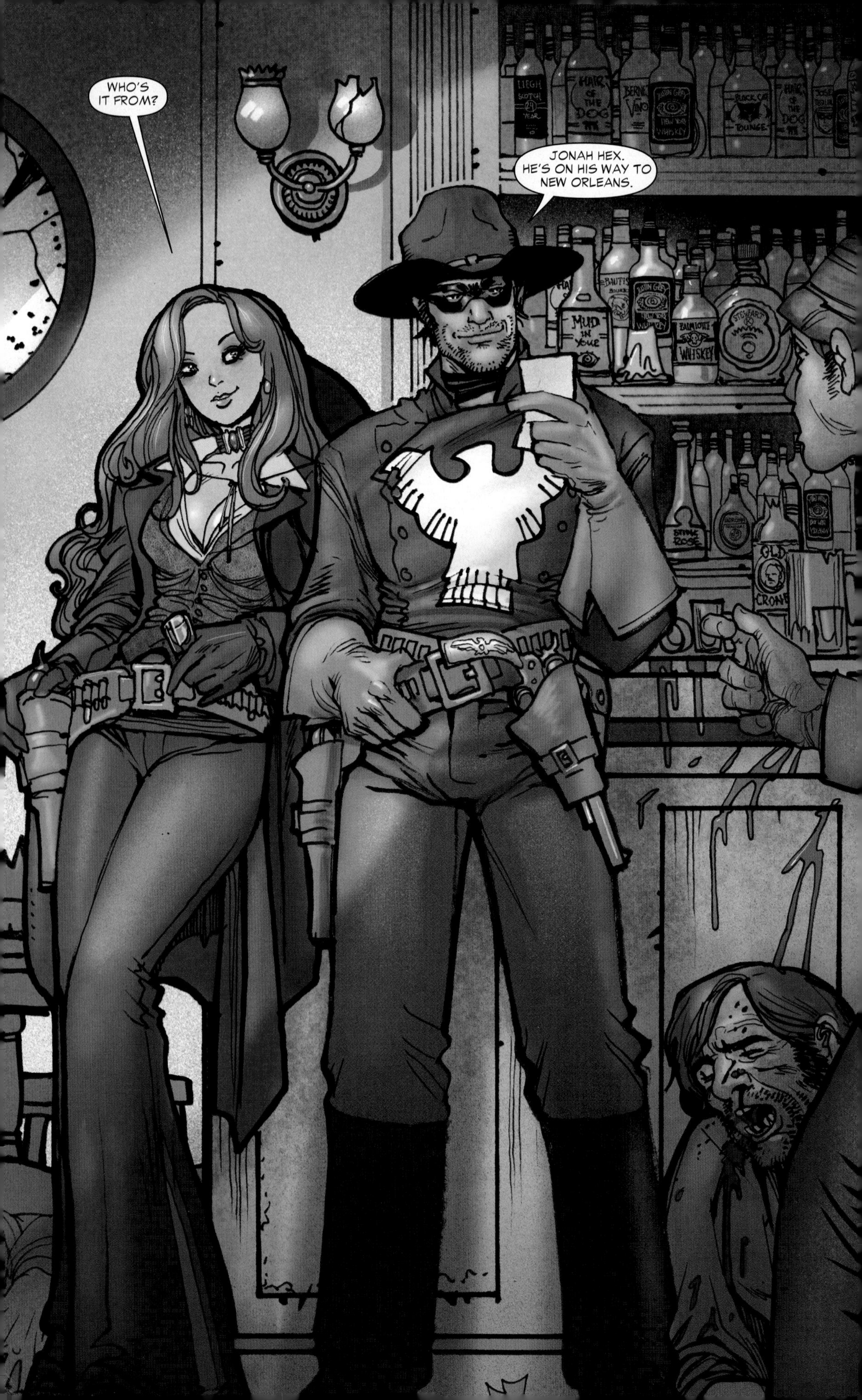
WHO'S IT FROM?
JONAH HEX. HE'S ON HIS WAY TO NEW ORLEANS.

EL DIABLO

140

JUSTIN GRAY
JIMMY PALMIOTTI
Writers

JORDI BERNET
Artist

ROB SCHWAGER
Colorist

ROB LEIGH
Letterer

THE BARBARY GHOST

156

JIMMY PALMIOTTI
JUSTIN GRAY
Writers

PHIL WINSLADE
Artist

DOMINIC REGAN
Colorist

ROB LEIGH
Letterer

THE BARBARY GHOST created by
JIMMY PALMIOTTI, JUSTIN GRAY & PHIL WINSLADE

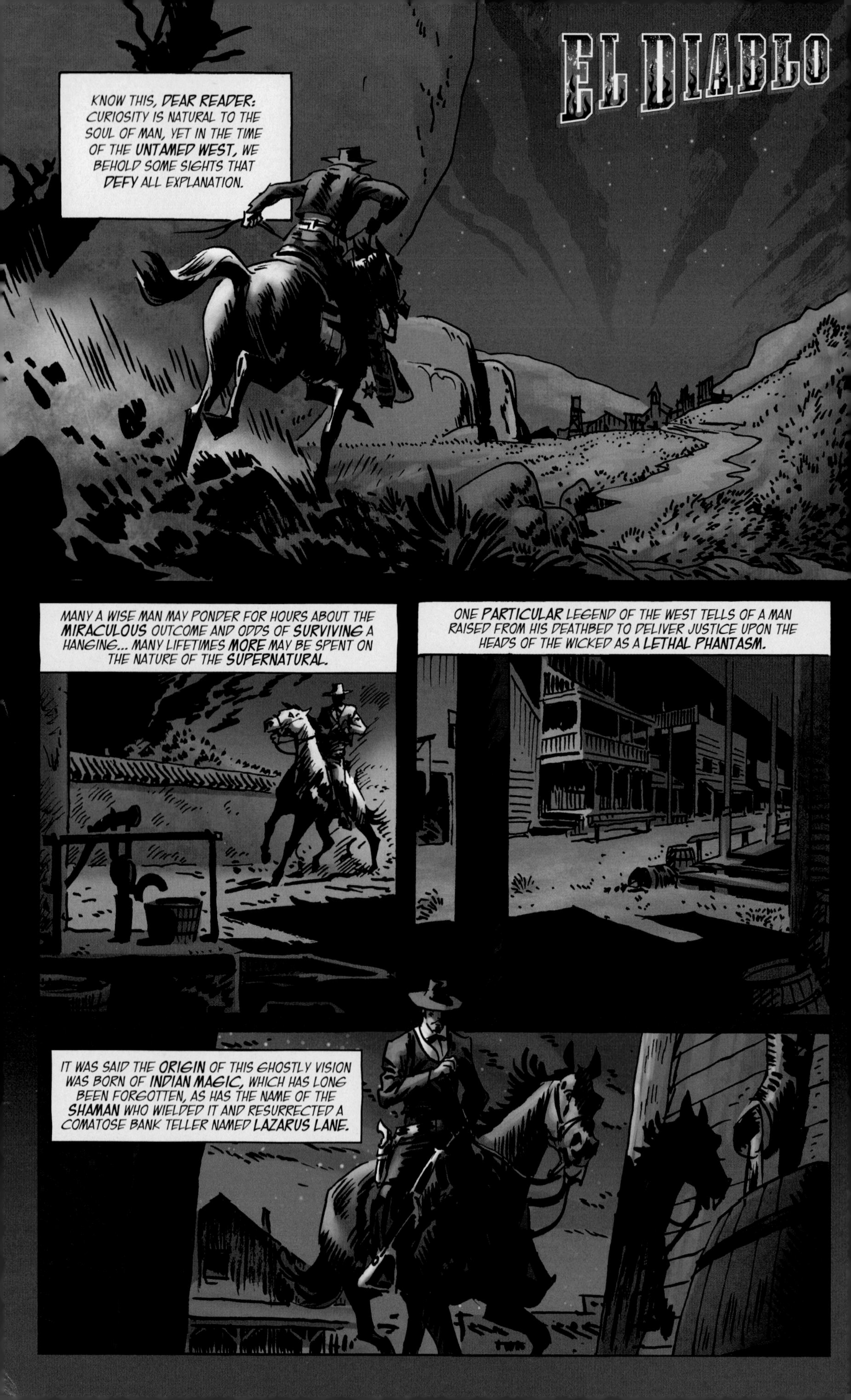
EL DIABLO
KNOW THIS, DEAR READER: CURIOSITY IS NATURAL TO THE SOUL OF MAN, YET IN THE TIME OF THE UNTAMED WEST, WE BEHOLD SOME SIGHTS THAT DEFY ALL EXPLANATION.
MANY A WISE MAN MAY PONDER FOR HOURS ABOUT THE MIRACULOUS OUTCOME AND ODDS OF SURVIVING A HANGING... MANY LIFETIMES MORE MAY BE SPENT ON THE NATURE OF THE SUPERNATURAL.
ONE PARTICULAR LEGEND OF THE WEST TELLS OF A MAN RAISED FROM HIS DEATHBED TO DELIVER JUSTICE UPON THE HEADS OF THE WICKED AS A LETHAL PHANTASM.
IT WAS SAID THE ORIGIN OF THIS GHOSTLY VISION WAS BORN OF INDIAN MAGIC, WHICH HAS LONG BEEN FORGOTTEN, AS HAS THE NAME OF THE SHAMAN WHO WIELDED IT AND RESURRECTED A COMATOSE BANK TELLER NAMED LAZARUS LANE.

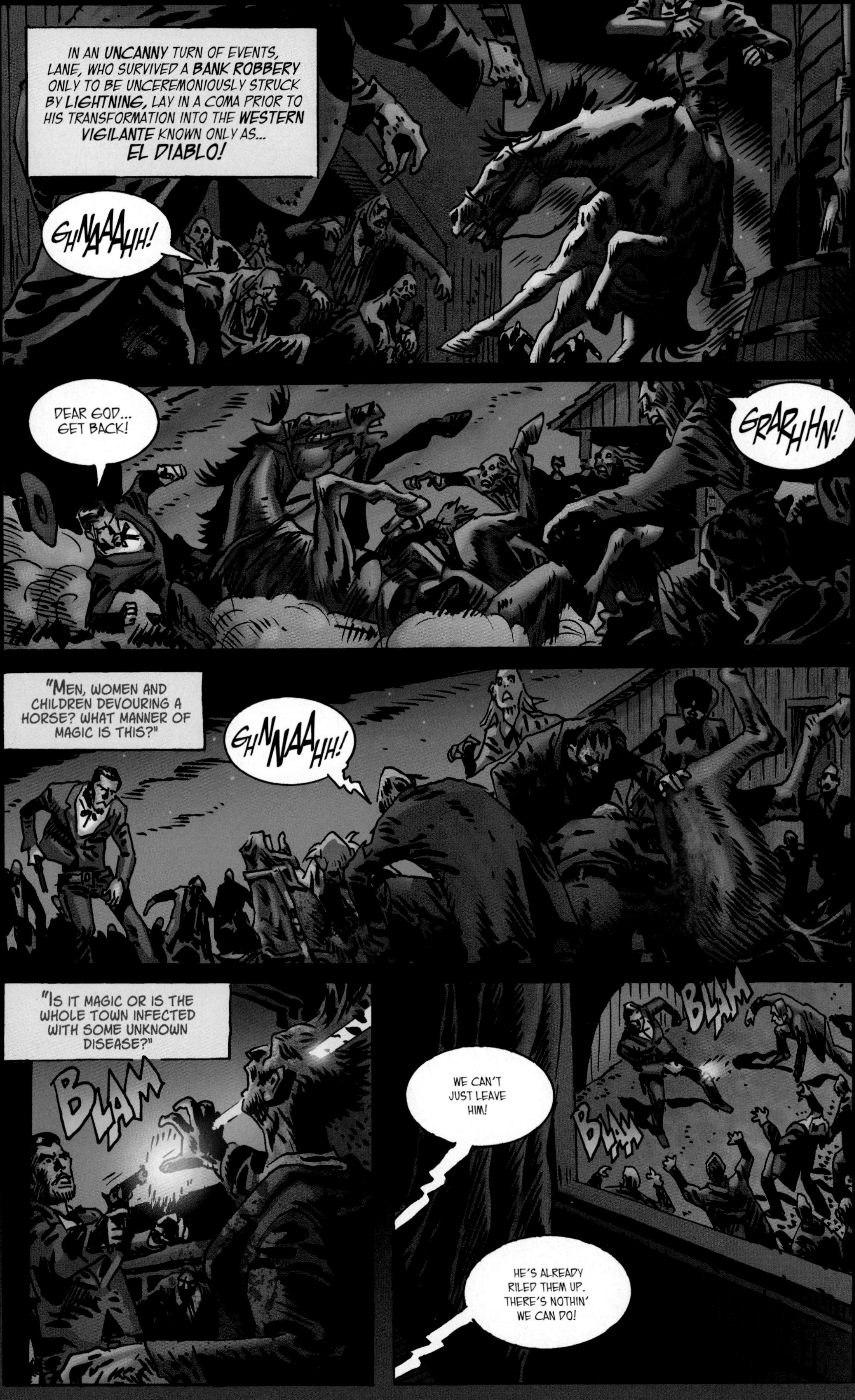
IN AN UNCANNY TURN OF EVENTS, LANE, WHO SURVIVED A BANK ROBBERY ONLY TO BE UNCEREMONIOUSLY STRUCK BY LIGHTNING, LAY IN A COMA PRIOR TO HIS TRANSFORMATION INTO THE WESTERN VIGILANTE KNOWN ONLY AS... EL DIABLO!
GHNAAAHH!
DEAR GOD... GET BACK!
GRARHHN!
"MEN, WOMEN AND CHILDREN DEVOURING A HORSE? WHAT MANNER OF MAGIC IS THIS?"
GHNNAAHH!
"IS IT MAGIC OR IS THE WHOLE TOWN INFECTED WITH SOME UNKNOWN DISEASE?"
BLAM
WE CAN'T JUST LEAVE HIM!
BLAM
BLAM
HE'S ALREADY RILED THEM UP. THERE'S NOTHIN' WE CAN DO!

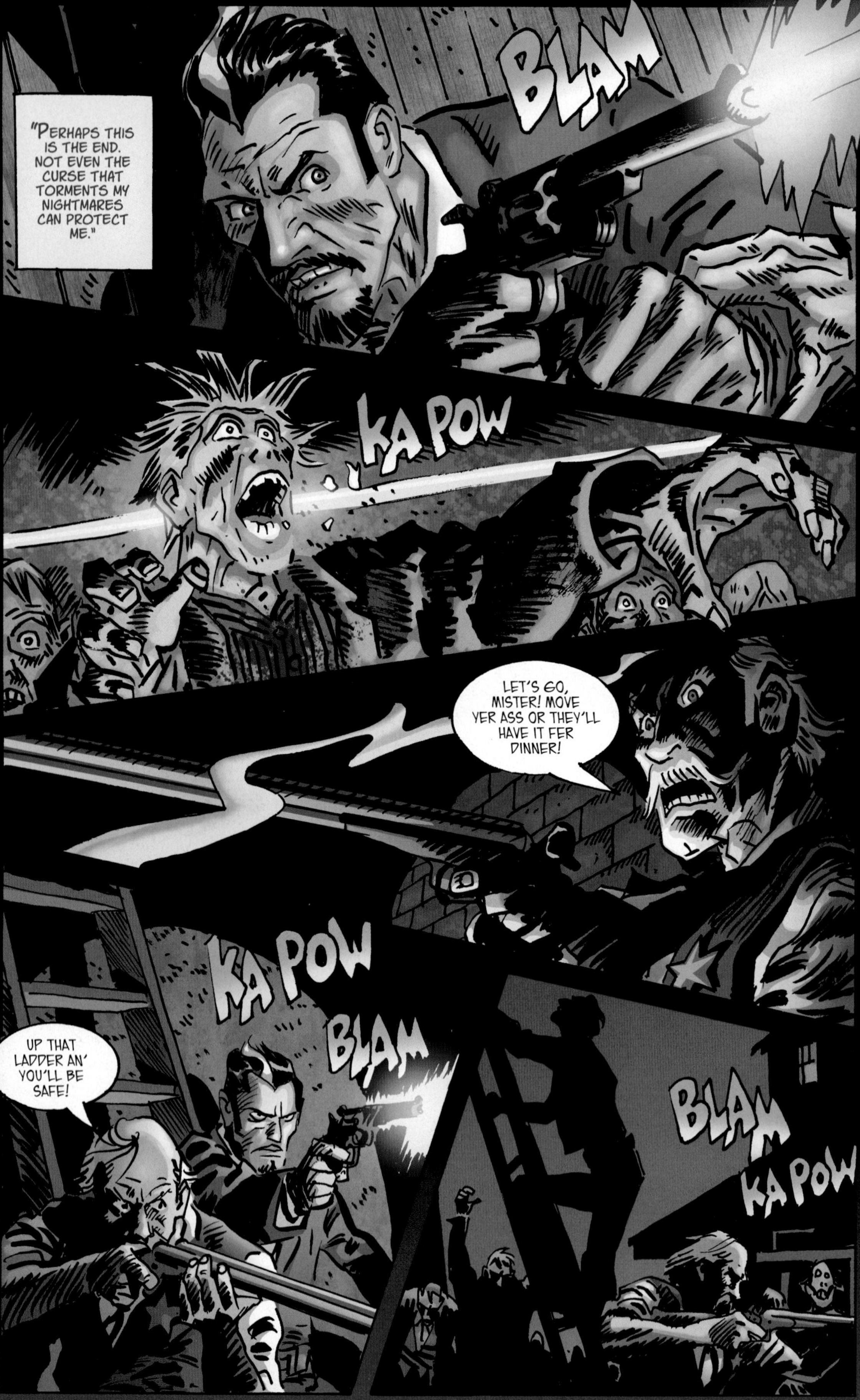
"PERHAPS THIS IS THE END. NOT EVEN THE CURSE THAT TORMENTS MY NIGHTMARES CAN PROTECT ME."
BLAM
KA POW
LET'S GO, MISTER! MOVE YER ASS OR THEY'LL HAVE IT FER DINNER!
KA POW
BLAM
UP THAT LADDER AN' YOU'LL BE SAFE!
BLAM
KA POW

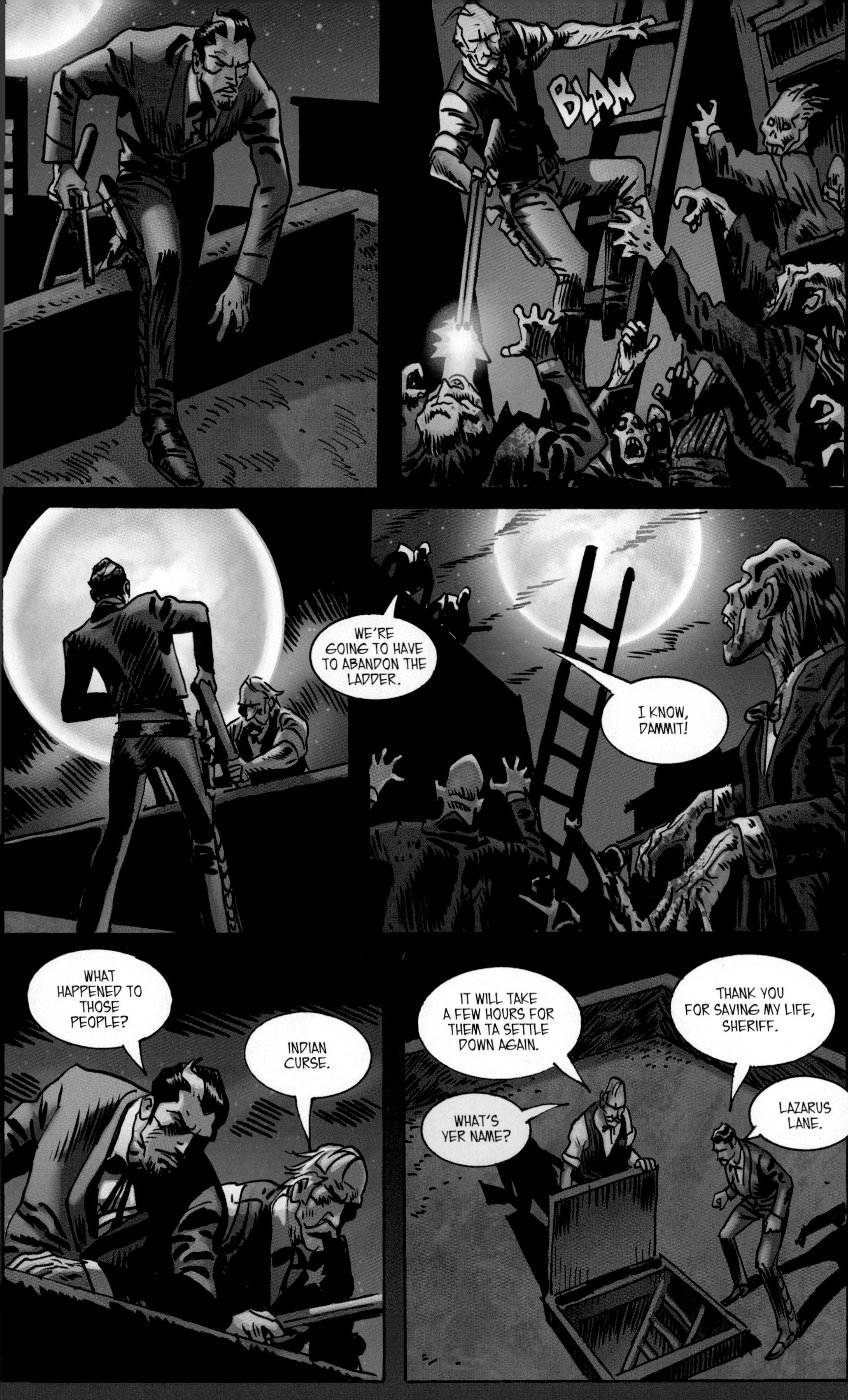
BLAM
WE'RE GOING TO HAVE TO ABANDON THE LADDER.
I KNOW, DAMMIT!
WHAT HAPPENED TO THOSE PEOPLE?
INDIAN CURSE.
IT WILL TAKE A FEW HOURS FOR THEM TA SETTLE DOWN AGAIN.
THANK YOU FOR SAVING MY LIFE, SHERIFF.
WHAT'S YER NAME?
LAZARUS LANE.

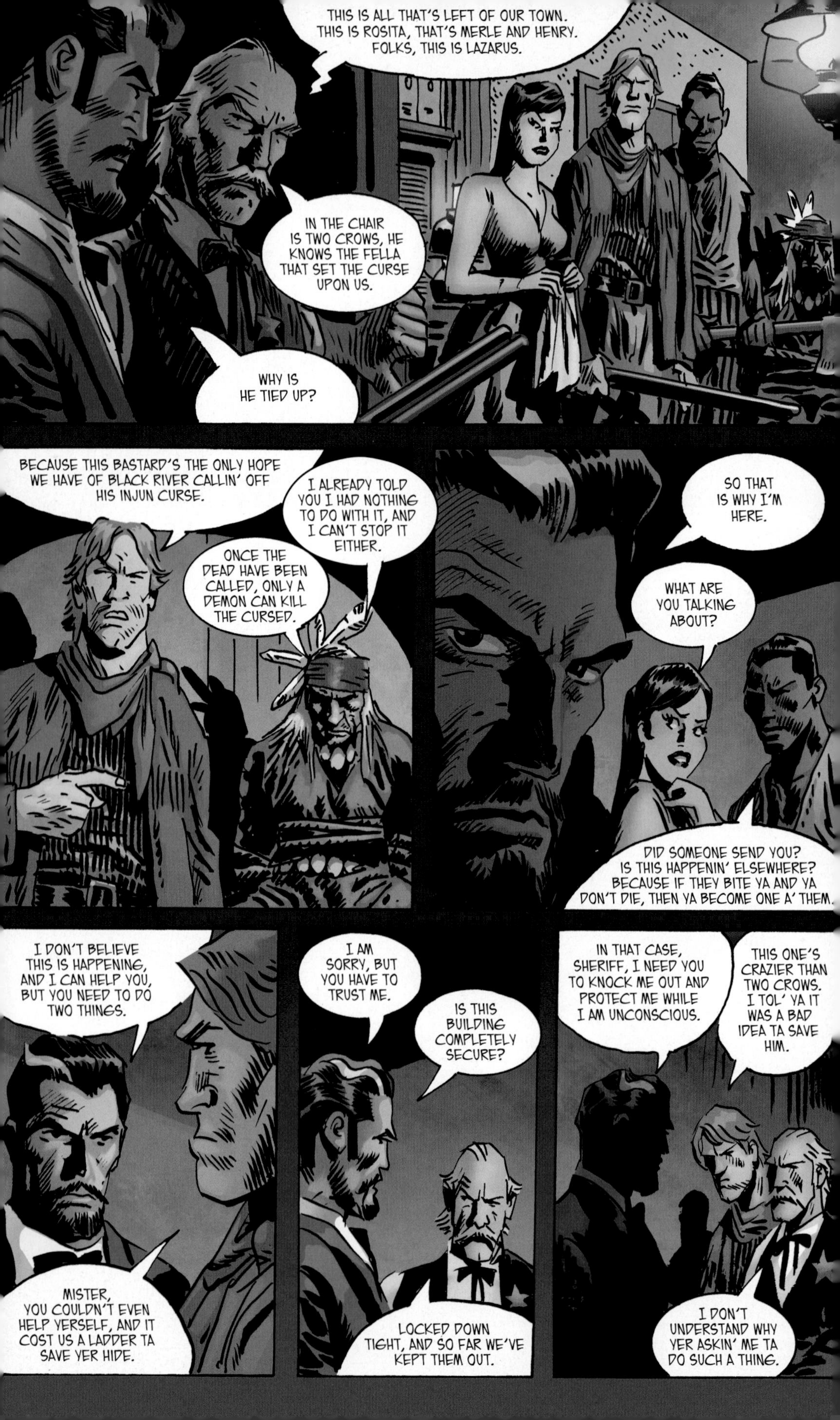
THIS IS ALL THAT'S LEFT OF OUR TOWN. THIS IS ROSITA, THAT'S MERLE AND HENRY. FOLKS, THIS IS LAZARUS.
IN THE CHAIR IS TWO CROWS, HE KNOWS THE FELLA THAT SET THE CURSE UPON US.
WHY IS HE TIED UP?
BECAUSE THIS BASTARD'S THE ONLY HOPE WE HAVE OF BLACK RIVER CALLIN' OFF HIS INJUN CURSE.
I ALREADY TOLD YOU I HAD NOTHING TO DO WITH IT, AND I CAN'T STOP IT EITHER.
ONCE THE DEAD HAVE BEEN CALLED, ONLY A DEMON CAN KILL THE CURSED.
SO THAT IS WHY I'M HERE.
WHAT ARE YOU TALKING ABOUT?
DID SOMEONE SEND YOU? IS THIS HAPPENIN' ELSEWHERE? BECAUSE IF THEY BITE YA AND YA DON'T DIE, THEN YA BECOME ONE A' THEM.
I DON'T BELIEVE THIS IS HAPPENING, AND I CAN HELP YOU, BUT YOU NEED TO DO TWO THINGS.
MISTER, YOU COULDN'T EVEN HELP YERSELF, AND IT COST US A LADDER TA SAVE YER HIDE.
I AM SORRY, BUT YOU HAVE TO TRUST ME.
IS THIS BUILDING COMPLETELY SECURE?
LOCKED DOWN TIGHT, AND SO FAR WE'VE KEPT THEM OUT.
IN THAT CASE, SHERIFF, I NEED YOU TO KNOCK ME OUT AND PROTECT ME WHILE I AM UNCONSCIOUS.
THIS ONE'S CRAZIER THAN TWO CROWS. I TOL' YA IT WAS A BAD IDEA TA SAVE HIM.
I DON'T UNDERSTAND WHY YER ASKIN' ME TA DO SUCH A THING.

TWO CROWS, YOU SAID A DEMON COULD SEND THEM BACK?

LOOK INTO MY EYES AND TELL THEM WHAT YOU SEE.

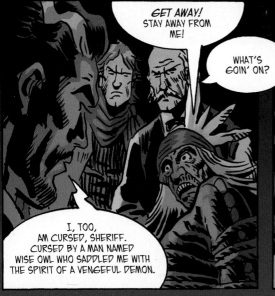

GET AWAY! STAY AWAY FROM ME!

WHAT'S GOIN' ON?

I, TOO, AM CURSED, SHERIFF. CURSED BY A MAN NAMED WISE OWL WHO SADDLED ME WITH THE SPIRIT OF A VENGEFUL DEMON.

EL DIABLO...

I NEED TO BE ASLEEP FOR THE DEMON TO RISE. HE IS YOUR ONLY HOPE OF STOPPING THE CURSE.

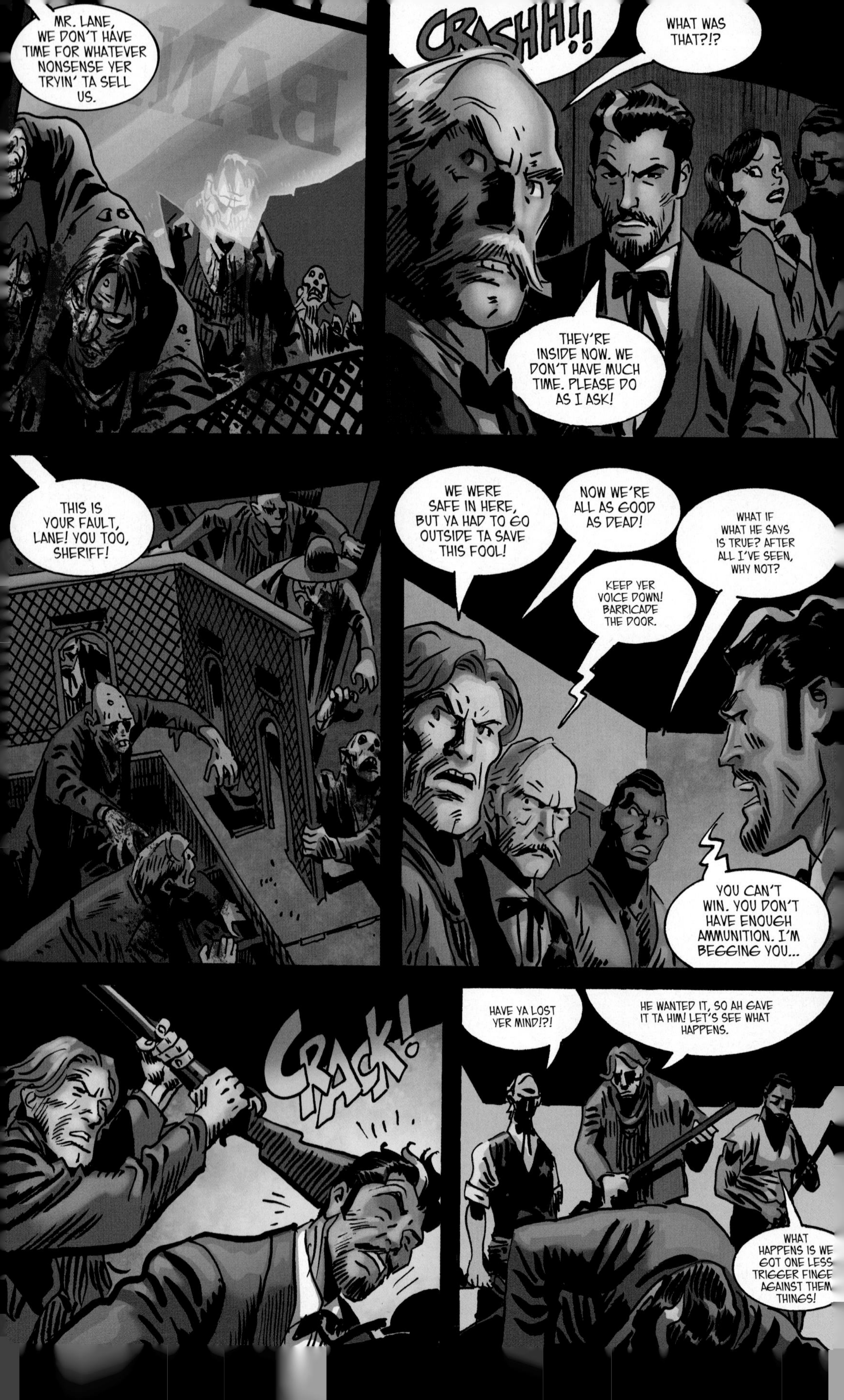

MR. LANE, WE DON'T HAVE TIME FOR WHATEVER NONSENSE YER TRYIN' TA SELL US.
CRASHH!!
WHAT WAS THAT?!?
THEY'RE INSIDE NOW. WE DON'T HAVE MUCH TIME. PLEASE DO AS I ASK!
THIS IS YOUR FAULT, LANE! YOU TOO, SHERIFF!
WE WERE SAFE IN HERE, BUT YA HAD TO GO OUTSIDE TA SAVE THIS FOOL!
NOW WE'RE ALL AS GOOD AS DEAD!
WHAT IF WHAT HE SAYS IS TRUE? AFTER ALL I'VE SEEN, WHY NOT?
KEEP YER VOICE DOWN! BARRICADE THE DOOR.
YOU CAN'T WIN. YOU DON'T HAVE ENOUGH AMMUNITION. I'M BEGGING YOU...
CRACK!
HAVE YA LOST YER MIND!?!
HE WANTED IT, SO AH GAVE IT TA HIM! LET'S SEE WHAT HAPPENS.
WHAT HAPPENS IS WE GOT ONE LESS TRIGGER FINGE AGAINST THEM THINGS!

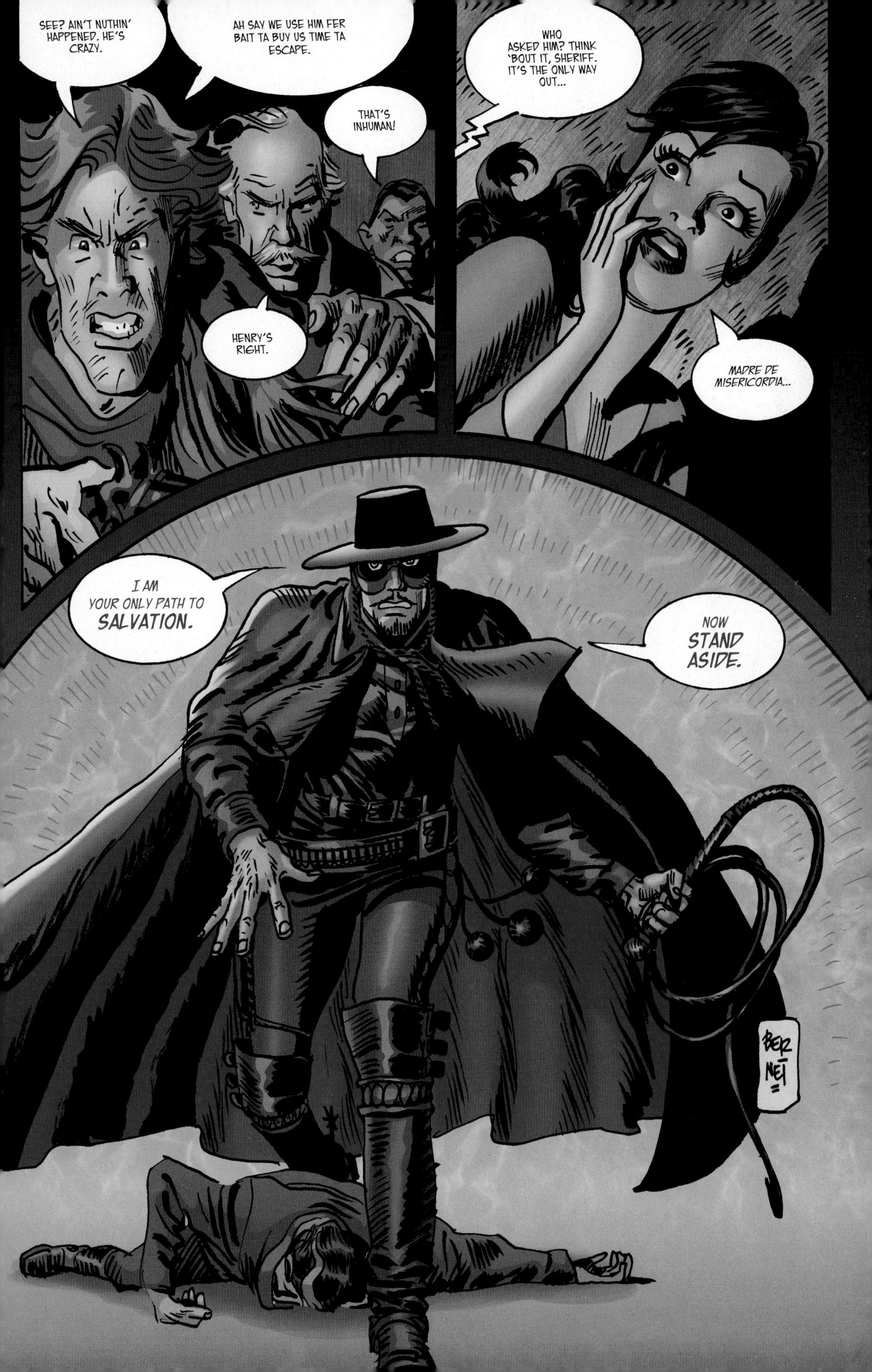
SEE? AIN'T NUTHIN' HAPPENED. HE'S CRAZY.
AH SAY WE USE HIM FER BAIT TA BUY US TIME TA ESCAPE.
THAT'S INHUMAN!
HENRY'S RIGHT.
WHO ASKED HIM? THINK 'BOUT IT, SHERIFF. IT'S THE ONLY WAY OUT...
MADRE DE MISERICORDIA...
I AM YOUR ONLY PATH TO SALVATION.
NOW STAND ASIDE.
BER NET

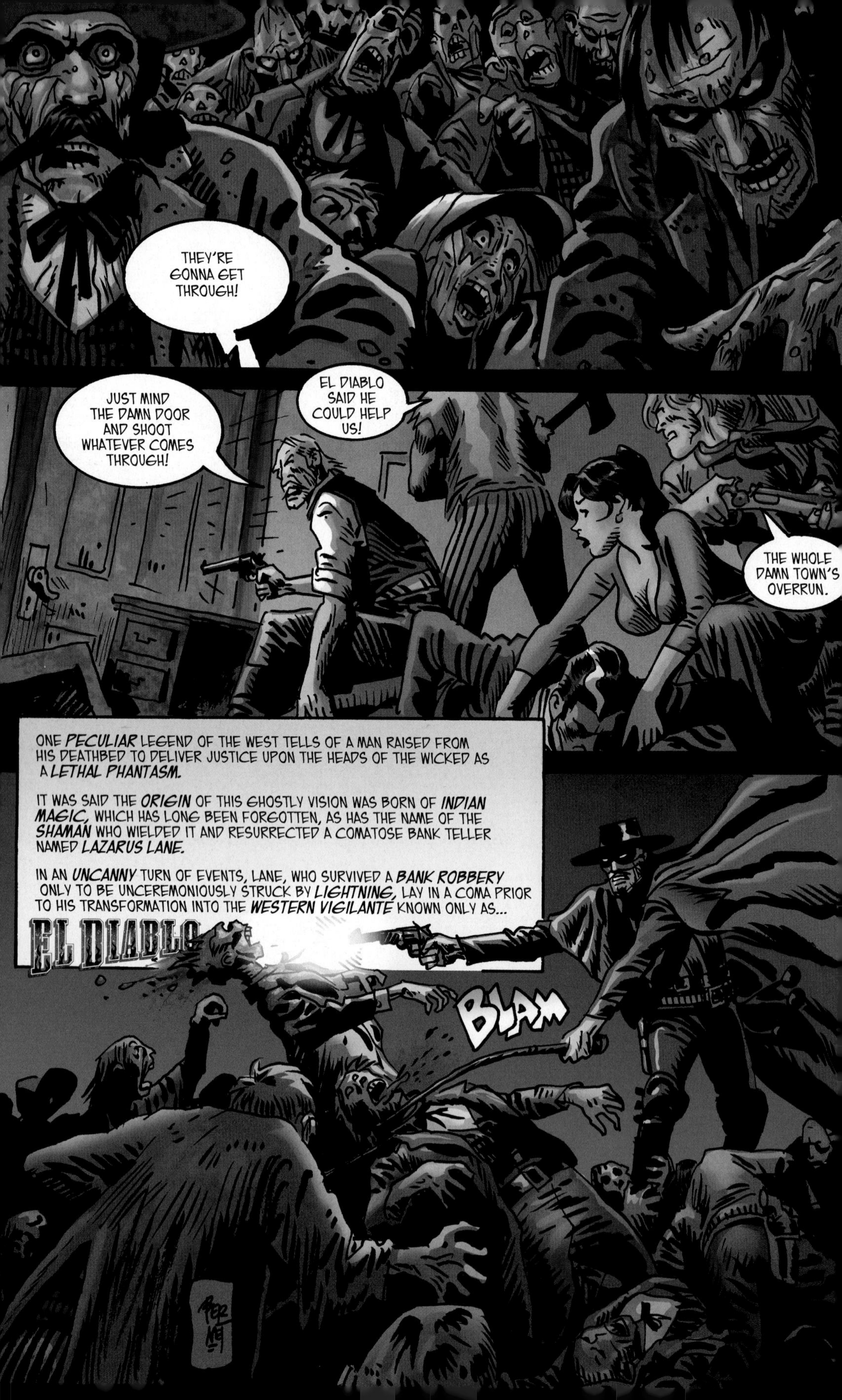
THEY'RE GONNA GET THROUGH!
JUST MIND THE DAMN DOOR AND SHOOT WHATEVER COMES THROUGH!
EL DIABLO SAID HE COULD HELP US!
THE WHOLE DAMN TOWN'S OVERRUN.
ONE PECULIAR LEGEND OF THE WEST TELLS OF A MAN RAISED FROM HIS DEATHBED TO DELIVER JUSTICE UPON THE HEADS OF THE WICKED AS A LETHAL PHANTASM.
IT WAS SAID THE ORIGIN OF THIS GHOSTLY VISION WAS BORN OF INDIAN MAGIC, WHICH HAS LONG BEEN FORGOTTEN, AS HAS THE NAME OF THE SHAMAN WHO WIELDED IT AND RESURRECTED A COMATOSE BANK TELLER NAMED LAZARUS LANE.
IN AN UNCANNY TURN OF EVENTS, LANE, WHO SURVIVED A BANK ROBBERY ONLY TO BE UNCEREMONIOUSLY STRUCK BY LIGHTNING, LAY IN A COMA PRIOR TO HIS TRANSFORMATION INTO THE WESTERN VIGILANTE KNOWN ONLY AS...
EL DIABLO
BLAM

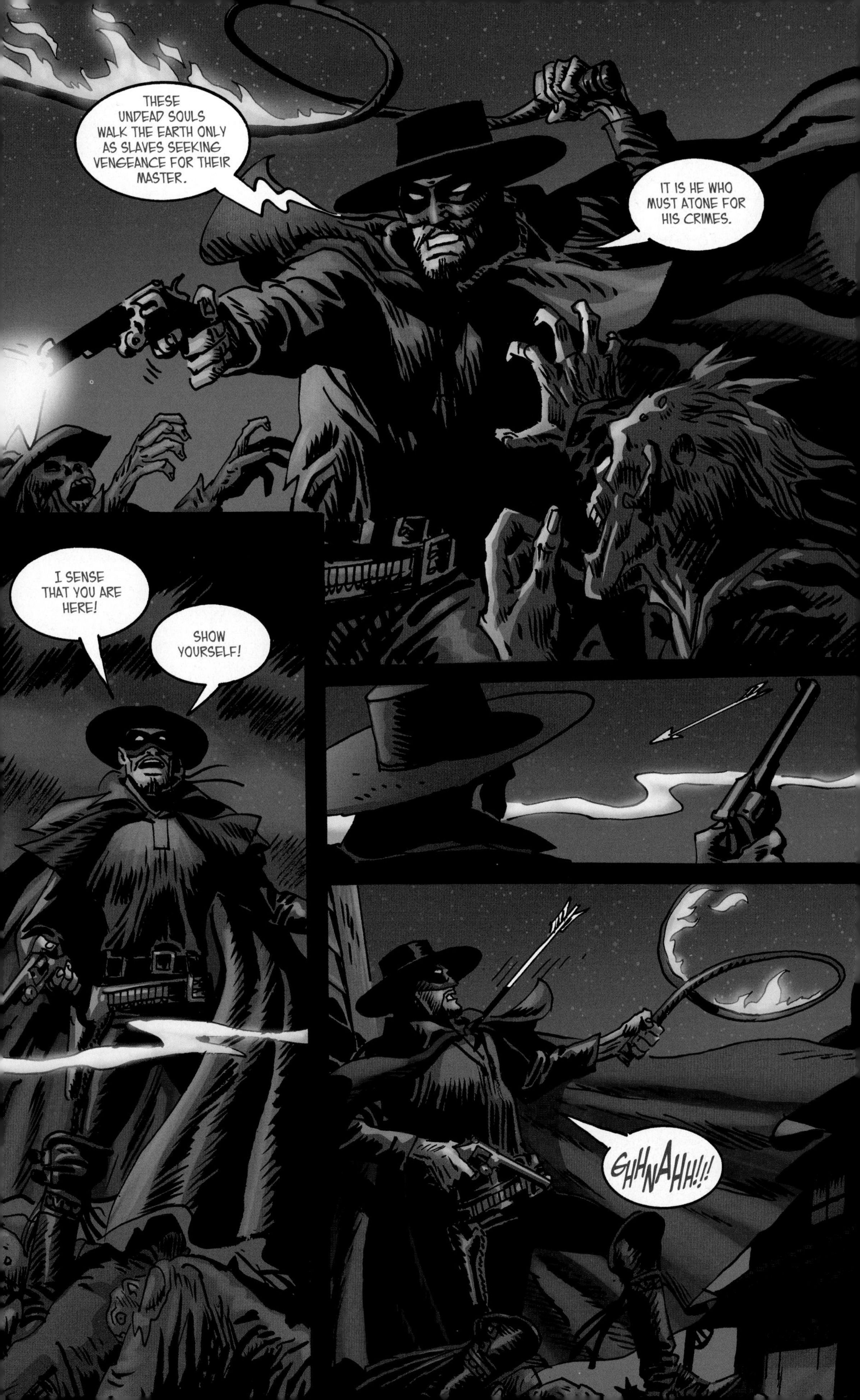
THESE UNDEAD SOULS WALK THE EARTH ONLY AS SLAVES SEEKING VENGEANCE FOR THEIR MASTER.
IT IS HE WHO MUST ATONE FOR HIS CRIMES.
I SENSE THAT YOU ARE HERE!
SHOW YOURSELF!
GHHNAHH!!!

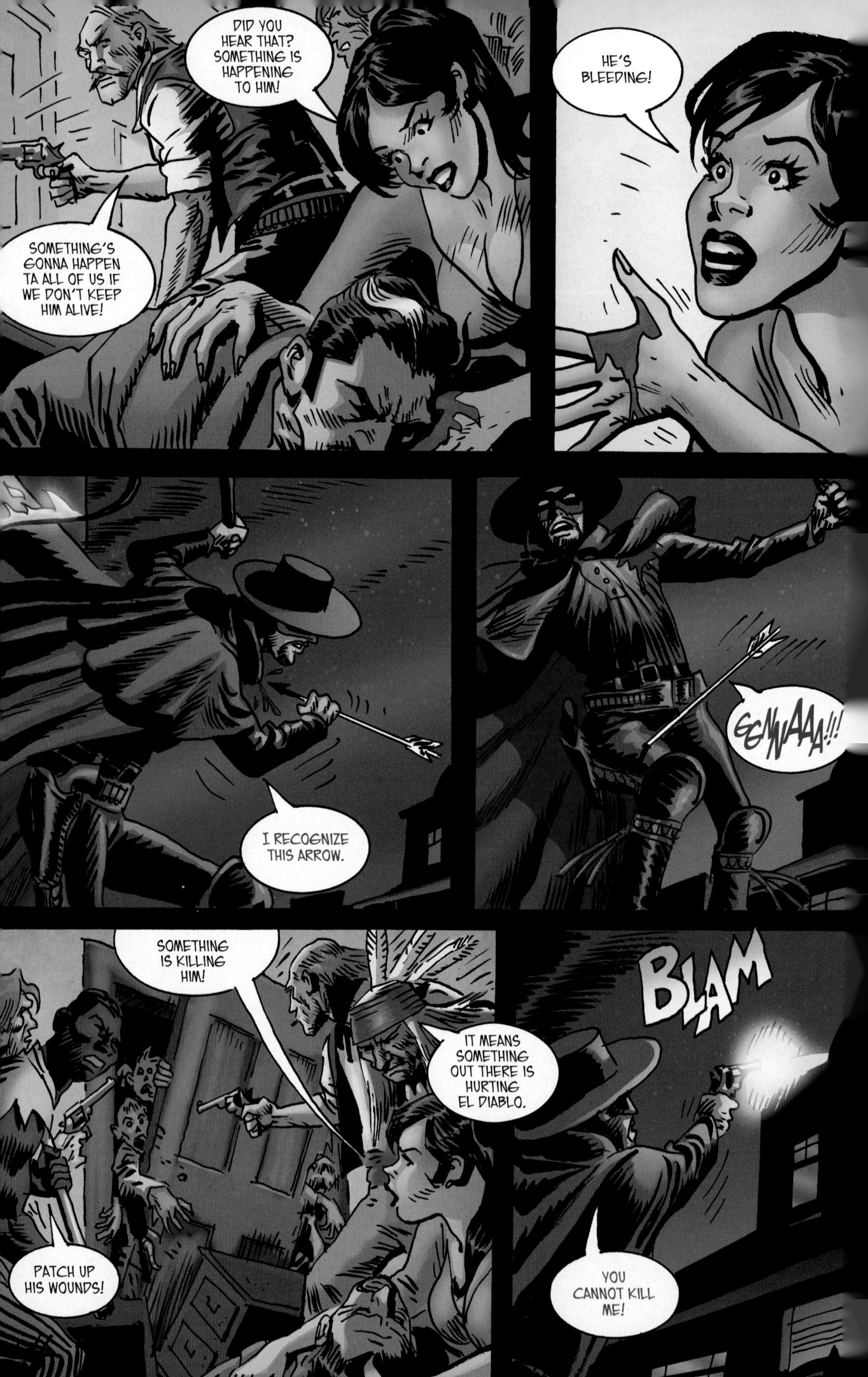
DID YOU HEAR THAT? SOMETHING IS HAPPENING TO HIM!
SOMETHING'S GONNA HAPPEN TA ALL OF US IF WE DON'T KEEP HIM ALIVE!
HE'S BLEEDING!
I RECOGNIZE THIS ARROW.
GGNAAAA!!!
SOMETHING IS KILLING HIM!
IT MEANS SOMETHING OUT THERE IS HURTING EL DIABLO.
PATCH UP HIS WOUNDS!
BLAM
YOU CANNOT KILL ME!

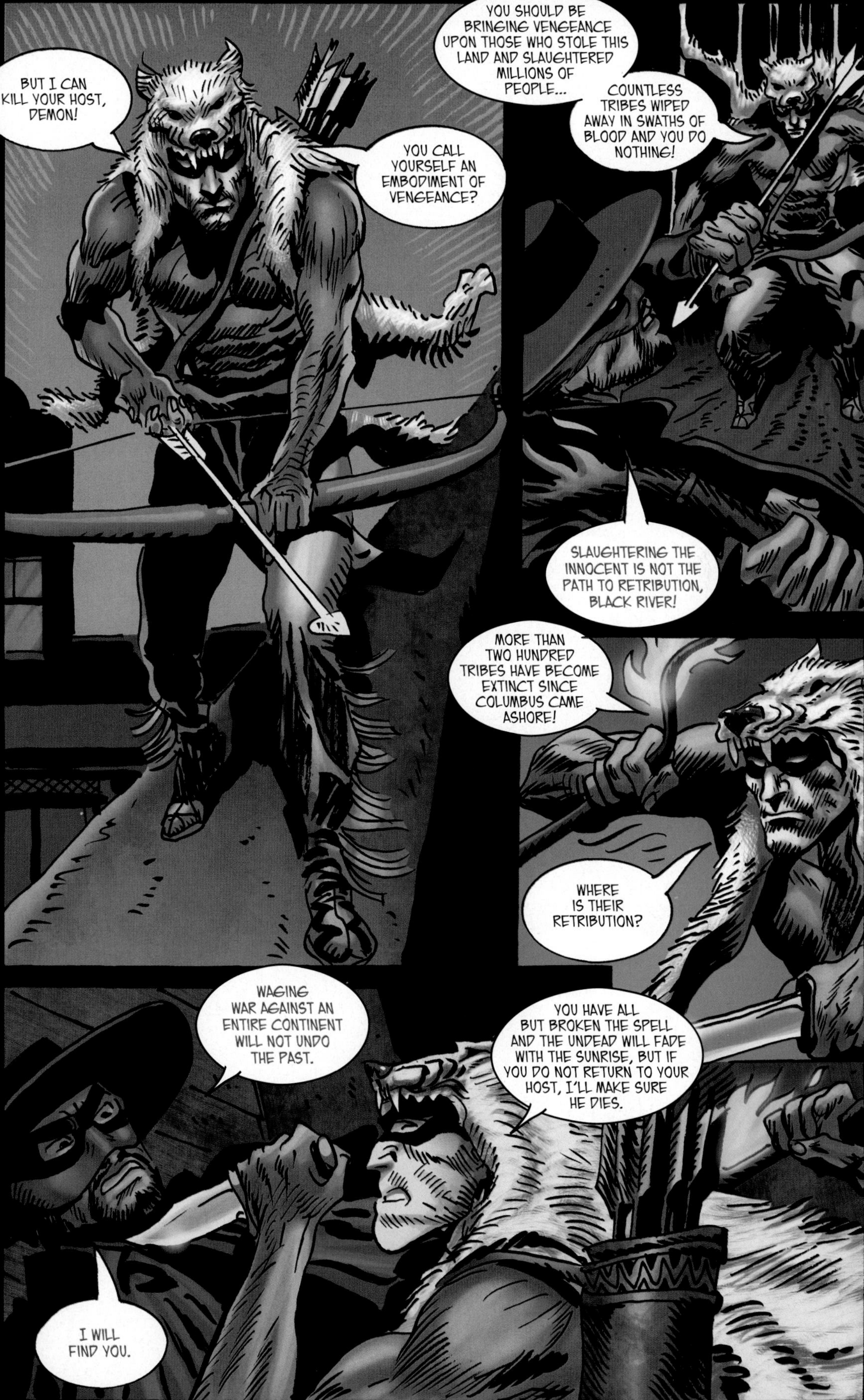
BUT I CAN KILL YOUR HOST, DEMON!
YOU CALL YOURSELF AN EMBODIMENT OF VENGEANCE?
YOU SHOULD BE BRINGING VENGEANCE UPON THOSE WHO STOLE THIS LAND AND SLAUGHTERED MILLIONS OF PEOPLE...
COUNTLESS TRIBES WIPED AWAY IN SWATHS OF BLOOD AND YOU DO NOTHING!
SLAUGHTERING THE INNOCENT IS NOT THE PATH TO RETRIBUTION, BLACK RIVER!
MORE THAN TWO HUNDRED TRIBES HAVE BECOME EXTINCT SINCE COLUMBUS CAME ASHORE!
WHERE IS THEIR RETRIBUTION?
WAGING WAR AGAINST AN ENTIRE CONTINENT WILL NOT UNDO THE PAST.
YOU HAVE ALL BUT BROKEN THE SPELL AND THE UNDEAD WILL FADE WITH THE SUNRISE, BUT IF YOU DO NOT RETURN TO YOUR HOST, I'LL MAKE SURE HE DIES.
I WILL FIND YOU.

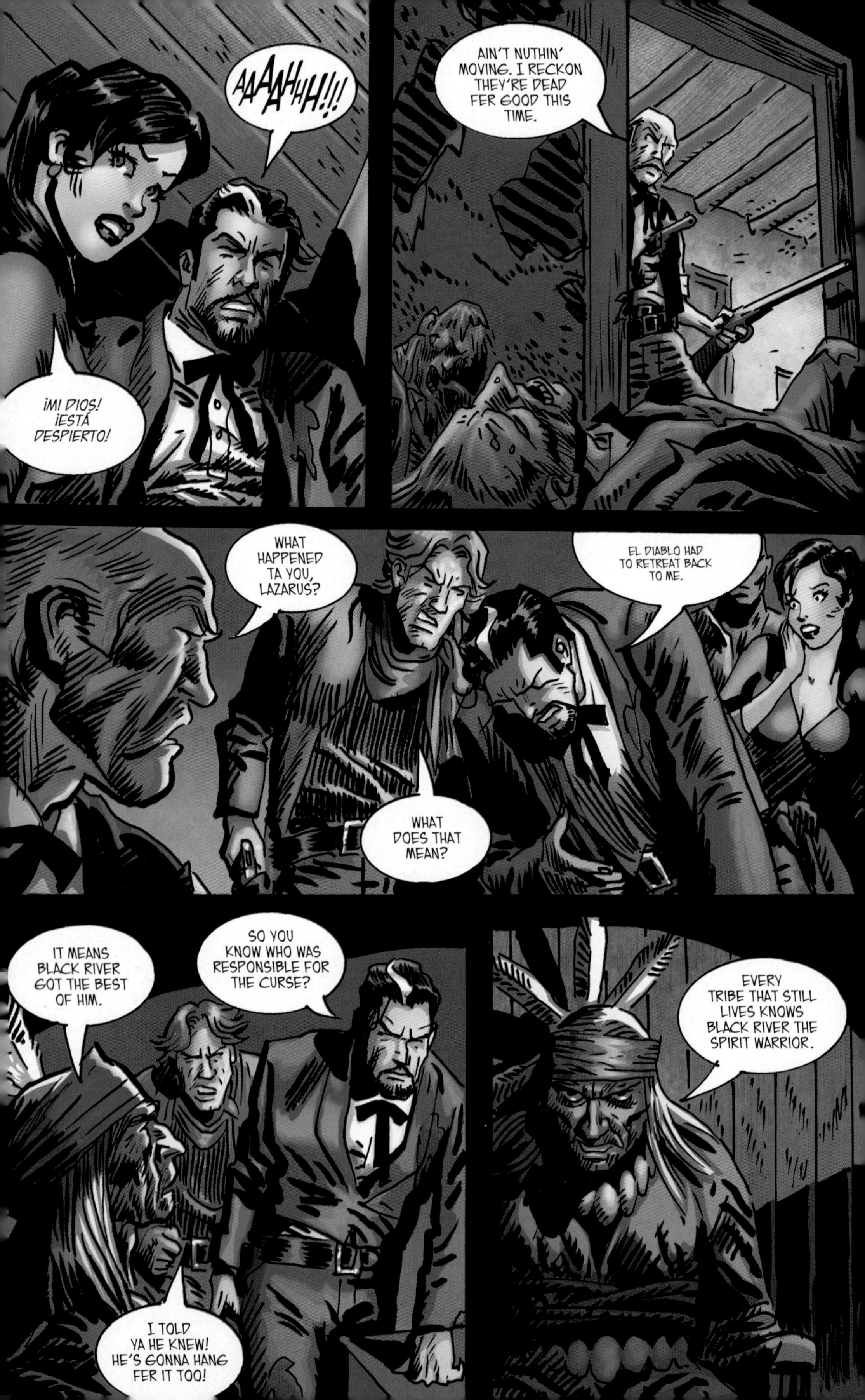
AAAAHHH!!!
¡MI DIOS! ¡ESTÁ DESPIERTO!
AIN'T NUTHIN' MOVING. I RECKON THEY'RE DEAD FER GOOD THIS TIME.
WHAT HAPPENED TA YOU, LAZARUS?
EL DIABLO HAD TO RETREAT BACK TO ME.
WHAT DOES THAT MEAN?
IT MEANS BLACK RIVER GOT THE BEST OF HIM.
SO YOU KNOW WHO WAS RESPONSIBLE FOR THE CURSE?
I TOLD YA HE KNEW! HE'S GONNA HANG FER IT TOO!
EVERY TRIBE THAT STILL LIVES KNOWS BLACK RIVER THE SPIRIT WARRIOR.

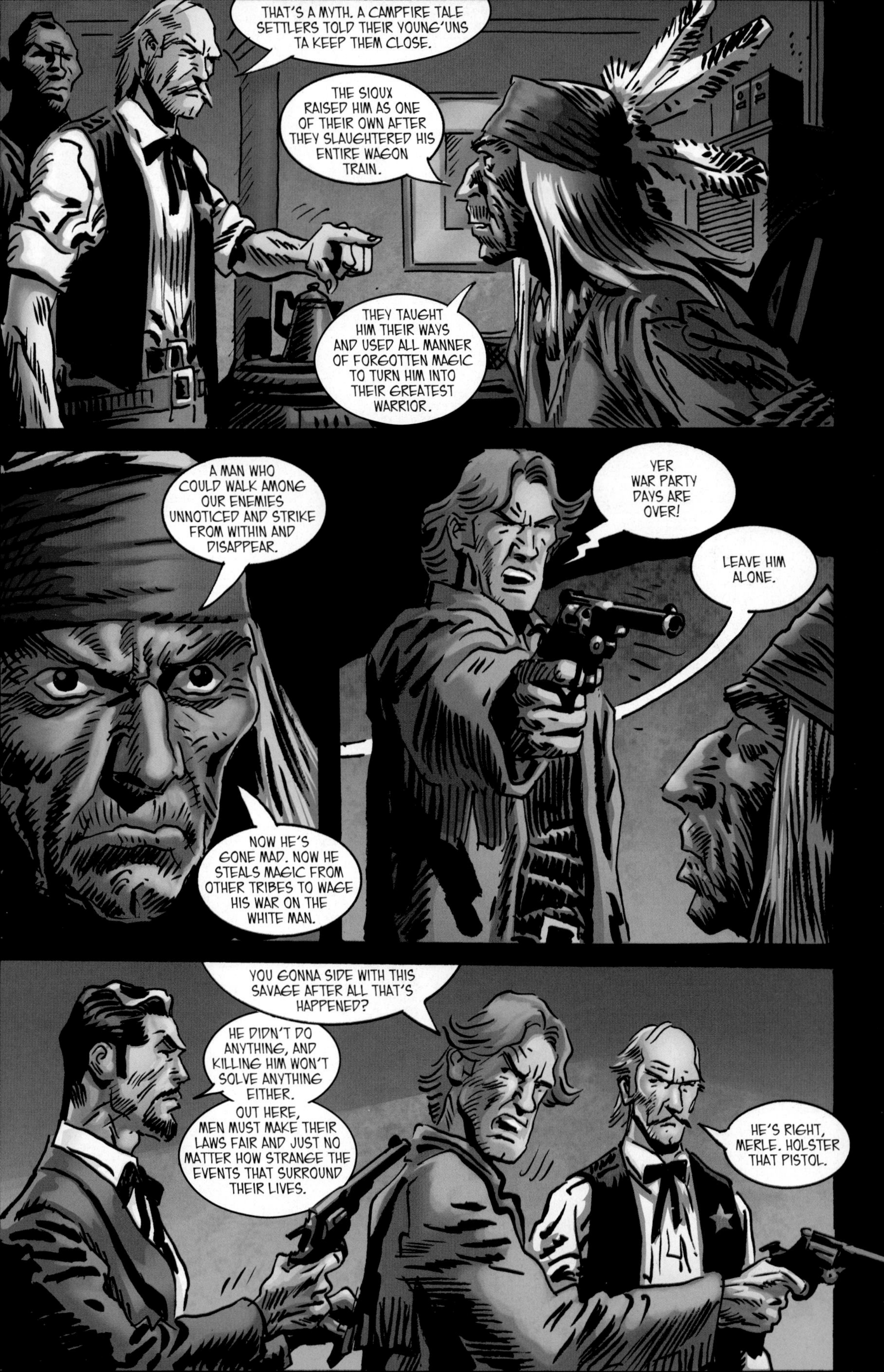
THAT'S A MYTH. A CAMPFIRE TALE SETTLERS TOLD THEIR YOUNG'UNS TA KEEP THEM CLOSE.
THE SIOUX RAISED HIM AS ONE OF THEIR OWN AFTER THEY SLAUGHTERED HIS ENTIRE WAGON TRAIN.
THEY TAUGHT HIM THEIR WAYS AND USED ALL MANNER OF FORGOTTEN MAGIC TO TURN HIM INTO THEIR GREATEST WARRIOR.
A MAN WHO COULD WALK AMONG OUR ENEMIES UNNOTICED AND STRIKE FROM WITHIN AND DISAPPEAR.
NOW HE'S GONE MAD. NOW HE STEALS MAGIC FROM OTHER TRIBES TO WAGE HIS WAR ON THE WHITE MAN.
YER WAR PARTY DAYS ARE OVER!
LEAVE HIM ALONE.
YOU GONNA SIDE WITH THIS SAVAGE AFTER ALL THAT'S HAPPENED?
HE DIDN'T DO ANYTHING, AND KILLING HIM WON'T SOLVE ANYTHING EITHER.
OUT HERE, MEN MUST MAKE THEIR LAWS FAIR AND JUST NO MATTER HOW STRANGE THE EVENTS THAT SURROUND THEIR LIVES.
HE'S RIGHT, MERLE. HOLSTER THAT PISTOL.

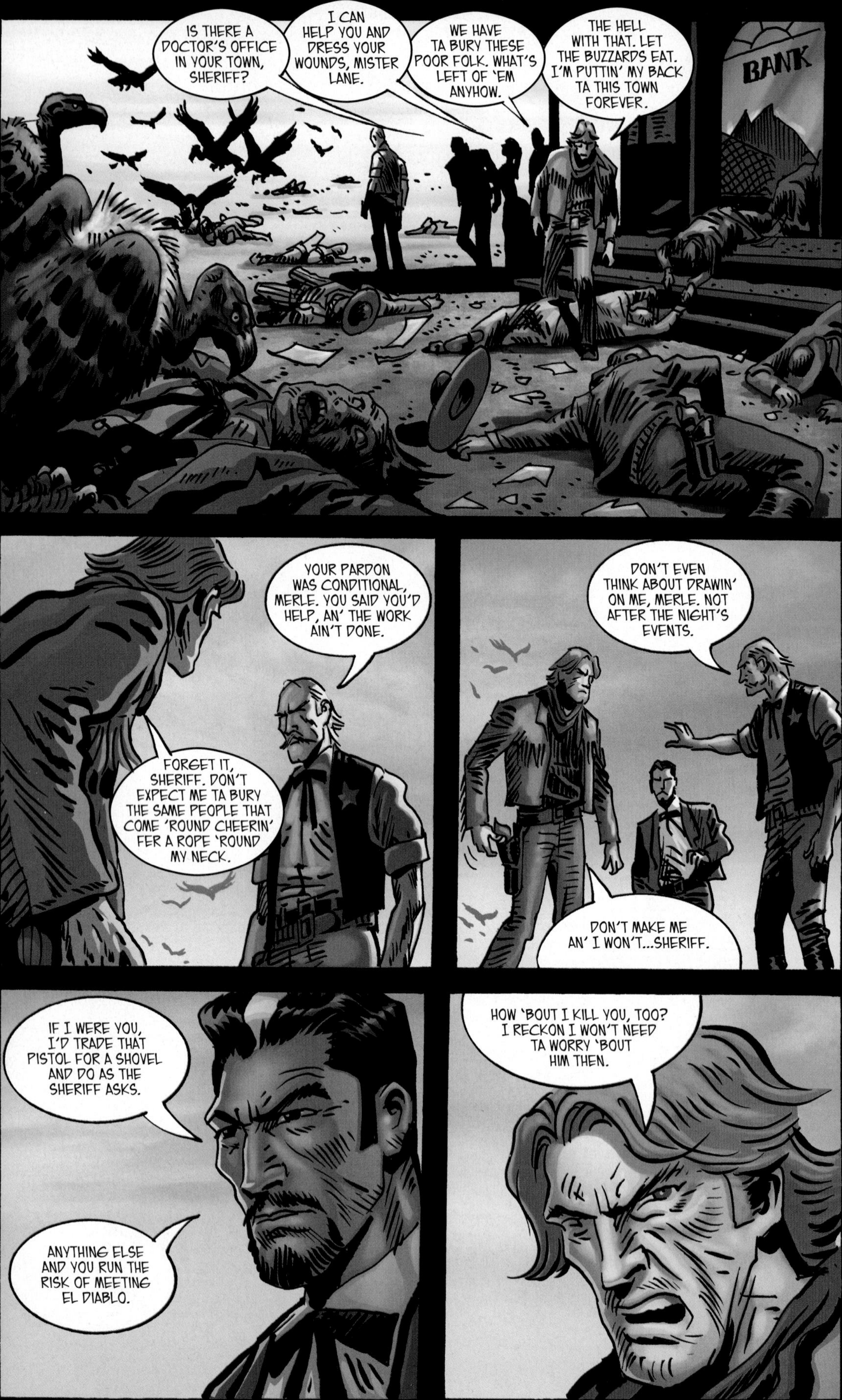
IS THERE A DOCTOR'S OFFICE IN YOUR TOWN, SHERIFF?
I CAN HELP YOU AND DRESS YOUR WOUNDS, MISTER LANE.
WE HAVE TA BURY THESE POOR FOLK. WHAT'S LEFT OF 'EM ANYHOW.
THE HELL WITH THAT. LET THE BUZZARDS EAT. I'M PUTTIN' MY BACK TA THIS TOWN FOREVER.
BANK
YOUR PARDON WAS CONDITIONAL, MERLE. YOU SAID YOU'D HELP, AN' THE WORK AIN'T DONE.
FORGET IT, SHERIFF. DON'T EXPECT ME TA BURY THE SAME PEOPLE THAT COME 'ROUND CHEERIN' FER A ROPE 'ROUND MY NECK.
DON'T EVEN THINK ABOUT DRAWIN' ON ME, MERLE. NOT AFTER THE NIGHT'S EVENTS.
DON'T MAKE ME AN' I WON'T...SHERIFF.
IF I WERE YOU, I'D TRADE THAT PISTOL FOR A SHOVEL AND DO AS THE SHERIFF ASKS.
ANYTHING ELSE AND YOU RUN THE RISK OF MEETING EL DIABLO.
HOW 'BOUT I KILL YOU, TOO? I RECKON I WON'T NEED TA WORRY 'BOUT HIM THEN.

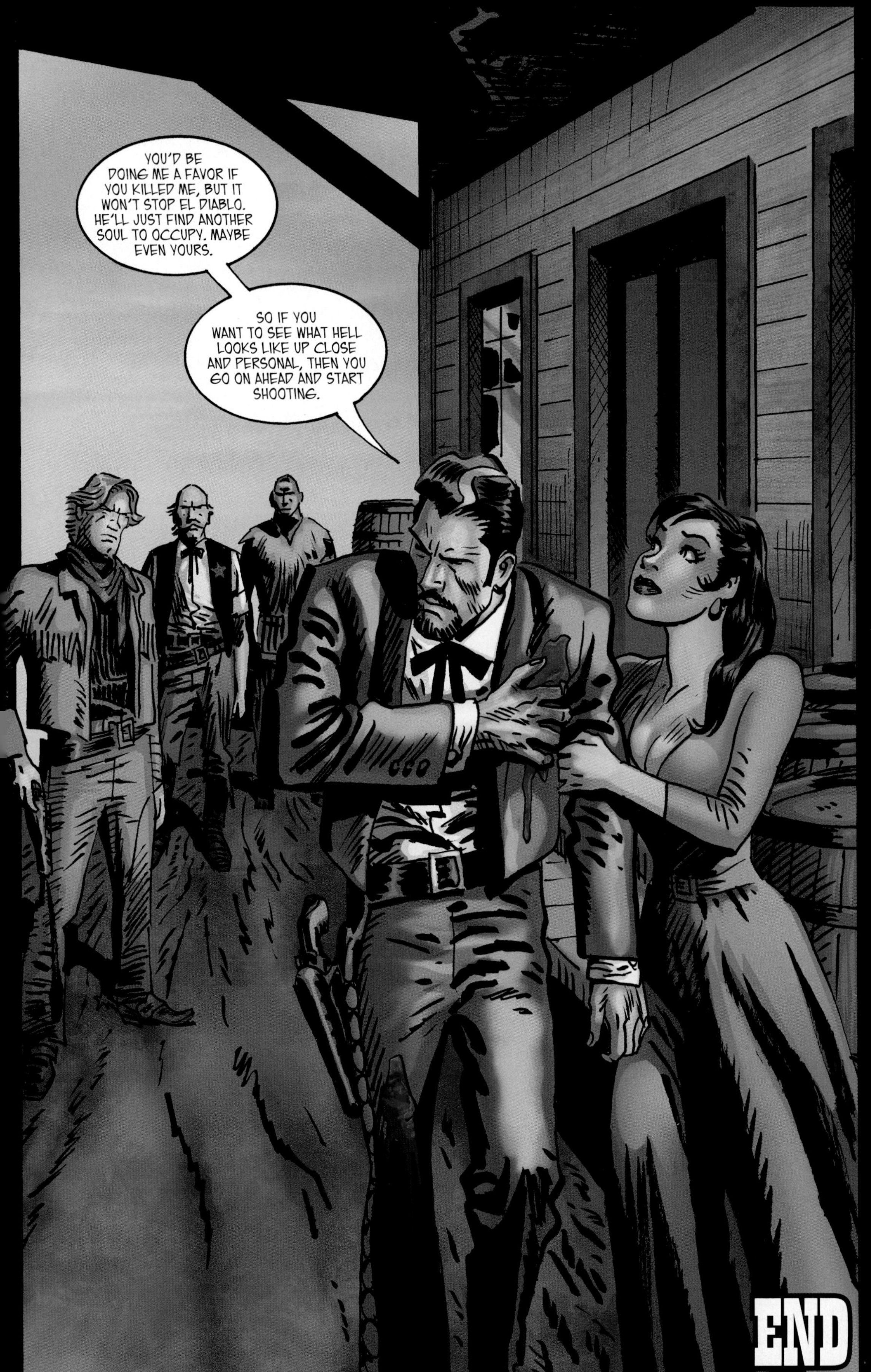
YOU'D BE DOING ME A FAVOR IF YOU KILLED ME, BUT IT WON'T STOP EL DIABLO. HE'LL JUST FIND ANOTHER SOUL TO OCCUPY. MAYBE EVEN YOURS.
SO IF YOU WANT TO SEE WHAT HELL LOOKS LIKE UP CLOSE AND PERSONAL, THEN YOU GO ON AHEAD AND START SHOOTING.
END

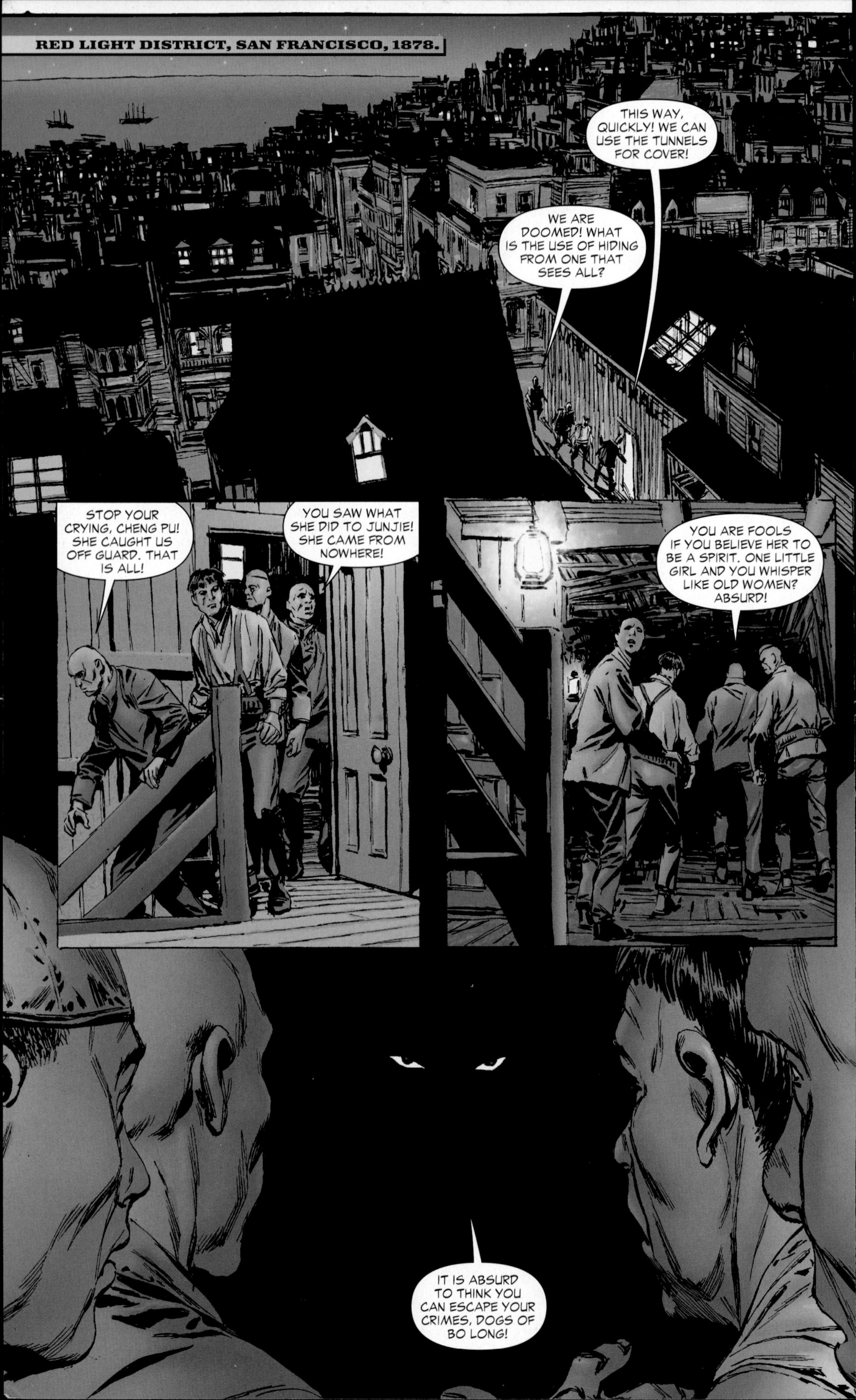
RED LIGHT DISTRICT, SAN FRANCISCO, 1878.
THIS WAY, QUICKLY! WE CAN USE THE TUNNELS FOR COVER!
WE ARE DOOMED! WHAT IS THE USE OF HIDING FROM ONE THAT SEES ALL?
STOP YOUR CRYING, CHENG PU! SHE CAUGHT US OFF GUARD. THAT IS ALL!
YOU SAW WHAT SHE DID TO JUNJIE! SHE CAME FROM NOWHERE!
YOU ARE FOOLS IF YOU BELIEVE HER TO BE A SPIRIT. ONE LITTLE GIRL AND YOU WHISPER LIKE OLD WOMEN? ABSURD!
IT IS ABSURD TO THINK YOU CAN ESCAPE YOUR CRIMES, DOGS OF BO LONG!

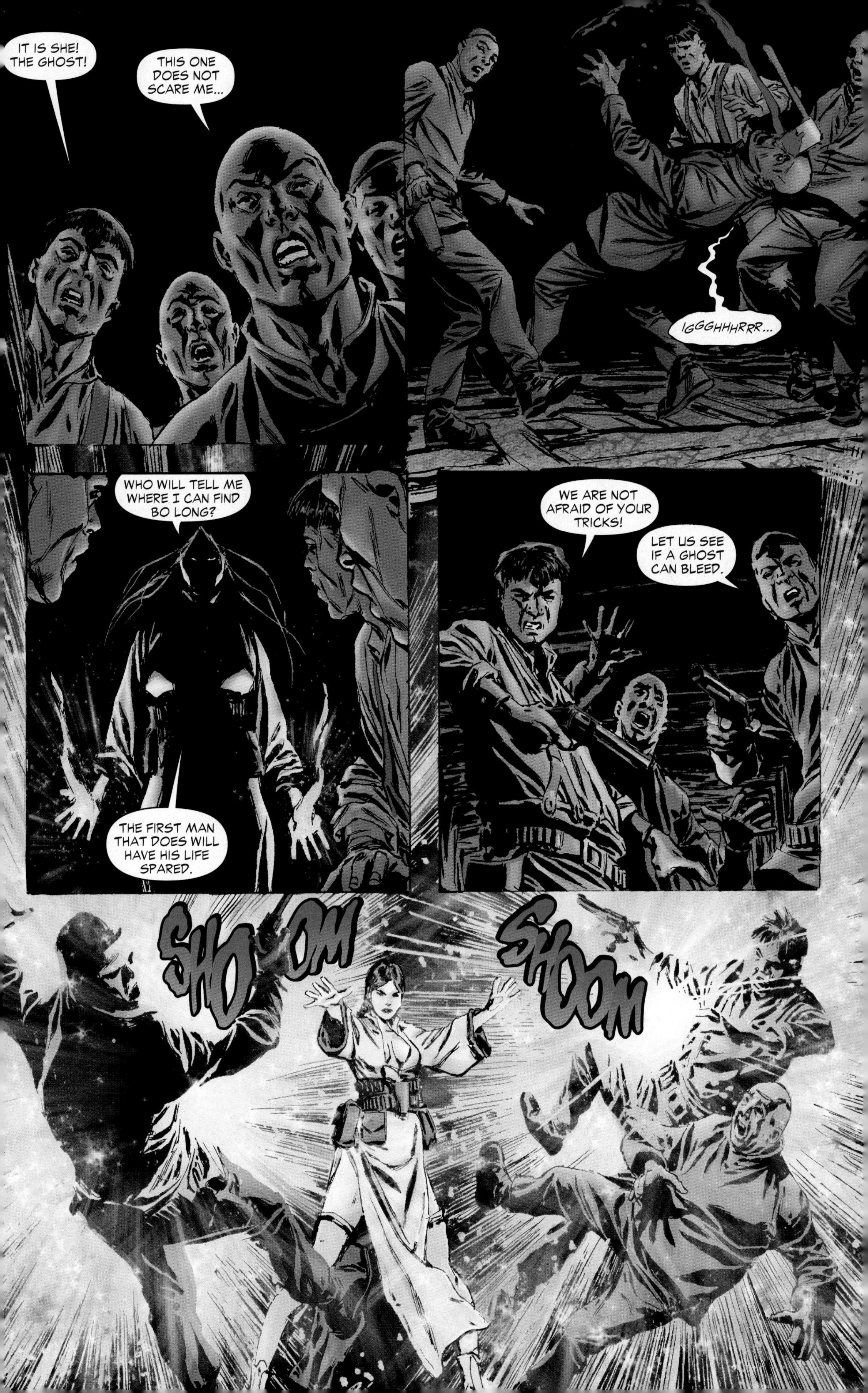
IT IS SHE! THE GHOST!
THIS ONE DOES NOT SCARE ME...
IGGGHHHRRR...
WHO WILL TELL ME WHERE I CAN FIND BO LONG?
THE FIRST MAN THAT DOES WILL HAVE HIS LIFE SPARED.
WE ARE NOT AFRAID OF YOUR TRICKS!
LET US SEE IF A GHOST CAN BLEED.
SHOOM
SHOOM

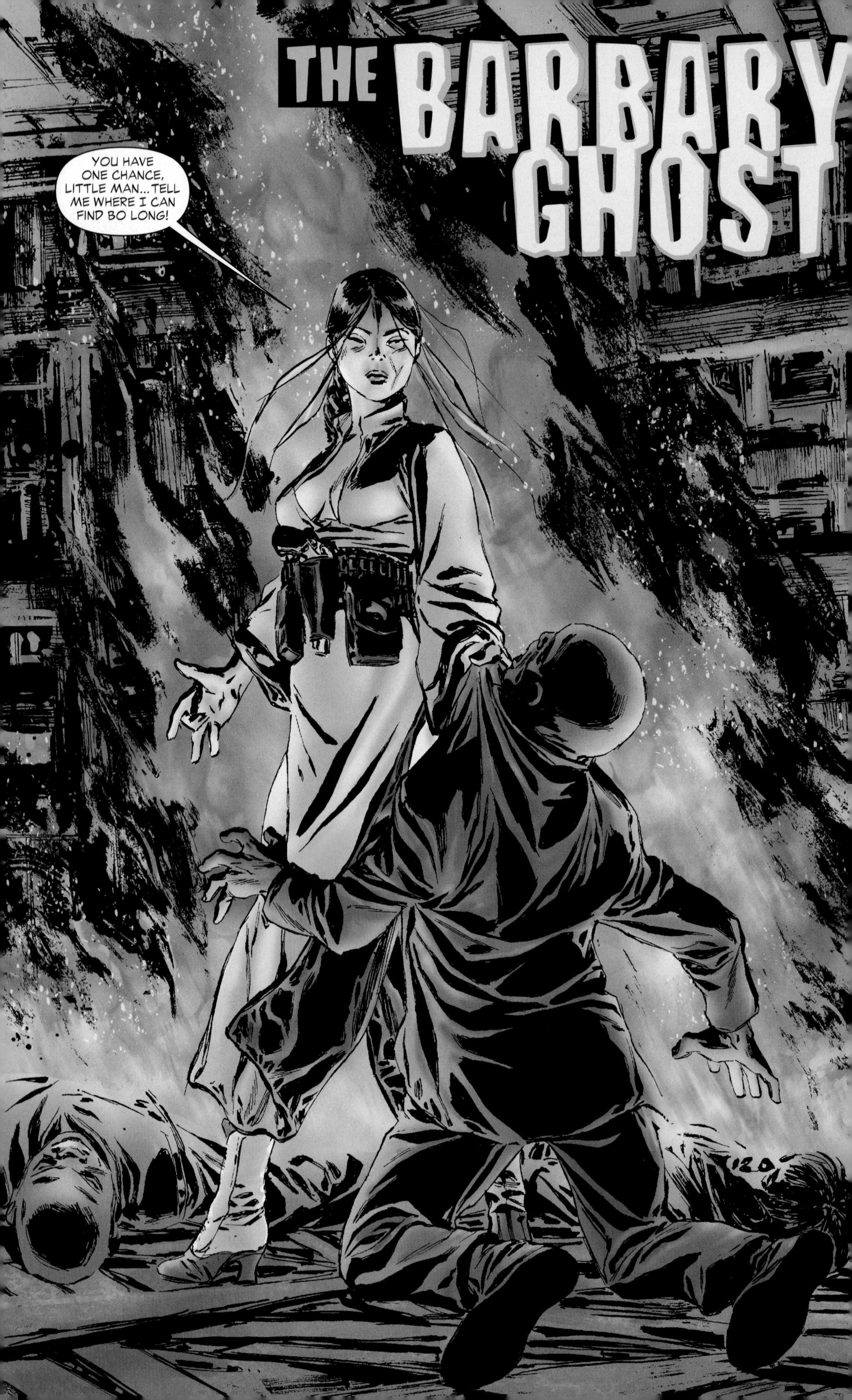
THE BARBARY GHOST
YOU HAVE ONE CHANCE, LITTLE MAN...TELL ME WHERE I CAN FIND BO LONG!

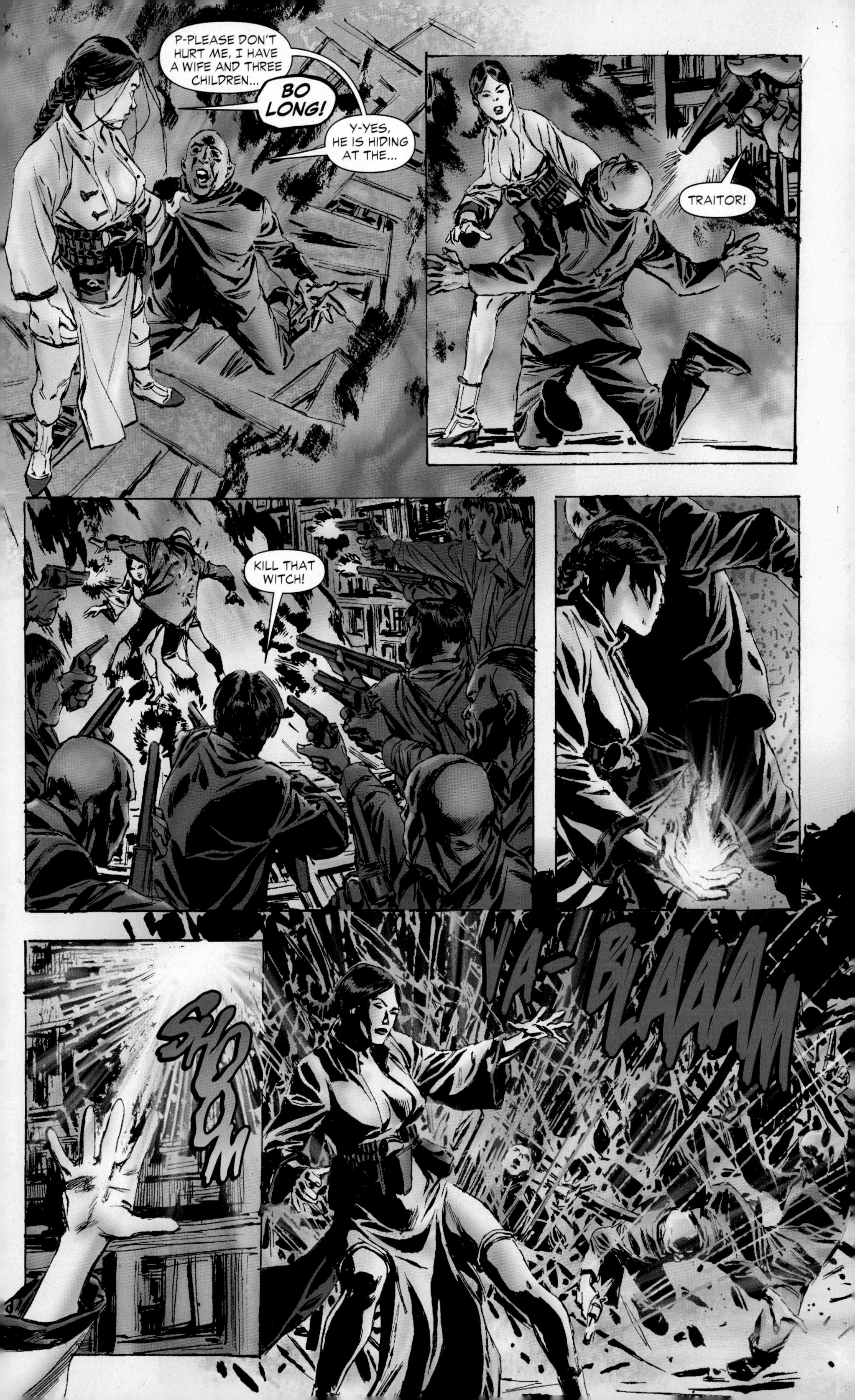
P-PLEASE DON'T HURT ME, I HAVE A WIFE AND THREE CHILDREN...
BO LONG!
Y-YES, HE IS HIDING AT THE...
TRAITOR!
KILL THAT WITCH!
SHOOM
VA-BLAAAM

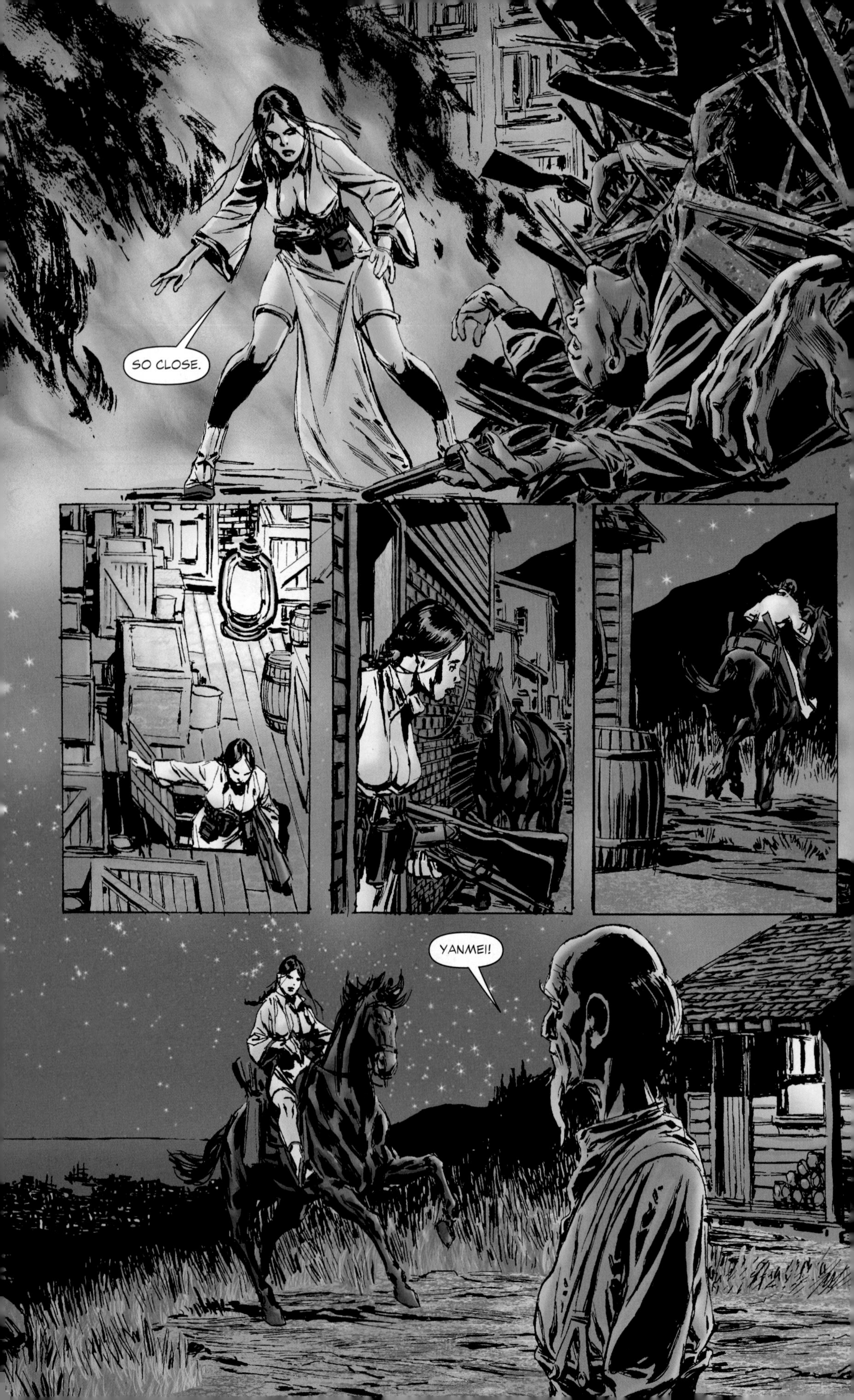
SO CLOSE.
YANMEI!

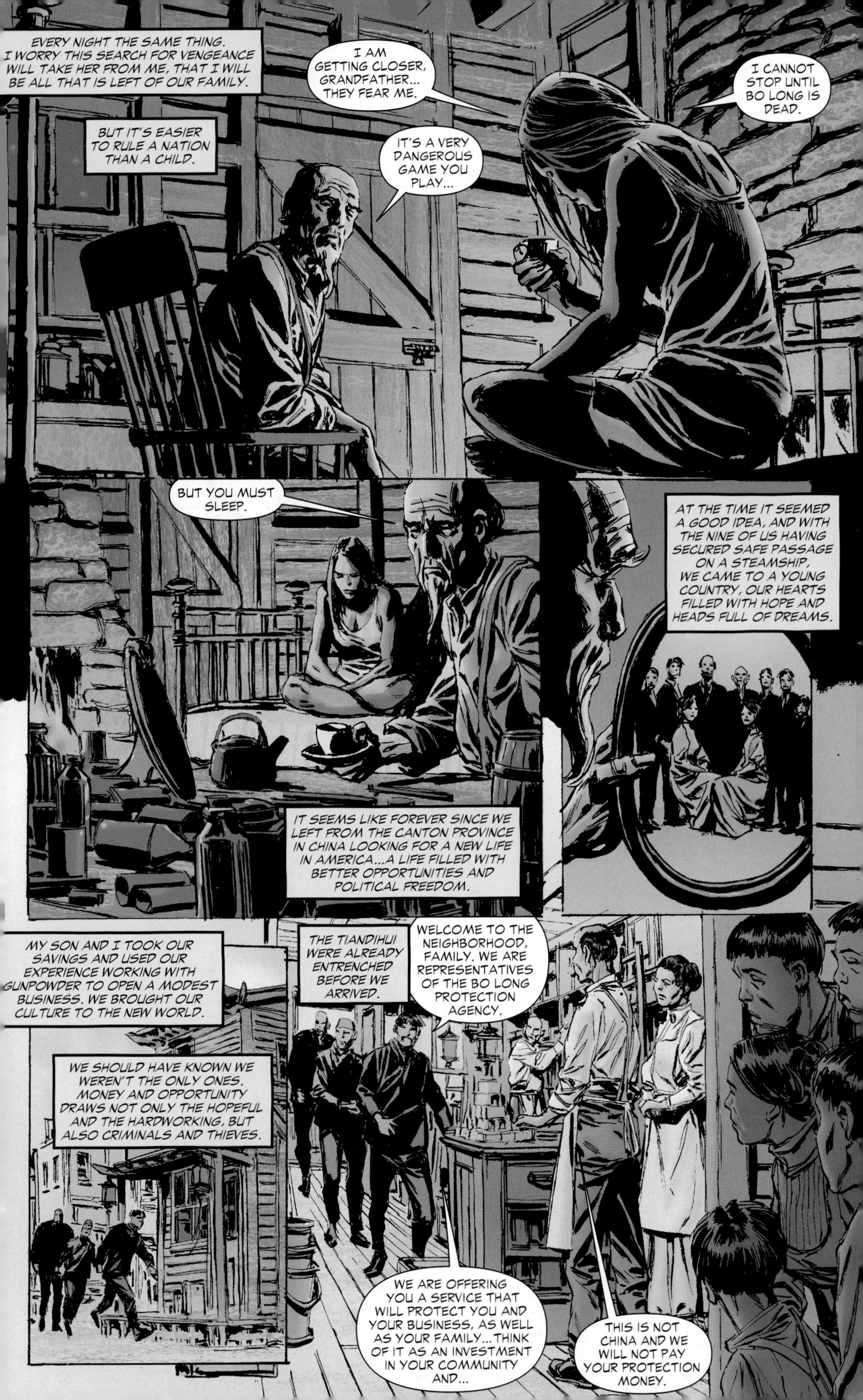
EVERY NIGHT THE SAME THING. I WORRY THIS SEARCH FOR VENGEANCE WILL TAKE HER FROM ME, THAT I WILL BE ALL THAT IS LEFT OF OUR FAMILY.
I AM GETTING CLOSER, GRANDFATHER... THEY FEAR ME.
I CANNOT STOP UNTIL BO LONG IS DEAD.
BUT IT'S EASIER TO RULE A NATION THAN A CHILD.
IT'S A VERY DANGEROUS GAME YOU PLAY...
BUT YOU MUST SLEEP.
IT SEEMS LIKE FOREVER SINCE WE LEFT FROM THE CANTON PROVINCE IN CHINA LOOKING FOR A NEW LIFE IN AMERICA...A LIFE FILLED WITH BETTER OPPORTUNITIES AND POLITICAL FREEDOM.
AT THE TIME IT SEEMED A GOOD IDEA, AND WITH THE NINE OF US HAVING SECURED SAFE PASSAGE ON A STEAMSHIP, WE CAME TO A YOUNG COUNTRY, OUR HEARTS FILLED WITH HOPE AND HEADS FULL OF DREAMS.
MY SON AND I TOOK OUR SAVINGS AND USED OUR EXPERIENCE WORKING WITH GUNPOWDER TO OPEN A MODEST BUSINESS. WE BROUGHT OUR CULTURE TO THE NEW WORLD.
WE SHOULD HAVE KNOWN WE WEREN'T THE ONLY ONES. MONEY AND OPPORTUNITY DRAWS NOT ONLY THE HOPEFUL AND THE HARDWORKING, BUT ALSO CRIMINALS AND THIEVES.
THE TIANDIHUI WERE ALREADY ENTRENCHED BEFORE WE ARRIVED.
WELCOME TO THE NEIGHBORHOOD, FAMILY. WE ARE REPRESENTATIVES OF THE BO LONG PROTECTION AGENCY.
WE ARE OFFERING YOU A SERVICE THAT WILL PROTECT YOU AND YOUR BUSINESS, AS WELL AS YOUR FAMILY...THINK OF IT AS AN INVESTMENT IN YOUR COMMUNITY AND...
THIS IS NOT CHINA AND WE WILL NOT PAY YOUR PROTECTION MONEY.

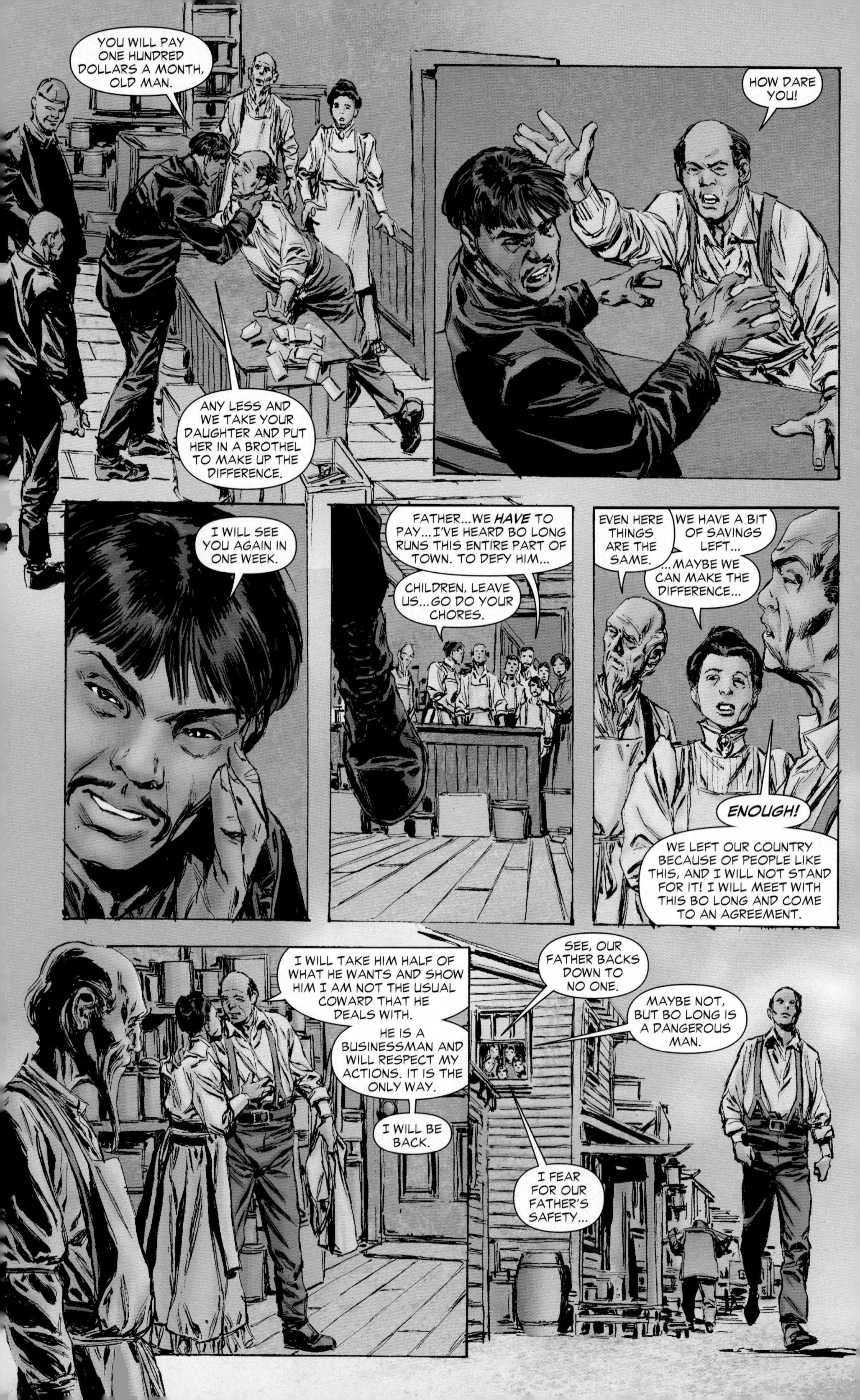

YOU WILL PAY ONE HUNDRED DOLLARS A MONTH, OLD MAN.
ANY LESS AND WE TAKE YOUR DAUGHTER AND PUT HER IN A BROTHEL TO MAKE UP THE DIFFERENCE.
HOW DARE YOU!
I WILL SEE YOU AGAIN IN ONE WEEK.
FATHER...WE HAVE TO PAY...I'VE HEARD BO LONG RUNS THIS ENTIRE PART OF TOWN. TO DEFY HIM...
CHILDREN, LEAVE US...GO DO YOUR CHORES.
EVEN HERE THINGS ARE THE SAME.
WE HAVE A BIT OF SAVINGS LEFT...
...MAYBE WE CAN MAKE THE DIFFERENCE...
ENOUGH!
WE LEFT OUR COUNTRY BECAUSE OF PEOPLE LIKE THIS, AND I WILL NOT STAND FOR IT! I WILL MEET WITH THIS BO LONG AND COME TO AN AGREEMENT.
I WILL TAKE HIM HALF OF WHAT HE WANTS AND SHOW HIM I AM NOT THE USUAL COWARD THAT HE DEALS WITH.
HE IS A BUSINESSMAN AND WILL RESPECT MY ACTIONS. IT IS THE ONLY WAY.
I WILL BE BACK.
SEE, OUR FATHER BACKS DOWN TO NO ONE.
MAYBE NOT, BUT BO LONG IS A DANGEROUS MAN.
I FEAR FOR OUR FATHER'S SAFETY...

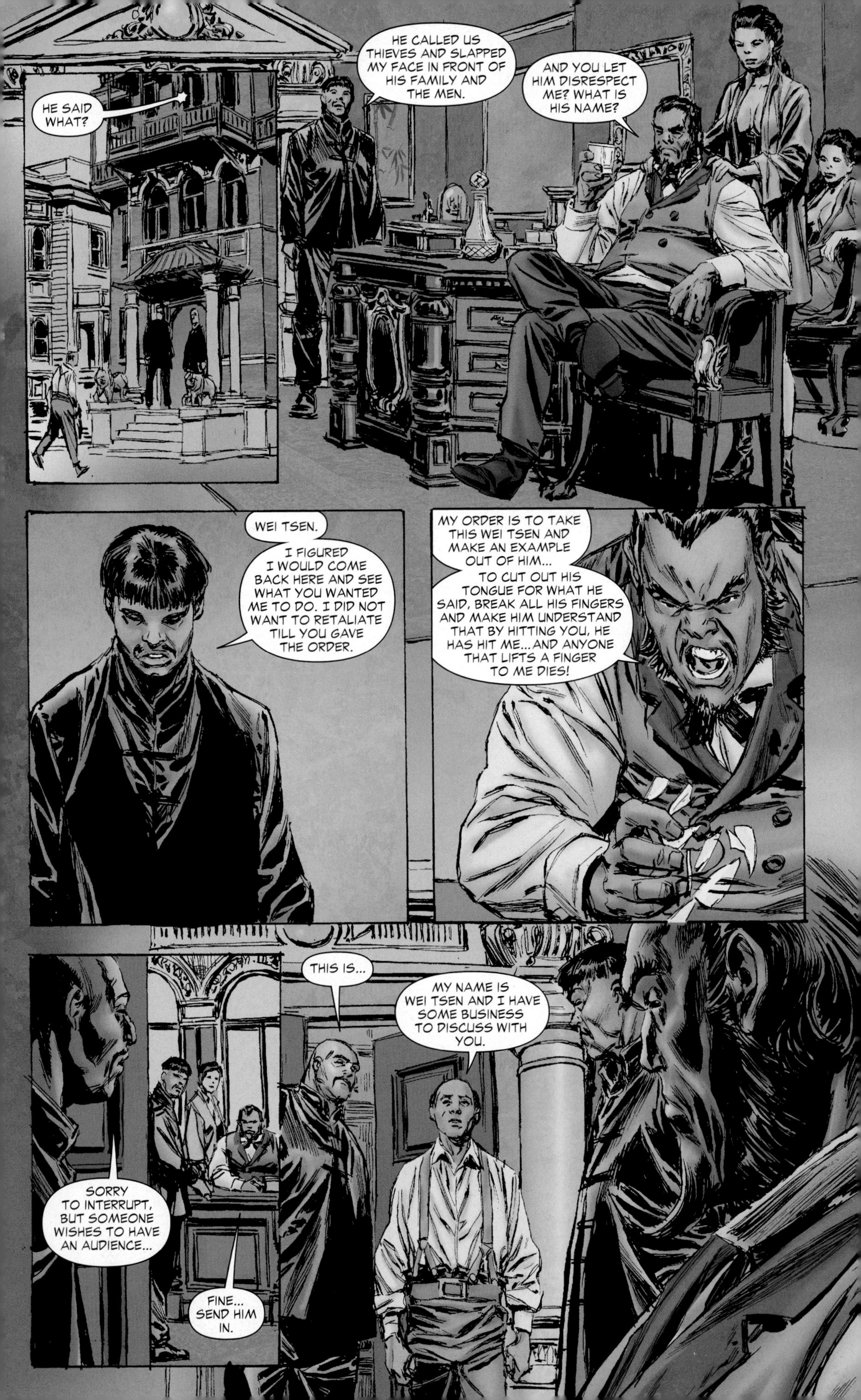
HE CALLED US THIEVES AND SLAPPED MY FACE IN FRONT OF HIS FAMILY AND THE MEN.
HE SAID WHAT?
AND YOU LET HIM DISRESPECT ME? WHAT IS HIS NAME?
WEI TSEN.
I FIGURED I WOULD COME BACK HERE AND SEE WHAT YOU WANTED ME TO DO. I DID NOT WANT TO RETALIATE TILL YOU GAVE THE ORDER.
MY ORDER IS TO TAKE THIS WEI TSEN AND MAKE AN EXAMPLE OUT OF HIM...
TO CUT OUT HIS TONGUE FOR WHAT HE SAID, BREAK ALL HIS FINGERS AND MAKE HIM UNDERSTAND THAT BY HITTING YOU, HE HAS HIT ME...AND ANYONE THAT LIFTS A FINGER TO ME DIES!
SORRY TO INTERRUPT, BUT SOMEONE WISHES TO HAVE AN AUDIENCE...
FINE... SEND HIM IN.
THIS IS...
MY NAME IS WEI TSEN AND I HAVE SOME BUSINESS TO DISCUSS WITH YOU.

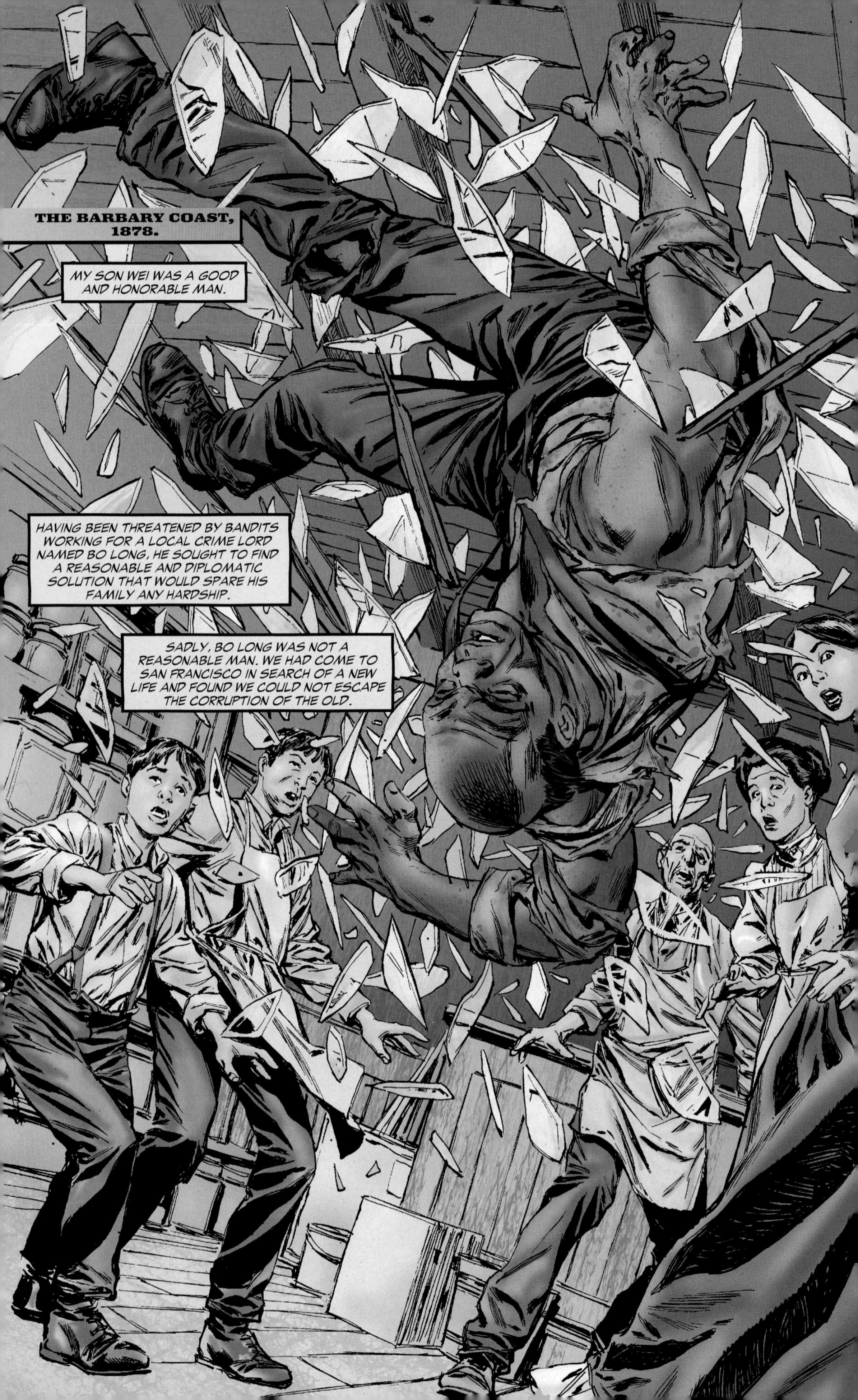
THE BARBARY COAST, 1878.
MY SON WEI WAS A GOOD AND HONORABLE MAN.
HAVING BEEN THREATENED BY BANDITS WORKING FOR A LOCAL CRIME LORD NAMED BO LONG, HE SOUGHT TO FIND A REASONABLE AND DIPLOMATIC SOLUTION THAT WOULD SPARE HIS FAMILY ANY HARDSHIP.
SADLY, BO LONG WAS NOT A REASONABLE MAN. WE HAD COME TO SAN FRANCISCO IN SEARCH OF A NEW LIFE AND FOUND WE COULD NOT ESCAPE THE CORRUPTION OF THE OLD.

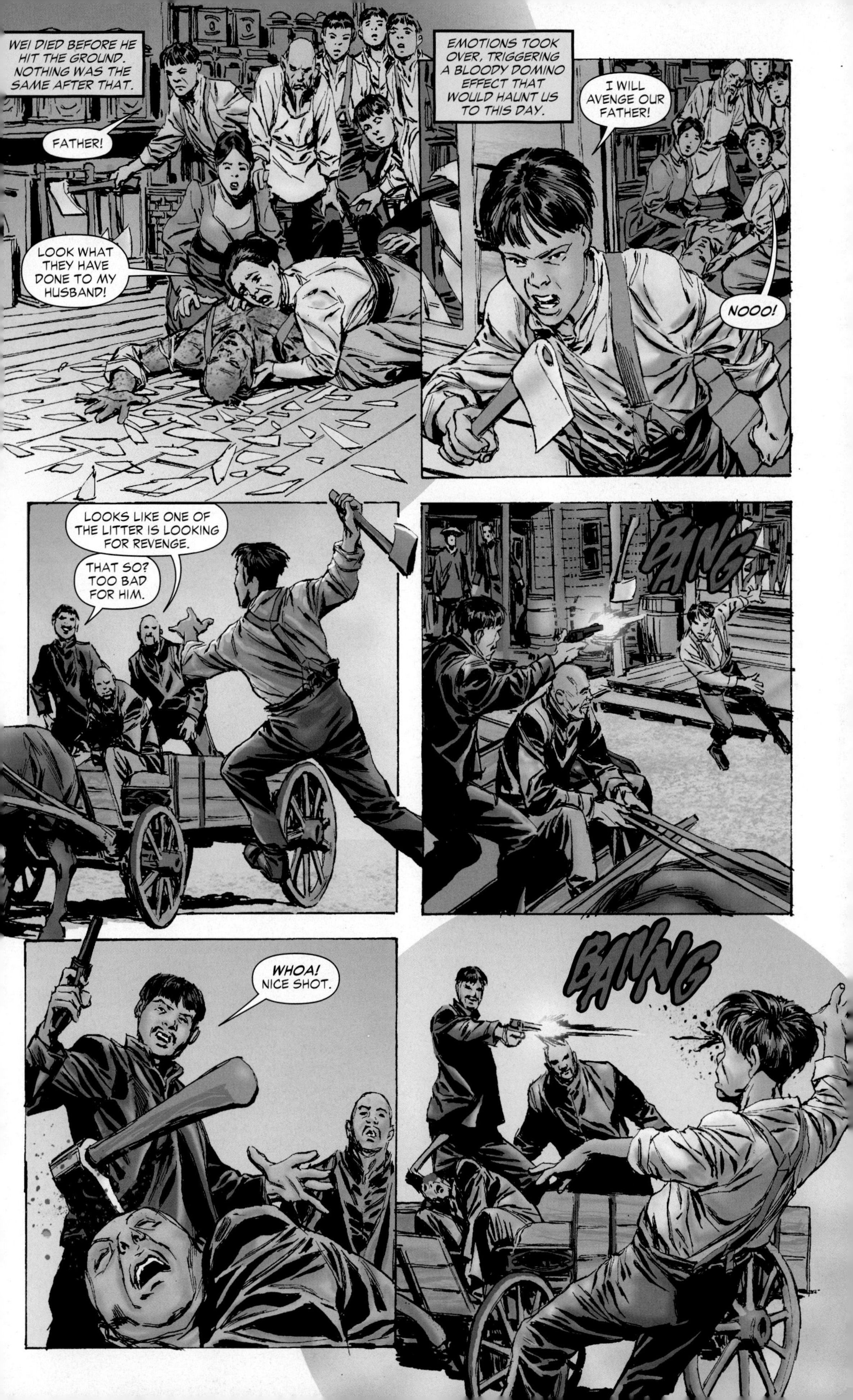

WEI DIED BEFORE HE HIT THE GROUND. NOTHING WAS THE SAME AFTER THAT.
FATHER!
LOOK WHAT THEY HAVE DONE TO MY HUSBAND!
EMOTIONS TOOK OVER, TRIGGERING A BLOODY DOMINO EFFECT THAT WOULD HAUNT US TO THIS DAY.
I WILL AVENGE OUR FATHER!
NOOO!
LOOKS LIKE ONE OF THE LITTER IS LOOKING FOR REVENGE.
THAT SO? TOO BAD FOR HIM.
BANG
WHOA! NICE SHOT.
BANNG

WE LOST TWO MEMBERS OF OUR FAMILY THAT DAY, AND UNFORTUNATELY, IT WAS ONLY THE BEGINNING.

IT IS SAID THAT HE WHO SEEKS REVENGE SHOULD DIG TWO GRAVES.

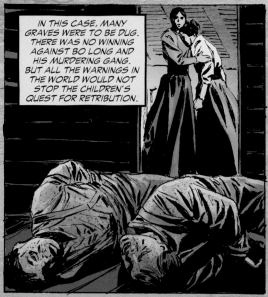

IN THIS CASE, MANY GRAVES WERE TO BE DUG. THERE WAS NO WINNING AGAINST BO LONG AND HIS MURDERING GANG. BUT ALL THE WARNINGS IN THE WORLD WOULD NOT STOP THE CHILDREN'S QUEST FOR RETRIBUTION.

FIVE SONS WERE MURDERED WITHIN TWO WEEKS...AND EIGHT OF BO LONG'S THUGS WERE KILLED IN THE EXCHANGES. THE BALANCE WAS OFF, AND BO LONG HAD TO MAKE AN EXAMPLE OF THE TSEN FAMILY.

MY DAUGHTER CAME TO ME AND SUGGESTED WE LEAVE WITH OUR REMAINING BELONGINGS AND OUR LIVES.

SHE ACQUIRED A SMALL PLACE OUTSIDE THE CITY WHERE WE WOULD BE SAFE. SHE TOLD ME THAT MY GRANDDAUGHTER WAS ALL SHE HAD LEFT AND ALL THE VIOLENCE HAD TO END.

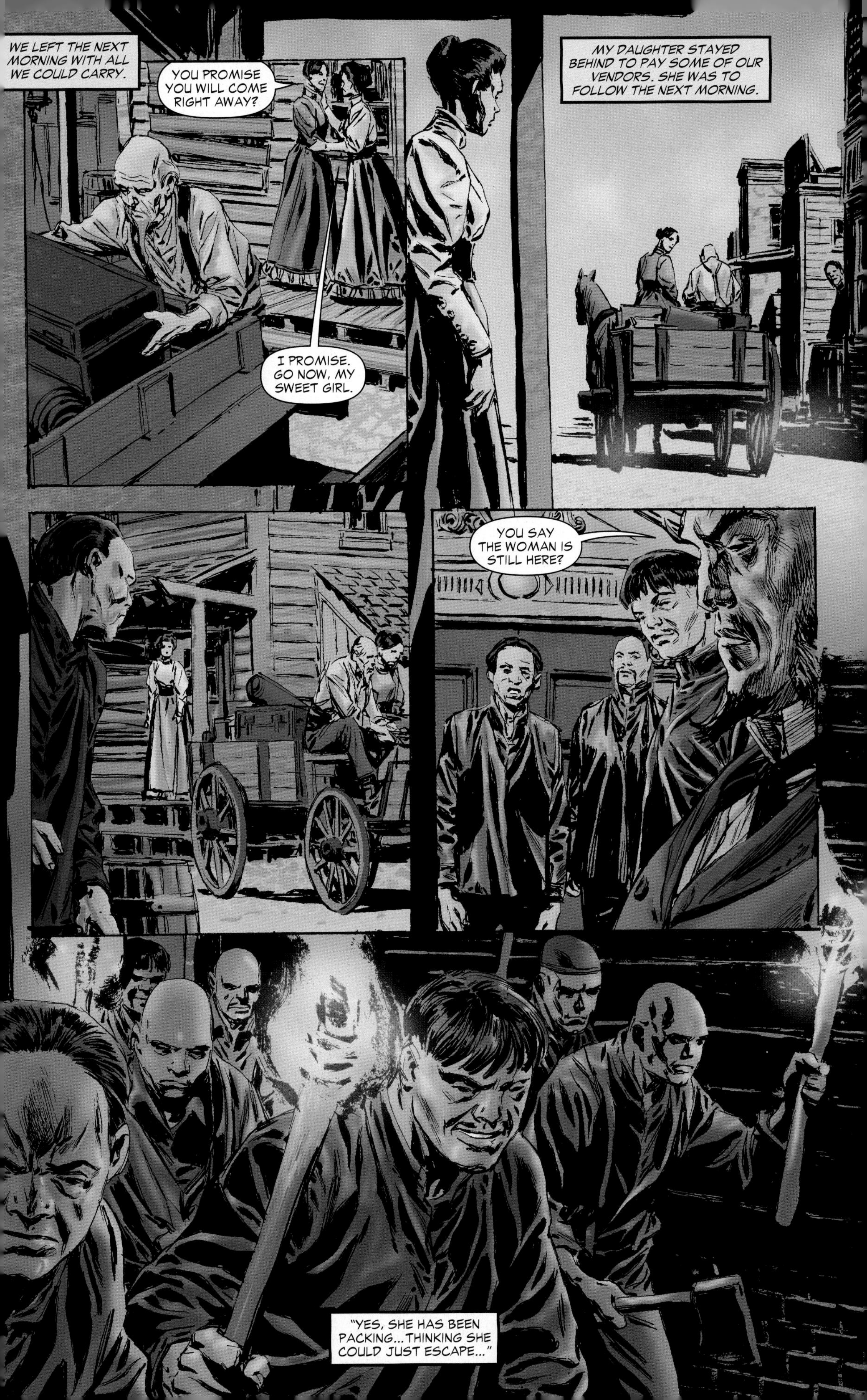
WE LEFT THE NEXT MORNING WITH ALL WE COULD CARRY.
YOU PROMISE YOU WILL COME RIGHT AWAY?
I PROMISE. GO NOW, MY SWEET GIRL.
MY DAUGHTER STAYED BEHIND TO PAY SOME OF OUR VENDORS. SHE WAS TO FOLLOW THE NEXT MORNING.
YOU SAY THE WOMAN IS STILL HERE?
"YES, SHE HAS BEEN PACKING... THINKING SHE COULD JUST ESCAPE..."

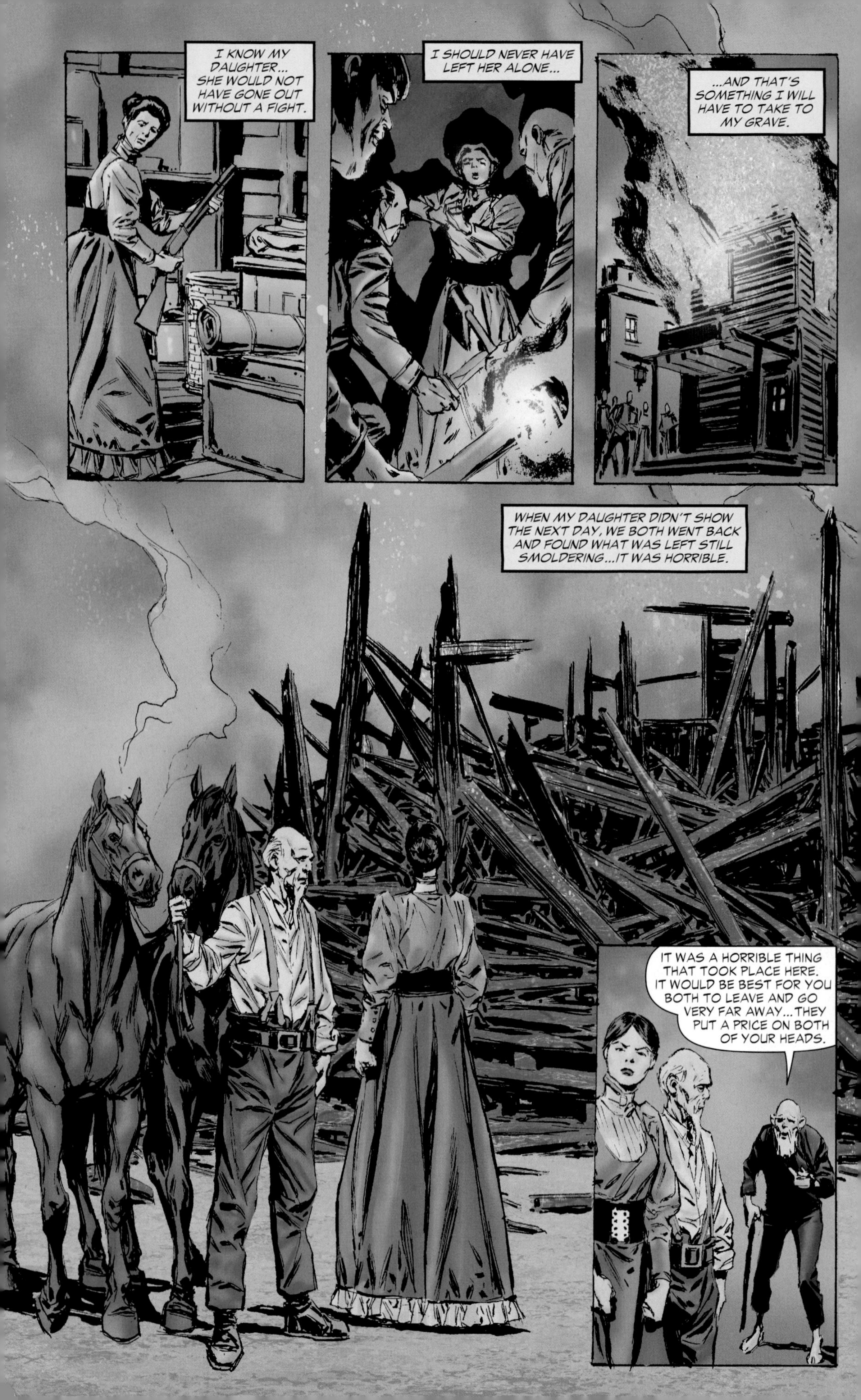
I KNOW MY DAUGHTER... SHE WOULD NOT HAVE GONE OUT WITHOUT A FIGHT.
I SHOULD NEVER HAVE LEFT HER ALONE...
...AND THAT'S SOMETHING I WILL HAVE TO TAKE TO MY GRAVE.
WHEN MY DAUGHTER DIDN'T SHOW THE NEXT DAY, WE BOTH WENT BACK AND FOUND WHAT WAS LEFT STILL SMOLDERING...IT WAS HORRIBLE.
IT WAS A HORRIBLE THING THAT TOOK PLACE HERE. IT WOULD BE BEST FOR YOU BOTH TO LEAVE AND GO VERY FAR AWAY...THEY PUT A PRICE ON BOTH OF YOUR HEADS.

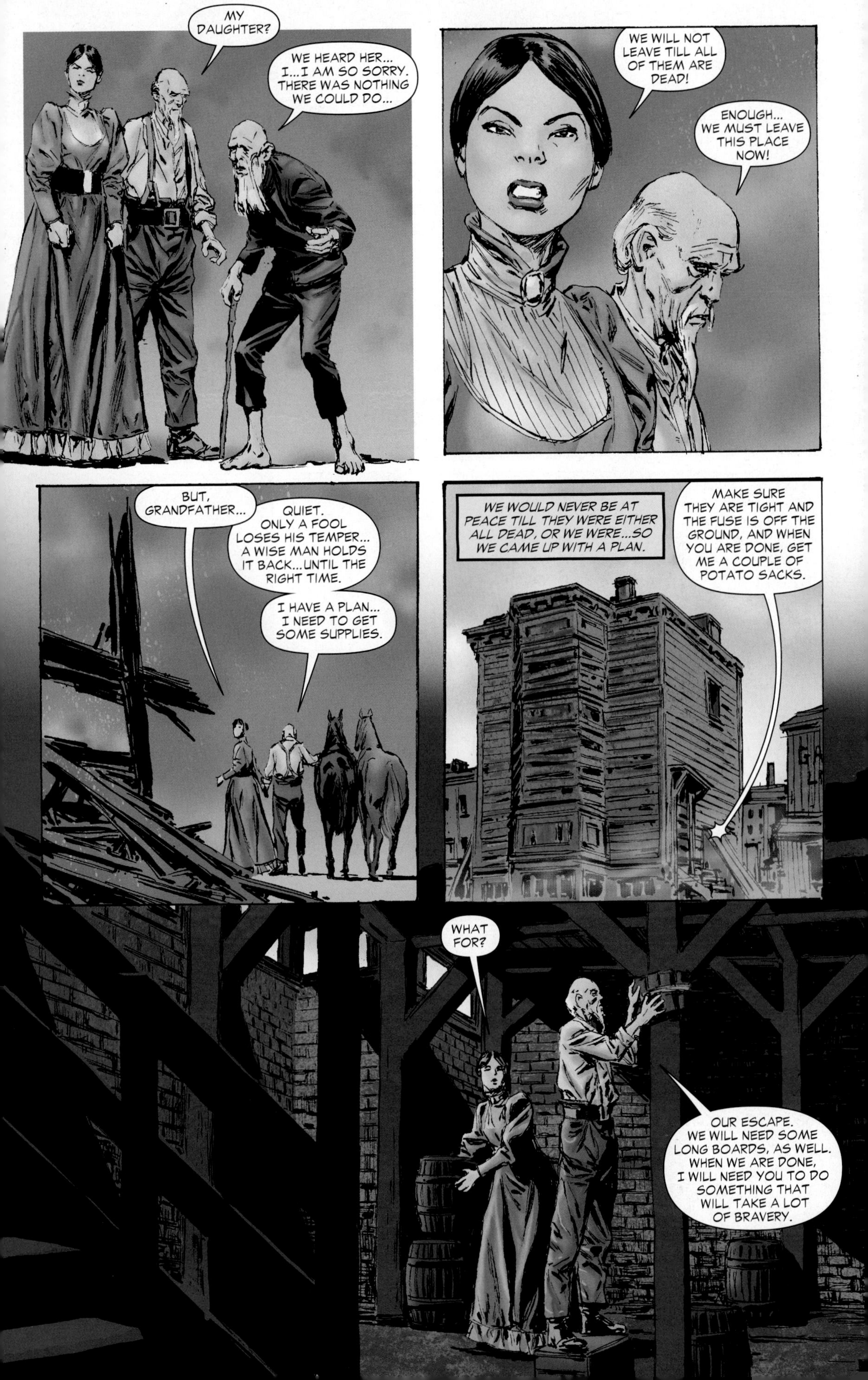
MY DAUGHTER?
WE HEARD HER... I...I AM SO SORRY. THERE WAS NOTHING WE COULD DO...
WE WILL NOT LEAVE TILL ALL OF THEM ARE DEAD!
ENOUGH... WE MUST LEAVE THIS PLACE NOW!
BUT, GRANDFATHER...
QUIET. ONLY A FOOL LOSES HIS TEMPER... A WISE MAN HOLDS IT BACK...UNTIL THE RIGHT TIME.
I HAVE A PLAN... I NEED TO GET SOME SUPPLIES.
WE WOULD NEVER BE AT PEACE TILL THEY WERE EITHER ALL DEAD, OR WE WERE...SO WE CAME UP WITH A PLAN.
MAKE SURE THEY ARE TIGHT AND THE FUSE IS OFF THE GROUND, AND WHEN YOU ARE DONE, GET ME A COUPLE OF POTATO SACKS.
WHAT FOR?
OUR ESCAPE. WE WILL NEED SOME LONG BOARDS, AS WELL. WHEN WE ARE DONE, I WILL NEED YOU TO DO SOMETHING THAT WILL TAKE A LOT OF BRAVERY.

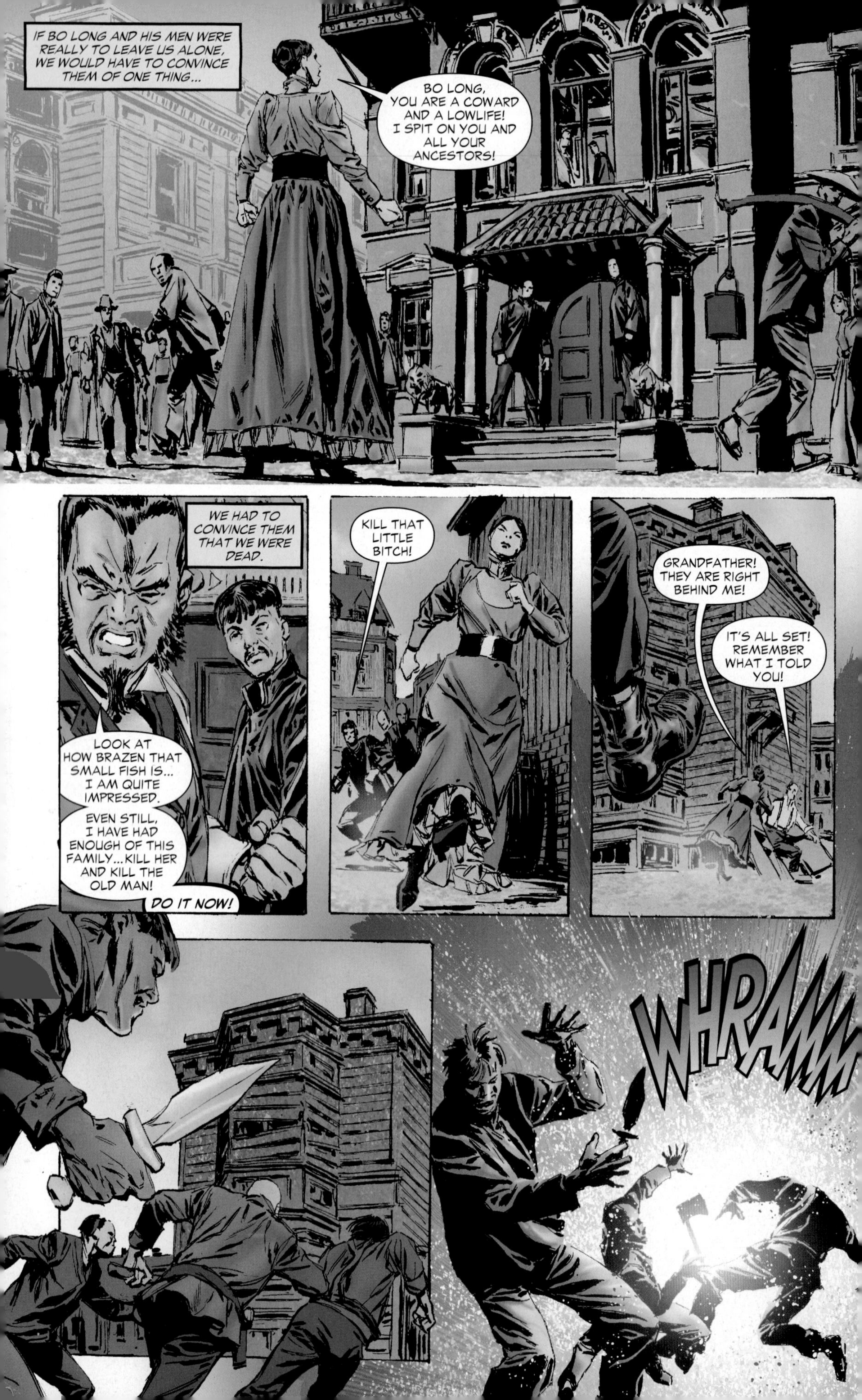
IF BO LONG AND HIS MEN WERE REALLY TO LEAVE US ALONE, WE WOULD HAVE TO CONVINCE THEM OF ONE THING...
BO LONG, YOU ARE A COWARD AND A LOWLIFE! I SPIT ON YOU AND ALL YOUR ANCESTORS!
WE HAD TO CONVINCE THEM THAT WE WERE DEAD.
LOOK AT HOW BRAZEN THAT SMALL FISH IS... I AM QUITE IMPRESSED.
EVEN STILL, I HAVE HAD ENOUGH OF THIS FAMILY...KILL HER AND KILL THE OLD MAN!
DO IT NOW!
KILL THAT LITTLE BITCH!
GRANDFATHER! THEY ARE RIGHT BEHIND ME!
IT'S ALL SET! REMEMBER WHAT I TOLD YOU!
WHRAMM

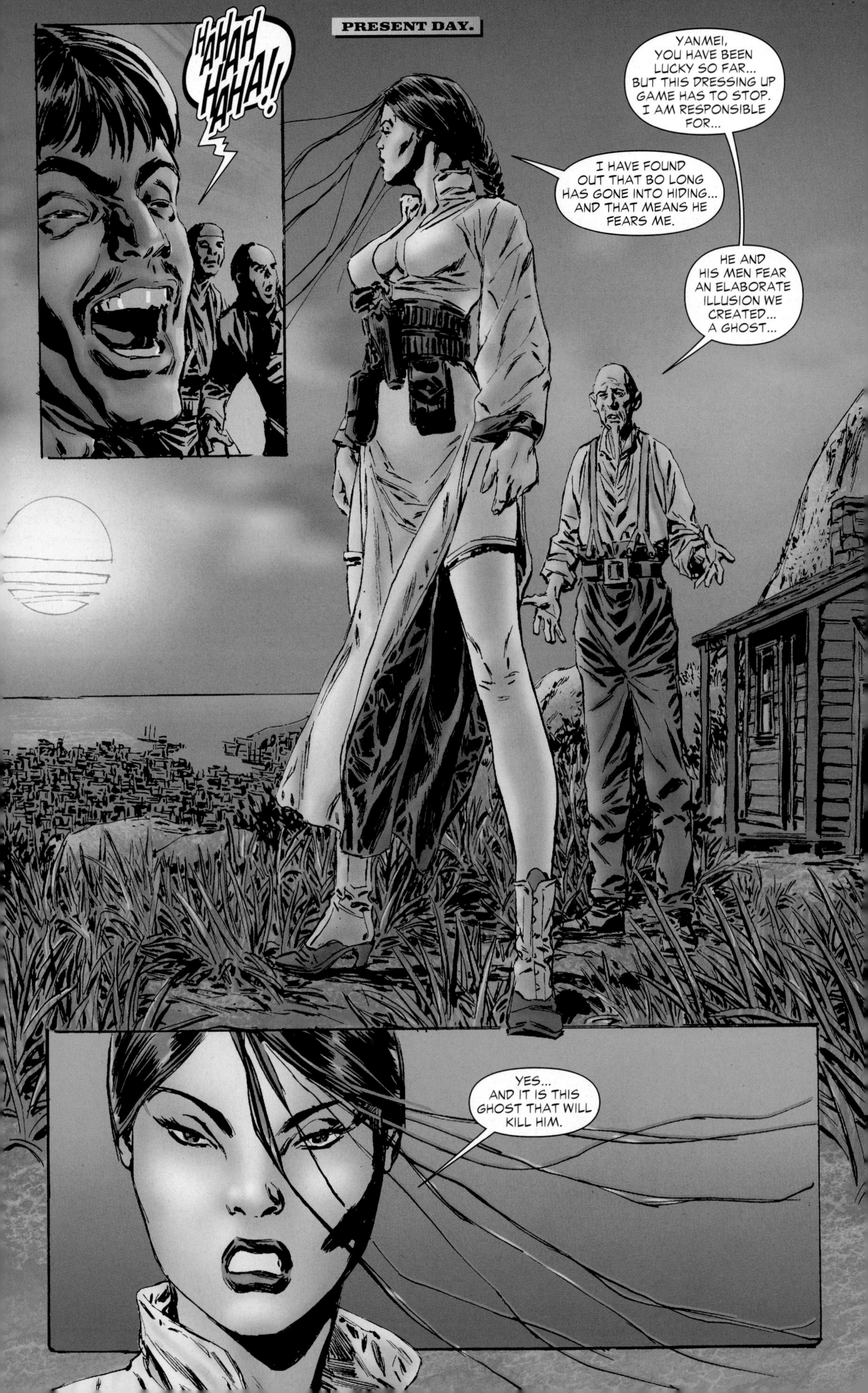
PRESENT DAY.
HAHAH HAHA HAHA!!
YANMEI, YOU HAVE BEEN LUCKY SO FAR... BUT THIS DRESSING UP GAME HAS TO STOP. I AM RESPONSIBLE FOR...
I HAVE FOUND OUT THAT BO LONG HAS GONE INTO HIDING... AND THAT MEANS HE FEARS ME.
HE AND HIS MEN FEAR AN ELABORATE ILLUSION WE CREATED... A GHOST...
YES... AND IT IS THIS GHOST THAT WILL KILL HIM.

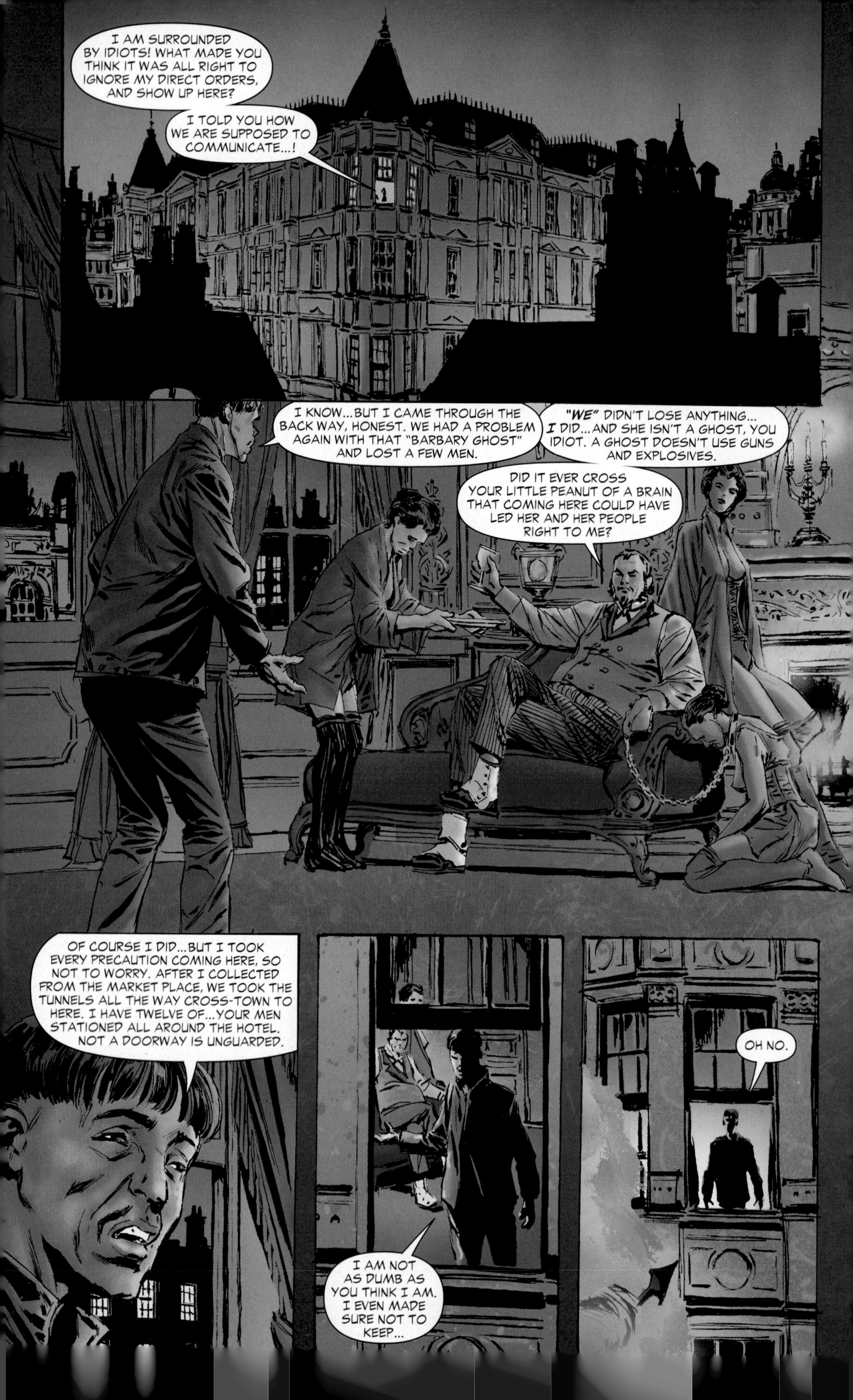
I AM SURROUNDED BY IDIOTS! WHAT MADE YOU THINK IT WAS ALL RIGHT TO IGNORE MY DIRECT ORDERS, AND SHOW UP HERE?
I TOLD YOU HOW WE ARE SUPPOSED TO COMMUNICATE...!
I KNOW...BUT I CAME THROUGH THE BACK WAY, HONEST. WE HAD A PROBLEM AGAIN WITH THAT "BARBARY GHOST" AND LOST A FEW MEN.
"WE" DIDN'T LOSE ANYTHING... I DID...AND SHE ISN'T A GHOST, YOU IDIOT. A GHOST DOESN'T USE GUNS AND EXPLOSIVES.
DID IT EVER CROSS YOUR LITTLE PEANUT OF A BRAIN THAT COMING HERE COULD HAVE LED HER AND HER PEOPLE RIGHT TO ME?
OF COURSE I DID...BUT I TOOK EVERY PRECAUTION COMING HERE, SO NOT TO WORRY. AFTER I COLLECTED FROM THE MARKET PLACE, WE TOOK THE TUNNELS ALL THE WAY CROSS-TOWN TO HERE. I HAVE TWELVE OF...YOUR MEN STATIONED ALL AROUND THE HOTEL. NOT A DOORWAY IS UNGUARDED.
I AM NOT AS DUMB AS YOU THINK I AM. I EVEN MADE SURE NOT TO KEEP...
OH NO.

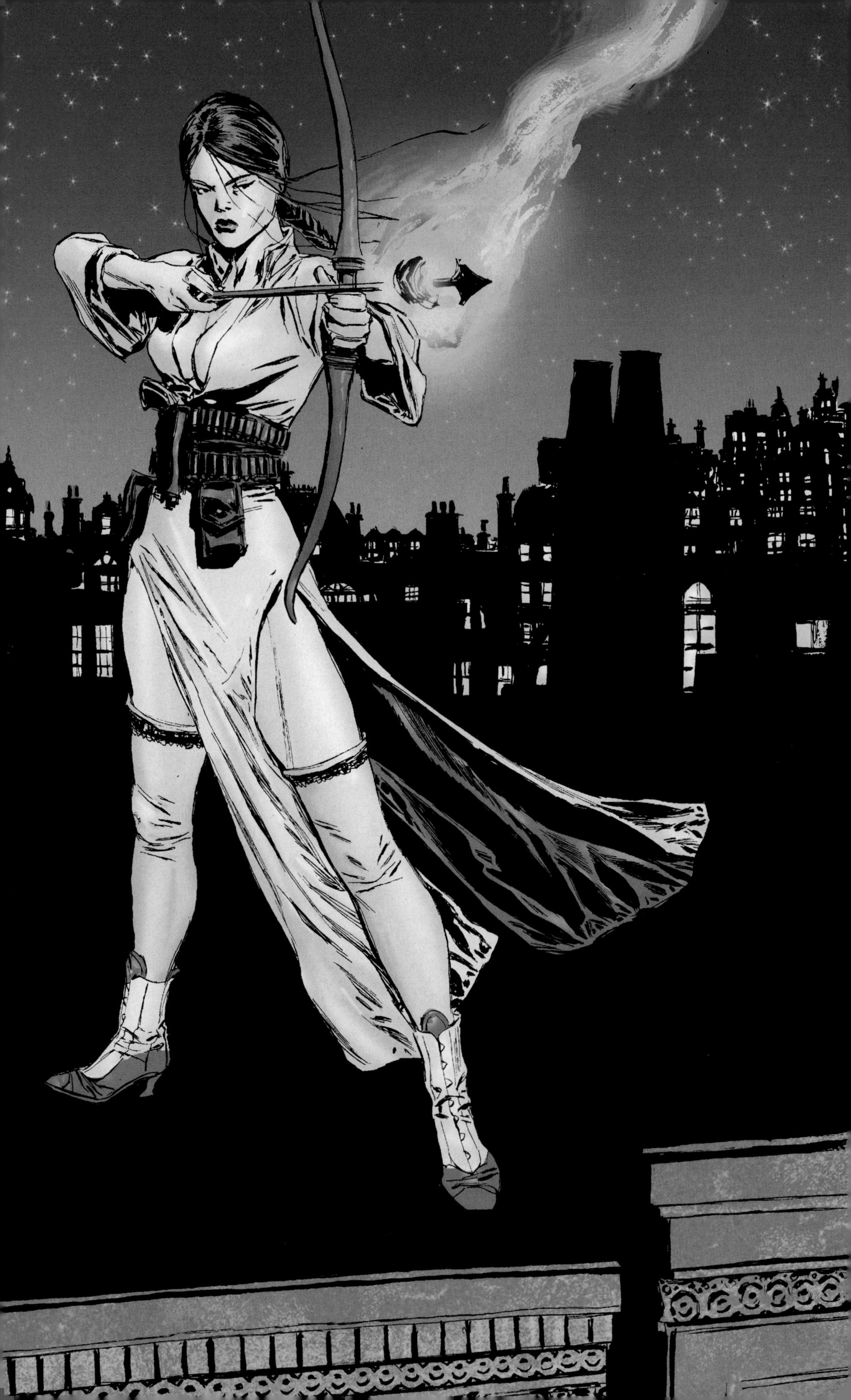

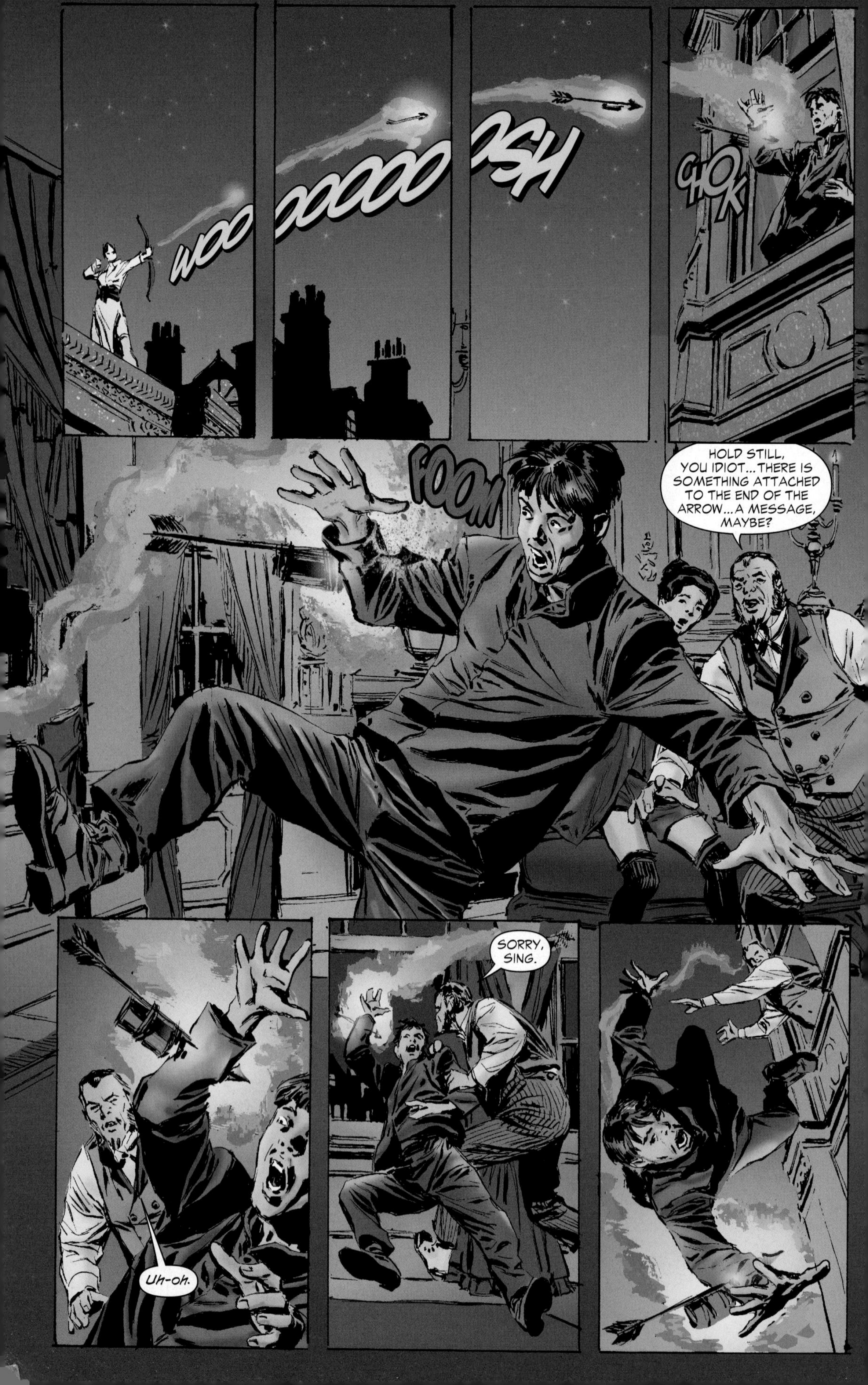
WOOOOOOOOOSH
CHOK
FOOM
HOLD STILL, YOU IDIOT...THERE IS SOMETHING ATTACHED TO THE END OF THE ARROW...A MESSAGE, MAYBE?
Uh-oh.
SORRY, SING.

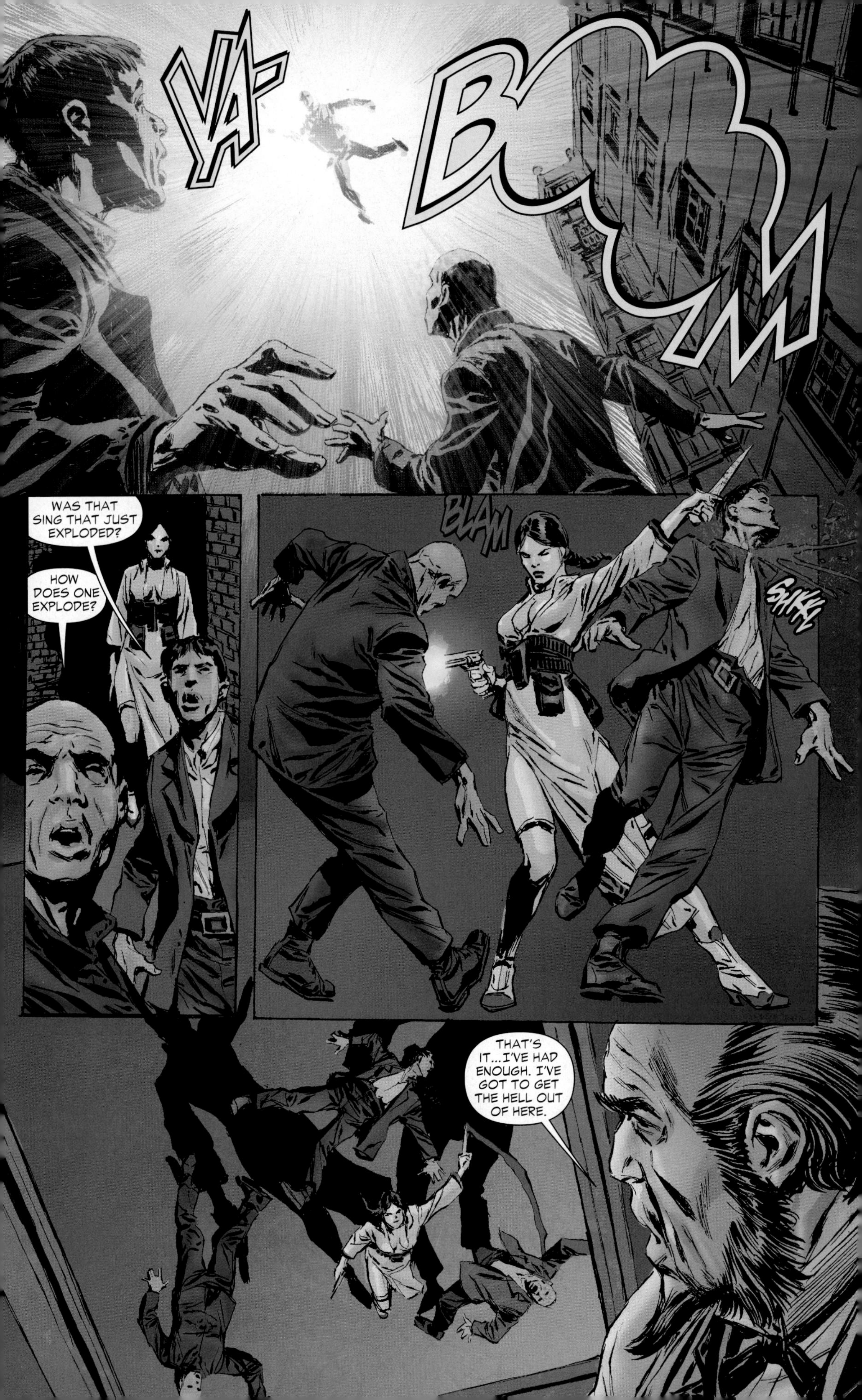
YA-BOOM
WAS THAT SING THAT JUST EXPLODED?
HOW DOES ONE EXPLODE?
BLAM
SHKK!
THAT'S IT...I'VE HAD ENOUGH. I'VE GOT TO GET THE HELL OUT OF HERE.

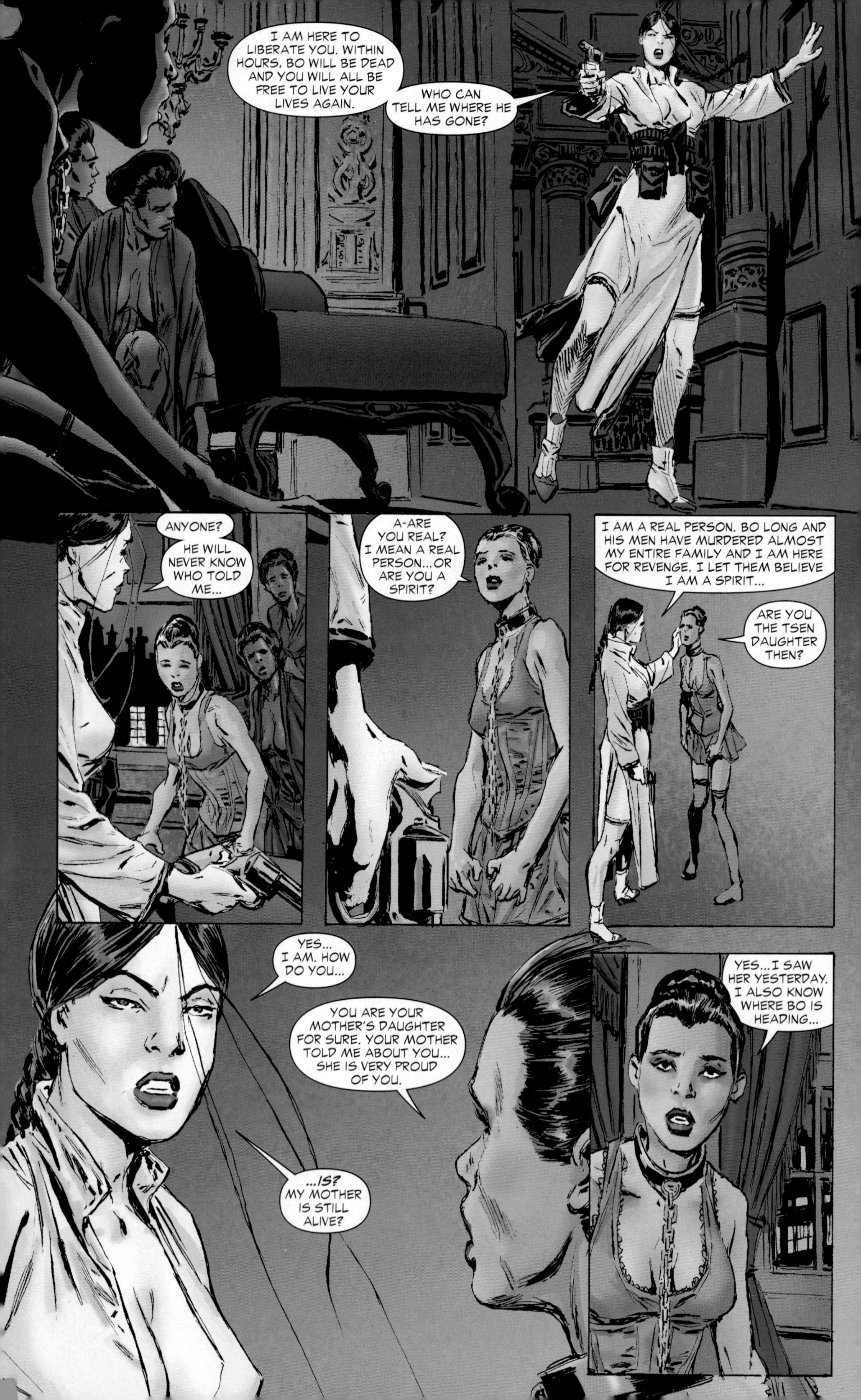
I AM HERE TO LIBERATE YOU. WITHIN HOURS, BO WILL BE DEAD AND YOU WILL ALL BE FREE TO LIVE YOUR LIVES AGAIN.
WHO CAN TELL ME WHERE HE HAS GONE?
ANYONE?
HE WILL NEVER KNOW WHO TOLD ME...
A-ARE YOU REAL? I MEAN A REAL PERSON...OR ARE YOU A SPIRIT?
I AM A REAL PERSON. BO LONG AND HIS MEN HAVE MURDERED ALMOST MY ENTIRE FAMILY AND I AM HERE FOR REVENGE. I LET THEM BELIEVE I AM A SPIRIT...
ARE YOU THE TSEN DAUGHTER THEN?
YES... I AM. HOW DO YOU...
YOU ARE YOUR MOTHER'S DAUGHTER FOR SURE. YOUR MOTHER TOLD ME ABOUT YOU... SHE IS VERY PROUD OF YOU.
...IS? MY MOTHER IS STILL ALIVE?
YES...I SAW HER YESTERDAY. I ALSO KNOW WHERE BO IS HEADING...

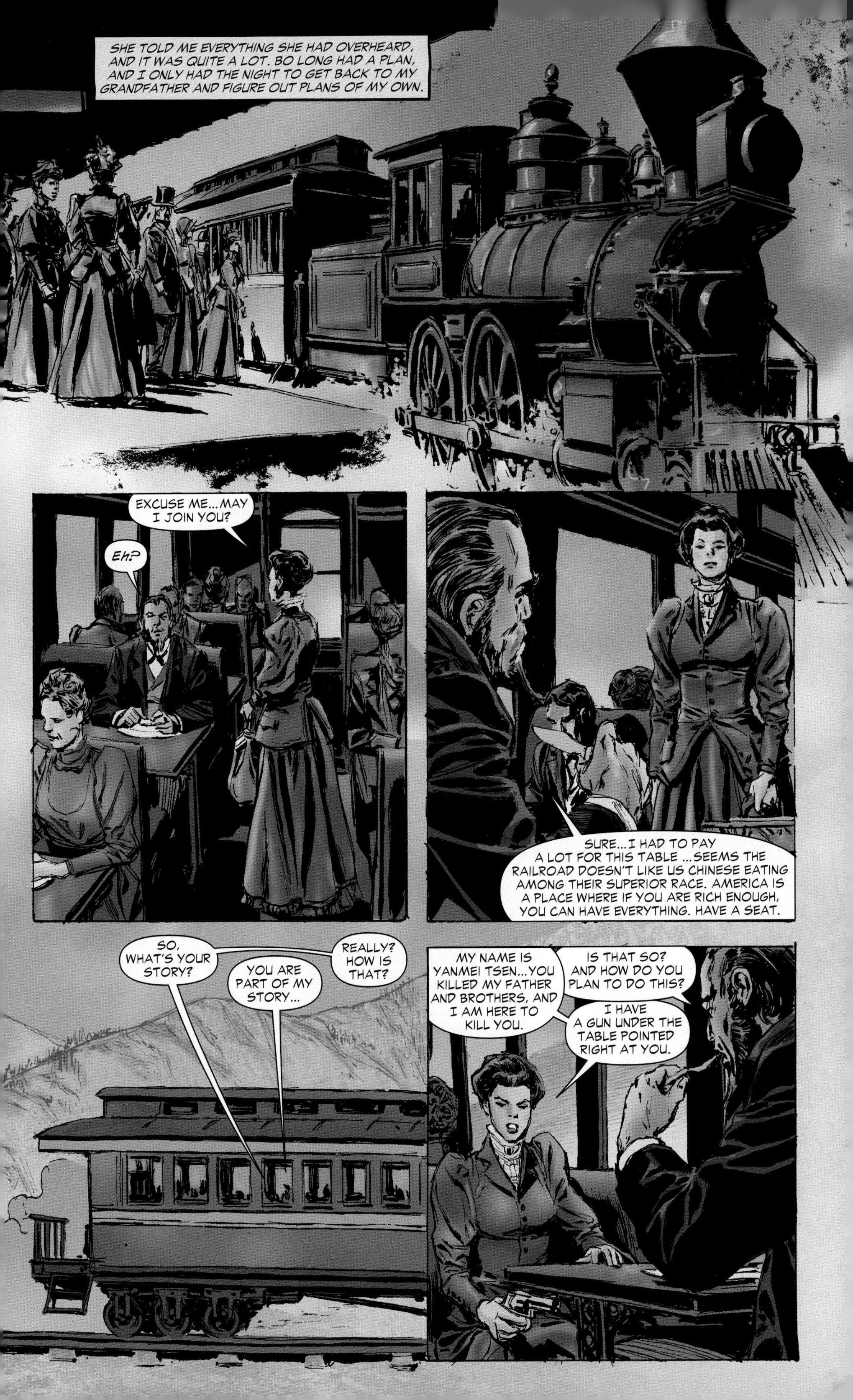
SHE TOLD ME EVERYTHING SHE HAD OVERHEARD, AND IT WAS QUITE A LOT. BO LONG HAD A PLAN, AND I ONLY HAD THE NIGHT TO GET BACK TO MY GRANDFATHER AND FIGURE OUT PLANS OF MY OWN.
EXCUSE ME...MAY I JOIN YOU?
Eh?
SURE...I HAD TO PAY A LOT FOR THIS TABLE ...SEEMS THE RAILROAD DOESN'T LIKE US CHINESE EATING AMONG THEIR SUPERIOR RACE. AMERICA IS A PLACE WHERE IF YOU ARE RICH ENOUGH, YOU CAN HAVE EVERYTHING. HAVE A SEAT.
SO, WHAT'S YOUR STORY?
YOU ARE PART OF MY STORY...
REALLY? HOW IS THAT?
MY NAME IS YANMEI TSEN...YOU KILLED MY FATHER AND BROTHERS, AND I AM HERE TO KILL YOU.
IS THAT SO? AND HOW DO YOU PLAN TO DO THIS?
I HAVE A GUN UNDER THE TABLE POINTED RIGHT AT YOU.

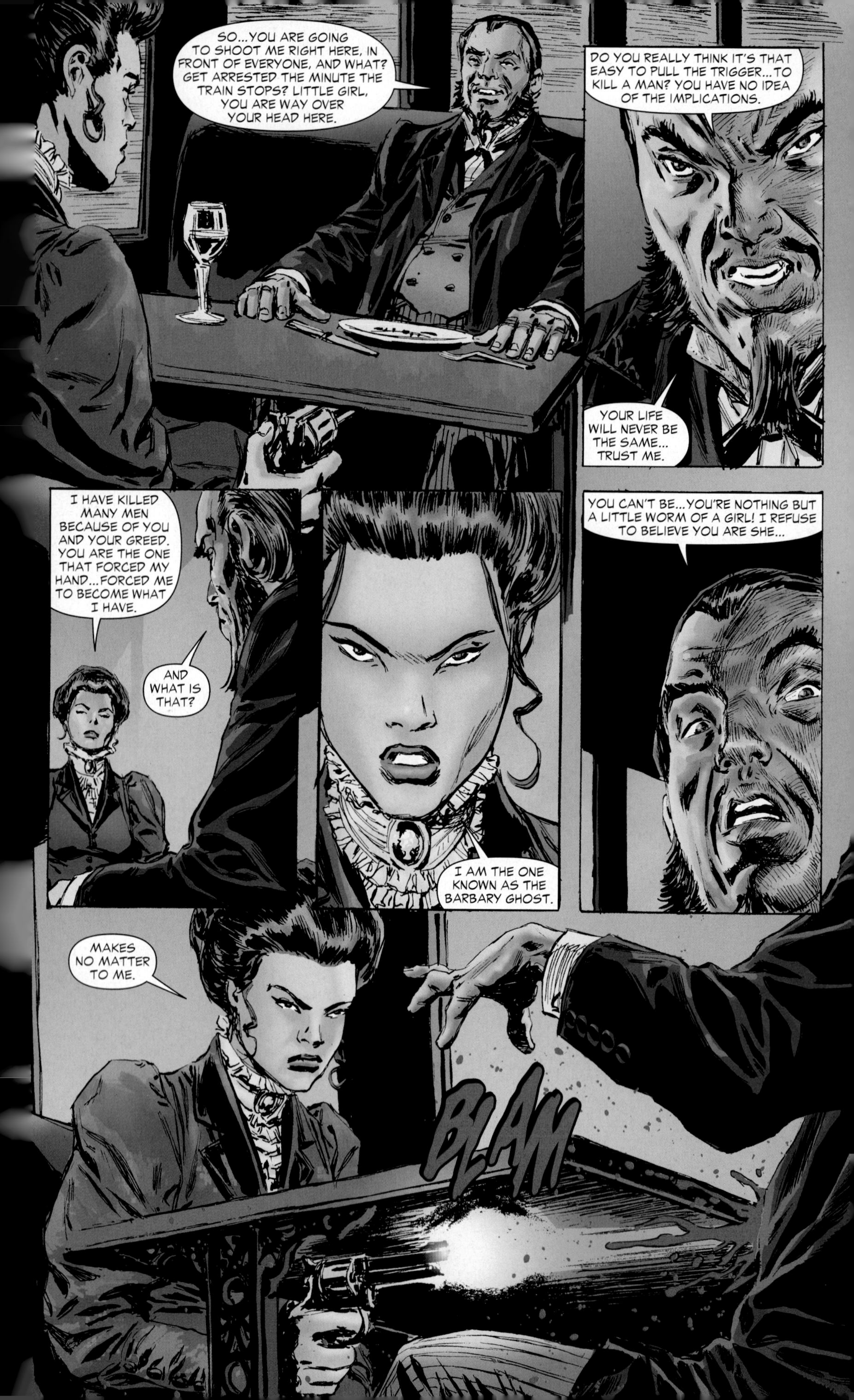
SO...YOU ARE GOING TO SHOOT ME RIGHT HERE, IN FRONT OF EVERYONE, AND WHAT? GET ARRESTED THE MINUTE THE TRAIN STOPS? LITTLE GIRL, YOU ARE WAY OVER YOUR HEAD HERE.
DO YOU REALLY THINK IT'S THAT EASY TO PULL THE TRIGGER...TO KILL A MAN? YOU HAVE NO IDEA OF THE IMPLICATIONS.
YOUR LIFE WILL NEVER BE THE SAME... TRUST ME.
I HAVE KILLED MANY MEN BECAUSE OF YOU AND YOUR GREED. YOU ARE THE ONE THAT FORCED MY HAND...FORCED ME TO BECOME WHAT I HAVE.
AND WHAT IS THAT?
I AM THE ONE KNOWN AS THE BARBARY GHOST.
YOU CAN'T BE...YOU'RE NOTHING BUT A LITTLE WORM OF A GIRL! I REFUSE TO BELIEVE YOU ARE SHE...
MAKES NO MATTER TO ME.
BLAM

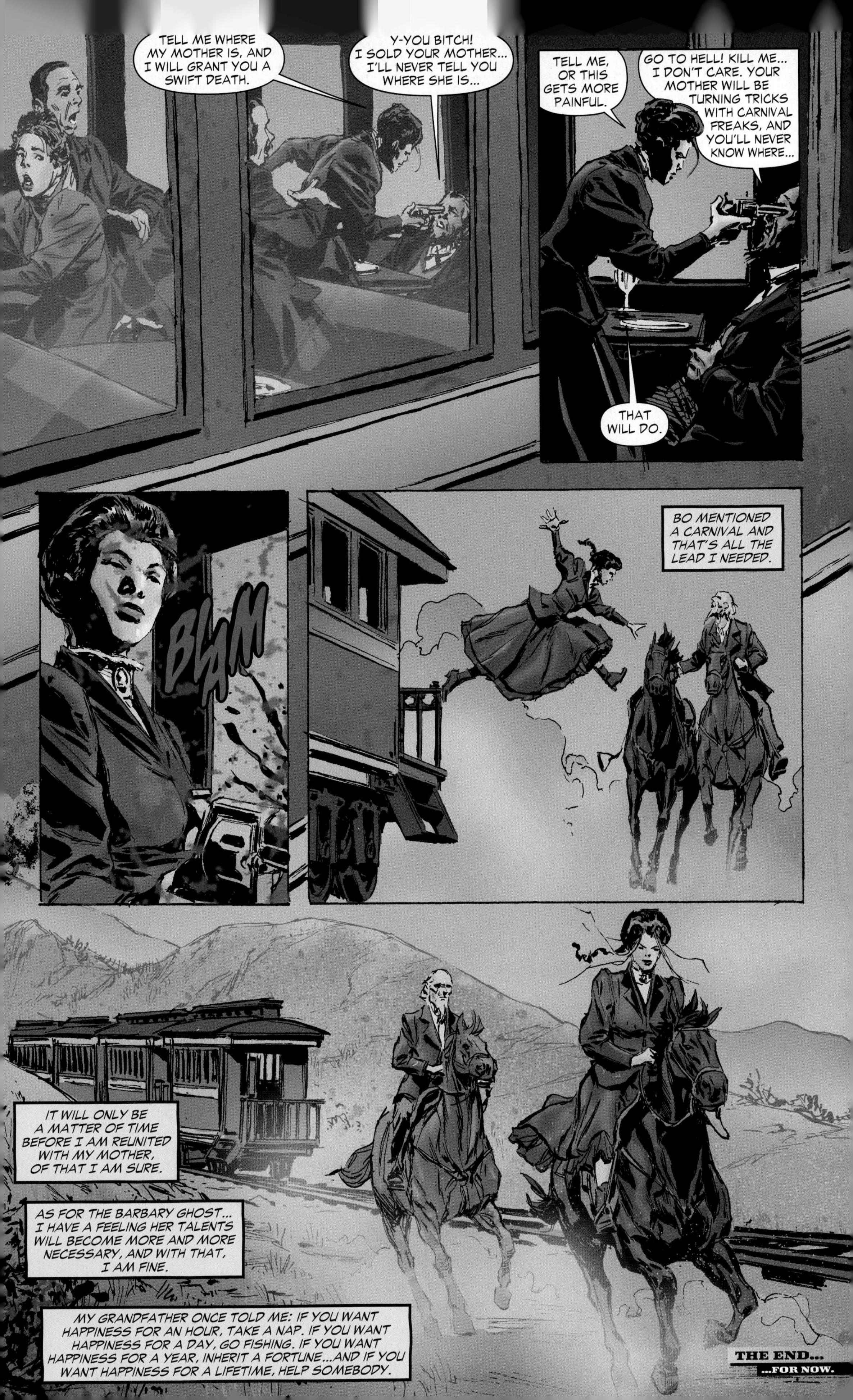
TELL ME WHERE MY MOTHER IS, AND I WILL GRANT YOU A SWIFT DEATH.
Y-YOU BITCH! I SOLD YOUR MOTHER... I'LL NEVER TELL YOU WHERE SHE IS...
TELL ME, OR THIS GETS MORE PAINFUL.
GO TO HELL! KILL ME... I DON'T CARE. YOUR MOTHER WILL BE TURNING TRICKS WITH CARNIVAL FREAKS, AND YOU'LL NEVER KNOW WHERE...
THAT WILL DO.
BLAM
BO MENTIONED A CARNIVAL AND THAT'S ALL THE LEAD I NEEDED.
IT WILL ONLY BE A MATTER OF TIME BEFORE I AM REUNITED WITH MY MOTHER, OF THAT I AM SURE.
AS FOR THE BARBARY GHOST... I HAVE A FEELING HER TALENTS WILL BECOME MORE AND MORE NECESSARY, AND WITH THAT, I AM FINE.
MY GRANDFATHER ONCE TOLD ME: IF YOU WANT HAPPINESS FOR AN HOUR, TAKE A NAP. IF YOU WANT HAPPINESS FOR A DAY, GO FISHING. IF YOU WANT HAPPINESS FOR A YEAR, INHERIT A FORTUNE...AND IF YOU WANT HAPPINESS FOR A LIFETIME, HELP SOMEBODY.
THE END...
...FOR NOW.

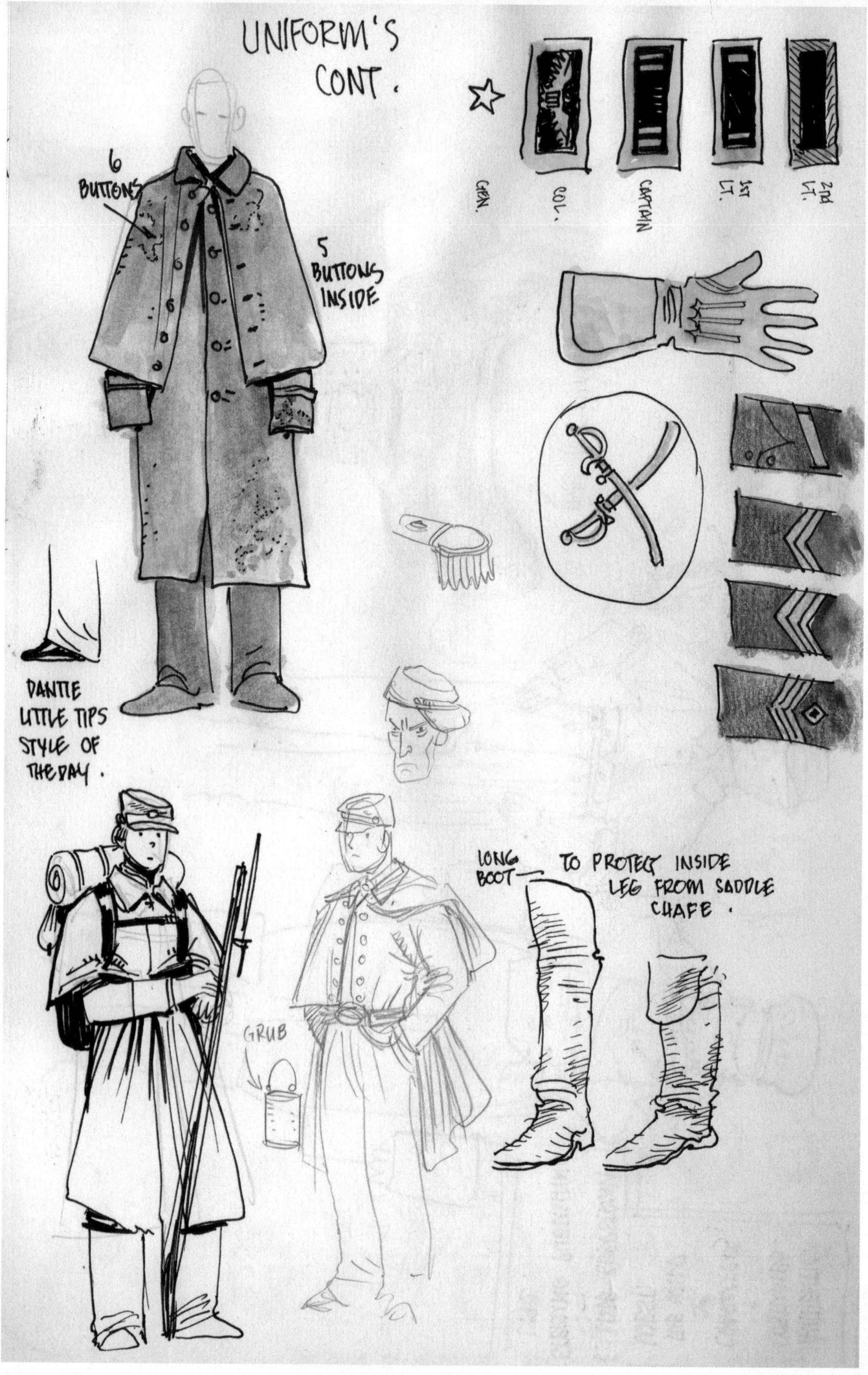
UNIFORM'S CONT.
6 BUTTONS
5 BUTTONS INSIDE
GEN.
COL.
CAPTAIN
1st LT.
2nd LT.
DANTIE LITTLE TIPS STYLE OF THE DAY.
GRUB
LONG BOOT
TO PROTECT INSIDE LEG FROM SADDLE CHAFE.

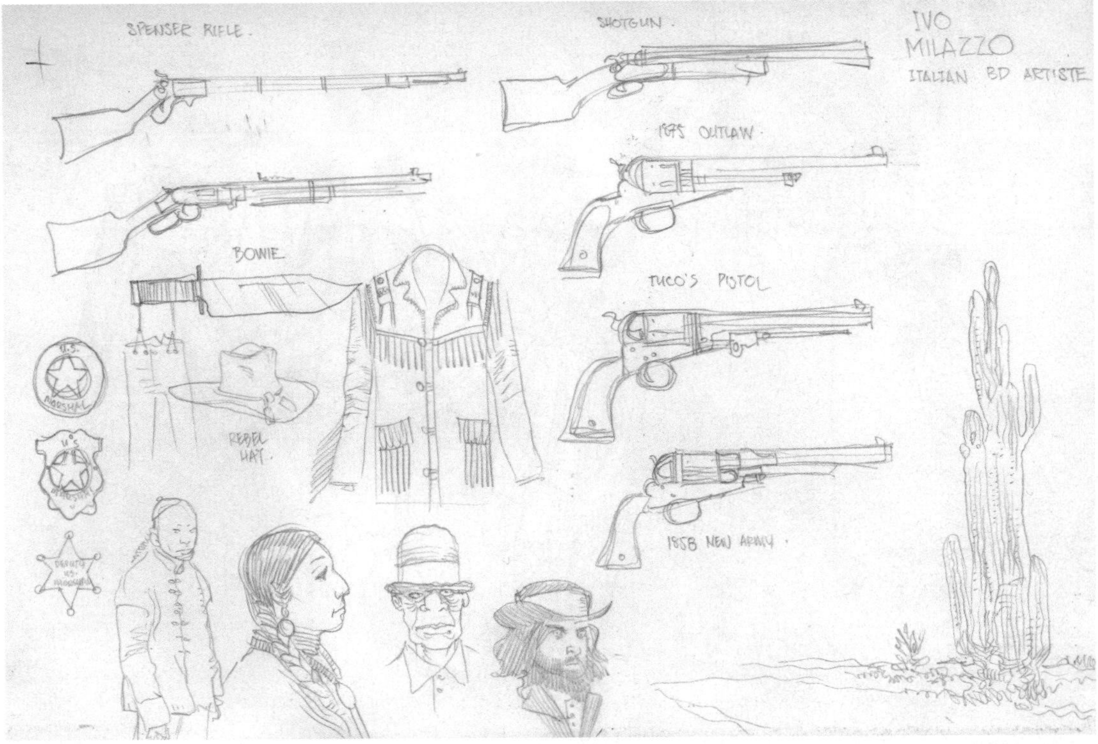
SPENSER RIFLE.
SHOTGUN.
IVO
MILAZZO
ITALIAN BD ARTISTE
1875 OUTLAW
BOWIE
TUCO'S PISTOL
REBEL HAT
1858 NEW ARMY

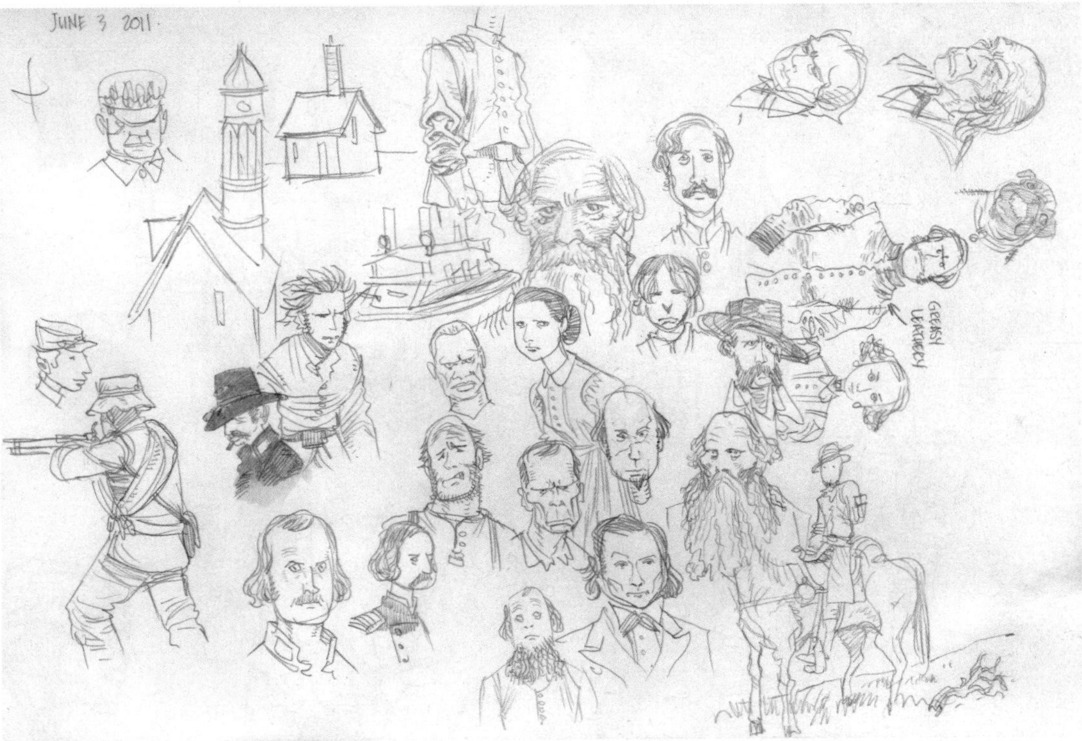
JUNE 3 2011.
GREASY
LEATHERY

GOTHAM'S
MIAGANI
· NATIVE ·

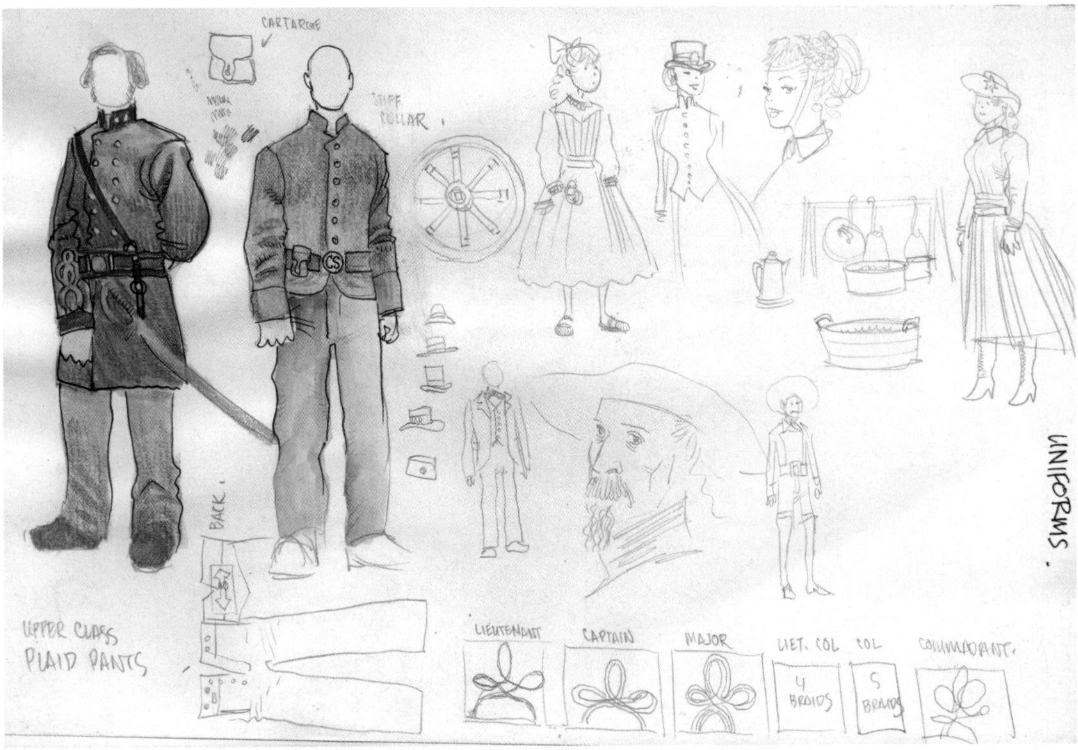
CARTARGE
STIFF COLLAR.
BACK.
UPPER CLASS
PLAID PANTS
LIEUTENANT
CAPTAIN
MAJOR
LIET. COL
4 BRAIDS
COL
5 BRAIDS
COMMANDANT.
UNIFORMS.

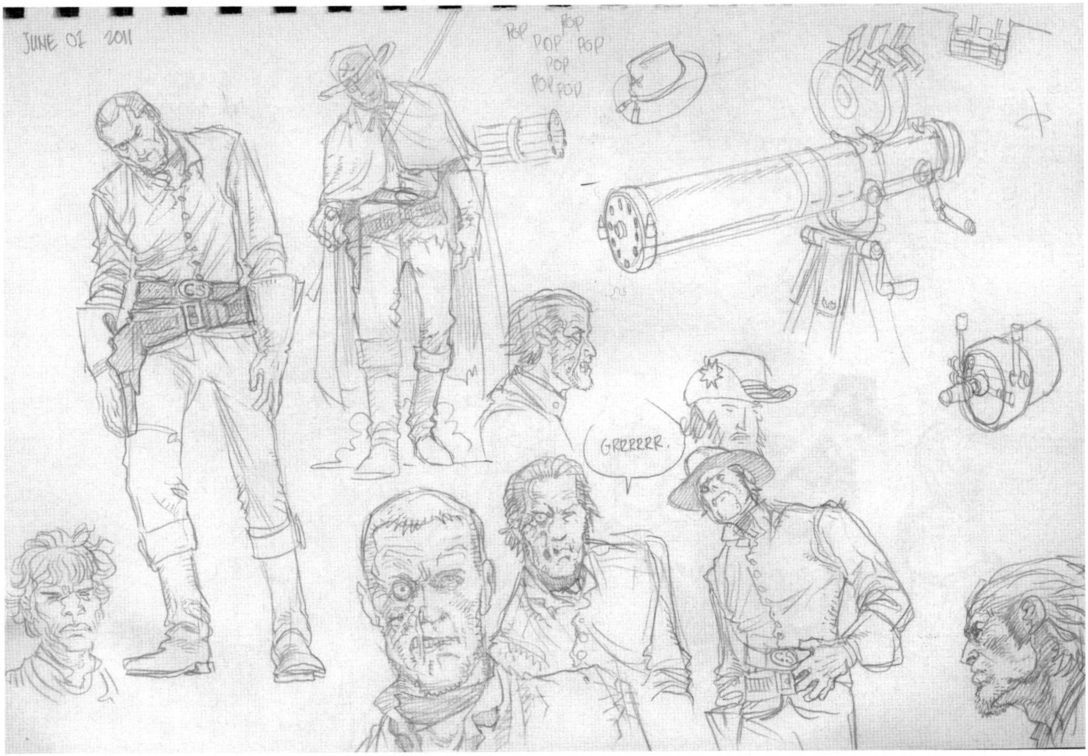
JUNE 07 2011
POP POP POP POP POP POP POP
GRRRRRR.

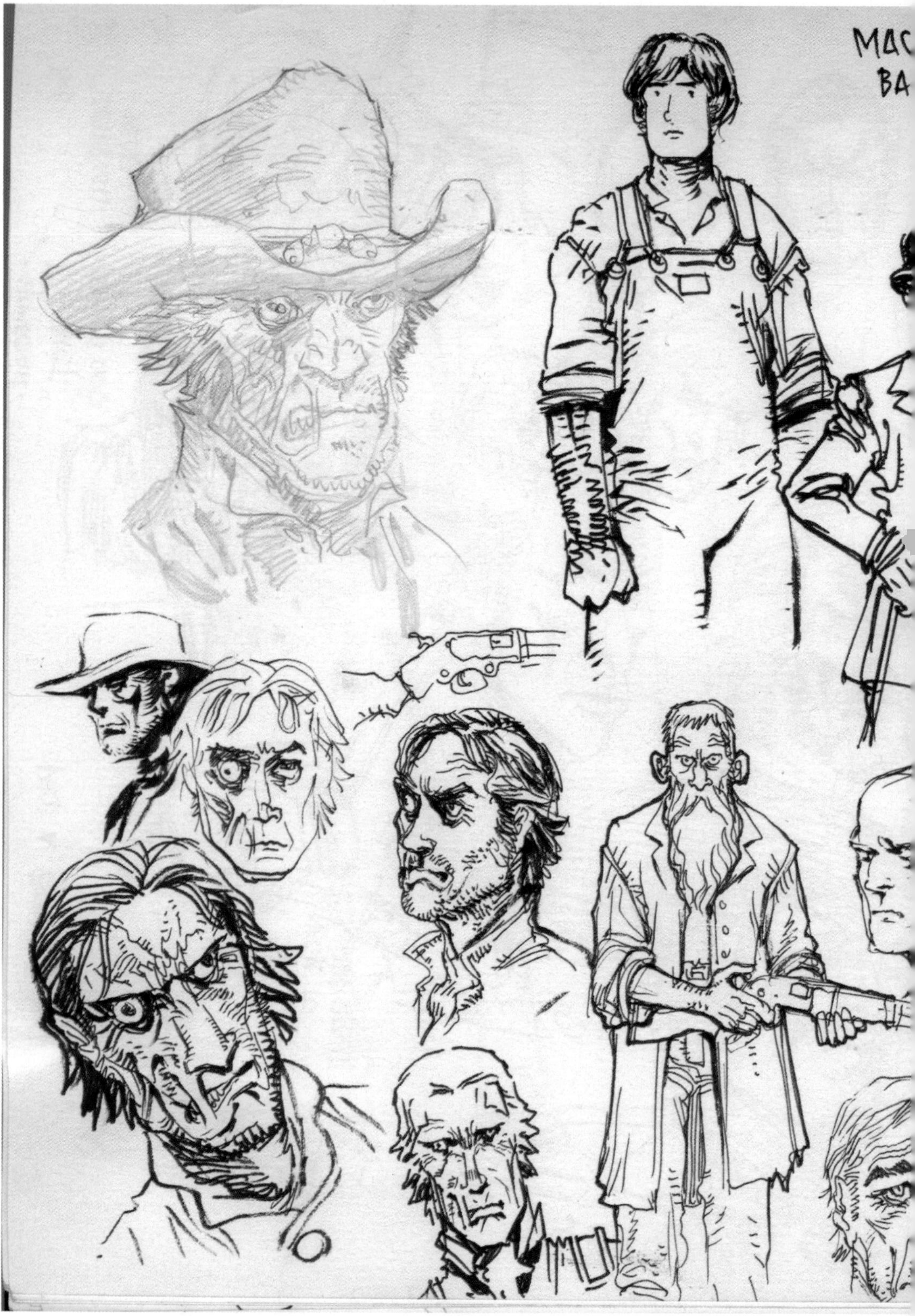
MAC
BA